STICKY SITUATIONS

Sticky Situations:

365 Devotions for
Kids and Families

BETSY SCHMITT

Tyndale House Publishers, Inc.
Wheaton, Illinois

Visit Tyndale's exciting Web site at www.tyndale.com

Copyright © 1997 by The Livingstone Corporation. All rights reserved.

Produced by The Livingstone Corporation; David R.Veerman, project editor.

Cover illustration copyright © 1997 by Dennis Jones. All rights reserved.

Scripture quotations are taken from the *Holy Bible,* New Living Translation, copyright © 1996. Used by permission of Tyndale House Publishers, Inc., Wheaton, Illinois 60189. All rights reserved.

Library of Congress Cataloging-In-Publication Data

Schmitt, Betsy.
  Sticky situations : 365 devotions for kids and families / Betsy Schmitt.
    p. cm.
  ISBN 0-8423-6550-8 (alk. paper)
  1. Family—Prayer-books and devotions—English.   2. Family—Religious life.   I. Title.
  BV255.S35 1997
  249—dc21   97-17526

Printed in the United States of America

02 01 00 99 98
9   8   7   6   5   4

INTRODUCTION TO *STICKY SITUATIONS*

Dear Parents:

The *Sticky Situations* devotional offers families a year's worth of situations to discuss and explore, meeting young people where they live: in the classroom, on the playground, at church, and at home. Through these situations, parents and children will be able to talk about various choices young people face daily and how God's Word can instruct and guide them on the right path.

There are many ways that your family can use this devotional. You may choose to read one situation for each day, or you may select entries that are relevant to real-life situations that your child may be experiencing. Or you may want to have the family select a verse from the index and then read that situation.

The situations can be used in a variety of ways as well. You may want to read the Bible verse first and ask your child how it relates to the situation before reading the choices. Or you could read the selection first and then have the child come up with his or her solution before you read the choices.

Talk about the situations before you discuss the choices. You may want to ask if the situation is something your child has experienced. If so, how did he or she feel about it? What choice did he or she make? Does it agree with biblical principles? Or perhaps your child has a friend who has experienced a similar situation. Ask how that friend handled the situation. Was it handled wisely? What would your child have advised the friend to do?

Talk about the choices. Some are obviously intended to be humorous, but others may require more consideration. Ask your child why one choice is better than another. Discuss the consequences of each choice, allowing your child to work through different scenarios.

Above all, pray with your child following a discussion. If a situation has hit close to home, you may want to pray for guidance and strength to handle the situation in God's way. Or a situation may represent a future temptation, requiring prayer for protection. Or you may simply want to pray for wisdom. As James reminds us, "If you need wisdom—if you want to know what God wants you to do—ask him, and he will gladly tell you. He will not resent your asking" (James 1:5).

—Betsy Schmitt

The Ring

Julie and Deb are good friends. Last Thursday, Deb received a beautiful opal ring for her birthday. At first Julie was happy for Deb—she showed genuine excitement and praised Deb's new possession. That wore off quickly, however, as their other friends made such a big deal over it. "Wow! What a gorgeous ring!" "Look at the way it reflects all the colors of the prism!" "It goes great with your eyes!"

Julie began to think about the ring a lot, wishing that she had one like it. And lately she has become annoyed at Deb, who always seems to be holding the ring out so that everyone can see it. Julie has become so frustrated that yesterday she even blurted out to her mother, "Deb and her stupid ring! That's all she ever talks about." What should Julie do?

Should she . . .

A. Save up all her money and buy a ring that is bigger and better than Deb's?

B. Forget about the ring, be happy for Deb, and be thankful for having her as a friend?

C. Tell her friends the ring is a fake?

D. Politely ask Deb not to wear the ring when the two of them are together?

E. Call Deb "Opal," compliment the beautiful "Deb" on her finger, and then laugh real loud at the joke?

 For help in knowing what Julie should do, read Exodus 20:17 and 1 Corinthians 13:4.

Getting Even

Wade is the big boy at school, and sometimes he takes advantage of his size and picks on smaller kids. Small and kind of shy, Tony is one of those picked-on kids. It seems as though Wade makes fun of Tony every day: before school, during lunch, after school, and even in some of his classes. Usually, Wade just calls Tony names, like "squirt," "nerd," and "shorty," but sometimes he knocks Tony's books out of his hands and even pushes him around.

Today, Tony stayed after school to work on a project with his science partner. It took longer than they had planned, so after finishing, the students and their teacher seem to be the only ones left at school (except for the custodians). As Tony walks alone down the deserted hallway toward the side entrance where his mom will pick him up, he sees a familiar light-blue jacket lying in the corner. Picking it up and looking closer, he sees the familiar sports team logo across the back and the pin on the front. It's Wade's jacket! No one is around to see what Tony will do.

Should he . . .
   A. Take the jacket home and then wear it to school in front of Wade and laugh at how stupid he must be to lose such a cool jacket?
   B. Take the jacket, cut off the sleeves with a knife, put it in a bag, and throw it on Wade's porch after dark?
   C. Take the jacket and have his mom drive by Wade's house so he can return it to him?
   D. Leave the jacket on the floor?
   E. Throw the jacket in the Dumpster in back of the school?

 For help in knowing what Tony should do, check out Luke 6:27-36.

The Star Player

Howard is the undisputed star of the basketball team. In fact, in an area where basketball is followed with a passion, Howard is the best player around. He has the potential to be named Mr. Basketball for the state, and he will be able to play college ball wherever he wants. Some people even think that with hard work, Howard will be able to make the NBA. Unfortunately, Howard has already adopted the attitude of a superstar.

On the court, Howard keeps up a steady stream of trash talk. Not only does he try to outplay his opponents, but he goes out of his way to humiliate them. Howard often embarrasses his own team with his showboat antics. A few of his teammates have tried to tell him to tone down his cocky attitude, but Howard dismisses such talk as jealousy.

The word is out that a college scout will be at the game tonight. Howard has been bragging all week to his teammates that the scouts are coming only to see him play. Right before the game, the team captain informs Howard that if he trash-talks against the other team and tries to showboat, his teammates will do whatever they can to keep the ball away from him—even if it means losing the game. Howard is floored. What do you think he should do?

Should Howard . . .
  A. Tone down his cocky behavior and just play the game?
  B. Tell the coach what is happening and let him handle it?
  C. Go out and try to humiliate his teammates by outplaying all of them?
  D. Trash-talk his own teammates for being such poor sports?
  E. Tell his coach he won't play with his teammates any more?

 Check out Isaiah 30:15 to see how Howard should respond.

3

We're Here to Praise Him!

Boy, has it been a bad week. Elaine can't remember having a worse week. Her mom has been in the hospital for some minor surgery. Elaine spent most of the week helping her younger brother and sister get ready for school. It wouldn't be so bad if they would listen to her—but no, they gave her a hard time all week. Then she had a huge test in history. She didn't study much for it and got a C minus. It's going to take a lot of hard studying to get that grade back up. Her orchestra instructor yelled at her Friday for forgetting her music (how was she supposed to remember everything with her brother and sister yelling at her!), and her best friend is mad at her because she couldn't go to the basketball game.

After arguing with her brother and sister to get ready for church on Sunday, Elaine walks into the worship service in a terrible mood. She's angry at her brother and sister. She's even angry at her mom for being sick. And, if she were totally honest, she would have to admit that she is angry at God for not taking care of all of these things. As the worship music begins, Elaine stews. She doesn't feel like singing, and she sure doesn't feel like praising God. What do you think Elaine should do?

Should she . . .
   A. Take a long walk in the neighborhood near the church to clear her thoughts?
   B. Spend the service plotting how she is going to get even with her brother and sister?
   C. Praise God despite her circumstances and because of who he is?
   D. Sing a few songs, without really thinking about what she is singing?
   E. Make a list of all the rotten things that went on this week, in case God hadn't noticed?

 To see how David responded during a difficult period in his life, read Psalm 70.

Pressed for Time

Friends, sports, television, friends, homework, friends, church, and friends keep Mike very busy. (Did I mention friends?) Lately the teachers have been piling on the work—tests, reports, projects—so Mike hasn't been able to spend as much time as he would like with his friends, especially Todd and Danny.

Mike's parents have a rule that he is to do his homework as soon as he comes home from school, before he does anything else, like watch TV, listen to music, or call his friends. After studying for a while, Mike hears his mom leave to go to the store. He knows the rules, but he is already sick of this homework. And he knows that his mom won't be back home for at least an hour. What do you think Mike should do?

Should he . . .
- A. Figure that a little television won't hurt and turn on his favorite show?
- B. Decide that he can concentrate on his homework better with background music and then turn on his stereo?
- C. Call his best friend on the phone and talk until he hears his mom's car in the driveway?
- D. Do his homework?
- E. Take his textbooks out to the backyard, throw them up in the air one at a time, and hit each one hard with a baseball bat? Then he can tell his mom that he was "hitting the books."

 The biblical principle that tells what Mike should do can be found in Colossians 3:20.

5

Found Treasure

Just the other day, Amber was thinking about how much she needed money. She had expenses: snacks, movies, and presents (to name just a few). She asked her parents for more allowance, but they said no. Amber even thought about selling some of her stuff in a garage sale or opening a lemonade stand (in January?). She was desperate.

As Amber goes home from school, she goes a different way, cutting through the field instead of walking around it. She sees something black sticking out of the snow. It looks interesting, so she goes to investigate.

It's a wallet with fifty dollars in it!

This is great, Amber thinks, *but now what should I do?* What do you think?

Should Amber . . .

    A. Carefully wipe her fingerprints off the wallet, put it back in the snow where she found it, and then quickly run away?

    B. See this as an answer to prayer—take the money and throw the wallet in the trash?

    C. Call the owner and give him his wallet, money and all?

    D. Take the money and then mail the wallet to the owner?

    E. Throw the wallet into a pond where a fish grabs it and flips it to another fish who flips it back to her—the world's first case of carp-to-carp walleting?

 To see what Amber should do, read Psalm 51:6.

My Hero?

Walking home from school, Chase and his friends are discussing their English assignment. Everyone has to write five paragraphs about their hero. It seems as though they all want to write about the hottest new basketball star. Chase isn't too sure he would call this guy a hero. Sure, he's the tallest player right now, and he has terrific moves on the court. All the boys are wearing the shoes he endorses. But off the court, the guy is a mess. He already has millions of dollars but is always whining about not making enough. And Chase read yesterday that this player only shows up to practice when he wants to and cuts down his teammates when they don't play well. A good basketball player? Yes. But a hero? Chase isn't too sure about that.

One of the boys notices that Chase has been quiet during the walk home. "Well, who are you going to write about?" his friend asks. Chase doesn't want to appear weird, but he doesn't agree with his friends. What do you think Chase should do?

Should he . . .
- A. Patiently explain the values he admires in a hero—honesty, integrity, humility, and godliness?
- B. Quickly agree with his friends so they will get on another topic?
- C. Say, "Batman! Now that's a hero"?
- D. Grab his friend's book and imitate the basketball star by slam-dunking it into the garbage can?
- E. Cough a couple of times and then point out the cool car going by?

 Read Psalm 101:5-6 to see the standards David set for his heroes of his land.

The Bike

Today is Greg's birthday, and he can hardly contain his excitement. For months he has been dropping hints about the really awesome twenty-speed bike displayed in the bike store downtown. Plus, he has been working hard in school and practicing his trombone whenever he comes home from school. He just knows his parents will come through.

As he walks into the kitchen, his mother casually asks him to take out the garbage. As Greg enters the garage, sure enough, there is the exact bike he has wanted for so long. Now that he has the ultimate bike on the block, what should Greg do?

Should he . . .
A. Brag about the bike all over school?
B. Hide the bike in the garage and save it for an emergency?
C. Ride the bike wherever he normally rides his bike?
D. Ride the bike all over the neighborhood so everyone will see it?
E. Purposefully get the new bike dirty so it looks like his old bike?

 For help in knowing what Greg should do, read Proverbs 18:12.

8

Secret Notes

Joe is a new boy in class, and Maddie thinks he's really cool. During science class, Maddie writes a secret note to her best friend telling her how much she likes this boy and how she would like to get to know him better as a friend.

Maddie doesn't know how it happened, but after class she discovers, to her horror, that her secret note ended up in the hands of Joe's best friend. Before the friend can pass the note along to Joe, what should Maddie do?

Should Maddie . . .

A. Demand the note back and threaten to level Joe's friend?

B. Tell Joe what was in the note?

C. Call Joe and tell him she was just kidding?

D. Quickly write ten more notes just like the first one and allow them to be found by other friends?

E. Deny she wrote the note, claiming someone had forged her handwriting?

 For help in knowing what Maddie should do, read Proverbs 12:17.

A Double Life

Olivia attends church every Sunday. She sings in the choir and helps out in the nursery. She's a regular at the youth group outings and contributes to the discussion during Sunday school. From all outward appearances, Olivia is a growing Christian. But on the other six days of the week, Olivia acts very differently. She runs with a fast crowd at school—the crowd that is known for using foul language and for causing trouble at school activities. Many of the students who hang out with this group were suspended from school for bringing liquor to the last school dance.

Olivia never mentions church to her friends at school. She knows exactly what they think about Christians. Often they make fun of those "churchy kids," some of whom are from Olivia's youth group. One day, one of Olivia's friends from church confronts her and tells Olivia that she is leading a double life. Olivia laughs it off, but her friend's comments make her think. Does it matter to God how she lives the other six days of the week? Isn't one day good enough for God? What do you think Olivia should do?

Should she . . .

A. Decide that going to church on Sunday is good enough for God?

B. Talk to her youth group leader about her "other life" and discuss if she needs to make changes in her lifestyle?

C. Let her friends at school know she is a Christian and see what happens?

D. Decide that her church friend is right and stop going to church?

E. Ignore what her church friend said—she's only being a spoilsport?

 Read Romans 2:5-8 to see how God views Olivia's lifestyle—on Sunday and during the week.

The Locker

Steve and Chris have a long-standing feud. The two can't be in the same room for more than five minutes before the first insult is hurled. Just the other day, Chris knocked over Steve's lunch tray. Not only did Steve have to clean up the mess, but he (not Chris) got into trouble with the lunch monitor. Now he has to eat lunch with the younger kids for an entire week.

Steve is walking down the hall, still fuming about the lunch-room incident. He notices that Chris's locker is open. What should Steve do?

Should he . . .
A. Walk past the locker and do nothing?
B. Look around to make sure nobody is watching and then trash the locker?
C. Close the locker before something gets stolen?
D. Grab one of those little kids he has to eat lunch with, stuff him into the locker, and then close the door?
E. Leave a nasty note in the locker, threatening ultimate revenge?

 For help in knowing what Steve should do, read Romans 12:19-20.

The "In" Crowd

Meg has a nice group of friends. They all get along and have a lot of fun together. But as far as being cool, Meg knows that according to the school's pecking order, her friends just don't cut it. So when the coolest kids in the school begin noticing her, she can't believe it.

At first it was just a smile and a friendly hello. Then one day they ask Meg to come join them for lunch. She sees her old friends sitting at their usual table, laughing and joking. Her seat is waiting for her there, at that table. What should Meg do?

Should Meg . . .

A. Walk past her friends and join the other group?
B. Try to keep the old friends by telling them, "We'll do lunch some other time"?
C. Stay with her friends and let popularity take care of itself?
D. Sneak around so her friends won't see her?
E. Eat lunch first with the cool kids, then hurry over and have a "second lunch" with her old friends?

 For help in knowing what Meg should do, read Romans 12:16.

Just a Minute

Caroline has finished her homework and has practiced her piano lesson for the afternoon. She pours herself a tall glass of cold milk, grabs a couple of cookies, and settles in for her favorite TV show. She eagerly anticipates this episode because the secret identity of the new character is going to be revealed.

Just as she sits down and tunes in the show, her mom asks her to take out the trash. What should Caroline do?

Should she . . .
   A. Say, "Just a minute" and stall as long as she can?
   B. Ask her mother nicely if she can take out the trash after the show is over?
   C. Pretend that she doesn't hear her mom?
   D. Tell her mother that it's her sister's turn to take out the trash?
   E. Get up immediately and do what her mom says?

For help in knowing what Caroline should do, read Ephesians 6:1.

13

The Invitation

Jeff is a quiet boy who usually keeps to himself. He doesn't join the other boys when they play after school on the playground. He keeps his nose in a book and rarely speaks to anyone. Consequently he doesn't have many friends. No one knows much about him, and no one bothers to find out. Everyone just assumes that Jeff is a weird guy who prefers to be by himself.

Lately, though, Jeff has been saying hi to Tim. Once he helped Tim with a difficult math problem. Today, Jeff asks Tim to come over after school for a snack. What should Tim do?

Should he . . .

    A.   Politely decline?

    B.   Make a comment about feeling sick and walk away?

    C.   Go for the food but leave as soon as he is able?

    D.   Go and try to get to know Jeff and his family?

    E.   Agree to go but remember a dentist appointment at the last minute?

 For help in knowing what Tim should do, read 1 Corinthians 14:1.

A Friend in Need

Vanessa's friend Shirley is going through a difficult time. Her mom and dad recently split up. Her dad moved out, and now her mom is working full-time. Shirley has to watch her younger brother and sister after school each day, make sure they get their homework done, and get dinner ready. It's a big load for such young shoulders. Shirley doesn't participate in any after-school activities anymore, and their friends rarely see her on the weekends because she's with her dad. Even worse, her grades are suffering. Vanessa knows that Shirley is afraid of flunking a couple of classes because she's too tired to study at night.

Vanessa and her friends were discussing Shirley's situation after school one day. They realized that their friend needed help, but they didn't know what to do. "What Shirley needs is for someone to give her a break," Vanessa told her friends. They quickly agreed, but before anything could be decided, one of the girls had to leave for flag practice. Shirley's plight was soon forgotten until later that night. As Vanessa is getting ready for bed, she thinks about her friend and wonders what she can do to help her. What do you think Vanessa should do?

Should she . . .
 A. Pray that God will bring some extra helpers to take the load off Shirley?
 B. Buy Shirley and her family a lottery ticket each week in hopes of winning "the big one" so they can hire a maid?
 C. Write Shirley a note of encouragement?
 D. Arrange with her friends to take turns watching Shirley's brother and sister, so Shirley can at least have more study time?
 E. Figure that Shirley's mom will do something about it after she sees Shirley's report card?

 Read James 1:22-27 to see what God says about people who listen to his Word but don't obey it by "doing."

15

The Sunday Matinee

After church, Lucas gets a call from his friends asking him to go to the Sunday matinee. It's a movie that Lucas has wanted to see for a long time, and it finally made it to the dollar theater. His friend can pick him up in half an hour and bring him home after the movie. Lucas asks his mom, who agrees as long as Lucas doesn't have any homework. He has youth group that night and probably won't be able to do any work that evening.

Lucas hesitates. He does have homework in his reading class. The only catch is that his reading teacher usually doesn't ask for the weekend homework until a day or two later. He knows a couple of his friends don't do the weekend homework until Monday during study hall, which is after the reading class. Lucas is sure he could finish his reading assignment during study hall, too. His friends all seem to get away with it. Why not him? What do you think Lucas should do?

Should he . . .

A. Tell his mom that he has no homework and go to the movie?

B. Tell his friend that he can't go because has to finish his reading homework?

C. Get up early Monday morning and finish his homework—without his mom seeing him?

D. Go to the movies and pray that his teacher doesn't collect the homework on Monday?

E. Take his reading homework to the movies with him?

 Check out Hebrews 12:11 for some helpful advice on what Lucas should do.

The Final Exam

Jodie rubs her eyes and looks at the clock. It's ten-thirty, time for her to be in bed. She has been studying for her math final since she got home from school, and her brain feels like mush. Jodie leafs through the book. She still has three chapters to go. She slumps in her chair. She can't possibly fit another number into her head. Besides, the ones already there are so jumbled around that it's not making sense anyway. Jodie decides to close the book for now, get some sleep, and get up early the next morning to study the remaining chapters.

What seems like minutes later, her mom is standing over her, shaking her. "Jodie, you've overslept. You'd better get up now or you'll miss the bus," her mom is saying. The word *overslept* sinks into Jodie's sleep-logged brain. It can't be true. Now she will have no time to study those last chapters. Jodie is in a panic. How will she ever pass her math final if she doesn't find the time to at least look over the chapters? Unfortunately, today is one of those days. There's not a spare moment to study.

During third period, her reading teacher asks if Jodie would mind taking a note to Mr. Simpson, who just happens to be Jodie's math teacher. Jodie takes the note over to his room. Nobody is around, so Jodie decides to leave the note on his desk. As she puts it on his desk, she notices the final exam—with answers—sitting in plain view. No one is around. What do you think Jodie should do?

Should she . . .
  A. Slip the exam under her sweater, take it to the library, make a copy, and return it before anyone notices it is gone?
  B. Quickly read the exam and try to memorize the questions?
  C. Walk away without looking at the exam?
  D. Tear up the exam so that Mr. Simpson will have to postpone the final?
  E. Just look at the sections in the exam covering the material she didn't have time to study?

 For help in knowing how Jodie should respond, look up Psalm 101:7.

17

The Substitute

Matt walks into English class Friday morning and immediately notices that something is different. The kids are all talking, walking around the room, and in general, just goofing off. He looks around for Mrs. Henry. Then Matt sees the reason for the confusion: There's a substitute teacher standing in front of the classroom trying to get the students' attention.

Slowly the kids take their seats, but the situation deteriorates. It's clear that the substitute doesn't have a clue what chapter the class is supposed to be studying. When she asks for help, the students give her a hard time, telling her it's the chapter the class studied last week. The chaos continues. Matt groans helplessly and wonders what he should do.

Should he . . .

    A. Join in, pretending to be someone else?

    B. Sit quietly and read a book, ignoring what is going on?

    C. Try to get the other kids to be nicer to the teacher?

    D. Scream, "I can't take it!" and run to the principal's office?

    E. Start taking down names to give to Mrs. Henry so he can get some brownie points when she returns?

 For help in knowing what Matt should do, read 1 Corinthians 13:4-5.

What a Week!

T he alarm rings, waking Shelby from a fitful sleep. She didn't sleep well last night, and it's no wonder. Shelby has a lot on her mind. This is going to be a difficult week. She has an audition on Thursday for the school play. Shelby has worked hard over the last several weeks to memorize her lines, and she wants the audition to be perfect. Then she has a big science test on Friday. Her final paper for the semester in English is also due that day—she has nearly completed it but needs to rewrite one section and type it on the computer.

That's only the major stuff coming up this week. Shelby also has all the routine activities that she somehow has to fit in. She spent most of last night lying awake, staring at the ceiling and wondering how she could possibly get everything done. Now, on top of all the work she has to do, Shelby is so exhausted that she doesn't even want to think about getting up. She wonders how she will make it through this week. What do you think Shelby should do?

Should she . . .
   A. Ask her mom to write her an excuse and stay home from school to get her work done?
   B. Ask her English teacher to give her an extension on her paper?
   C. Put the pillow over her head and go back to sleep?
   D. Spend more time worrying about what she has to do?
   E. Devise a daily plan of what she needs to accomplish each day, and trust God to get her through—one day at a time?

 Colossians 2:6-7 will shed light on how Shelby can get through this difficult week.

The Comic Book King

Milt is an admitted comic book fanatic. He loves them. Every spare minute he will pull out his newest super-hero comic and plunge into the fantasy world. Milt not only likes to read comic books, but he also is an avid collector, with his collection now numbering more than five hundred comics of all varieties. Milt and his friend, when they can convince their parents to take them, go to comic book shows. There they buy, exchange comic book favorites with other fans, and hear the latest news in the comic book industry. To Milt, collecting and reading comic books is a fun hobby.

Lately Milt has been wondering about the time he devotes to this hobby. In Sunday school last week, his teacher was talking about putting God first and spending time in God's Word. Milt had to confess that the last time he sat down and opened his Bible was at Christmas. Throughout the week, Milt has prayed and considered making a few changes in his habits. He decided to reduce the amount of time he spends reading comic books and to devote more time to quality reading—particularly his Bible.

On his way home from school, Milt passes by his favorite comic book store. This place is a true gold mine for finding those hard-to-find collector editions. Milt is about to enter the store to see if they have the newest Spiderman comic when he remembers his decision. This would be a good time to start disciplining himself. But what would one more comic book hurt? What do you think Milt should do?

Should he . . .

A. Take a deep breath and keep walking past the comic book store?

B. Start his new reading discipline tomorrow?

C. Quickly peek into the store. If he doesn't see the comic book he wants immediately, run out?

D. Have a friend go in the store to check out the inventory. Then only if there's something good will he go in to buy it?

E. Forget about his decision—after all, what harm is there in collecting and reading comic books?

 To find out how Milt can resist temptation, read 1 Timothy 6:11-12.

The Loan

Lindsey borrowed a dollar from Elizabeth several weeks ago. Lindsey promised to pay Elizabeth back right away but apparently has forgotten all about it. When Elizabeth sees Lindsey in the lunch line today, she remembers the loan and Lindsey's promise. Elizabeth could use the money to buy that extra piece of pizza. What should Elizabeth do?

Should she . . .

A. Not say anything about the money and figure that if Lindsey pays it back, fine; if not, that's fine, too?

B. Nicely remind Lindsey about the dollar?

C. Tell other kids that Lindsey owes her money and won't pay it back?

D. Demand that Lindsey pay back the dollar immediately?

E. Drop big hints about how she could buy that extra pizza if only she had a dollar?

 For help in knowing what Lindsey should do, read Luke 6:34.

Lights Out!

It is a cold, windy day and it's just beginning to snow. Jean is on her way into the store to pick up a gallon of milk for her mom when she notices a car with its lights on. The driver is nowhere to be seen. Jean's mom is waiting for her because they have to get home for a quick supper before choir. She really needs to hurry. What should Jean do?

Should she . . .

   A. Say, "I wonder how long his lights will last" and keep walking?

   B. Try the doors, get in, check out the tapes, and take a few?

   C. Try the doors, get in, and turn off the lights?

   D. Try the doors and finding them locked, take down the license plate number and report it to the store cashier?

   E. Leave a note saying "You should be more careful. Leaving your lights on can run down the battery"?

 For help in knowing what Jean should do, read Matthew 7:12.

All the Right Moves

Malcolm is a talented basketball player. He is one of the stars on the team. A lot of the younger players look up to Malcolm, and he enjoys staying after practice to help the newer kids improve their game. He's a patient teacher and hopes to be a coach eventually. Today, when Malcolm came to practice, he noticed a new kid on the court. Malcolm introduced himself and let the new kid know that if he needed any help, he would be available.

When practice gets underway, Malcolm quickly realizes that he had underestimated the new boy's skills. He is good and has some moves that Malcolm has never seen before. Without showboating, the new boy puts on a ball-handling and shooting clinic. Malcolm can't help but be impressed. After practice, the new boy offers to show Malcolm some of those moves. "I watched you during practice, and you're good. I bet you could pick up these moves real fast," the boy tells Malcolm. What do you think Malcolm should do?

Should he . . .

A. Act insulted and walk away?

B. Tell the new boy that he will think about it?

C. Watch the new boy carefully and try to copy his moves on his own?

D. Tell the boy he has his own style, thank you, and doesn't need to learn anything else?

E. Gratefully accept the boy's offer to learn those new moves?

 Check out Acts 18:24-28 to see how Apollos, a gifted speaker, handled an offer to improve his message.

The Sick Classmate

Mr. Spencer, Lauren's homeroom teacher, looks as though he has something serious to tell the class. As everyone settles into their seats, Mr. Spencer tells the class that one of their classmates, Emily, is very sick and will be out of school for some time. Mr. Spencer says the doctors aren't quite sure what is wrong with Emily. She was in the hospital for tests last week, and her family is awaiting the results.

Emily already has missed a week of school. Lauren doesn't know Emily very well, and although she feels badly for Emily, she doesn't know what to do.

Should she . . .
- A. Not do anything because Emily is not in her group of friends?
- B. Decide it's too late to send Emily a card—after all, she has been gone a week already?
- C. Call Emily's parents to ask if she could bring Emily's schoolwork to her?
- D. Stay as far away from Emily as possible because she doesn't want to catch Emily's illness?
- E. Send get-well cards to all her friends "just in case"?

 For help in knowing what Lauren should do, read James 4:17.

Doubting Ray

Jeff's friend Ray has been coming to church since he was four years old. He has heard all the Bible stories time and again. He knows about Jesus. He's heard it all. But Ray is beginning to question some of the stories in the Bible. He's just not so sure anymore about what he's hearing at church and what he's reading in the Bible.

One Sunday after church Jeff and Ray are riding bikes. Out of the blue Ray asks Jeff if he believes everything he hears about Jesus. Before Jeff can answer, Ray hurriedly says that he's really not so sure about all he hears in church and reads in the Bible. Ray obviously wants to talk about his doubts with Jeff. What should Jeff do?

Should he . . .
  A. Help Ray find answers to his questions?
  B. Argue with Ray and tell him that his questions are dumb?
  C. Decide not to spend any more time with Ray because he might be a bad influence?
  D. Gasp, ride away as quickly as possible, and tell the pastor as soon as he can?
  E. Start praying really loudly over Ray that he would have greater faith?

 For help in knowing what Jeff should do, read Jude 1:22.

Shooting Hoops

Ross is a loud, obnoxious boy in Brian's class. Although Brian doesn't know Ross well, he doesn't like Ross because Ross always has to be the center of attention. Ross tends to make jokes at others' expense and boss kids around. He is just not fun to be with.

Brian usually tries to stay away from Ross. Today on the playground, however, Ross comes over to Brian and asks if he wants to shoot some hoops after school. What should Brian do?

Should he . . .
- A. Make up an excuse and stay home instead?
- B. Go just to beat Ross and show him up so Ross won't invite him back?
- C. Go—although he doesn't want to—and try to be nice to Ross?
- D. Laugh in Ross's face and say, "Are you kidding?" and walk away?
- E. Say OK, and then "forget" to show up?

 For help in knowing what Brian should do, read Ephesians 4:2.

26

Guess Who's Coming to Dinner?

Russ can't believe his ears. His mother's old college room-mate is coming for the weekend. If that's not bad enough (Russ will get kicked out of his room for Mrs. Spencer), she is also bringing her obnoxious son, Oliver. Ollie, as his mom calls him, is a real pain. Last time they visited, Oliver broke two of Russ's new Terminators, spilled paint and blamed it on Russ, pulled the dog's tail until she almost bit him (serves him right), and generally created havoc wherever he went. And that was only for a day! Russ can't imagine what Ollie might do over an entire weekend.

To make matters worse—if that's possible—Russ had planned to go over to his friend's house to try out his new remote-controlled truck. They had just built the most awesome obstacle course in his friend's backyard and have been waiting all week to test the truck. Instead, Russ will be stuck with Oliver the entire weekend. He may as well spend both days in school. That would be more enjoyable. How will he ever going to survive this week-end? What do you think Russ should do?

Should he . . .
   A. Hide all his expensive equipment, including his remote-controlled truck, in the basement so Oliver can't get his hands on it?
   B. Share his other stuff with Oliver, and offer to take him to his friend's house to test-drive the remote-controlled truck?
   C. Refuse to play with Oliver?
   D. Tell his mom that he's really sick and shouldn't be around other people? He may have to stay in his room, but at least he'll be away from Oliver.
   E. Ignore Oliver the entire weekend?

 Check out 1 Peter 4:9 to see how Russ should respond.

27

Early Edition

Tyler plans to spend the night with his best friend, Lou. They have a whole evening of entertainment planned: a couple of videos, the newest computer game, some comic books to flip through. Before Tyler leaves, his mother reminds him to wear his gloves and hat. It's January, and the weathermen are all predicting frigid temperatures for the night and morning.

The evening has been great so far. The new computer game is totally cool. The boys swapped a couple of comic books and then topped off the night with a *Star Wars* marathon. It's late when they both finally tumble into bed.

Before he knows it, Tyler is rudely awakened. Lou is shaking his foot, trying to get him up. "Come on, wake up. I've got to do my newspaper route. Let's get going," Lou insists. Bleary-eyed, Tyler looks at the clock. It's only 6 A.M. Tyler never said he would help Lou. In fact, Lou never asked him. What's he going to do now?

Should he . . .
  A. Help Lou without grumbling?
  B. Help Lou for several houses and then fake an attack of frostbite?
  C. Try to ignore Lou and sleep in?
  D. Help Lou out but ask him politely to ask first the next time?
  E. Tell Lou he'll go on the condition that Lou pay him for the work?

 For help in finding out how Tyler should act, read Philippians 2:14-15.

Egg-spectations

Garrett is the most popular boy in Brendan's class. Everyone wants to sit with him at lunch and be his friend. When it's time to decide what to do at recess, Garrett typically leads the way. Whatever Garrett decides, the gang generally goes along with.

Brendan likes Garrett, too, and wants to be his friend. He joins in whatever games Garrett and his friends play. One afternoon, Garrett suggests that the group egg Mrs. Smith's house that night. Mrs. Smith is one of the strictest teachers in the school and not very popular. Nobody likes Mrs. Smith—or at least no one admits he does. What should Brendan do?

Should he . . .

A. Volunteer to get the eggs?

B. Laugh and pretend to go along with the idea?

C. Explain that it would be wrong and walk away?

D. Suggest a less messy prank?

E. Say he's allergic to eggs and can't be around them at all?

 For help in knowing what Brendan should do, read Proverbs 1:10.

Stolen Goods

While eating lunch at school the other day, Jared happened to overhear one of the boys bragging at the other end of the table. Jared almost didn't believe what he was hearing—the boy was telling his friends about the candy bars he had stolen from the snack bar. Usually Jared would think that such claims were just a bunch of hot air, but then the boy began passing out the candy bars to his friends. The boy and his friends laughed as they enjoyed their stolen treats. Looking quickly around the lunchroom, Jared saw the assistant principal on the far side of the room, breaking up a fight. No one had seen the boy and the candy bars except for Jared.

That night at home, Jared was uneasy about what he saw, and he wondered what to do about the situation. The next day he sat at the same table, keeping an eye out for the boy. Sure enough, the boy came back.

Today, he has stolen several dozen large cookies. Jared knows that he has to do something, but what?

Should Jared . . .
A. Go to the principal and tell him what he saw?
B. Stand up and yell, "Stop, thief!" in the middle of the cafeteria?
C. Ignore the situation. The staff will discover what's happening sooner or later?
D. Hire the biggest kid in school to get after this boy to stop stealing?
E. Write an anonymous note to this boy and threaten to tell the police if he doesn't stop stealing?

 Take a look at Leviticus 19:11 for the biblical principle to guide Jared's response.

Show a Little Respect

The students at Ginny's school are hopping mad. The other day the principal announced that there would be no more class trips this year. It seems that on the last school trip, a half dozen students decided to leave their group and go their own way instead. They got lost, and the teachers and chaperones spent several frantic hours searching for them. Those students were punished individually, but the principal canceled all the other trips for this year.

As editor of the school newspaper, Ginny is receiving letter after letter from angry students about the new policy. Some of the letters offer helpful ideas. Others are downright nasty and disrespectful. Ginny is pressured by her newspaper staff and her friends to run some of the letters—the nastier, the better. Ginny doesn't agree with the principal's decision, and she is disappointed. One of her classes was supposed to go to the new water park this spring as part of its science project, but now the class can't go. Ginny has to admit many of the nastier letters are pretty funny, but she wonders if it is right to print them. What do you think Ginny should do?

Should she . . .

A. Print the nastiest letter she can find to let the principal know how unpopular he has become?

B. Print one or two of the milder letters—the principal will get the point?

C. Write a scathing editorial about how mean the principal is and call for his resignation?

D. Express her, and her classmates', opposition in a thoughtful and respectful editorial that clearly presents their views?

E. Put all the letters together and send them to the principal anonymously?

 For help in knowing how Ginny should respond, look up 1 Peter 2:13.

The Terminator

Jonathan doesn't quite know why, but Ben, the school bully, has it in for him. And that's not good news. Ben, simply put, is immense. He's three times as big as Jonathan and looks like Arnold Schwarzenegger. He's the terror of the entire school and apparently has taken a personal interest in making Jonathan's life miserable.

It started with name-calling, but Ben is getting increasingly aggressive. He keeps bothering Jonathan and trying to pick a fight with him. The last couple of days, Ben has been waiting for Jonathan outside school, calling him a wimp for not fighting. What should Jonathan do?

Should he . . .
- A. Totally avoid Ben at all costs?
- B. Hit Ben as hard as he possibly can?
- C. Ignore Ben's comments and keep his cool?
- D. Look for ways to be nice to Ben?
- E. Pay ten of the biggest kids he knows to beat up Ben?

 For help in knowing what Jonathan should do, read Proverbs 19:11 and Luke 6:27-36.

The Sweater Swap

Paula searches through her closet looking for something to wear with her khaki skirt. Her sister's new red sweater would look really cool. Since Marge has already left for school, Paula decides to go ahead and "borrow" it. After all, what Marge doesn't know won't hurt her. Paula gets home first from school anyway, so she can put the sweater back in Marge's closet before her sister gets home. Marge will never know.

Everyone likes Paula's "new sweater," and things are going just fine until math class. Paula jumps up quickly to turn in her assignment and catches the sweater on a loose screw on the side of her desk. To her horror, it makes a huge hole in the sleeve. Marge's sweater is ruined. What should Paula do?

Should she . . .
   A. Hang the sweater in Marge's closet before she gets home and say nothing?
   B. Buy another sweater like the ruined one and hang it in the closet?
   C. Put the sweater in the wash and blame the washer for ruining it?
   D. Stuff the sweater under her bed and see if Marge misses it?
   E. Tell Marge what she did and offer to buy her a new sweater?

 For help in knowing what Paula should do, read Proverbs 29:25.

Heard It through the Grapevine

Susan and her friends are finishing lunch when Amy walks up. "Have you heard?" Amy begins excitedly. She then proceeds to tell everyone at the table some juicy news involving another girl in Susan's math class. Susan doesn't know the girl very well, but she knows that the girl has been the subject of hurtful gossip before. The girl is rather quiet, but Susan's friends think she is a snob.

Amy takes great relish in passing along the latest dirt on this girl. Susan knows that the story isn't true because she was in class when this incident supposedly happened. But Susan's friends listen intently, laughing and making wisecracks about the girl. What should Susan do?

Should she . . .

A. Hurry after lunch to find her best friend and pass the news along?

B. Tell everyone at the lunch table not to believe the story because she knows it's not true?

C. Listen quietly and decide not to tell anyone the gossip?

D. Add to the story and make it even more wild?

E. Tell everyone a wild story about Amy?

 For help in knowing what Susan should do, read Proverbs 18:17 and Proverbs 18:8.

The Challenge

Kurt and Eric have gotten into a big argument. Eric is such a know-it-all; he has just insulted Kurt's favorite college team. Although Kurt knows better, he can't let this comment slip by, and the argument grows. Some pretty tough words are exchanged, and finally, Eric challenges Kurt to a fight after school. When the bell rings for class, Eric storms away.

Many of Kurt's and Eric's friends witnessed the entire exchange. Kurt is expected to meet Eric after school on the soccer field. By the end of the school day, everyone is talking about the fight. Some of Kurt's friends are even taking bets on how it will turn out. What should Kurt do?

Should he . . .

A. Meet Eric on the soccer field and fight him?

B. Meet Eric on the soccer field and try to work things out without fighting?

C. Gather some of his friends to help take on Eric?

D. Put balloons in his sleeves to make it look as though he has massive muscles?

E. Not go to the soccer field and slink around school for the next several weeks, hoping that Eric will forget all about their argument?

 For help in knowing what Kurt should do, read Proverbs 29:8 and Matthew 5:9.

The Tough Guy

Adam is always getting into trouble at school. Nobody messes around with him, and he will fight anybody who gets in his way. A lot of kids look up to Adam because everyone seems to be afraid of him.

Sam notices that some of his friends are beginning to follow Adam. They admire how "brave" he is and think it's cool that nobody pushes him around. Sam fears that he will lose all his friends unless something changes. What should he do?

Should he . . .

A. Wish he were as brave as Adam and try to act tougher with people, just like Adam?

B. Not only avoid Adam and his group but also pray for them?

C. Organize his own gang and challenge Adam and his friends to a fight?

D. Write "Adam is a jerk" on the bathroom wall?

E. Start spreading false rumors about Adam so no one will like him?

 For help in knowing what Sam should do, read Proverbs 3:31.

5

Don't Believe It

Wait until you hear the latest," Lara whispers to Charlotte as they take their seats in class. The teacher walks in, so Charlotte will have to wait until after class to hear Lara's latest gossip. If there is some dirt to pass around about anyone, Lara will have it. She is the class busybody, always sticking her nose where it doesn't belong. The worse the news is, the more Lara relishes passing it along. This latest piece of gossip must be pretty juicy because Lara is practically glowing.

During the class, Charlotte forgets about Lara and her news. As she leaving the room, however, Lara catches up to her. "Hey, I've got something to tell you, remember?" she begins. Then Lara proceeds to tell her how Charlotte's best friend was caught cheating on a math test and will not be allowed to participate in the academic contest on Saturday. Charlotte knows that her friend is an honest person. She can't imagine her cheating on a math test—especially since math is her best subject. Charlotte realizes that Lara is standing there waiting for her to react. What do you think Charlotte should do?

Should she . . .
- A. Tell Lara that she knows her friend would not cheat, so the rumor is totally false?
- B. Figure that although Lara is exaggerating, there must be some truth to the rumor?
- C. Find her friend and demand to know why she was cheating?
- D. Pass the gossip along to her other friends?
- E. Demand proof of Lara's story because she accused her friend?

 For help in deciding how Charlotte should handle gossip about her friend, read 1 Corinthians 13:6-7.

Spilled Beans

Joy feels terrible about what happened at lunch today. She and her friends were sitting around after they had eaten when the subject of boys came up. Somehow, the conversation turned to Joy's best friend, Darcy. One of the girls began speculating about which boy Darcy liked in their math class. Well, she came up with the wrong name. Rather than leave it at that, Joy blurted out the name of the boy Darcy *does* like. One thing lead to another, and by the end of the day, the school was buzzing with the latest news.

Darcy was so mad at Joy that she didn't even wait to walk home with her after school. Joy knows that she should have kept her big mouth shut, but it's too late. If only Darcy would give her a chance to at least apologize. The phone rings, and it's Darcy. Before Joy can get in a word, Darcy blasts her. She really lets her have it. Joy is completely taken aback. She knows she was wrong to say anything, but does she deserve a tirade like this? Darcy finally quiets down and is waiting for a response. What do you think Joy should say to her?

Should she . . .
   A. Admit quietly that she was wrong and ask Darcy to forgive her?
   B. Let Darcy have it back—full blast!?
   C. Tell Darcy it really was another girl at the table who spilled the beans?
   D. Get so mad at Darcy for blasting her that she vows never to speak to her again?
   E. Hang up—and wait for Darcy to calm down?

 Check out Proverbs 15:1 to find out how Joy should respond.

The Good Old Days

At dinner, Dustin mentions a problem that he is having with his friend Steve. He and Steve have been friends for a long time, but recently Steve has been a bit aloof. Dustin is puzzled by this and doesn't know what to do. Dustin's father begins to offer some suggestions for what Dustin might do. His father relates that when he was that age, he and his best friends went through a similar situation.

Dustin has heard stories about his dad and his boyhood friends many times before. What should Dustin do?

Should he . . .

  A. Listen quietly and think about what his father is saying?

  B. Quickly change the subject and ask his father how was his day at work?

  C. Roll his eyes and say, "Please, Dad, not again"?

  D. Pretend to listen, saying, "Hmmmmm" and "Yeah" while thinking about Pez dispensers?

  E. Jump up from the table, saying, "Hey, I forgot I have twenty pages of math homework to do. I'd better get started"?

 For help in knowing what Dustin should do, read Proverbs 12:15 and Proverbs 21:16.

8

Channel Surfing

I t has been an exhausting day at school, and Jenny is looking forward to coming home and relaxing for a while before doing her homework. After a quick snack, Jenny grabs the *TV Guide* and notices that a really interesting show is on the public television channel. *Perfect!* she thinks, switching on the tube.

A half hour later, her brother, Dale, walks in the door. He grabs a handful of cookies, plops down in front of the TV, picks up the remote control, and starts channel surfing. What should Jenny do?

Should she . . .
A. Glare at Dale for the rest of the evening as though he is an alien from another planet?
B. Get up and start her homework instead of watching TV?
C. Get into an argument over who should have control of the TV that lasts until their mother breaks it up and sends them both to their rooms?
D. Politely ask Dale to turn the channel back to the program she was watching?
E. Grab the remote control and throw it out the window so that neither of them can watch what they want?

 For help in knowing what Jenny should do, read Proverbs 17:14.

The Windfall

After school, Rick always brings in the mail. Today he notices a letter for him in the stack. It's from his Uncle Ken, his favorite uncle! Rick can hardly wait to open the letter. Uncle Ken travels a lot and always has interesting stories to relate. And sometimes Uncle Ken tucks in a little surprise for Rick.

Rick opens the letter excitedly. Sure enough, a twenty-five dollar check drops out. *This is great!* thinks Rick. Now that he has this little windfall, what should he do?

Should Rick . . .

A. Run right out and spend the money on baseball cards and candy?

B. Throw away the check and forget about it?

C. Cash the check for one-dollar bills and stick the money in his wallet so it looks like he is loaded?

D. Save all of the money to buy a new computer game?

E. Put some money aside for church, put some in the bank, and put the rest in his wallet?

 For help in knowing what Rick should do, read Proverbs 10:16.

Looking for Answers

Today is Tucker's first day in his new school. His family moved in the middle of the school year, and Tucker is joining his new classes in midstream. He's not sure what they are studying at his new school. Tucker could be ahead of his classmates—or he could be way behind. He was more than a bit nervous entering his first class of the day, English. As he has gone through the day—social studies, reading and science—Tucker has begun to feel more comfortable. The topics are different than what he has studied already, but it appears that he will be able to pick them up quickly.

The kids have been friendly to Tucker, and his new teachers are very nice. He is feeling more confident by the time he enters his math class. Tucker's confidence vanishes, however, as the math teacher announces a pop quiz on multiplying fractions. At his old school, they were just starting fractions. This wasn't covered yet. Tucker isn't sure what he should do. He doesn't want to call attention to himself, and he doesn't want to appear stupid in front of his new classmates. Tucker glances around. The boy next to him is writing furiously. He seems to know what he's doing, and Tucker can easily see his paper. What do you think Tucker should do?

Should he . . .
    A. Go to the desk and admit to the teacher that he doesn't know anything about multiplying fractions?
    B. Copy off the boy's paper next to him and ask his parents for help later?
    C. Guess at the answers?
    D. Tell the teacher that he has to leave early for a dentist appointment?
    E. Crumple up his quiz paper and try to make a basket in the garbage can?

 Read Proverbs 11:2 and Proverbs 16:18 for guidance on how Tucker should respond.

Facing Unjust Criticism

Carson is having a difficult time getting along with the band instructor, Mr. Parke. Carson enjoys music, and he practices his clarinet faithfully. He's not the best player in the clarinet section, but he's not the worst, either. Carson always gets to band on time and has never missed a rehearsal. For whatever reason, however, Mr. Parke seems to pick on him. Last week, for example, the students were having a hard time settling down to play. At least three or four kids in the clarinet section were still talking when Mr. Parke raised his baton. But whom did Mr. Parke single out and punish? Carson. And he wasn't even one of the culprits.

Today is the worst. The clarinet section is having trouble with a certain passage. Mr. Parke stops the entire band and asks the section to play. The clarinets manage to get through it, but it is obvious to everyone in the band that there were a few clunkers. Mr. Parke yells at the clarinets and then asks Carson to play the difficult passage. Carson has practiced that passage many times, and he can play it. But playing it under the fierce gaze of Mr. Parke is a different story. With pounding heart and sweaty hands, Carson gives it his best shot, but it is a total disaster. He can't hit a right note. The entire band laughs, and Carson feels utterly humiliated. What do you think he should do?

Should Carson . . .
A. Throw a tantrum, firing his clarinet through the bass drum?

B. Say nothing but give Mr. Parke a dirty look?

C. Go to the guidance counselor and ask to switch from band to shop class?

D. Pray about the situation and ask God for strength to help him through this problem?

E. Start a petition drive to have Mr. Parke fired?

 Read 1 Samuel 1:6-10, 15-18 to find out how Hannah handled unjust criticism.

12

Math Problem

Randy's friend Pat is struggling in math class. The big test is on Friday. Pat knows that Randy is really good in math, so he asks Randy if he will help him after school today. Randy says he will. Later that day, Randy's friend Terry asks him to come over after school to try out his new video game. It just happens to be the game that Randy really wants to get for himself, and he would love to try it out. As he is about to say yes, he remembers his promise to Pat. What should Randy do?

Should he . . .
 A. Say nothing to Pat and go to Terry's house?
 B. Tell Pat he can't come over because he has to go right home, then go over to Terry's house?
 C. Tell Terry, "I'd like to, but I can't because I have something else to do" then help Pat as he promised?
 D. Pay Terry to help Pat while he gets to play video games?
 E. Ask Terry if Pat can come over too and help Pat between games?

 For help in knowing what Randy should do, read Proverbs 12:22.

The Group Project

Every year, Dalton's school sponsors a science fair. This year, the students in Dalton's science class are assigned to a group project. Each group has been given broad guidelines for the project and instructions how to do it. But the instructions are very specific about one thing—each member of the group must contribute to the project. At the first group meeting, Dalton was selected to head the project team. It took the group the rest of the meeting time to select a topic, assign different parts of the project to various team members, and set up a schedule to complete the project on time.

During the first several meetings in the early phases of the project, it became obvious to Dalton that one member of the group was not pulling his weight. The boy never came to the first meeting. The second time, he came late and had forgotten his materials. Dalton let it slide because there still was plenty of time to complete the project. But now the project is due in two weeks, and the boy still has yet to do his part. The rest of the group is grumbling and demanding that Dalton do something about it. Dalton realizes that something needs to be done, but he doesn't know what to do. What do you think he should do?

Should Dalton . . .

A. Call the boy and yell at him for not doing his part of the project?

B. Kick the boy off the project and report him to the teacher?

C. Do the project himself and cover for the boy?

D. Ask the boy how he can help him get his part of the project done and then be sure to call him frequently to encourage him to participate?

E. Turn in the project with the boy's part missing so everyone will know he didn't do it?

 To know how Dalton should handle this situation, read 1 Thessalonians 5:14.

14

Practice Makes Perfect

Before leaving for the store, Amanda's mother tells her to practice the piano while she is gone. Amanda plays for about three minutes and then stops to get a drink of water. On her way into the kitchen, Amanda catches a bit of the TV show her brother is watching. She stops to watch awhile. Suddenly she remembers that she should be practicing. Amanda jumps up and gets back to the piano. She sits back down just as her mother walks in the door.

Her mother looks in and asks Amanda if she has practiced. What should Amanda do?

Should she . . .
- A. Say yes and let it go at that?
- B. Say, "Not really. I started but then started watching TV"?
- C. Answer with a silly grin, "Sure, Mom, I practiced"?
- D. Ignore her mother?
- E. Promise that she will practice double the next day?

 For help in knowing what Amanda should do, read Proverbs 28:13.

15

Hoop Dreams

It's the final seconds of the basketball game, and Kyle is having a great game. Everything seems to be going for him tonight. The game is close, however, and it comes down to the last few seconds. Tom passes the ball to Kyle, and he shoots it in for the winning basket.

The crowd goes wild, and all of Kyle's teammates surround him and give him high fives. After the game, just about everyone comes up and tells Kyle how great he was. Kyle goes home feeling really good about himself. Now that he's the star, what should he do?

Should Kyle . . .
    A. Keep practicing hard and play with teamwork? (After all, Tom did pass him the ball.)
    B. Feel really proud of himself and begin to hang around with only the kids who think he's cool?
    C. Think he's the new Michael Jordan and start shooting all the time?
    D. Tell everyone, "See you at the slam-dunk contest"?
    E. Start taking applications for the Kyle Fan Club?

 For help in knowing what Kyle should do, read Proverbs 27:2.

The Slumber Party

Andrea invites several friends for a sleepover. The girls arrive and settle in for a great night of polishing nails, trying new hairstyles, and listening to some CDs. Andrea happens to look out the window and sees Heather walking up to the door. Heather lives down the street, but Andrea did not invite her to the party. It's obvious, however, that Heather knows all about the party, because she is carrying her sleeping bag and an overnight case. What should Andrea do?

Should she . . .
  A. Quickly turn off the porch lights, get everyone quiet, ignore the doorbell, and pretend that no one is home?
  B. Let Heather in but treat her rotten all evening?
  C. Say, "I didn't invite you!" and turn Heather away?
  D. Tell Heather it's really not a sleepover but a math study session?
  E. Invite Heather in and welcome her to the party?

 For help in knowing what Andrea should do, read Titus 3:2.

The Clique

Jackie is good friends with a group of girls, including Catherine, Christina, and Jamie. This group eats lunch together every day, and they go to the basketball games after school together. They all tried out for the field hockey team and made it! It's a fun group of girls, and Jackie really enjoys being with them.

But lately, Jackie has noticed that Catherine and Jamie are becoming more bossy. Usually they decide what the group will do, where they will go after the basketball game, and who will be invited. Now they have decided they don't like Christina. Jackie and Christina are particularly close because they have been friends since elementary school.

Today at lunch, while Christina is in the lunch line, Catherine and Jamie start cutting her down. What should Jackie do?

Should she . . .
  A. Listen quietly?
  B. Laugh and agree with what Catherine and Jamie are saying?
  C. Defend Christina, explaining that what the two are saying isn't true?
  D. Try to change the subject by talking about the cute new boy in math class?
  E. Start cutting down one of Catherine and Jamie's friends?

For help in knowing what Jackie should do, read Proverbs 3:3-4.

The Stock Boy

Lance recently got an after-school job at the neighborhood grocery store. It's a small store, and his dad's friend owns the place. Lance usually comes in three times a week to help stock the shelves. His parents have agreed to let him work as long as Lance keeps his grades up and participates in other activities. Lance likes it, but it is hard, physical work, requiring a lot of lifting and carrying. When Lance gets home, he is exhausted.

Today, Lance walks into the store already tired. Last night he stayed up late to study for a test. Then he went to school early for the student Bible study. He hopes that there's not too much to do today. Lance is greeted with the unwelcome news that a huge shipment just arrived. Lance and the other stock boy have to unpack everything and stock the shelves. Lance sighs. The other boy is already getting down to work and enthusiastically tosses him a can. "Hey, if we both work hard, we can get this done in no time," he calls out. Lance stares at the stacks of boxes. He really doesn't want to work today. He would rather take it easy and let this guy do the work. As long as it gets done, does it matter who does more of the work? Besides, this guy has plenty of energy for both of them. What do you think Lance should do?

Should he . . .
- A. Help stock the shelves . . . but very slowly?
- B. Do a bit of stocking but take plenty of long breaks?
- C. Regardless of his feelings, pitch in and get the job done, doing his share of the load?
- D. Put a couple of cans on the shelves, then tell the other boy he needs to leave early?
- E. Tell the boy he sprained his arm in gym and can't do too much lifting? He will have to supervise today!

 Read 2 Thessalonians 3:6-7 for Paul's instructions about lazy workers and hard work.

The Baby-sitting Blues

Scott has been looking forward to spending Friday night with a couple of friends, watching videos, playing computer games, and just hanging out. Nothing definite has been set, however. Scott has mentioned it to his friends, but no one has committed to it yet.

When Mrs. Johnson calls Scott Thursday evening, desperately looking for a baby-sitter, Scott inwardly groans. He can hear the pleading in her voice, but what about his plans for Friday evening? What should Scott do?

Should he . . .

A. Have his mother call back and say that he has important business to attend to Friday night?

B. Say that he has a bad cold and shouldn't be around babies?

C. Suggest another friend who might be able to baby-sit for Mrs. Johnson?

D. Tell Mrs. Johnson he needs to check his calendar. Then quickly call his friends to make definite plans and then tell Mrs. Johnson, "Sorry, I have plans"?

E. Change his plans and baby-sit for Mrs. Johnson?

 For help in knowing what Scott should do, read Galatians 6:2-3.

20

Spreading the Word

Kim's best friend, Alexa, doesn't go to church. She knows that Kim is very involved with church, singing in the choir, attending youth group every Sunday night, and working in the Sunday school nursery. Kim also is a student leader at the early morning Bible study held at school. While Kim doesn't hide the fact she goes to church and the Bible study, she never has discussed spiritual matters with Alexa.

Today, as the two girls are walking home from school, Alexa starts asking Kim questions about church. She wants to know what goes on during the church service, what the pastor is like, and if Kim enjoys going to church. Finally, after several minutes of easy questions, Alexa asks Kim to explain why she believes in Jesus. Kim, who has easily answered the other questions, is caught off guard. What should she do?

Should Kim . . .

    A. Quickly change the subject and ask what Alexa is doing this weekend?

    B. Say, "I don't know. I was raised that way"?

    C. Say, "Jesus *who*"?

    D. Explain how Alexa can know Christ too?

    E. Tell Alexa she'll get the church's pastor to give her a call?

 For help in knowing what Kim should do, read 1 Peter 3:15.

Fire!

Peter is walking home from school. Preoccupied with thoughts of the big history test coming up on Wednesday, he hardly notices that he's more than halfway home. Then, to his utter amazement, he sees fire coming from a basement window in the neighbor's house.

Peter looks quickly around and sees no one else on the street. The neighbor's house appears empty, too. The flames are shooting out the window. What should Peter do?

Should he . . .
A. Run and get his camera?
B. Get a stick and some marshmallows?
C. Hope that someone else will call the fire department and go on home to study for the test?
D. Run and get a bucket of water to douse the flames?
E. Go to the nearest phone and call the fire department?

 For help in knowing what Peter should do, read Leviticus 19:18.

Pet Peeves

Anne Marie has finished basketball practice and is in a hurry to get home. Today is her friend's birthday party, and she has just enough time to get home, change, wrap the present, and go. Anne Marie runs into the house and upstairs, changes in record time, and then comes down to wrap her gift. As she puts the finishing touches on the present, she looks at the clock. Great, she thinks, ten minutes to get to the house.

As Anne Marie is about to leave, her mom comes in holding the dog's dish and says, "Aren't you forgetting something?" Anne Marie groans. It's her turn to feed and walk the dog. She will never make it to the party on time. What should she do?

Should Anne Marie . . .

    A. Ask her little brother to take care of the dog this time?

    B. Take the dog for the long walk he needs and then feed him, even though she will be late for the party?

    C. Run a couple of blocks with the dog, throw a biscuit in the dog's dish, and dash off to the party?

    D. Leave for the party and figure she'll take care of the dog later?

    E. Take the dog with her to the party and feed him birthday cake and ice cream?

 For help in knowing what Anne Marie should do, read Proverbs 12:10.

And Today's Topic Is . . .

In history class, Stephanie's teacher is discussing the religions of the world. The teacher asks for volunteers to explain what they believe. One boy, whose family is Vietnamese, shares his Buddhist beliefs. Another student explains her Islamic faith. Another classmate says his family is into the New Age movement. No one, however, has volunteered to explain Christianity.

Stephanie is a Christian. She is active in her church and truly loves the Lord. But does she really have to explain her faith now? She looks around the classroom but sees no one about to volunteer. The teacher looks like she's about to go on with the lesson. What should Stephanie do?

Should she . . .
- A. Look around and laugh softly, trying to be cool?
- B. Volunteer and explain how she accepted Christ as her Savior?
- C. Slump in her seat and hope the teacher doesn't see her?
- D. Make up a religion and explain it as a joke?
- E. Figure that everyone in the room knows about Jesus and doesn't really need to hear it again?

 For help in knowing what Stephanie should do, read Luke 9:26.

The Birthday Gift

Hunter's older brother is turning sixteen tomorrow, and Hunter wants to find the perfect birthday gift. His mom offered to buy it for him, but this year, Hunter wants to pick something out by himself. He doesn't want it to be a "kid" gift, either. He wants to get something more "mature." Hunter asked his best friend to help him look around for a gift after school today. His mom dropped the two boys off at the mall and promised to return in an hour. The boys drifted into store after store. Nothing struck Hunter as appropriate. He doesn't want to get his brother another book or a new leather belt. Finally, the boys turn into a small novelty shop that has all sorts of unique gifts. Hunter is excited. Now this store has possibilities!

As the two boys browse, Hunter's friend notices a section in the back that is partially blocked off from the rest of the store. A sign reads Adults Only. Hunter's friend nudges him toward the section. "Hey, I bet you'll find something for your brother in there." Hunter is unsure whether they should go into that section, but his friend urges him on. "You said you wanted to find something your brother will really like. Well, I bet you'll find it in here." Since no one is watching, Hunter and his friend go in. Immediately Hunter realizes that this material is intended for adults only. What should he do?

Should Hunter . . .

A. Browse along with his friend, looking for a grown-up gift?

B. Trash the section by pulling all the dirty books, tapes, and novelty items from the shelves and run from the store?

C. Take a quick look at everything in the section as long as he is there?

D. Tell his friend that if they don't leave now, an alarm will sound?

E. Tell his friend they have no business being in that section and that they had better go?

 Read 1 Timothy 4:12 for help in knowing how Hunter should respond in this situation.

The Big Hurt

Alan is walking home from school thinking about his science project. When he gets home he wants to get started on it right away because he has a piano lesson at 4:30 P.M. Alan glances at his watch. He should make it home in five minutes. That would give him enough time for a snack before he needs to hit the books.

Just then, Alan sees a small boy fall off his bike. The boy ends up under his bike and is crying. Alan looks around to see if the boy's mother is anywhere around. He sees no one, and it appears that the boy has scraped himself badly. What should Alan do?

Should he . . .
   A. Ignore the child because he doesn't know the boy? (Besides, it's not his problem.)
   B. Point at the boy and laugh?
   C. Stop and see what he can do to help?
   D. Compliment the boy on his nice bike?
   E. Give the boy a tissue for his scrapes, then hurry home?

 For help in knowing what Alan should do, read Luke 10:30-37.

Making Fun

Lisa and her friends always sit at the same table for lunch. They are among the oldest kids in the school, and it's an unwritten rule that no one else can sit at that table. Lisa and her friends spend their lunchtime goofing around with each other, telling jokes, or comparing horror stories from gym class. Typically, they ignore any students younger than themselves.

Lately, however, some of Lisa's friends have been picking on a younger student. This girl is small for her age, rather bookish, and extremely shy. She sits by herself for lunch. While the girl never has said anything to Lisa's friends, some of them seem to enjoy making fun of her and calling her names. Lisa can tell this is making the girl very uncomfortable and unhappy, but these are her friends. What should Lisa do?

Should she . . .
 A. Stick up for the girl and ask her friends to stop making fun of her?
 B. Say nothing as her friends continue to have fun at this girl's expense?
 C. Start talking about something else to distract her friends?
 D. Walk away, saying she doesn't like to hear her friends cut other people down?
 E. Report her friends' behavior to the lunchroom monitor?

 For help in knowing what Lisa should do, read Psalm 82:4

The Woodcutter

Nathan is rummaging around in his father's workshop when he notices his dad's special hunting knife lying on the table. His dad had been sharpening it, and Nathan thinks it looks sharp enough to chop some wood in the backyard. Although he has been told by his dad not to handle the knife, Nathan decides to take it outside.

Just as Nathan is about to start chopping wood, his father comes out and asks Nathan what he is doing with his special hunting knife. What should Nathan do?

Should he . . .

A. Say, "I found the knife outside and was going to return it to the workshop"?

B. Say, "What knife?"

C. Admit that he took the knife to chop wood?

D. Say he was cleaning the knife to surprise his dad?

E. Say, "Oops! I thought I picked up the hatchet"?

 For help in knowing what Nathan should do, read Proverbs 12:19.

On Time

It never fails. Anita's friend Marcie is always late. The car pool has to wait at Marcie's house in the morning at least ten minutes before she's ready. After school it's no better. Without fail, Marcie always comes out last. No one is quite sure what she is doing. It's a complete mystery to everyone. When Anita plans to go to the movies with Marcie, she tells her to be ready twenty minutes ahead of everyone else—and Marcie is still late. The situation seems hopeless!

This week should present a real challenge. Marcie will be spending the week with Anita while her parents are out of town. In preparation for the spring concert, the two girls have some special band rehearsals scheduled before school begins each morning. Anita does not want to be late for the rehearsals. But she's afraid she will be unless she can get Marcie moving in the morning. What do you think Anita should do?

Should she . . .

A. Nag Marcie every morning until she gets up and continue to nag her until she is out the door?

B. Splash cold water on Marcie's face every morning?

C. Tell Marcie that if she's not ready, the car will leave without her?

D. Set Marcie's alarm clock two hours early, so she will be ready?

E. Patiently work out a plan together that will enable Marcie to be ready to leave on time?

 Read Proverbs 27:15-16 to find out how God regards a nagging friend.

On the Air

Lizzie has invited Miranda to come over after school. Miranda is one of the most popular girls in Lizzie's class, and Lizzie is really excited that Miranda is coming over to her house. The two girls share a lot of common interests—both play soccer, enjoy collecting key chains, and have the same American Girl doll. Lizzie can't wait to show Miranda her collection and the cool outfits her aunt has made for her doll.

After a quick snack, the girls bound up the stairs to Lizzie's room. Lizzie closes the door to keep out her pesky brother and turns on the radio for some tunes. The two girls are spending an enjoyable time talking and listening to the music when Miranda gets up to change the radio station. "Hey, have you ever listened to this guy? He's totally cool," Miranda says. Lizzie listens for a minute and realizes this is the DJ who does all the dirty talking. She knows her parents don't approve of these dirty-talking DJs, but this is the first time Miranda has come over. What should Lizzie do?

Should she . . .
- A. Say and do nothing?
- B. Keep the radio on but go into another room?
- C. Say she would rather listen to something else and turn the radio dial to another station?
- D. Explain why she doesn't like to listen to that station and ask if it would be OK to listen to another popular music station?
- E. Pull the plug on the radio and tell Miranda it's broken?

 For help in knowing what Lizzie should do, read Philippians 4:8.

The Shortcut

Greg only has an half hour before he has to baby-sit for Mrs. Meyer's three-year-old son. Greg glances at his watch. Not a minute to lose. He's halfway home when he decides to take a shortcut through a neighbor's yard. It looks like nobody is at home, so it won't hurt. Besides, the shortcut will save at least two minutes.

It turns out that Greg was wrong. The neighbor was home and saw him cut through the yard. Worse yet, the neighbor has called Greg's dad. Now his dad is asking Greg about the incident. What should Greg do?

Should he . . .

    A. Say he was in a hurry to get home to do his chores?

    B. Say he was trying to catch up with a friend who needed help?

    C. Say his neighbor is a grouch, always complaining about something?

    D. Admit he was taking a shortcut and promise not to do it again?

    E. Say he took a wrong turn coming home from school and was lost?

 For help in knowing what Greg should do, read Proverbs 21:2.

The Cutting Edge

Justine gets along with just about everyone in her classes. But one girl in science really gets on Justine's nerves. She has a high-pitched voice, and she always sounds as though she is whining. This girl never understands anything the teacher says the first time. She is constantly asking the teacher to explain the assignment again—even the most simple ones. Whenever she asks a question—which is usually every day—it's almost like fingernails being scraped down a blackboard.

At lunch, Justine and her friends are discussing the science assignment. Someone brings up the girl's name, and a couple of the girls start imitating her whiny question. Later as Justine is walking home, she thinks of a joke about the girl to tell to the group. They would love it! Justine is laughing to herself as she thinks about the joke and her friends' reaction. She can't wait to get to lunch tomorrow.

The next day, however, Justine begins to wonder about telling her friends the joke. Maybe she shouldn't do it. *But it really is harmless,* she thinks, *isn't it?* What do you think Justine should do?

Should she . . .
- A. Forget about the joke—how would she feel if kids were making up jokes about her?
- B. Tell only one friend who will be sure to spread the joke around?
- C. Go ahead and tell the joke to her friends at lunch—the girl will never find out?
- D. Come up with a whole bunch of jokes about the girl for her friends' amusement?
- E. Write funny things about the girl on the bathroom walls?

 Read Luke 6:37-38 to find out what Jesus would say about this situation and what Justine should do.

You've Got a Friend

Julie has lots of friends, but she would rather spend time with Grace than anyone else. Grace is fun to be around. She and Julie share a lot of the same interests, and no one can make Julie laugh like Grace can. They are the closest of friends—"best friends forever," they always tell everyone. Sometimes, however, Julie has to admit, Grace can act a little crazy, but that's why Julie likes her. She's always ready to try something new.

In school this morning, one of Julie's friends said she saw Grace drinking a beer behind the school the other day. Julie doesn't want to believe it, but later that day, Grace hints about something she's tried that Julie "absolutely will love!" She asks Julie to meet her and a bunch of other kids down by the playground after school. Julie knows the other kids' reputations, and they're not good. In fact, Julie knows that one of the kids has been grounded for stealing drinks from his parents' liquor cabinet. Julie is certain that Grace has been drinking. What do you think Julie should do?

Should she . . .

A. Gently confront Grace about what she has heard?

B. Keep quiet and pretend that she has never heard anything about the drinking?

C. Write Grace an anonymous letter threatening to inform her parents if she doesn't stop drinking?

D. Make up an excuse not to meet with Grace after school, and then avoid Grace until she comes to her senses?

E. Find another "best" friend without telling Grace why?

 For help in knowing how God wants Julie to respond, read Ezekiel 2:3-7, where God gave Ezekiel a message to relay to the people about what they were doing wrong.

5

Setbacks

Tamara and her friend are partners on an English project. Each pair is to research an author and present a poster about that author to the class, telling the class why they should read this particular author's books. Tamara and her friend have spent the last several weeks reading different books, researching, and planning their poster. They worked all weekend to put together the project. Tamara is pleased with the results. She's confident that with a good presentation today, she and her partner will receive an A.

When Tamara walks into her English class, she can tell that something terrible has happened. Her friend looks awful. She doesn't say anything, but points down at the posterboard. It is covered with crayon marks! Her friend tells Tamara that her little brother got into her room and "colored" their poster for them. Tamara is distraught. All that hard work! What will the teacher say? They can't turn in a posterboard looking like that. What do you think Tamara should do?

Should she . . .
- A. Tell the teacher that it's all her friend's fault their posterboard is ruined and that she should not be penalized for it?
- B. Start screaming at her friend for being so careless?
- C. Accept what has happened and work out a plan with the teacher to redo the poster?
- D. Ask the teacher for another partner?
- E. Demand that her friend remedy the situation since it was her fault that the poster got ruined?

 To see how Joseph handled setbacks in his life, read Genesis 39:19-23.

Room Service

Leslie is excited. Her best friend called to see if she wants to go to the mall today. Leslie has saved some money from baby-sitting, and there's a great sale on sweaters at her favorite store. Of course she wants to go! Leslie's friend will pick her up in a half hour. Now all she has to do is tell her parents.

Leslie bounds down the stairs and bursts into the kitchen. Perfect. Her mom and dad are at the kitchen table, finishing their morning coffee. Before Leslie can get a word out, her mom reminds Leslie that she needs to clean and dust her room before she can leave the house. Leslie groans. Now she'll be late for her friend. And what about the sale? All the good sweaters will be gone before she can get there. What should Leslie do?

Should she . . .

    A. Lightly run the dustcloth over her bedroom furniture then zoom out the door?

    B. Nail the door to her room shut and run out of the house?

    C. Call her friend and tell her she'll meet her at the mall after she does her chores?

    D. Sneak out of the house without doing her jobs?

    E. Pay her younger sister to clean and dust her room for her?

 For help in knowing what Leslie should do, read Proverbs 13:4.

The New Girl

Justin can't help but notice the new girl in his math class. She and her family have moved in recently from California. She's cute, with a great smile and a friendly personality. Justin hasn't talked to her much, but whenever she sees him in the hall she smiles and says hello. Justin finds himself really looking forward to math class (not his favorite subject!) so he can see her.

Justin decides that he really wants to become friends with this girl, but he doesn't quite know how to go about it. Justin doesn't want to ask his friends for advice. They'll just tease him. He's never really done this before. What should he do?

Should Justin . . .
  A.   Knock the books out of the girl's arms as she walks out of class?
  B.   Drop a real mushy note in the girl's locker?
  C.   Talk to the girl and act friendly toward her whenever he gets a chance?
  D.   Give gifts to the girl so she will like him?
  E.   Find out who the girl's best friend is and tell her how he feels?

 For help in knowing what Justin should do, read Ephesians 5:1-2.

Finders Keepers, Part 1

Mack and his friend are hanging out after school. It's a warm spring afternoon, so they decide to walk over to the park and mess around there for a while. They spend some time chasing each other on the playground equipment. After a half hour of running, the boys flop down on the grass under a shady tree for a rest.

Mack picks up a twig to twirl when he suddenly notices a five-dollar bill at the base of the tree. He points out the money to his friend. Just as Mack is about to jump up and get the bill, his friend beats him to it and claims ownership. Mack is stunned. He saw the five-dollar bill first, but his friend insists that the money is his. Now what should Mack do?

Should he . . .

A. Not say anything and let his friend have the money?

B. Keep his cool and suggest that he and his friend split the money?

C. Insist that the money is his because he saw it first?

D. Argue for a while and then go home mad, vowing never to play with that friend again?

E. Challenge his friend to a fight—winner take all?

 For help in knowing what Mack should do, read Proverbs 13:2.

Great Expectations

Emmet's dad is one of the leading businessmen in the community. He is known throughout the town for his good business sense, his strong civic responsibility, and his generous donations to local charities. Everyone in town (and at school, for that matter) knows Emmet's dad. Emmet loves his dad, but unfortunately for Emmet, everyone expects him to be exactly like his dad. He is expected to run for student government in school and to follow his father's footsteps into the family business.

Instead, Emmet wants to blaze his own trail. What he wants to do is to try drama. He has been involved in a few skits at church that were presented to the Sunday school classes. Emmet enjoys being on stage and becoming another character. His Sunday school teacher said that Emmet had a gift for acting. Emmet wants to audition for the school's spring drama production, but his dad thinks that he should devote his time to learning the family business and spending his spare time at the family store. Emmet wants to obey his father, but he also wants to explore new ventures. What do you think Emmet should do?

Should he . . .
- A. Forget about the drama production for now and help out at his dad's store?
- B. Go ahead and audition without telling his dad; if he gets the part, it will be too late for his dad to disagree?
- C. Try to talk with his dad about his desire to try out acting?
- D. Get a friend of his to work at the store in his place during auditions?
- E. Rebel and refuse to work at his dad's store ever?

 Read Acts 16:11-15, 38-40 to see how Lydia defied expectations of her day and did her best for God.

Partners in Prayer

Elliott has been attending a Bible study at his school that meets every day before classes begin. It's a fun group, and Elliott enjoys going. Some of the coolest teachers in the school are the advisors, and there are about thirty to forty kids that show up each week. The group has been studying prayer, and Mr. Wilson, one of the teacher-advisors, has recommended that each student find a prayer partner. Elliott and his friend Clay decide to pair up. So far, the boys have shared a few prayer requests with each other—mostly praying for tests, sick relatives, and other easy requests.

But tonight when his friend calls, Elliott is alarmed. Clay sounds very upset. When Elliott asks what's wrong, Clay nearly breaks down over the phone. In a voice filled with emotion, Clay explains that his mom and dad are separating. They have been having huge fights lately, and tonight his mom just walked out the door. Clay is scared and confused, and he is asking if Elliott will pray for him during his quiet time. Elliott mumbles, "Yeah, sure" and quickly hangs up. *Boy, this is heavy stuff,* Elliott thinks. He's not sure if he is equipped to pray for something that big. What do you think Elliott should do?

Should he . . .
- A. Get down on his knees and immediately pray the best he can that God will help Clay and his family straighten out their problems?
- B. Go find the nearest adult—and fast? This is grown-up stuff, not kids' stuff.
- C. Mumble a quick prayer before he goes to bed and then forget about it?
- D. Call his pastor and ask him to pray for Clay?
- E. Go find a book of prayers and look up one that will fit the occasion?

 Check out 1 Samuel 12:23 and Philippians 4:6 for the biblical principles that should guide Elliott's response.

Truth and Consequences

As Betsy is getting ready for school, her mom reminds her to come home right after school. Betsy needs to watch her little brother while Mom goes to a meeting. Betsy gives a quick nod and runs out the door as she spies her friend walking by. In social studies class, the teacher hands out an assignment that the class can either do alone or with another student. Betsy and her friend decide to work on the assignment together.

The teacher has given them the weekend to get the project done, but Betsy's friend wants to get started on the project right away. She asks Betsy to come over to her house so they can use her computer to look up some information. Betsy agrees but then remembers that her mom wants her to come home right after school. Betsy decides to go to her friend's house anyway. Her mom can take her brother to the meeting with her; besides, this is schoolwork. Her project is more important than Mom's meeting.

When Betsy gets home an hour later, her mom is waiting for her in the kitchen. She doesn't look at all happy with Betsy and wants to know where Betsy has been. What should Betsy tell her?

Should she . . .

A. Pretend she lost her voice and was looking for it?

B. Say, "School got out an hour late today"?

C. Admit what she did and accept her punishment?

D. Say, "Bullies chased me, and I barely escaped with my life"?

E. Tell her mom that the project is due tomorrow and that she just had to go over to her friend's house today to work on it?

 Read Psalm 32:1-5 to see how Betsy should respond.

Going to Church

Ned and his family attend church every Sunday. It's definitely not an option to stay home just because it has been a busy weekend or because something else comes up. Ned has grown in his faith during the past year, and he really looks forward to Sunday. Ned enjoys the music during worship, the fellowship with his youth group friends, and the challenges he receives from his Sunday school teacher. Sunday worship has become an important part of his life, not just something his parents make him do.

Today at school a friend asks Ned to spend the night at his house Saturday and then go fishing with him and his dad on Sunday. They want to get an early start so they can get back in time for the big football game on TV. Ned tells his friend he can't go because his family goes to church on Sunday. His friend can't believe it and wants to know why Ned goes to church all the time. How should Ned answer him?

Should he . . .

A. Shrug and say, "My parents force me to go"?

B. Say, "I don't know"?

C. Pretend he didn't hear the question?

D. Say, "Because my faith is important to me"?

E. Say, "Oh, you wouldn't understand" and walk away?

To see how Ned should react, read 2 Timothy 1:8.

The Birthday Present

For weeks Angela has been waiting for her birthday. She and her friends already celebrated with a roller-skating party. Now it's time for her family party. She is brimming with excitement. To this point, Angela has received a new CD player, some clothes for school, and a silver necklace, but she can tell that her parents have another surprise in store. As Angela waits in anticipation, her parents proudly present her with a rectangular package. They explain that this gift will become one of her most treasured possessions, a gift she can use throughout her life.

Angela can hardly wait. Her curiosity is piqued. The present has all the appearances of a thick book. She opens it to discover a new leather-bound Bible. Angela already has a Bible, but it's a paperback version designed for younger kids. This really is beautiful! Angela thanks her parents and takes it to her room. She leafs through the new Bible and thinks about her parents' words. Now that she has this new Bible, what is she supposed to do with it?

Should Angela . . .

A. Put the Bible in her closet with all the other books she has never read?

B. Read the Bible every day so she can learn more about God and what he wants her to do?

C. Keep the Bible on her desk so that she will remember to bring it to church on Sunday?

D. Keep the Bible by her bed as a good-luck charm?

E. Put the Bible in a box and bury it in the backyard because it is a treasure?

 Read 2 Timothy 2:15 to know what Angela should do with her new Bible.

Surfing the Net

For the past several weeks, Henry has been totally absorbed in his family's new computer. He has already mastered all the computer games and has learned how to make really cool party invitations. But the most fun is surfing the Internet. The computer came with a month-long trial of the service, and Henry is hoping his parents will continue their subscription. So far, he has found several sports Web sites, a Web site devoted to trading baseball cards, and some cool chat rooms for kids. Henry's parents have established well-defined guidelines for using the Internet, and so far there haven't been any problems.

Today at lunch, Henry overhears some boys at the next table talking about "this really cool Web site. You've gotta see it to believe it!" Henry catches up to the boy who was talking about it and asks for the address. The boy looks at him closely and says, "Well, I guess it's OK." When Henry gets home, he grabs his cookies and milk and heads back to the computer. He easily finds the Web site the boys were all talking about, but when he gets into it, he immediately realizes that the material there is X-rated. What do you think Henry should do?

Should he . . .
A. Write down the Web site address and tell his friends all about it?
B. Download the information at the Web site and print it out to show his buddies?
C. Quickly find a more appropriate place to surf?
D. Visit some of the other sites listed at this particular address?
E. Take a quick look to see what this Web site is all about?

 Read 1 Timothy 6:11 to find the biblical principle that should underlie Henry's response.

15

Decisions, Decisions

Aaron's friend Gordon has been talking about this neat summer camp. He brought over the camp brochures, and, sure enough, it looks really cool. There's horseback riding, swimming, canoeing, and hiking. Gordon is planning to go, and he has asked Aaron to go with him. Aaron's parents have said he can go if he wants. But that's the problem. Aaron doesn't know if he wants to go.

It does sound like a lot of fun. Aaron would really like to go canoeing and horseback riding. But he is on the swim team and would miss several important meets if he were to go to camp. Aaron has been trying to improve his stroke times so he can make it into the big season-end meet, and this would mean fewer opportunities to make those times. Plus, he wants to help at his church's vacation Bible school, which takes place at the same time as the camp.

Aaron is really confused. He's not sure what to do. Gordon has been pressing him for an answer because they have to send in the registration soon. Aaron is beginning to panic. What should he do?

Should Aaron . . .
- A. Keep putting off his answer until it's too late?
- B. Worry about the situation and think up all sorts of solutions, none of which will work. Finally as a last resort, pray for wisdom?
- C. Pray, asking God to show him what he wants and to help him make the right decision?
- D. Flip a coin?
- E. Ask his other friends what he should do?

 For help in knowing what Aaron should do, read James 1:5.

16

The Talent Show

Marie has always loved singing. Even as a little girl she would spend hours singing to herself, her dolls, her mom, and whoever would listen. Her parents would encourage her, telling Marie that she had a true gift for singing. So when Marie's school plans a talent show she is thrilled. This is her opportunity to sing for a real audience. Marie's parents are enthusiastic about the talent show as well. Dad plays piano as Marie practices day after day. Mom buys her a new dress for the show.

Finally the big night arrives. Marie nervously waits backstage for her turn. She goes over and over the words to her song in her mind. Finally, her name is announced. Taking a deep breath, she walks onto the stage. As the familiar notes sound, Marie forgets about her nervousness. She forgets about the eyes looking at her. She simply smiles and begins to sing. As Marie finishes, the audience breaks into applause. Gratefully, Marie acknowledges their cheers with a small bow.

As Marie walks out of the school with her parents, she is greeted by friends. One after another they tell her the same thing: "Marie, you were great up there. You really sing well." Marie smiles broadly. What should she do with all this attention?

Should Marie . . .
- A. Politely answer, "Thank you"?
- B. Laugh uncontrollably?
- C. Say, "Well, actually, I've done a lot better"?
- D. Respond, "Yes, I know"?
- E. Roll her eyes and say, "Oh, that. It was nothing really"?

 To know how Marie should respond, read Romans 12:3.

The New Pastor

Karl's church recently hired a new pastor. Their former pastor had retired after serving at the church for the past twenty-five years. Karl really enjoyed his former pastor. He had a great sense of humor and enjoyed joking around with the young people. He was a great fisherman, too, and often would go along with the youth group when they went on canoe trips. Karl also enjoyed the pastor's sermons.

The problem, however, is that Karl just can't get used to the new pastor. He is always so serious—he hardly ever seems to smile. (At least, he doesn't when Karl has been around.) Whenever someone asks a question, he has a peculiar habit of rubbing his nose before he answers. And his sermons! Whoo boy, are they boooring. Some of Karl's friends did a great imitation of the new pastor in Sunday school last week and everybody laughed. Karl's not sure what to do when his friends start making fun of the pastor. How do you think he should react?

Should Karl . . .

A. Laugh the loudest when his friends do their pastor imitation?

B. Report his friends to the Sunday school superintendent?

C. Get together with his friends after Sunday school to make up some even better jokes about the new pastor?

D. Ask his mom and dad if they can go to a new church?

E. Suggest to the class that they invite the new pastor to join them one Sunday so they can get to know him?

 To know what Karl should do, check out 1 Thessalonians 5:12-13.

The Gross Joke

Ray and his friends are at the park after school. They're playing a spirited game of Capture the Flag, when an older boy from their school asks to join in. Ray knows the boy only slightly. He has a reputation for being a bit rowdy, but this is not school. The boys say sure, and the game continues. Ray's team finally succeeds in capturing their opponent's flag. The boys flop down on the ground, breathless.

The boys are talking about the upcoming big game at the high school, when a girl they know from school walks by. She's a shy girl, and Ray doesn't know her very well. But the older boy begins telling a gross joke, using the girl as the subject. Ray looks around. His friends all seem intent on listening to the joke. Ray feels very uncomfortable. What should he do?

Should Ray . . .

A. Listen carefully and laugh loudly with the rest of the boys?

B. Tell another joke that is even more gross than the first one?

C. Try to change the subject?

D. Tell a good clean joke?

E. Defend the girl's honor and challenge the older boy to a squirt-gun duel?

 For help in knowing how Ray should react, read Philippians 4:8.

We're Number One!

It's the big soccer game today. Beth's team is playing its archrivals, the Buttonwood Barons. It promises to be a close game. Both teams are enjoying winning seasons, and the winner today most likely will go on to win the city championship. Beth and her team have prepared long and hard for the game. Beth in particular has spent long hours at home working on her skills. Now it's time to take the field.

Midway through the game the score is tied. Players on both teams are giving it their all. It's a tough, scrappy match. The players are near exhaustion as the match draws to a close. With under a minute remaining in the game, the score still tied, Beth's team is awarded a penalty kick. Beth is to take the shot. As each team prepares itself for the shot, Beth mentally reviews how she will approach the shot. The whistle blows. Beth makes her approach, kicks the ball hard and watches as it sails past the outstretched arms of the Barons' goalie. Beth's team emerges the victors as their opponents are unable to score again.

Beth can hardly believe it. Not only did her team win the game, but she scored the winning goal. What a day! Beth looks across the field at the dejected Baron players. What should she do?

Should Beth . . .
   A. Laugh at the other team?
   B. Cry uncontrollably?
   C. Run around the field with her index finger raised high, yelling, "We're Number One!"?
   D. Congratulate the other team on playing a good game?
   E. Go up and tell the goalie how poorly she played the shot?

 To know how Beth should respond, read James 4:6.

20

Standing Firm

C had's English class is studying a novel in which the main character is an atheist. The discussion today focuses on the character's system of beliefs and how that guided the decisions he made later in the novel. A few students, in defending the character's actions, say they, too, are atheists. Chad, who has been a Christian since he was a young boy, offers a different opinion of the character as viewed from a person who believes in Jesus. Some of the students start to argue with Chad, but the bell rings. The teacher reminds the class of their homework assignment as the students gather up their books.

After class, Chad walks down the hallway discussing the assignment with his friend. A couple of students who had been debating him in class come up behind Chad and start making fun of him. "Hey look, it's Churchy Chad. Hey, Chad, you gonna preach a sermon tomorrow? This boy's a real Jesus Freak." As the students continue to taunt Chad, a crowd begins to gather. Chad is really embarrassed. What should he do to stop the students from heckling him?

Should Chad . . .

A. Threaten to beat up the kids if they don't stop?

B. Make up even worse nicknames about the students who are making fun of him?

C. Ignore the kids' comments, try to be nice to them, and pray that they will become Christians?

D. Hit the kids with his Bible?

E. Report the mocking students to the school hall monitor?

 To find out how Chad should respond, read Romans 12:14.

Exposed!

The other day in school Jeremy saw a large brown envelope lying on the floor. It was obvious that someone had dropped it. The envelope was very dirty because it had been walked on and kicked around. But Jeremy saw something that looked suspiciously like money sticking out of the envelope. He picked up the envelope, and much to his surprise, he discovered that the envelope was filled with money—one-hundred dollars in fives, tens, and twenties. Jeremy couldn't believe his good fortune. He pocketed the money and walked away. Later that day, however, an announcement was made over the public-address system that some money was missing that the Home Ec Club had collected from the bake sale that morning; anyone finding the money should let the club know. Jeremy didn't say anything and kept the money.

Today, however, one of Jeremy's good friends catches up to him as he's walking to school. He tells Jeremy that he saw him in the hall picking up something the day the money was missing. His friend confronts Jeremy and says he believes that Jeremy found the money. Jeremy is startled. He was sure no one saw him that day. What should he do now?

Should he . . .
A. Offer his friend half the money if he promises to keep quiet?
B. Tell his friend he did find the money, but he's been too busy to return it?
C. Confess that he took the money and give it back today?
D. Tell his friend he was just picking up some trash that day; he didn't see any money?
E. Tell his friend that he found the money but spent it already, so his friend better keep quiet about it?

 Check out 2 Samuel 12:1-13 and Psalm 51:3-4 to see how King David responded when confronted about his sin by his friend.

True Confessions

Missy and her friends are having a slumber party. After watching a video, they begin getting ready for bed. They turn off the lights and settle down for a late-night chat. In the darkened room, they begin to share stories about the worst thing they ever did. A couple of stories are silly: short-sheeting their brother's bed; hiding the teacher's book; pulling a prank on a camp counselor. One of the girls, who Missy doesn't know very well, giggles nervously and says, "Well I can top that. That's all kid stuff." She then proceeds to tell the girls that whenever she needs some makeup, she goes to the drugstore and slips it into her pocket. "It's no big deal," she says. "My mom won't buy it for me, and the store is not going to miss one silly little lipstick. I never take anything big—just little stuff." Missy doesn't know what to make of this. She knows that the girl is known for exaggerating. She also knows that this girl had a purse full of makeup that she brought to the party. If she is stealing, maybe Missy ought to say something to someone. What do you think Missy should do?

Should she . . .

    A. Disregard what the girl said as another exaggeration?

    B. Tell everyone she knows at school about what this girl said?

    C. Call the girl a thief and keep a close watch on her purse when the girl is near?

    D. Talk with the girl privately later and tell her that what she is doing is wrong and that she needs help?

    E. Ask if the girl can pick up some mascara for her the next time she's in the store?

 In Leviticus 19:17 the Bible teaches us how to confront sin in someone else.

Reckless Words

One of Patty's friends has a good appetite. In fact, Kayla eats more than all the girls at the lunch table combined. If anyone has something left over, they automatically hand it over to Kayla. She is a big girl, tall and husky, and never seems self-conscious about her eating habits. She enjoys a good meal. Lately, however, the boys have been making fun of Kayla. They call her "Amazon Girl" and other names. Kayla tries to ignore them, but Patty can tell that the boys are starting to bother her. She's been rather quiet at lunch and not eating as much.

Today they are serving submarine sandwiches—one of Kayla's favorites. She is still in the lunch line while Patty and her friends start to eat. The sandwiches are a real favorite at the school because they are so big. One of the girls announces she is stuffed and can't eat another bite. Without thinking about it, Patty says, "Oh, don't worry. Just give it to you-know-who. She'll eat anything!" The girls all laugh but stop quickly when they realize that Kayla has heard every word and has run out of the lunchroom in tears. Patty feels terrible. What do you think she should do?

Should Patty . . .

A. Avoid Kayla for a couple of weeks and hope Kayla forgets about what she said?

B. Tell Kayla it was only a joke; she didn't mean to hurt her feelings?

C. Apologize to Kayla and let her know she feels awful about her reckless words?

D. Tell Kayla she was talking about someone else and that she misunderstood?

E. Tell Kayla she is hypersensitive and needs to lighten up?

 Check out Proverbs 12:18 and James 3:6 to see what kind of person watches his or her words carefully.

24

The Fashion Patrol

Valerie and her mom recently went clothes shopping for some new spring clothes. Valerie picked out a really cute skirt with butterflies on it and a matching top. It fit great, and Valerie couldn't wait to wear it to school.

The first warm spring day, Valerie wears her new skirt and top to school. She feels really good about herself until she sees Mary and her friends. Mary begins making fun of Valerie's new outfit. She and her friends start laughing at Valerie and making loud comments about "getting a net to catch those tacky butterflies."

Other kids are beginning to notice the commotion, and Valerie feels just awful. What should Valerie do?

Should she . . .

    A.   Scream, "Shut up!" and run away?

    B.   Make a joke about the clothes they are wearing?

    C.   Pull out a squirt gun and start to chase them?

    D.   Ignore their comments and walk away?

    E.   Run home real fast and change clothes before anyone else can make fun of her outfit?

 For help in knowing what Valerie should do, read Proverbs 19:11.

Just One Drink

Angela's new friend Jean is planning to run for class president. Jean asks Angela if she can come over after school to help make campaign posters and hear Jean's speech. After checking with her mom, Angela agrees to go home with Jean the next day right after school. The two girls get off the bus and walk the four blocks to Jean's house. Jean takes out her key and lets them into the house. "Where is everybody?" asks Angela. Jean explains that her mom and dad usually don't get home till around six o'clock, but that it's OK. She is allowed to have friends over while they are out.

The girls get right to work. They make a half dozen posters, all with catchy slogans. Jean practices her speech. Angela offers a few suggestions, and Jean likes the improvements. It's getting close to five o'clock before the girls take a break. "How about a drink?" asks Jean. Angela asks for a cola, but Jean says, "No. I mean a real drink. You know, from the bar. My parents have oodles of stuff here." Angela is caught off guard. What should she do?

Should Angela . . .
   A. Politely take a small drink because she wants to be Jean's friend?
   B. Say, "Sure," and play bartender?
   C. Tell Jean she has to go home now?
   D. Refuse, and encourage Jean not to drink either?
   E. Call the police and report Jean?

 For help in knowing what Angela should do, read Proverbs 23:20-21.

Singing the Blues

Sign-ups for the spring musical were just posted at school. Until this year, trying out for the musical has been a highlight of the school year for Felicia. Every year Felicia tries out for the musical and, typically, gets the best role. Until this year, that is. Now she drags her feet to where the sign-up sheets are posted. Sure enough, right at the top of the list is Melissa Dean. And she is trying out for the same role that Felicia wants to have.

Melissa is a new girl at school, and word has it that she has a beautiful voice. Felicia never has heard her sing, but everyone in Melissa's music class says she is fantastic. Felicia feels a bit ill as she looks at the sign-up sheet. What if she doesn't get the part? She never has had any real competition before. It just isn't fair. What should Felicia do?

Should she . . .

    A. Tell everyone, "Melissa's not so good"?

    B. Do her best at the tryouts and be happy no matter which part she gets, knowing she did all she could?

    C. Look for a chance to show up Melissa during the tryouts?

    D. Tell her teacher she doesn't want to be in the musical this year?

    E. Tell Melissa that she shouldn't even try out because she won't get a good part?

 To know how Felicia should act in this situation, read Romans 12:10.

27

The Perfect Pen

Mr. Smith, Dan's math teacher, is leaving for a new position at the end of the school year. Mr. Smith is one of Dan's all-time favorite teachers. He has helped Dan a lot with his math during the school year. Thanks to Mr. Smith's help, Dan is now able to take the accelerated math course next year. Dan really wants to give Mr. Smith something special as a going-away present. He knows that Mr. Smith likes unusual pens, so Dan hopes to find just the right pen for him.

Today, Dan is at the mall with his friend Morgan. The two of them are just browsing through the shops when Dan sees it. It's the perfect pen for Mr. Smith! As Morgan browses through the magazines at the front of the store, Dan takes a closer look at the pen. It's really neat, and Dan knows that Mr. Smith would really like it. He looks for a price tag and then groans as he reads the price—forty-five dollars. That's way too much. Dan had planned to spend about twenty-five dollars. But how can he pass up this pen? Dan looks around. There's no one near him in the store. It would be so easy to just slip the pen into his pocket. What should Dan do?

Should he . . .
- A. Say, "Oh, well" and keep shopping, knowing that he might find another more reasonably priced pen that Mr. Smith would like more?
- B. Quickly slip the pen into his pocket and then casually walk out of the store?
- C. Switch the price tag of the pen with that of a cheaper item and then pay the lower price?
- D. Point to a customer leaving the store, tell a salesperson he saw the person take something, wait for the salesperson to leave, and take the pen?
- E. Buy Mr. Smith a cheaper pen but tell him that he really wanted to buy him a more expensive one?

 To know what Dan should do, read Exodus 20:15.

The English Test

Mrs. Todd is known for giving the toughest tests in the English department. Today's test is no exception. In fact, it should be about the most difficult test that Jason has had all year because it covers material that the class has studied since September. Jason has spent hours studying for this test. All that is left to do now is to take it. Jason is glad he has Mrs. Todd's class first period. He can get it over with as soon as possible—and hopefully before he begins to forget everything he has studied! After taking the test, Jason walks out of Mrs. Todd's class and breathes a sigh of relief. It was tough, but Jason felt that he did pretty well. At least he doesn't have the test hanging over his head the rest of the day.

At lunchtime, Jason's friend Freddie asks him about the test. Jason tells him it was OK and leaves it at that. Freddie, who has yet to take the test, asks Jason what questions are included. He hasn't had much time to study because of hockey practice and band rehearsals after school. Jason knows that if Freddie hasn't studied much he will have a hard time passing the test. Jason would hate to see Freddie flunk the test. After all, Freddie is the star goalie for the school's hockey team, and he can't play if he doesn't pass his classes. What should Jason do?

Should he . . .
- A. Tell Freddie all the questions on the test to help him out?
- B. Give Freddie the wrong questions to teach him not to cheat?
- C. Say nothing but offer to help Freddie study for the test?
- D. Give Freddie just one or two questions but then say he can't remember the others?
- E. Tell Freddie that it wouldn't help because Mrs. Todd is making a new test for her afternoon classes?

 To know what Jason should do, read Proverbs 20:10.

29

The Real Race

Theo never considered himself a prejudiced person. He gets along with everyone and tries to be respectful of different people. But lately he's beginning to wonder. Recently, the school boundary lines have been redrawn in his town. Now Theo attends a school with kids from different racial backgrounds. Since the beginning of school several fights have broken out between different racial groups. Theo has not been personally involved in any fight, but today, as he was walking home, a group of kids of another race called him names.

The more Theo thinks about the incident, the angrier he becomes. He didn't even know any of those kids. How dare they say those sorts of things about him? Without realizing it, Theo begins thinking badly of them and about how he can get back at them. He has been invited to a party this weekend, which he was planning to attend. Now he doesn't think he wants to. After all, some of "those kind" of kids will be there. Theo isn't so sure that he wants to mingle with them. What do you think Theo should do?

Should he . . .

A. Not go to the party and start spreading rumors about "those kind" of kids?

B. Get a group of his friends to go with him to the party and ambush the group who had called him names?

C. Write nasty things on the school walls about those other kids so they won't want to go to the party?

D. Go to the party and try to reach out to kids of another group to get to know them?

E. Vow never to have anything to do with people from different racial backgrounds?

 To discover what Theo should do, read John 4:4-30, which tells how Jesus responded to a woman from a group that was hated by the Jews.

30

Benched!

Pamela kicks the ground in disgust. What an awful practice. She kept missing all the passes, and when it was her turn to try heading the ball into the goal, she completely missed the ball. Then, to make matters worse, when the team practiced penalty kicks, Pamela's shoe came flying off as she tried to kick the ball. Things couldn't get much worse . . . or could they?

As Pamela gathers up her books, her coach calls her over. In a soft voice, Coach Ellen explains that she is making up the lineup for the next game, and well, Pamela isn't on it. Coach Ellen explains it may only be temporary—especially if Pamela practices hard—but for the next game at least, Pamela is on the bench.

Pamela chokes back the tears. How is she going to tell her friends, not to mention her parents? Pamela has been a starter on the soccer team ever since last season. How can she tell them she just lost her starting spot? Sure, she hasn't really been devoting a lot of time to practicing. And she's been distracted by trying to get out of practice as soon as she can to baby-sit for her neighbors. But she's been on the team longer than some of the other girls. *It isn't fair!* she storms. How should Pamela handle this?

Should she . . .
- A. Quit the team in disgust?
- B. Stay on the team but have a bad attitude and not try hard?
- C. Keep a good attitude, work harder at practice, and make the most of her game time?
- D. Sneak into the gym at night and deflate all the soccer balls?
- E. Watch her replacement like a hawk and point out all her mistakes to the coach in hopes of regaining her spot?

 For help in knowing how Pamela should handle this situation, read Romans 8:28.

Pop Quiz!

Melinda stifles a yawn. Boy, this history class is so booorring. She glances at the class—half an hour to go. Her thoughts turn to after school. She has jazz band right afterward, and then she has to catch the activity bus so she can get home in time to baby-sit for Mrs. Johnson. Melinda begins to daydream about what she will buy with her baby-sitting money when her ears catch the word *quiz*. What? Did her teacher really say that? Melinda looks up, startled. Sure enough, her history teacher is passing out paper and telling the students to close their books. The quiz will cover chapters three and four.

Melinda groans. She didn't get a chance to review those chapters last night although the teacher had hinted strongly that the students might want to do that. What will Melinda do now? A bad grade on this quiz could really bring her average down. And if she doesn't do well in history, her parents will make her drop out of band. Melinda glances around the room. Some of her classmates look panicked. But Bobby, sitting next to her, looks quietly confident. And why not, thinks Melinda glumly, he is the smartest boy in history class. Melinda puts her name at the top of the quiz. She stares blankly at the sheet. How is she going to pass this test? What should Melinda do?

Should she . . .
A. Pretend to get sick and ask to be sent home?
B. Make sure the teacher isn't looking, then quickly glance at Bobby's paper to get the right answers?
C. Take the test and do the best she can?
D. Explain her situation to the teacher and ask if she can take the quiz tomorrow?
E. Pull the fire alarm so that everyone will leave the room and the teacher will have to reschedule the quiz?

 To know how Melinda should handle this situation, read Proverbs 11:1.

A Full Recovery

Austin has come down with a spring flu, just as baseball practice at school has started. For the past ten days, Austin has been really sick. He has had a constant headache, a high fever, and a sore throat. His body aches all over, and he feels too weak to even watch TV. Although Mom takes Austin to the doctor, there is very little the doctor can do to help him. Basically, Austin needs to get lots of rest and drink plenty of fluids. Every night before going to bed, his parents come in to pray with him. Austin is grateful for their prayers asking God to help heal him. When he is lying in bed, Austin prays, too, asking God for a full recovery.

When Austin wakes up the next morning, he immediately notices that his headache is gone. His mom takes his temperature and it is back to normal. Austin's appetite is back, and after a huge breakfast he feels ready to conquer the world. And why not? He's gotten plenty of rest these past ten days. Austin is definitely well, and he feels great. Now that he is back on his feet, what should Austin do?

Should he . . .
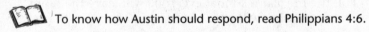

- A. Mumble, "It's about time!" and catch up on all the batting practice he missed?
- B. Hurry to tell his best friend how much vitamin-C therapy helped him?
- C. Pretend he's still not feeling 100 percent so he can get an extra day off school?
- D. Thank God for making him better and tell his best friend how God answered his family's prayers?
- E. Complain to anyone who will listen about his "terrible doctor" because it took him so long to recover?

To know how Austin should respond, read Philippians 4:6.

To Tell the Truth

Gemma is really mad at Ellen, her best friend. Ellen forgot all about their plans to study for the math test after school yesterday. Instead she went to the library with Cindy. When Gemma brought this up to her in the hall today, Ellen just laughed and said that Gemma was a true space case. "Space case, for sure," steams Gemma. Ellen didn't even say she was sorry. Now she is off with Cindy again, so Gemma can't make plans with her for after school today. Gemma spends all of English class stewing about the situation.

After school Gemma and her friends are talking, waiting for Ellen to join them. Cindy walks up, and before Gemma even thinks what she is saying, she tells Cindy that Ellen already has gone home and doesn't want to be her friend anymore. Cindy looks like she is about to cry and runs off. Gemma hurries home before Ellen can discover her lie. Another friend catches up with her and tells her that she was wrong to say what she did to Cindy. Gemma stares at her. What should Gemma do?

Should she . . .
  A. Argue with her friend and defend what she said because Cindy deserved it?
  B. Say, "You must not have heard me right," then explain what she "really said"?
  C. Yell, "Some kind of friend you are!" and stomp away?
  D. Tell her friend that she was only just joking and that it was Cindy's problem because she couldn't take a joke?
  E. Thank her friend for being honest and helpful—although the truth hurts, Gemma needed to hear it?

 To know how Gemma should respond, read Proverbs 27:6.

The Last-Minute Report

Blake works well under pressure—at least that's what he tells everyone. If there's a paper due in three weeks, he doesn't sweat it until the night before it's due. So far, Blake's system has worked because he continues to get good grades on his assignments. This time, however, Blake may be in for a rude awakening. His social studies teacher told the class to report on a city within their region of states. Each student picked a different city and has to report on its cultural offerings, education system, and points of interest, among other information. Many of Blake's classmates wrote letters to local chambers of commerce to get information about their cities. Some are drawing maps and gathering photos and other information for their report. Not Blake. His plan is to hit the library the day before the paper is due and throw it all together the night before.

When Blake goes to the library, however, he discovers that there is very little information about the city he has chosen. The librarian suggests that Blake contact one of the automobile travel associations, but Blake knows his mom doesn't have time to take him over there this afternoon. There are only a few sentences about his city in the social studies book—certainly not enough to write a five-page paper! Blake is starting to panic. What do you think he should do?

Should Blake . . .

A. Make up the information—his teacher probably won't be able to check out all the facts?

B. Prepare an elaborate story about how three weeks ago he wrote to the chamber of commerce, but his letter obviously got lost in the mail?

C. Borrow a social studies paper his brother turned in last year for the same teacher and hope the teacher doesn't remember it?

D. Tell the teacher that he doesn't have his paper ready because he waited until the last minute and couldn't find any information—and accept the consequences?

E. Say "Hey, the dog ate it"? (Or was it the guinea pig this time?)

 For help in knowing what Blake should do, read 1 Chronicles 21:8 to see how David responded when he had acted irresponsibly.

The Job

Kris wanted to earn a little extra spending money, so she asked the manager of the convenience store if he had any work that she could do on Saturdays. The manager knows Kris because she lives nearby and is a frequent customer. He also knows that he needs extra help cleaning the store and the storage room. So he offers to pay Kris minimum wage for working on Saturday mornings, from eight until noon.

The job works out great. The work isn't boring or too difficult, and it doesn't interfere with schoolwork, church, or her activities. After a few months, however, Kris begins to tire of the routine. Some mornings she is very sleepy and would rather sleep in. On other days, she just doesn't feel like working. But she likes the money, so she keeps at it.

One sunny Saturday (the first great weekend of spring), some of Kris's friends organize a trip to a state park about two hours away. They want to leave at nine in the morning. Kris really wants to go, but she knows that she has to work. Kris talks it over with the store manager, and he agrees to let her leave as soon as she takes out all the trash and sweeps out the store. Kris knows that sweeping alone usually takes her an hour.

When Kris arrives at eight to begin work, the manager goes to run some errands, leaving only Kris and the clerk in the store. What should Kris do?

Should she . . .

    A. Do the best job she can, even if it means missing the outing with her friends?

    B. Work twice as fast by sweeping with a broom in each hand and wearing brushes on both feet?

    C. Do a quick sweep of the floors, avoiding the corners and hiding dirt under the carpet?

    D. Start working hard, then pretend to get sick so she can go home and wait for her friends to pick her up?

    E. Just pretend to work and later, when the boss says something about the place being dirty, blame the clerk and customers for messing everything up again?

 To see how Kris should respond, read Colossians 3:23.

The Party Invitations

Melanie answers the phone. Kara wants to know if Melanie can come to her party Saturday night. Melanie doesn't know Kara real well although she is in several of Melanie's classes and sits next to her in science. The girls talk occasionally after school, and Kara seems like an interesting person. The kids that Kara hangs around with aren't really Melanie's type, although she doesn't mind being with them. Melanie glances at her calendar. Nothing's happening Saturday, and it could be fun. It would be a good chance to get to know Kara a little better. She tells Kara yes and jots down the time and directions to Kara's house.

The next day in school, Melanie's best friend, Annie, grabs her in the hallway. She tells Melanie about the coolest party she's planning for this Saturday night, and Melanie just has to come. Without thinking, Melanie says yes, and the two girls begin to plan the party. Melanie promises to help Annie with the guest list that evening. When Melanie gets home, she goes to the calendar to write down the time for Annie's party. Oh no! How could she have forgotten about Kara's party? She just can't miss Annie's party—Annie is her best friend. What should Melanie do?

Should she . . .
   A. Tell Kara that she can't come and go to Annie's party?
   B. Go to Annie's party and simply not show up at the first party?
   C. Go to Kara's party, pretend to get sick, and then go over to Annie's party?
   D. Try to convince Kara that she should move her party to Friday night because more kids would be able to come?
   E. Go to Kara's party because she said she would?

 For help in knowing what Melanie should do, read Psalm 25:21 and Proverbs 11:20.

Money in the Bank?

Phoebe has been diligently saving money for college. A few years ago, her parents helped her devise a savings plan so when the day comes and she goes off to school, she will have enough money. After setting aside a certain portion for church and for weekly school expenses, Phoebe puts all her money from baby-sitting, chores around the house, and birthday gifts into the bank. She already has saved quite a bit, and there are still many years left before college. By then she should have thousands in her account!

Today while shopping at the mall with her friends, Phoebe sees a personal computer on sale. She has wanted a computer for some time now, but it was always too expensive. After quickly calculating, Phoebe figures that she has just enough money saved in her college fund to pay for the computer, and she knows that she can easily get the money out. The computer will be on sale for another couple of days. If she buys it, that would deplete her college fund, but she still has lots of time to build it up again. What should Phoebe do?

Should she . . .
- A. Call her grandmother and ask Nana to buy the computer for her? (It is a good cause!)
- B. Take the money out of her college fund and buy the computer? After all, it is her money, and the computer will help her in college, too.
- C. Decide to set aside money that she now uses for entertainment and clothes and save for a computer?
- D. "Borrow" from her college fund to buy the computer and tell her parents that she will repay the fund later?
- E. Ask her parents to charge the computer and explain that she will repay them?

 To know what Phoebe should do in this situation, read Proverbs 21:20.

7

The Bible Study

Brent is a new believer, who, through the encouragement and support of a few close friends, is growing in his newfound faith. Brent's parents don't attend church, so one of his buddies usually picks him up on Sundays and takes him there. Another friend gave him a new Bible and has been taking him to the Bible study that meets before school on Mondays. Having never been in a Bible study before, Brent is discovering so much. He enjoys getting into God's Word and learning more about faith in the Lord. Someday, he thinks, he wants to invite his other friends to the Bible study.

The Bible study runs a bit late today, and Brent is hurrying down the hall to his locker before first period class. He bumps into another student and drops his books all over the hall. As he's picking up his books, he hears some of his friends laughing, "Hey, whose is this? Who's the holy roller around here?" Brent looks up to see his friends kicking his Bible down the hallway. "Hey, this makes a great hockey puck." Brent feels sick watching his friends. What do you think he should do?

Should Brent . . .

    A.   Kick the Bible down the hall and yell, "Score!"?

    B.   Hurry to class and hope his Bible is in one piece when he returns?

    C.   Pick up the Bible and say that he had better take it to the lost and found?

    D.   Explain to his friends that it's his Bible and much too valuable to kick around?

    E.   Start screaming at his friends to stop kicking around God's Word!?

 Check out Romans 1:16 to see how Brent should respond in this situation.

Overtime!

I t's Saturday evening, and Curtis has been invited over to his friend's house for dinner and games. Curtis's parents agree to let him go but say that he must be home by nine o'clock so he can get ready for church the next morning. Curtis says, "No problem" and runs down the street to Al's house. After a quick dinner, the boys go down to the basement. Al just got the latest video game and can't wait to play it with Curtis. Before they know it, the boys are deeply engrossed in the game. Al has won the first three games, but Curtis is finally getting the hang of it. Curtis wins the next three. He wants to call it quits, but Al pleads with him for just one more game. Curtis agrees.

Just one more game turns into another game . . . and then another . . . and then another. After the tenth game, the boys are still tied. Al suggests one final game to determine the ultimate winner. Curtis agrees and happens to glance at the clock. It's ten o'clock! Oh, no. He was supposed to have been home an hour ago. Boy, is he going to be in big trouble when he gets home. Al has the game all set up, ready to go. Curtis can't give up now. What should he do?

Should Curtis . . .
   A. Go ahead and play the last game and then go home, pretending he didn't know he was late?
   B. Stop to call his parents, apologize, and ask for permission to stay until the game is finished?
   C. Sneak in the back door of his house, go to his room, and pretend that he has been there for an hour?
   D. Change his name?
   E. Tell his parents there was a power outage at Al's house and that all the clocks were wrong?

 For help in knowing how Curtis should handle this situation, read Proverbs 23:22-25.

Common Ground

Anew family is moving into the house where Sherry's best friend used to live. Sherry is anxious to meet the new family because she hopes they have a girl her age. She misses having a good friend nearby. Sherry rides her bike down the street to take a look as the movers unload the van. She doesn't see anyone around, but there are some definite signs of a girl her age. She sees a purple ten-speed bike, pink-and-black roller blades, and some cheerleading pom-poms in the garage. Sherry is feeling very optimistic.

Later that afternoon, Sherry takes another ride past the house on her bike. This time some of the family members are outside talking to their new neighbors. Sure enough, there's a girl who looks about Sherry's age. But Sherry's heart sinks as she realizes that her new neighbors are from a different ethnic group from hers. Maybe they don't speak English. Maybe the girl doesn't know anything about the latest rock group or the hottest books out right now. Maybe she doesn't even like pizza. The one neighbor sees her and calls Sherry over to meet the new girl. When they are introduced, Sherry can't even pronounce the girl's name. What do you think Sherry should do?

Should she . . .
  A. Pretend to be going to the store for her mom and can't stop?
  B. Say hello and then rush off to tell her other friends about the weird girl who moved in?
  C. Ask the girl if she wants to ride bikes? (After all, that purple ten-speed must be hers.)
  D. Be pleasant but stay away from the new girl because she's different?
  E. Say, "Boy, that is a weird name. Where did you get that"?

 Before Sherry makes a big mistake, read 1 Corinthians 9:22 to see how she should respond.

10

The Accused

Marilyn is first into the locker room after soccer practice. She wants to change as quickly as possible because she wants to catch her math teacher before he leaves. Marilyn is having trouble with geometry and needs some extra help. Mr. Wolf usually is good about staying after school with students, so Marilyn is confident that she can see him. The locker room is quickly filling up with the rest of the team. The noise level in the locker room grows, but Marilyn picks up a distinctive wail among the girls in the next stall. Curious, she goes over to see what has happened.

Josie is visibly upset. It appears that someone has stolen money from her jeans' pocket. The situation worsens as two other girls in the same locker area as Josie discover that they have money missing as well. Ms. Andrews, the soccer coach, hurries over. She questions the girls and then goes back into her office. As Marilyn is gathering up her books, Ms. Andrews calls her into the office. "I think you know something about these thefts," Ms. Andrews begins. At first Marilyn is confused. Then it becomes clear that Ms. Andrews thinks she has stolen the money because she was the first one in the locker room after practice. Marilyn is stunned. What should she do?

Should Marilyn . . .
  A. Plead the fifth amendment and demand to see a lawyer?
  B. Calmly state the truth and trust God for the outcome?
  C. Cry and plead for mercy?
  D. Figure there's no way to prove her innocence, so offer to be the coach's slave if she'll forget the whole incident?
  E. Accuse another girl on the team?

 For help in knowing what Marilyn should do, read 1 Peter 3:16.

Unlocked Secrets

Erin promises her friend Taylor that she will wait for her after school while Taylor tries out for jazz band. Erin hopes Taylor makes it. Erin has been in jazz band for two years, and she has really enjoyed the experience. If Taylor makes it, this will be a great year.

Erin stands outside the room, getting a bit impatient. She listens to the muted sounds of instruments while absentmindedly fiddling with a combination on someone's locker. *If she doesn't finish soon, I'm going,* thinks Erin, giving the combination another twirl. Suddenly the locker pops open. Erin starts in surprise. She looks around. No one has seen her fooling with the locker. What should Erin do?

Should she . . .
A. Say, "Oops" and relock the locker?
B. Look in the locker, switch stuff around just for fun, and then close it?
C. Shut the locker and try the same thing with another one?
D. Put her head inside to hear how good the echo is?
E. Write an anonymous note saying how messy the locker is and leave it for the person to find the next day?

 To find out what Erin should do, read Titus 3:8.

And the Answer Is . . .

Marcus's English teacher is notorious for springing pop quizzes. Everyone in the class knows this fact, but some of his classmates don't take it very seriously. So far, they haven't had one pop quiz. To be safe, however, Marcus has made it a practice to review the day's English lesson each night.

When Mrs. Wagner announces a pop quiz today in class, Marcus smiles to himself. He is ready. But most of his classmates are squirming nervously. A few kids desperately leaf through their textbooks, as if they will glean some knowledge in thirty seconds or less that will help them pass the quiz.

As Mrs. Wagner distributes the quizzes, Marcus notices his friend across the aisle trying to get his attention. Roger is not a good student and really has to work hard to get passing grades. He looks very worried—obviously he hasn't even read last night's assignment. Roger drops his pencil on the floor and leans over toward Marcus. "Hey," he whispers. "Can you help me out here? Can I look at your paper for the answers? I can't fail this quiz." Marcus is concerned. He likes Roger. Roger's a good friend, and he sure does look worried. Mrs. Wagner hands Marcus his test. What do you think Marcus should do?

Should he . . .
  A. Answer in a loud voice, "No, that would be cheating"?
  B. Move his arm and slide the quiz to the edge of the desk so Roger can get a good look?
  C. Politely whisper no and keep his paper hidden from Roger's line of sight as he takes the quiz?
  D. Write down all the wrong answers on purpose to teach Roger a lesson?
  E. Pretend he can't hear Roger and ignore him?

 For help in knowing what Marcus should do, read Proverbs 8:1-8.

Behind the Scenes

Alice is really nervous. Today the church choir director is posting the list of choir members who will receive solo parts for the spring choir concert. Alice truly loves to sing, especially in church. Last year she was too young to try out, and this year she has her heart set on singing a particular song. It's a perfect range for her voice, and the words are so inspirational. Alice knows she can do a good job.

A crowd of choir members has gathered around the list. As Alice walks up, she hears one girl congratulate her friend on getting . . . Alice's song. Alice's heart sinks a little, but she gives herself a pep talk. *That's OK*, she thinks. *Maybe I got another song.* When she finally gets close enough to read the list, her name is nowhere to be found. She didn't get even a small solo. Nothing. Alice walks away very sad and disappointed. Before she leaves choir, the director asks her to come over.

What he says surprises Alice. Mr. Stone begins, "Alice, I know you wanted a solo part, but I've noticed that you are very organized. I would like you to assist me as a stage manager for the spring production. It's a big job, but I know you can do it. What do you think?" Alice is quiet. It's not what she had in mind. It would be working behind the scenes, not out in front singing. What do you think she should do?

Should Alice . . .
- A. Storm out of the room, saying she quits because she didn't get a solo?
- B. Agree only if Mr. Stone gives her a big part in the Christmas show?
- C. Convince her parents to go to another church where she can sing solos?
- D. Laugh at Mr. Stone and say, "Me, organized? You should see my room"?
- E. Tell Mr. Stone that she will do whatever she can to help make the spring concert a great production?

 To know what Alice should do, read 1 Corinthians 12:5.

The Great Debate

Carlos sighs. Here comes Kevin, that new kid with the obnoxious "know-it-all" attitude. It looks like Kevin wants to sit with Carlos and his friends for lunch. Kevin is not such a bad kid. It's just that he has to have the absolute last word about everything. Name the topic, and Kevin knows just about all there is to know—or at least he thinks so. Carlos glances at the clock. Oh, well. At least there isn't too much time left before lunch is over.

As Kevin sits down, the conversation switches to football. Immediately Kevin begins to expound about the latest football poll, ranking the top twenty-five teams. His favorite team, of course, is ranked number-one in the country. Carlos listens with half an ear until Kevin begins to critique Carlos's favorite team. His ears perk up as Kevin explains why this team doesn't even deserve to be on the same field as his football powerhouse. Carlos does a slow burn. *Now this is too much,* he thinks. *He can't get away with that!* What do you think Carlos should do?

Should he . . .

   A. Call Kevin's team a bunch of cheaters who paid the pollsters to be number one?

   B. Walk away and let Kevin think what he wants—after all, it's only football?

   C. Come back the next day with a stack of statistics to prove Kevin wrong?

   D. Challenge Kevin to a fight after school if he doesn't take back what he said about his team?

   E. Argue with Kevin and don't stop until he gets the last word?

 To know what Carlos should do, read 2 Timothy 2:23.

The Grass Looks Greener

Mickey gets up early so he can get his chores done. As soon as he is finished, he's going to ride his bike over to Zachary's house. Zachary is a new kid at school, and word has it that he lives in a huge house in the nicest part of town. Mickey believes it because Zachary always has the latest stuff for school: the most expensive calculator, the best athletic shoes, the coolest new jacket. Mickey can hardly wait to see where Zach lives. It must be awesome.

Whatever Mickey expected, it is nothing compared to what he sees when he rides his bike up the stone-laid driveway. Zachary's house isn't huge—it's humongous! Mickey's mouth hangs open as Zachary leads him into the house. The foyer, with its two-storied window and crystal chandelier, looks like an art gallery. There is an immense living room with a grand piano. Zachary leads his friend to the computer loft overlooking a huge kitchen area and great room with floor-to-ceiling windows.

The boys have a great time playing with all of Zachary's stuff (and he has quite a lot of it), but Mickey notices that Zachary's parents haven't come in to say hello. When he asks about it, Zachary tells him that they are on a weekend trip, and his nanny is watching Zachary and his brothers. Mickey is impressed. He never knew anyone with a real live nanny before.

Back home, Mickey sees his house in a different light. Sure, it's nice, but now he thinks it's kinda small. Mickey is quiet at the dinner table as he mulls over the differences between his home and Zachary's house. Finally his dad asks him what's on his mind. What should he say?

Should Mickey . . .

A. Ask his parents why they live in such a dump?

B. Ask his parents if they can move over to Zachary's neighborhood?

C. Tell his parents about all the cool things that Zachary has in his house?

D. Tell his parents that when he grows up he's going to live in the most expensive house he can find?

E. Tell his parents about Zachary's house but say he is thankful for the love and support he finds in his home?

 Check out Luke 12:15 to see how Mickey should respond.

16

Sharing

Shannon and her mom spent Saturday afternoon cleaning out her closet. Shannon tried on all her winter clothes from last year and put aside all the clothes that no longer fit her. Eventually she had three bags of clothes, a winter coat, and a good pair of hardly worn boots that she can no longer wear. Shannon asks her mom if she can sell her old things in a garage sale, with the hope of making enough money to buy herself a really cool jean jacket. Her mom agrees, and they set a date for the sale at the end of the month.

The next week in school, Shannon notices a new girl who is rather quiet. The other kids in Shannon's class have begun making fun of her because the girl wears the same outfit three or four days in a row. Shannon sees this girl several times during the week, and it's true. She doesn't seem to have much of a wardrobe. Shannon begins to think about the bags of clothes in her closet—everything is in pretty good shape and probably would fit this new girl. But if she gives the clothes to this girl, what about the garage sale? She won't be able to buy the jean jacket for herself. What should Shannon do?

Should she . . .

A. Forget about the girl and sell the clothes? The new girl probably wouldn't like her taste in clothes anyway.

B. Befriend the new girl and eventually invite her over and let her try on what she wants?

C. Tell the new girl about a great secondhand shop where she can buy clothes for less money?

D. Sell her clothes at the garage sale, and whatever doesn't sell give to the new girl?

E. Buy something for the new girl with the money she gets from the garage sale—if there's anything left over after she buys herself the jacket?

 To know how Shannon should respond, check out Romans 12:13.

The Class Picnic

As class president, Claire is in charge of the annual picnic. She decides on the location, helpers, food, and entertainment—all the details. It's a big job, and Claire wants to start planning now so that everything will run smoothly. She announces a meeting after school for anyone who wants to help with the picnic. To her surprise, about twenty kids show up for the meeting.

The group quickly votes on food, games, and the date. The next big question is location. Brett raises his hand and offers to have the picnic at his home. He has a pool, a deck, a screened-in porch, and a big yard for playing games. *Well,* thinks Claire, *that seems to settle it.* But then she notices a girl with her hand up in the back of the room. Rachel wants to offer another suggestion for where to hold the party. Everyone in the room knows that Rachel doesn't have a pool, deck, or big yard. The group is eager to accept Brett's offer and doesn't even want to listen to Rachel. What should Claire should do?

Should she . . .
  A. Offer to let Rachel be in charge of cleanup?
  B. Tell Rachel that the decision already has been made (because no one could do better than Brett's offer)?
  C. Allow Rachel a chance to offer her suggestion and give equal consideration to both options?
  D. Politely listen to Rachel and then say, "Thanks, but no thanks"?
  E. Ignore Rachel and go on with the rest of the meeting?

 To find out how Claire should respond, read Deuteronomy 1:17.

That's No Excuse

Hugh slams his books down on the lunch table and sits down with a sigh of disgust. "What's the matter with you?" his friend asks. "Oh, I've got gym next period, and we're doing line dancing," he says with a grimace. "I can't believe we have to do this." Hugh dejectedly eats his sandwich as if he were having his last meal. One of his buddies sits down next to him. "I don't know why you're so bummed out about this. It's simple to fix," he says. He pulls from his pocket a note signed by his mom excusing him from gym. "Wow, how did you get your mom to write that?" Hugh asks, admiring the note and wishing he had one. "She didn't. I wrote it. And you can too. Everybody is doing it," the boy says confidently. He tells Hugh how to type the note on the library computer and then forge his mom's signature. Hugh glances at the clock. He has fifteen minutes before gym. Certainly that's enough time to get to the library to write the note. And it sure would get him out of stupid line dancing. And if everybody is doing it, then how can he possibly get into trouble? What do you think Hugh should do?

Should he . . .
- A. Call his mom and ask her to quickly drive over with a written excuse to miss gym?
- B. Write the note and forge his mom's signature, bandaging his arm for special effect?
- C. Go to gym class and suffer through line dancing?
- D. Get his friend to forge his mom's signature?
- E. Tell the gym teacher that he will do three hundred push-ups if only he doesn't have to do the line dancing?

 To see what Hugh should do, read 2 Kings 17:7-9, the story of what happened to the Israelites when they followed the evil customs of the people surrounding them.

19

The Hospital

Harry is puzzled. Why is he being paged to the school office? He didn't forget his lunch this morning, or his instrument. There weren't any permission slips due. Oh well, he'll find out soon enough. As Harry approaches the office, he can see his dad and little sister waiting for him. This is strange, he thinks. It gets even stranger as he sees his sister is crying. Now he hurries to the office. When he walks in, his father gets up and quietly says, "I'm sorry, Harry, but there's been an accident. Mom was hit after dropping you off at school. She's in the hospital, and we all need to get over there as soon as possible."

The scene at the hospital is a blur. His mom is already in the operating room. Harry sits waiting with his sister and father. There are many people stopping in to see the family—friends from the neighborhood, other family members, and people from their church. Harry can hardly believe this is happening to him, to his family. He feels scared, alone, and confused. He doesn't know where to turn, what to do. What should Harry do?

Should he . . .

A. Run hysterically from the hospital?

B. Hide his feelings and pretend to be brave in front of his sister and dad?

C. Blame himself for his mom's accident because he didn't take the bus that morning?

D. Refuse to talk to anyone, including God, about what he is feeling?

E. Pray, telling God how he feels and trusting him to care for his mom and family?

 For help in knowing what Harry should do, read Psalm 62:8.

After-School Activity

Both of Brock's parents work—his mother got her job when he started first grade. For many years, Brock went to a day-care center after school. But now that he is older, Brock asked if he could come home after school by himself and wait the two hours before his mom arrives. After much discussion his parents agreed, but with strict guidelines: Brock has to come right home; he is not allowed to go to any friend's house without clearing it with his parents a day ahead of time; no friends are allowed at his house; he has to call Mom as soon as he gets home. For the past two months, the arrangement has worked beautifully. Brock has enjoyed the freedom of coming home. He has felt responsible, letting himself in, fixing his snack, and doing his homework.

Now, however, Brock is beginning to feel a bit relaxed about his routine. In fact, he has to admit, it's a little boring all by himself. His friends often invite him to come over, but, so far, Brock has observed the rules and made arrangements for another day. But sometimes things come up. Today, a friend from school walks home with Brock and mentions he is going down to the bookstore to look at the new Thriller Spy books that recently came in. Brock would love to get his hands on one of them. His friend invites him to come along. It's really tempting. What do you think Brock should do?

Should he . . .
   A. Tell his friend no; he will have to wait until his mom gets home?
   B. Ask his friend to buy him one of the books and then stop by the house to drop it off?
   C. Go home, call his mom first, and then go to the store?
   D. Go to the store with his friend and tell his mom he forgot to call?
   E. Call his mom on his friend's cell phone while he's on his way to the store?

 Read James 1:13-16 to see the source of Brock's temptation and to know what he should do.

21

Third Chair

Ian kicks the couch as he walks into the family room. He slumps into the chair and lets out a loud, long sigh. *It doesn't matter,* he thinks. *It just doesn't matter.* Ian can't even remember a time when he felt so discouraged. For the entire year in band Ian has tried really hard. He has put in extra hours practicing; he has taken an hour lesson every week from a great trumpet teacher. He has worked hard to improve his playing.

Ian felt he had been making progress. Just the other week, his band instructor complimented him on his tone. And when each of the kids had to play a particularly difficult passage in one piece of music, Ian was the only one to get it right. So why did his band instructor put him back on third part again? Ian just can't understand it. When he went to look at the chair assignments after try-outs, Ian thought there was a mistake. But when he checked it closer, sure enough, he was assigned to playing third trumpet—again. Ian feels so discouraged, he hardly knows what to do. What should he do?

Should Ian . . .

A. Talk to the band instructor and demand that he be placed at first or second chair?

B. Quit the band and take up basket weaving?

C. Stop tooting his own horn, melt his trumpet down, and sell the raw metal?

D. Continue to work hard at trumpet, thanking God for the musical gifts that have been given to him?

E. Decide to take up drums and beat it?

 To know how Ian should respond, read Psalm 42:5-6.

22

In the Middle

Kristen is in the middle of a major disagreement. Her two closest friends, Jill and Laurel, are quarreling. Actually, that's putting it mildly. The two girls had a huge fight and are not even talking to one another. Worse yet, each girl wants to pull Kristen into the middle of the fight by choosing sides. At first, Jill pulled Kristen aside and told her how Laurel is such a snitch and can't be trusted. Then Laurel grabbed Kristen and told her how Jill exaggerates everything and is overly sensitive. Kristen is confused and frustrated and wants to scream.

Something will have to give, however, because tomorrow is Kristen's birthday party, and both girls have been invited. Jill already has told Kristen that she won't be there if Laurel comes. And Laurel has told Kristen that she can forget being her friend if she insists on inviting Jill. Kristen comes home near tears, knowing that her party will be ruined. What do you think she should do?

Should Kristen . . .

A. Call both girls and tell them she's "uninviting" them to the party?

B. Pick a side and decide if the other girl doesn't like it, tough luck? At least she'll have one close friend left.

C. Tell each of them they can decide what they want to do, but that she intends to invite both of them to her party and hopes that each will come?

D. Cancel the party until the two friends can make up?

E. Tell each girl that she values her friendship and hope she will at least listen to the other girl's side of the situation?

 Read James 3:18 to see how Kristen should respond.

The Sick Mom

Barrett needs to work on his social studies assignment. Each student has to pick a state and make a chart of its natural resources—and it's due tomorrow. If Mom can take him to the store right after his snack and before soccer practice, Barrett should be able to get the project done after dinner and still have plenty of time to watch TV. As Barrett walks into his house, he calls out for his mother. But there's no answer.

Barrett walks into the kitchen. No Mom. He checks the sewing and laundry rooms. Where can she be? Finally he goes upstairs. His mom is in bed! "What's the matter?" he asks. In almost a whisper, Barrett's mother explains that she has the flu and asks if he would mind calling the Smiths for a ride to soccer practice. Barrett agrees and heads downstairs. Now he's in a fix. How will he get the poster board for his project? *Poor Mom. She's looking pretty bad,* he thinks. What do you think Barrett should do now?

Should he . . .
  A. Get down on his knees next to the bed and beg his mom to take him to the store?

  B. Ask if there is anything he can do for his mother? Then he can call the Smiths to ask if they can give him a ride to soccer practice, stopping at the store for poster board quickly on the way.

  C. Pray for his mom to get well quickly so she can take him to the store for his project?

  D. Get his snack, go to soccer, and forget about his mom because she'll be better soon?

  E. Use his mom's sickness as an excuse to not do the social studies project?

 For help in knowing what Barrett should do, read 1 John 3:18.

Moving On

Darren knows it is trouble when his dad calls a family meeting. As soon as he sits down at the kitchen table, he knows what's coming. "Well, kids," his father begins, "I just got this great promotion. . . ." A groan goes up from his brothers and sisters. "Oh no!" "Do we have to move?" "You promised this was the last time," the chorus goes on. But after the initial din, it becomes clear that Darren and his family are moving before the end of the school year.

Darren is angry and confused. He doesn't want to move—that much he knows. He just got into the honor band; he made the football team; he's has lots of friends. How could Dad do this to him? What if his new school doesn't have a band program—or at least one like his school does now? What kind of kids go to the new school? What if they don't like him? Where will they go to church, and what if they don't have a youth group like his church does? The countless questions swirl in his mind. He just doesn't know what to do with this bombshell. What do you think Darren should do?

Should he . . .
   A. Go on a hunger strike until his dad comes to his senses and cancels the move?
   B. Absolutely refuse to go and make plans to live at a friend's house?
   C. Whine and complain about the move for the next three months?
   D. Trust that God will meet his family's needs in their new home, school, and church?
   E. Try to convince his dad not to move by sharing his hurt feelings and making him feel guilty?

 To know how Darren should respond, check out Philippians 4:19 and 1 Peter 5:7.

Taught to Pray

Mr. Bradstreet is an awesome Sunday school teacher. He's funny, he's interesting, but most important, he's honest. When Mr. Bradstreet teaches, he really shares what the Lord is doing in his own life. Courtney looks forward to the class, and she is growing by leaps and bounds in her faith. So when Mr. Bradstreet taught a ten-part series on prayer, Courtney was listening. Sure, Courtney said her prayers at night. Didn't everybody? But a consistent time alone with the Lord? Well, she didn't exactly do that, she had to admit.

At the end of the series, Mr. Bradstreet challenges each of his students to pick a prayer goal for the next month. They are supposed to turn in their goal to Mr. Bradstreet next Sunday. Courtney is excited. Mr. Bradstreet's messages have struck a chord with her, and she is eager to become more deeply involved in prayer. The only question is how to get started. What do you think Courtney should do?

Should she . . .
    A. Keep praying before she goes to sleep at night—and keep dozing off in midsentence?
    B. Vow to get up every morning at five o'clock to pray for an hour?
    C. Decide that she really needs to grow a bit more in her faith before she can tackle such a serious spiritual discipline as prayer?
    D. Read more books about prayer?
    E. As a starting point, set a goal to pray for five minutes, three times a week in the morning?

 For help in knowing what Courtney should do, read Psalm 5:3.

Personal Best

Linda and Judy are good friends. They do everything together, usually without any problems, except when it comes to swim team. There's something about being in the pool that brings out the competitive streak in both girls. The girls have been on the same swim team for three years. And although Linda is a year older, Judy is by far the better swimmer of the two. While they always cheer for one another as they swim their races, just once Linda would like to get a faster time than her friend.

One of the biggest meets of the year is tonight. Linda has been swimming well lately, and she feels good about her chances. Although they will be in a couple of relays and other individual events, they both will be swimming butterfly. Linda is excited because this is becoming one of her strongest strokes. This could be it, she thinks. This could be the night she finally beats Judy. Linda swims in the first heat, and she wins it with her best time ever in the butterfly. Judy swims next. She finishes first, too, but her time is slower. Judy's expression tells her disappointment. Linda realizes that she finally did it! She finally beat Judy's time. Now what should Linda do?

Should she . . .

A. Congratulate Judy on swimming a good race?

B. Run around the pool deck, shouting "Yes! I did it!"?

C. Immediately run up to Judy and tell her, "I beat you. I got a faster time than you"?

D. Not say anything to Judy but make sure she sees her ribbon with the winning time on it?

E. Whenever the subject of the "butterfly" comes up, act as though the discussion is about insects?

 Check out Jeremiah 9:23-24 to know how Linda should respond.

New and Unusual

The kids in the youth group are buzzing. Obviously something is up, and Todd is missing out. He goes to one friend and asks, "What gives?" His friend gives a quick nod over to the corner of the room. "Check out the new kid."

Todd glances over. *Whoa! That is one strange dude,* thinks Todd. The boy has a long ponytail extending to the middle of his back, with a large streak of magenta-colored hair. He sports several earrings in one ear and what appears to be a tattoo on his upper arm.

The boy is standing by himself, and, so far, no one has approached him. The talk is circulating. "He's from the city." "He came out here to live with his mother—his parents are divorced." "His older brother plays in a punk band." "He has a sister who has her eyebrows and nose pierced." The unspoken question remains: *What is he doing here? He can't possibly be a Christian, looking like that. Or could he?* Todd feels a bit sorry for the guy. He looks so obviously out of place. What do you think Todd should do?

Should he . . .

    A.   Go over to the boy and introduce himself and some of his friends from the youth group?

    B.   Ask him where he gets his hair done?

    C.   Make snide remarks about the boy's appearance to his friends?

    D.   Mention that his ear has a familiar ring to it?

    E.   Avoid him at all costs?

 Check out Romans 15:7 for help in knowing how Todd should respond.

The Paper Chase

For the past three weeks, Vanessa has been working diligently on her term paper. This is the major social studies assignment given to each student, and it counts for 50 percent of her final grade. Vanessa already has spent many hours in the library researching her topic. She has worked on an outline for her paper, which she had to revise three times before her teacher would accept it. Now all that's left to do is write the paper.

Vanessa began writing over the weekend. She has finished her introduction and the first three main sections of the paper. Now it's Wednesday, and Vanessa is almost done. She has one last section to complete before writing her conclusion. But Vanessa is tired. She looks at the stack of notecards and her dog-eared outline. All of a sudden the task seems overwhelming. She can't think of a thing to write. If she doesn't get it done today, she'll have to cram everything in tomorrow because the paper is due Friday. Vanessa is close to tears. How is she going to get this all done? What do you think Vanessa should do?

Should she . . .

A. Wait and cram all the work in tomorrow—after all, she works well under deadline pressure?

B. Pray that God will give her the strength to continue and finish the project today?

C. Write her teacher a note saying the computer "ate" her term paper and ask for an extension?

D. Turn the paper in as it is, assuming that the teacher won't read the whole thing?

E. Get her doctor to write her a medical excuse for not finishing her term paper?

 To know how Vanessa should respond in this situation, read Isaiah 40:29-31.

29

Mother's Day

It is a busy time of the school year for Chuck. He has extra choir rehearsals at church for the spring musical. He also has been practicing hard for the band's solo contest coming up at school. The big science project is due at the end of the month. Chuck and his friends also have been planning some after-school practices to get in shape for baseball.

As Chuck is finishing his homework and getting ready to practice, his dad comes into his room. He reminds Chuck that Mother's Day is in less than two weeks. With everything going on, what should Chuck do?

Should he . . .

A. Give his mom a used pack of gum?

B. Wait until the last minute and then run out to get her a card and a candy bar?

C. Talk with his dad about what Mom might like, make a list of three things he can afford, and plan a time to go shopping for the gift?

D. Write his mom a poem telling her all the things he appreciates about her, working a little bit each night until it's done?

E. Give his mom an IOU for a gift until he finally has the time to shop?

 For help in knowing what Chuck should do, read Proverbs 13:16.

Never Too Young

Tonight at youth group, a missionary from one of the islands off New Zealand gave a talk. He spoke about his work there among the natives, translating the Bible and teaching them about Jesus. The missionary has been out on the mission field for three years and is back in the United States for a brief time to raise more financial support. He told many funny stories about learning the customs of the people, as well as inspirational life-changing testimonies. The missionary ended his talk by telling the young people that there are opportunities for them to get involved in mission work. He challenged the group to get involved!

Afterwards, the group talks about the missionary's challenge. One girl remarks how she could never live that long without the comforts of home. Another boy says he wants to get involved in mission work—right after he graduates from college. Still another girl says she believes that, as a group, they can get involved in mission work right now. Claudia is skeptical. Her mom won't let her go shopping at the mall by herself, never mind going clear across the world to some other country! She still takes a teddy bear to bed with her. How can she help anyone else? What should she offer to the discussion?

Should Claudia . . .
 A. Suggest they find a local food bank or family in their own community that they can help?
 B. Say, "We're only kids. What can we do to help other people?"
 C. Offer to buy a lottery ticket for the missionary?
 D. Suggest they talk about this next month because they have to plan their next party first?
 E. Form a committee to look into it—like the adults do?

 Read Acts 23:12-22 to see how Paul's nephew, a young boy, helped his uncle's mission work.

Saturday Chores

After a tough week at school, Nate is looking forward to the weekend. He comes home, drops his books on the table, and lets out a long sigh. *Oh, the joy of doing absolutely nothing,* he thinks. *Sleeping in . . . watching some serious TV. . . maybe trying out one of his new computer games.*

After dinner that night, Nate's dad says he really needs Nate's help with the yard work on Saturday. Dad is going out of town for a week and really wants to get the yard cleaned up before he goes. Nate knows what this means—raking, pulling weeds, mowing the grass. Nate moans inside. This is not exactly what he had in mind for the weekend. What should he do?

Should Nate . . .

    A. Jump out of bed Saturday morning, get dressed, and ask what he can do to help?

    B. Stay in bed and try to sleep until noon to avoid most of the work?

    C. Develop a sudden limp and explain he hurt his leg in gym class?

    D. Get up real early and cut the grass with his fingernail clippers, one blade at a time, to surprise his dad?

    E. Pay the boy down the street to do the chores?

 For help in knowing what Nate should do, read Proverbs 22:29.

Down, but Not Out

Caleb gets off the bus humming. It's been a good week at school. He aced his science test, and his English teacher gave the entire class an extension on their term paper. To top it all off, pizza was featured for lunch today. It doesn't get any better than this. Walking up to his house, he notices his dad's car in the driveway. Strange, his dad doesn't usually get home this early.

When Caleb walks in the door, he immediately notices the tension in the air. *Something's not right,* he thinks. Both his mom and dad are sitting together, not saying much, but looking very serious. Caleb hurries in. "What's up? Why are you home so early?" he asks. Dad answers that he lost his job this afternoon. Caleb is stunned. If his dad's not working, who's going to pay the bills? How will they eat? Where are they going to live? What is going to happen to them as a family? Caleb can't think of a thing to say. Dad tells Caleb not to worry. *Yeah, sure,* he thinks, and he leaves the room. Caleb wonders why this had to happen to him and what he can do about it. What should Caleb do?

Should he . . .
   A. Try to find some part-time jobs to earn a few extra dollars for the family?
   B. Worry himself sick about the financial situation?
   C. Get mad at his dad for not doing a good enough job?
   D. Trust that the Lord will help him and his family make it through these tough times?
   E. Become hysterical as he considers all the bad things that could happen to his family?

 Check out Isaiah 54:10 to know how Caleb should respond to this situation.

Study Guide

Clint has a big test in science this Tuesday. His teacher has given the students a study guide and plenty of time to prepare for the test. She has advised the class to start studying over the weekend because it will be difficult to prepare for all the material on the test in one night. So Clint brought his science book and study guide home. When he walked in the door after school on Friday, he dropped his book in his room and ran out to meet his friends. It's the weekend! Freedom!

At breakfast on Saturday, his mom asks if he has any homework. Clint mentions the test. His mom suggests that he study some that morning and then right after church on Sunday since he has youth group Sunday night. The family is having company on Saturday night, and Clint has a soccer game on Saturday afternoon. Clint assures his mom that he will take care of it and get the studying done—sometime that weekend. Clint's mom looks skeptical, but she says nothing more about the test or studying. What do you think Clint should do?

Should he . . .
  A. Cram for the test on Monday night?
  B. Take his mom's advice and study a little bit each day?
  C. Sleep with his science book under his pillow to help him absorb the information during the night?
  D. Study for five minutes on Saturday morning and another five on Sunday. His mom never said how long he should study?
  E. Tell his mom that he has a photographic memory so he has it all down now?

 Check out Proverbs 16:20 to see what Clint should do.

The Last Game

Skip warms up his pitching arm with his best friend, who just happens to be the catcher. It's a beautiful spring day—perfect for baseball. And this should be a special day, too. During the season Skip has developed into a pretty good pitcher. He's got good speed on his fastball, and he has struck out more batters than any other pitcher on the team. Skip hears that the high school coach is coming to the game to take a look at the players. Skip really wants to do his best to get a head start on next year. The team already has won its division and will move on to the city championships, so the game doesn't mean much. But Skip is eager to go out and play ball!

While Skip tosses a few to Glen, he notices that two of the younger guys on the team also are warming up. That's interesting, he thinks. Maybe the coach is going to take him out a few innings earlier to give him some rest before the championship game. That's OK with Skip. He could use the rest, and besides, the high school coach is bound to come down earlier than later. Right before game time, Skip takes a look at the lineup. He quickly goes down the list once, then twice. He doesn't see his name. Skip goes to the coach and asks if there's been a mistake. Coach Henderson shakes his head. He wants to give the younger guys a chance and rest Skip for the big game. Skip is furious. What about the high school coach, he thinks. All his plans are going down the tubes. How do you think Skip should handle this situation?

Should he . . .

  A. Argue with the coach about his decision and demand to play?

  B. Agree to sit this one out and offer to help the younger guys with their pitching?

  C. Throw his mitt into the dugout with disgust and sulk the entire game?

  D. Sit on the bench but vocally express his anger with the coach to anyone who will listen?

  E. Threaten to quit if the coach won't let him at least pitch a couple of innings?

 To know how Skip should respond, read Psalm 37:8-9.

5

The Guilty Goalie

Sheila's soccer team is on the verge of winning its first state tournament. Her team has never advanced this far, and getting the trophy will be a real coup. Sheila can sense the excitement mounting on the sidelines as parents and teammates cheer them on. The score is 2-1, with less than a minute left. Sheila has played an outstanding game at goalie, making numerous saves in the last five minutes of play as their opponents have mounted a furious attack to try to tie the score.

Shiela gets ready for a final shot goal as the opponents break up her team's attack and send the ball down the field toward her. There's a flurry of activity in front of the net. In a flash, Sheila spies the ball hurtling toward her. She leaps into the air, but the ball sails overhead into the goal and goes through a hole in the back of the net. Everything happened so quickly and the shot was so hard that not even the referee saw what happened. He whistles the ball out of bounds—not a goal! The other team protests strongly. Sheila sees her team erupt in victory. But Sheila knows that the other team is right. They did score a goal. But if she tells the ref, the game will be tied. What do you think Sheila should do?

Should she . . .
   A. Join in the celebration with her teammates?
   B. Tell the ref what she saw and that the ball really did go into the goal?
   C. Tell the other team that they are a bunch of poor losers for complaining?
   D. Figure it's part of the game if the ref blew the call?
   E. Tell her coach about it and let him decide what to do?

 Check out Jeremiah 17:11 to see what may motivate Sheila to make the right decision.

The Camp-Out

Brad and his church youth group are on a weekend camping trip at a state park about two hours from home. Brad has never camped out before and is really looking forward to the experience. He and his father assemble all his camping gear. Brad arrives right on time as the group is ready to depart. The entire group is excited about all the hiking and other activities planned for the weekend.

After what seems like forever, the youth group finally pulls into the state park, and the park ranger tells them how to get to the campsite. After a ten-minute drive on dusty dirt roads, the group arrives at its site. It's a beautiful spot nestled in the woods, close to a bubbling stream. Brad can't wait to hike along the trails and try out his new boots. As the kids gather up their gear, the adult leader explains that everyone is supposed to help prepare the campsite, fix the meals, and clean up. He announces that after everyone gets their gear unpacked, it will be time to get ready for supper. Brad really would rather do some exploring while it's still light out instead of fixing dinner. What should he do?

Should Brad . . .

   A. Pretend he has a bad cold and tell the leader that if he cooks he'll give everyone else his germs?

   B. Sneak off into the woods and go exploring, leaving all the work to the others?

   C. Pretend to work but run off at the first opportunity when no one is looking?

   D. Say he'd rather go hunt elk?

   E. Ask what he should do and then do his part before doing anything else?

 For help in knowing what Brad should do, read Proverbs 20:4.

Sleeping In

Minda stayed up late last night, putting the finishing touches on her costume for Drama Club. She snuggles down deeper in her bed as her mom's voice calling her to get up penetrates her sleepy mind. Pulling the pillow over her head, she tries to ignore the sounds of morning—the radio downstairs, her mom emptying the dishwasher, her sister rummaging in the bathroom. Ignoring her mom's calls, Minda thinks groggily to herself, *Five more minutes, just five more minutes.* Five minutes stretches into ten, and then fifteen. When Minda finally rouses herself, she realizes that she has just fifteen minutes to get dressed and get out the door.

Racing around her room, she throws her clothes on and grabs her books. Then she hurries downstairs. As she walks into the kitchen, Minda knows that even if she gulps down her breakfast in one minute, she will never make it to school on time, unless, of course, her mom drives her. Minda knows that she's in trouble now. This is the second time she has been late this week. With as contrite an expression as she can muster, she asks her mom if she will please drive her to school. To Minda's utter amazement, her mom calmly says, "No, you will have to walk. I have a meeting to attend, and I can't be late. I told you to get up an hour ago." Minda is outraged! She's going to be late for sure. How can her mom be so inconsiderate? If her mom hurries, they can both be on time, can't they? How can her mom do this to her? What do you think Minda should do?

Should she . . .
- A. Get on her hands and knees on the kitchen floor at her mom's feet and promise to never, never, never be late again—if only her mom will take her to school?
- B. Throw a tantrum until her mom relents and drives her to school?
- C. Go back to bed?
- D. Accept the consequences of sleeping in—and get walking?
- E. Hitchhike to school?

 Read Proverbs 19:20 to see what Minda should have done in the first place.

8

Future Plans

Today at school, the science teacher invited an oceanographer to come and talk with the students. Chip thinks it is fascinating, studying the ocean, going down to depths where no human has ever ventured. Could there be a more exciting career? Of course, Chip felt that way when he heard the meteorologist (chasing down tornadoes sounds great), and the doctor (healing others would be so cool) address their class as part of a series on careers involving science. All these careers sound so exciting to Chip. Each week it seems as though he has a new career that he wants to pursue.

Then there was this missionary at church, and he was totally awesome. But if Chip decides to do that, what about medicine, oceanography, or chasing tornadoes? The more Chip thinks about it, the more confused he becomes. He knows that college is several years away, but he needs to begin planning the types of courses he should take in high school to prepare himself. But prepare himself for what? Then he comes right back to the same question—what is he going to be when he grows? Chip gets discouraged as he tries to make sense out of his future. What do you think Chip should do?

Should he . . .
 A. Make a dartboard with his career choices on it and throw a dart to choose one?
 B. Give up, frustrated, and decide not to go to college?
 C. Trust that God has a plan for his life and that God will guide him in the right direction?
 D. Talk with his best friend, Alex, about some of his interests and ask him for advice?
 E. Put off any decision for now—he's much too young to be thinking about the future?

 For help in knowing how Chip can deal with the future, read Jeremiah 29:11.

Turning the Other Cheek

Tina is captain of the soccer team, and this is one of the biggest games of the season. Her team is well-coached and prepared for the game, but it soon becomes obvious that their opponents are out for blood. Whenever they can get away with a cheap shot, they take it. Unfortunately, for Tina and her teammates, the refs never seem to catch them at it. During the first half of play, Tina gets a pass and has a clear break—only one person is standing in her way. But the girl trips her from behind. Instead of scoring, Tina is shaken up and taken out of the game.

Although the score is tied, during half-time, Tina's teammates are really down. They are roughed up, discouraged, and angry. After the coach finishes talking with the girls about their second-half strategy, one of Tina's friends starts whispering to the other girls. She is urging them to trip, kick, and hurt their opponents whenever they can—in other words, to play dirty like the other team is doing. Tina is not so sure. She wants to get back into the game, but she wants to play the game on her terms, not the opponent's. As captain, what do you think Tina should do?

Should she . . .
    A. Agree with her friends and fight fire with fire during the second half?

    B. Get out on the field, and as soon as she sees that girl who brought her down, nail her?

    C. Hand the refs some glasses so they can see the fouls being committed?

    D. Set the tone for her team by urging them to play as cleanly and fairly as possible?

    E. Refuse to go back out on the field because the other team is a bunch of cheaters?

 To know how Tina should respond, read Matthew 5:39.

Spin the Bottle

Juanita is going to her first boy-girl party tonight. She can hardly wait. She and her friends have been talking about the party for days. Every "cool" kid in her class will be there. Juanita was surprised to receive an invitation, but her best friend knows the hostess. Juanita has planned her outfit carefully and has rearranged her hair at least a dozen times before it's time to go. Her dad drives Juanita and her friend to the party and leaves with a final, "Have a good time. Be good!"

The party is going full force by the time they arrive. Juanita and her friend make their way down the stairs to a darkened basement. When their eyes adjust, they can see a number of kids dancing. Most are hanging around the snack table, talking. A few disappear, giggling, into a room off the main area. Juanita asks one of the boys who has just emerged from the room what's going on. He smiles and says, "Why don't you come in and see? It's just a game of Spin the Bottle. You don't want to miss it, do ya?" Her friend tugs on Juanita's arm. "Come on. I want to see who's in there. We don't have to do any kissing." Juanita does not have a good feeling about this. What do you think she should do?

Should Juanita . . .
A. Tell the hostess's mom what's going on?
B. Tell her friend that she would rather not and find something else to do?
C. Go in but run screaming from the room if the bottle points to her?
D. Pretend she's feeling ill and ask to go home?
E. Tell her friend that she will watch her play?

 Check out Colossians 3:5 for some good advice on how Juanita should handle this problem.

The Science Project

Last week Mr. Henley gave the guidelines for the final science project. This is the big year-end project that everyone in the seventh grade has to complete. The grade on this project will count for more than half of the final grade in science for the year. Everyone in Caitlin's class is talking about it—at lunch, during gym class, before band rehearsal. It's all anyone is thinking about. After school one day, Caitlin and her friend were discussing the science project. Caitlin mentioned an idea that she had for the project. She had seen a couple of books at the library on the topic and thought she could develop a good project from the material. Her friend nodded her head but said nothing.

Over the next several days, Caitlin worked on her idea. She needed to do a little more research, however, before she could decide whether her project would work. She went to the library to check out those books that she had found earlier. To her dismay, however, she discovered that the books were already checked out. Her spirits sank as she realized that someone else was doing a project on the same topic. So she was back to square one and had to come up with another idea.

Today in school, Caitlin noticed a library book on her friend's desk. The title caught her eye. It was one of the books she had been looking for at the library. When Caitlin confronts her friend, she discovers that her friend has stolen her idea. Caitlin is furious! She feels like stealing the books and hiding them. It's payback time! Or is it? What do you think Caitlin should do?

Should she . . .
  A. Report her friend to the science teacher as a "project thief"?
  B. Go ahead, steal the books and hide them so her friend can't finish her project?
  C. Tell all her other friends that this girl stole her science project idea so they will be mad at her too?
  D. Quit talking to this girl and count her as an enemy from now on?
  E. Forgive her friend and give her all the research Caitlin had collected on the project?

 Read Deuteronomy 32:35 and Proverbs 25:21-22 to know how Caitlin should respond in this situation.

12

The Accident

Jessie finishes her Saturday chores. It's a beautiful spring afternoon, perfect conditions for a bike ride. She calls up her friend, and they decide to meet at the park and ride along the bike trail by the river. Jessie packs some water bottles and PowerBars for a quick energy snack. Jessie tells her mom and dad her plans for the afternoon, and off she goes.

To get to the park from her house, Jessie has to cross one particularly busy street. There's a traffic light and crosswalk, so it's not too dangerous if you pay attention. As Jessie approaches the intersection, she sees a car speeding through the intersection just as the light turns red. There's a terrific crash as the speeding car plows into another car making a left turn. Jessie watches in horror as shards of glass fly through the air. What should Jessie do now?

Should she . . .

A. Say, "How cool!" and wait for the explosion?

B. Ride to the nearest house and call for help?

C. Ride away quickly?

D. Go get her friend at the park so she can see the excitement?

E. Ride back to her house as fast as she can, run up to her room, and lock the door so that she will be safe?

 For help in knowing what Jessie should do, read James 4:17.

13

The Team Captain

Sally has been playing softball since third grade. She has become a very good pitcher and a decent hitter. She enjoys the game and looks forward to when they play softball in gym class. Today the P.E. teacher chose Sally and another girl as team captains for softball. It's quite an honor for Sally. Miss Crews typically names the strongest players in the class as captains. Sally feels proud as her name is called.

Moments later, Sally doesn't feel quite the same. Miss Crews announces that the captains will take turns choosing classmates for their teams. Sally knows there are several girls in the gym class, including her good friend Connie, who can't play very well. They usually get chosen last because no one wants them on their team. Sally always feels sorry for these kids when the other girls are picking teams. Now *she* has to do it! How should Sally handle this situation?

Should she . . .
- A. Keep choosing the better players to build the strongest team possible?
- B. Choose some weaker players earlier than usual so they'll feel like an important part of the team?
- C. Suggest that Miss Crews divide the class into teams instead?
- D. Choose the strongest team and then play terrible on purpose so the weaker players will think they are better?
- E. Tell Miss Crews she's really not that good at softball and really shouldn't be a captain?

 The biblical principle that tells how Sally should respond can be found in Colossians 3:12.

Beauty Is in the Eye . . .

Gail really admires her friend Mollie who always looks as though she has just walked off the page of a teen fashion magazine. Mollie always dresses in the latest fashion, with the coolest shoes and accessories. Gail can't remember when she has ever seen Mollie in a pair of old jeans and T-shirt. If there's any question about the proper thing to wear for any occasion, Mollie has the answer. She's always suggesting ways for Gail to dress up her outfits, but Gail just can't seem to get the hang of it. Mollie practically had a fit the day Gail wore the wrong color scarf. Mollie corrected that fashion no-no right away.

Today, when Gail walks into school, she notices something different about Mollie. Then it hits her. Mollie is wearing makeup—not just a little, but lipstick, blush, mascara, eye shadow, the whole works. She grabs Gail and drags her into the girls' bathroom. Mollie offers to "make over" Gail. Gail is unsure. She and her mom have discussed this before, and it was decided that Gail could start wearing a little makeup in high school (and definitely not eye shadow!). Mollie is very insistent that Gail give it a try. What do you think Gail should do?

Should she . . .
 A. Let Mollie put on the makeup and wash it off before she goes home?
 B. Politely tell Mollie that she is not allowed to wear makeup until high school?
 C. Start laughing at Mollie and ask her when the circus got into town?
 D. Try just a little bit of makeup to see how it looks?
 E. Tell Mollie that she is allergic to makeup and will break out in hives if she puts some on?

 For help in knowing what Gail should do, read 1 Peter 3:3-4.

15

Unconditional Love

It has been a couple of weeks since Marla has seen her friend Beth-Ellen at church. The two girls attend different schools, but they usually catch up with each other in Sunday school class. Marla is a little worried about her friend. Beth-Ellen tends to get sick easily, and Marla hopes nothing serious is wrong with her. A few days later, Marla spots Beth-Ellen coming out of the grocery store. She's by herself, and Marla calls over to her, "Hey, where have you been? I've missed you." For a minute it looks as though Beth-Ellen will turn and run away, but she slowly approaches Marla.

"Uh, hi," Beth-Ellen offers. Again Marla asks where she has been and if everything is OK. Beth-Ellen looks nervously around and then bursts into tears. It turns out that she has gotten herself into some real trouble. She and some friends were goofing around after school and decided it would be fun to write dirty sayings about the teacher on the walls. They were caught, suspended from school, and forced to pay for the damage they had done.

It's obvious that Beth-Ellen deeply regrets her part in the prank. Marla says she's sorry to hear about Beth-Ellen's troubles at school, but wants to know when Beth-Ellen will be at church. Beth-Ellen stares at her in disbelief. "I can't go back to church. How could God possibly love someone like me who has done something as terrible as I did?" she exclaims. Marla is caught off guard by her friend's reply. What do you think she should do?

Should Marla . . .

A. Tell Beth-Ellen that God is a loving and merciful father who is always ready to forgive?

B. Suggest that Beth-Ellen pray a bit harder and ask God a few more times to forgive her?

C. Agree with Beth-Ellen that maybe it is a good idea to stay away from church for a while? After all, what will the other kids think about what she did?

D. Write Beth-Ellen off as a friend because she obviously isn't a Christian if she wrote those kinds of words on the school walls?

E. Thank Beth-Ellen for the great idea and ask where she bought the spray paint?

 For help in knowing what Marla should do and how much God loves his repentant children, read Zephaniah 3:17 and 1 John 1:9.

16

Making the First Move

A new girl recently moved into the house across the street from Felicia. So far, Felicia has only seen her from a distance, but she knows the girl is about her age because Felicia has seen her around school. Felicia has been so busy with softball season that she hasn't been around much. She hasn't had a chance to go over and meet this new girl. A couple of her friends have met her but haven't had much to say about her.

Felicia doesn't know if she is shy or a snob. One time Felicia saw her outside and grabbed her coat to go over to talk with her, but the girl ran inside. If Felicia didn't know better, she might think that the girl was trying to avoid her. If the new girl wants to meet her, why doesn't she come over and introduce herself, Felicia wonders? Maybe she thinks she's too good for this neighborhood. Felicia has heard that she wears expensive clothes and has one of those expensive new jackets. The more Felicia thinks about it, the more she doesn't want to introduce herself after all. What do you think Felicia should do?

Should she . . .
A. Make the first move and go over to introduce herself before they graduate from high school?
B. Spread rumors that the new girl is a rich snob?
C. Wait for the new girl to make the first move—after all, this is Felicia's turf?
D. Send the new girl a Christmas card?
E. Stay on her own side of the street and wave every once in a while?

 Read Acts 9:26-28 to see what Barnabas did when Saul was new in town.

Baseball Burnout

Art slumps wearily in the backseat of the car. "So, how was practice?" his dad asks cheerfully. Art mumbles a response. The flood of questions continues: How did he do? Did he strike anyone out at practice? Did his arm feel good? Did he get any hits? How's his pitching coming along? Art grunts a one- or two-word answer to each question. All he wants to do is go home, take a shower, put on his music, and forget about baseball for one day. He's tired of it!

Art has played baseball ever since he was on a T-ball team in kindergarten. His dad played semi-pro as a pitcher and has enthusiastically monitored Art's progress over the years. Art does have talent for playing the game, but he's burned out. The stakes are getting higher; the coaches are more demanding; his dad's expectations are higher than ever. Art wants to escape from it all! If only he could quit. But what would he tell his dad? What do you think Art should do?

Should he . . .

A. Begin to play so poorly that he doesn't make the team?

B. Secretly quit without telling his dad and hang out after school until practice is over?

C. Try to talk with his dad about the pressure he is feeling in playing baseball right now?

D. Pretend that he has a sore shoulder and can't play anymore?

E. Tell his dad that he wants to take up a new sport—like lawn bowling?

 Read Philippians 3:13-14 to find out how Paul was able to persevere despite adversity and burnout.

Trash TV

Everyone in Guy's class is talking about the new cop show on TV. According to Guy's friends (who haven't missed an episode), the show is filled with blood-and-guts scenes, lots of shootings and killings, and even some great swearing. His friends know all the characters; at lunch, they sit and talk about these TV personalities as if they know them personally. Guy has to be the only one in the entire school who hasn't seen the show. He has asked his parents if they could let him see one episode, but they explained that the show received terrible reviews in a Christian parent magazine. They also pointed out that two young boys tried to copy one of the scenes from the TV show and were severely injured. They have strictly ruled out this show as off-limits to Guy and his brother.

Tonight is the climatic ending to the show's season. Guy's friends have been talking about the possible endings for days. Tonight, Guy's parents are going out for a church meeting, leaving him in charge. Guy figures that when his parents leave, he will have just enough time to get his younger brother to bed and watch the show. How will his parents ever know? What do you think Guy should do?

Should he . . .
  A. Tape the show and save it for when he's old enough to make his own decisions about what shows to watch?
  B. Tune in the show but close his eyes (and ears) at all the gory parts?
  C. Obey his parents and forget about watching the show?
  D. Don't watch the show but have his friends fill him in on all the details?
  E. Go ahead and tune in—what can watching one TV show hurt?

 Take a look at Ephesians 4:21-23 to know how Guy is expected to behave.

19

Spreading the News

Robyn can tell that something is wrong with her best friend, Holly. She has been unusually quiet on the bus trip home from school. When Robyn invites Holly in for a snack, Holly uncharacteristically says she has to hurry home. *What gives?* thinks Robyn. *Holly never has to get home in a hurry for anything.* Robyn doesn't think any more about it until the phone rings later that afternoon. It's Holly, and she wants to meet Robyn at their meeting place.

When Robyn arrives, Holly is already there. Robyn can tell just by looking at Holly that she has been crying. "What's the matter, Holly?" she asks as she rushes to hug her friend. In a torrent of tears and words, Holly explains that her mom and dad have been fighting for months now and are splitting up. Her dad is moving out on Saturday. Robyn is shocked. She never noticed anything wrong when she was over at Holly's house. This is just awful. Robyn doesn't know what to say but just listens as Robyn pours out her feelings and tells her what has been going on.

The next day in school, Holly barely talks to any of their other friends. At lunch, one of their friends comments on Holly's behavior. "What is going on with her anyway? Is she sick or something?" the friend questions. Robyn knows Holly hasn't talked to anyone else about this. What should she do?

Should Robyn. . .

A. Simply say that Holly is going through a tough time right now and needs some time to herself?

B. Fill all her friends in on the juicy gossip about Holly's parents?

C. Tell her other friend, "It's none of your business"?

D. Make up another story about Holly to keep the girls off track?

E. Shrug and say, "I don't know"?

 Check out Proverbs 25:19 for help in knowing how Robyn should respond.

The Prayer Chain

Derek recently moved into a new town. Even though he has been attending school for about two months and regularly attends the church's youth group, he really hasn't made any friends. He misses his old friends and school. It has been a tough two months for Derek. When he comes home from school, he spends a lot of time in his room, listening to music or throwing the ball outside with his dog. There have been a few guys at church that seem nice, but so far no one has invited him over to do anything. He sure could use a few friends.

Today, Derek receives a call from his old youth group leader. Mr. Martin listens as Derek tells him about how lonely he is. "Well, Derek, I know it has been tough. The entire group has been praying that you will meet some good friends. I know the Lord will answer that prayer," he explains.

Derek dejectedly hangs up the phone. *A lot of good that does,* he thinks. He has been praying, too, but it sure seems as if those prayers have been hitting the ceiling and going nowhere. He's not so sure anyone is listening anymore! What do you think Derek should do?

Should he . . .

A. Just give up because it has been two months already and obviously nothing is happening?

B. Keep on praying and trust that God will work things out because God is good and his timing is perfect?

C. Figure that his friends will do his praying for him?

D. Make up different prayers because maybe he isn't asking the "right way"?

E. Decide that maybe he isn't meant to have friends in his new home?

 To know how Derek should respond, read Luke 18:1-8.

It's in the Stars!

Vicki has been invited to a friend's house for a slumber party. All the girls in her class have been invited, and everyone has been talking about it for days. It's a '60s theme, and Vicki and her friends have been bugging her mom to dig out some old bell-bottoms for them to wear. Vicki even got a few of her dad's old albums to take with her—although there probably won't be anything to play them on. It's fun to look at the album covers and see all the crazy clothes they wore way back then.

The evening passes quickly as the girls have a dance contest, a '60s scavenger hunt, and play some games. Vicki scored the highest on her '60s IQ test—her mom and dad will be real proud. Finally it's time for the girls to quiet down and find a spot on the floor to sleep. As they settle in, one of the girls brings out a horoscope book and some tarot cards. The other girls gather around to check out their "sign." One of the girls says that she reads her horoscope every day and that the tarot cards can predict the future. Vicki never paid much attention to astrology, and she is curious. What do you think Vicki should do?

Should she . . .

    A. Ask one of the girls to tell her future with the tarot cards?

    B. See where the horoscope is in the paper so she can read it every day to check out how accurate it really is?

    C. Start praying really loud because these girls are dabbling in witchcraft?

    D. Tell her friends they are all crazy to believe in something as stupid as astrology?

    E. Politely decline to get involved in astrology, saying she believes that God, who made the stars, is the one in control?

 For help in knowing how Vicki should respond, read Deuteronomy 4:19 and Deuteronomy 18:10-12.

Looks Aren't Everything

From the day that Lyle walked into first grade, he has been the tallest boy in the class. It was bad enough back then. He always had to stand in the back row for the class picture. So when the class lined up according to height, Lyle immediately went to the back of the line. He thought that as everyone grew, some of the other kids would catch up to him. But Lyle continued to grow as well. Nobody ever caught up with him.

Things have gotten worse for Lyle. Not only is he still the tallest student in the school, but he is also the skinniest. And his ears tend to stick out because his face is so thin. And because he doesn't know what to do with his arms and legs, Lyle tends to be awkward. He tried out for basketball once, but he got so tangled up with the other players that he spent more time on the floor than anyplace else.

The kids all make fun of him. They call him "Stork," "Scarecrow," "Stick," or sometimes "Ichabod." He hates that nickname the most because he thinks Ichabod Crane was a real dork. Sometimes Lyle gets very discouraged. At times, it feels as though he will be like this forever. What should Lyle do to help him through this tough time?

Should he . . .

   A. Eat lots of PowerBars and milk shakes to gain some weight?

   B. Start working out in the gym to build up some muscles?

   C. Make up some awful nicknames for his worst tormentors and start calling them names?

   D. Take comfort in knowing that God doesn't judge based on appearances; instead, he looks at a person's character and heart?

   E. Find someone who is worse off than he is to pick on?

Check out 1 Samuel 16:7 to find out how Lyle should respond.

Too Hard to Handle?

Christopher is scared. His parents seem to be fighting all the time. He's really worried that they will get a divorce or will separate. Then what will happen to his brother and him? Lately, things have gotten so bad that he doesn't want to go home. Christopher had been hanging out at his friend's house, but his friend's mother is starting to get suspicious. She has been asking him questions about his mom and dad and all that stuff. So now he hangs out at the library until he absolutely has to be home.

Christopher thinks about his home situation all the time. He really would love to talk to someone about it, but his best friend just wouldn't understand—he has such a perfect family. Christopher would feel weird talking about it. He tried to talk to his youth group leader and got as far as telling him there's a problem, but then someone interrupted them. Besides, he already knows what his youth group leader will say: "Take your problems to God; he will help you." The problem is that Christopher doesn't think even God can get his parents to stop arguing. What do you think Christopher should do?

Should he . . .

A. Write to "Dear Abby" and hope that she will answer his letter?

B. Continue to worry and lose sleep about his home situation?

C. Find the time to talk with his youth group leader; at least he will be able to unload a little bit?

D. Trust and believe that God is bigger than any problem he could ever encounter?

E. Pretend that everything is OK and just try to get through each day?

 Read Jeremiah 32:27 for a verse that will help Christopher during this difficult time.

The Pizza Party

Last Sunday the youth choir performed at all three services for its year-end finale. Everyone worked hard to prepare for the performance. There were several extra rehearsals, including one on Saturday morning. All the choir members did very well on Sunday, and the choir director was pleased with the performance. Liza is glad the performance is over. Now she can concentrate on preparing her solo for the big chorus competition at school.

There is still one more choir meeting, when members turn in their music and talk about their plans for next year. The choir director thanks everyone again and then announces that it's time for the pizza party. Liza forgot all about the party. And she is sure that her mother didn't sign her up for pizza. Liza walks to the room where a number of her friends already have their food. "Come on, Liza, we're saving you a seat." The pizza sure smells good, and it looks like there is plenty of it. No one seems to be checking any list. What do you think Liza should do?

Should she . . .

   A. Help herself to a couple of pieces—she deserves it!?

   B. Ask the director if she can participate, even though her mom didn't sign her up?

   C. Ask one of her friends who did sign up to get her some pizza?

   D. Wait around until the end and eat what's left over?

   E. Yell at her mom when she comes to pick her up for forgetting to sign her up?

 Read Romans 14:23 for some wise words on how Liza can keep a clear conscience.

The Hidden Magazines

If Earl doesn't hurry, he will be late for his baseball game. He knows that if he doesn't get to the ball field at least ten minutes before the game, he will be benched. Earl has been playing pretty well lately, and he doesn't want to blow it with his coach. The only problem is he can't find his mitt. It's not in the garage or in the laundry room where Earl usually drops his stuff when he gets home. He tears his room apart looking for his glove, but it is nowhere to be found. Earl pauses a moment, sits on his bed, and takes a deep breath. Now, when was the last time he saw his mitt?

Then it suddenly dawns on Earl that he let his older brother use his glove for his pickup game last weekend. Of course, his brother has it. Earl asks his mom where his brother is, and she informs him that his brother went out with a couple of his buddies and won't be back until five o'clock. That leaves only one alternative—he has to look for the glove in his brother's room. This normally is off-limits territory for Earl, but these are desperate times. He rips through his brother's closet. No mitt. Next he checks under the bed. There it is, on top of a pile of magazines. Earl pulls out the magazines to get his mitt. One of the magazine covers catches his eyes. It's one of those dirty magazines! Earl quickly checks the others—it's a whole pile of dirty magazines. What do you think Earl should do?

Should he . . .
   A. Take the pile of magazines and hide them in his room so he can read them later?
   B. Take the pile of magazines down to his mom?
   C. Use this knowledge as blackmail against his brother?
   D. Later, gently confront his brother with what he has discovered?
   E. Ignore what he has found and get going to the game?

 Read Job 31:1 and Philippians 2:15-16 for verses that will help Earl in handling his discovery and that he can share with his older brother.

26

Choosing Friends

Lori is a pretty, outgoing girl who makes friends easily. She is involved with her church's youth group and really enjoys being with her friends at church. They all believe in Christ and want to live the right way. They have a fun time when they get together, whether it's playing games or doing a Bible study. Lori always feels good after she has been with her "church friends." But Lori only sees those friends on Sundays. The kids in her youth group all go to different schools. It's rare for them to see each other during the week outside of church.

Lori has a big group of friends at school, too. She enjoys them because they are fun and they like her, but it's different. None of her school friends are Christians. They seem to tune Lori out when she speaks about going to church. They don't make fun of her, but Lori can tell that they don't understand it either. Because they aren't Christians, her school friends often say and do things that she doesn't agree with. Sometimes she feels downright uncomfortable around them. Sometimes Lori feels as though she is being pulled in two different directions. What do you think Lori should do?

Should she . . .

    A. Ditch her church friends? (After all, she spends more time at school.)

    B. Find ways to get together with friends from church other than on Sundays and make an effort to form close friendships there?

    C. Just leave things as they are? Her school friends aren't that bad, after all.

    D. Invite her school friends to church so they can get to know Jesus?

    E. Flip a coin to decide which group of friends to associate with?

 For the biblical principle underlying how Lori should respond, read 2 Corinthians 6:4-7.

27

Your Witness

Brittany is truly worried about her friend Nicole. Nicole is not a Christian, and lately she has been hanging around kids who have a reputation for being real party animals. A few times, Brittany has tried to arrange to get together with Nicole, but she has always been busy with her new group of friends. Brittany feels her friend slipping away and heading in a direction that could mean trouble. Brittany has been praying for Nicole for some time now. She has been asking God for an opportunity to witness to Nicole and share her faith in Christ.

The perfect opportunity presents itself today. Nicole asks Brittany if she would like to come over for dinner and a sleepover. *That's perfect,* thinks Brittany. *God is really answering prayer here.* Before she goes over to Nicole's house, she prays again for the right opportunity during the evening. After dinner, instead of watching a movie, the two girls start talking, catching up with each other. The conversation gradually turns to Nicole's new group of friends and how different they are from her other friends. Brittany sees an opportunity to point out what makes her different and shares her faith in Jesus with Nicole. Nicole gives a few halfhearted grunts as Brittany talks and then makes a small joke about being a Holy Roller. Brittany is crushed. The timing was so right; the opportunity was there, just as she prayed. She is really discouraged now. Were her witness and prayers really worth it? Should she have even bothered? How do you think Brittany should respond?

Should she . . .
- A. Give up on Nicole; after all, she gave it her best shot?
- B. Realize that her job is to share her faith and trust God to do the rest?
- C. Argue with Nicole about what exactly she means by "Holy Roller"?
- D. Start telling Nicole all the things that are wrong with her new friends?
- E. Get insulted by Nicole's joke and leave?

 Check out Acts 20:24 to know how Brittany should respond in this situation.

28

Justice Is Served?

Dominic is one of the meanest kids Bert has ever met. He's one of the biggest students in school, and he throws his weight around. He takes every opportunity he gets to make life miserable for someone else. Dominic picks on all the little kids walking home from school. He teases the girls so cruelly that they usually end up running to the playground aide in tears. Nobody likes him. His only friends are the ones he can intimidate into hanging out with him. Bert and his friends try to avoid Dominic and not get in his way. That's the only way to stay out of trouble because when Dominic is around, it means trouble.

Today on the playground, there is a loud crash. Someone broke a window. Immediately the playground aide summons Dominic and orders him to the principal's office. Dominic keeps protesting that he didn't do it, but his pleas fall on deaf ears. Actually, in this particular case, Dominic didn't do it. Bert saw him, right before the crash, on the opposite side of the playground from the broken window. There is no way Dominic could have done it. A lot of other kids also know that Dominic is not responsible. *But hey, he's such a bully,* they think, *he deserves whatever punishment he gets.* Bert is no Dominic fan, that's for sure, but he wonders if he should tell what he saw to the playground aide. What do you think Bert should do?

Should he . . .
A.   Keep quiet like the other kids—this creep needs to be taught a lesson?
B.   Tell the playground aide a few days later—after he is sure that Dominic has received his punishment?
C.   Forget about it? Dominic would just beat him up anyway for not telling sooner.
D.   Tell the playground aide that Dominic was not responsible for the broken window?
E.   Write an anonymous letter to the principal telling him the truth about the situation but include a long list of other "crimes" that Dominic has committed?

 To know how Bert should respond, read Leviticus 5:1.

29

A Little Help from My Friends

Blair is planning a big end-of-the-year picnic for the band at her house. She asked a couple of her friends to help her plan the food, decorations, games, and music. Blair's friends were enthusiastic about the party. Together they planned a menu, made lists of stuff to buy for decorations, and wrote down possible games they could play. Blair felt confident that with the help of her friends this would be a terrific party. The week before the party, she asked her friends to help prepare the food and decorations. Each time she brought up a specific request, however, her friends seemed to be busy. Blair passed it off because it was a busy time of year, and she prepared the food and decorations herself.

She definitely needed her friends, however, to help her set up everything on the day of the party. She called everyone the night before, and each one promised to be there a couple of hours early to help. The day of the party, Blair got up early and started getting the backyard ready. It was a beautiful day; that was one thing she didn't need to worry about! Blair worked hard throughout the morning, but still no friends showed up. She couldn't believe they forgot about it. Where were they? After finally enlisting her mom and brother to help her, Blair managed to get everything ready. She was exhausted and angry at her friends. She didn't even want to have the party now. When it was time for the party to begin, sure enough, her two friends were among the first to arrive. What do you think Blair should do?

Should she . . .

A. Tell her friends she's disappointed they weren't able to help her with the party but to enjoy themselves anyway?

B. Spill sodas on her friends and ruin their day too?

C. Tell everyone who will listen how she managed to plan the party all by herself?

D. Tell her friends they aren't welcome at her party?

E. Ignore her friends during the party?

 To see what Blair should do, take a look at Matthew 26:30-46 to see how Jesus responded when he was let down by his friends.

30

"I Spy"

Beau is staying after school today to help his science teacher clean out the cabinets for the summer. His science teacher is a cool guy, and Beau enjoys hanging out with him and talking about stuff. As they are working, another teacher walks into the room and tells his teacher about the eighth grade student caught smoking outside the school. The teacher sees Beau standing there and immediately stops talking and walks out of the classroom. Beau is dying to know who the kid is. With only three days left until graduation, this infraction could mean that kid won't graduate.

An hour later Beau and his teacher finish cleaning the room. His teacher gives Beau a box of supplies that need to be returned to the office. On the way, he sees a boy waiting outside the principal's office. Beau can't quite make out who it is so he pretends to drop something to get a better look. It's Owen Carlson, an eighth grader who is constantly getting into trouble. This must be the one who got caught smoking! If it's true, then Owen won't graduate. That hasn't happened in the school in a long time. Beau has the hottest story in the school. What do you think he should do?

Should Beau . . .

  A. Forget the whole incident?
  B. Get home as soon as he can to start calling his friends with the news?
  C. Wait to tell others until he can confirm whether Owen actually is the one caught smoking?
  D. Run back to tell his teacher he knows who is not going to graduate this year?
  E. Fill the boy's locker with discarded cigarette butts as a prank?

 Check out Joshua 22:10-34 and Acts 11:1-4, 15-18 to see what can happen when people jump to conclusions.

Many Thanks

Jordan can hardly believe that it's already June and time to move up to the next grade in Sunday school. He's looking forward to joining the new class, but he has to admit that Mrs. Nolan has been a good teacher. They really did a lot of neat things this year—they went caroling at Christmas to a nearby nursing home; they put on a skit about Daniel in the lion's den for the younger kids (Jordan got to be the lion); they even put out a Bible times newspaper.

Jordan is especially thankful for Mrs. Nolan's prayer time. Each Sunday, Mrs. Nolan would take prayer requests and then set aside time for the class to pray for one another. It really helped Jordan the time his dad broke his leg, knowing that Mrs. Nolan and his classmates were praying for his dad—and for him. Yeah, he sure will miss Mrs. Nolan. And Sunday is their last class together. What should Jordan do?

Should he . . .

A. Send Mrs. Nolan a card with a note thanking her for her dedication and hard work?

B. Mumble, "Outta here" as he leaves Mrs. Nolan's class for the last time?

C. Thank Mrs. Nolan because his mom told him to?

D. Knit Mrs. Nolan a beautiful sweater out of cat's hair (Yuck!)?

E. Do nothing because, as everyone knows, kids in the youth group are too cool to miss anyone?

 For help in knowing what Jordan should do, read Proverbs 16:24.

1

Family Feud

Lately, Vic has been struggling in math. His mom has been spending a lot of time helping him with his math homework after school and reviewing what was covered in class. Vic's mom and dad made an agreement with him: He could go out with his friends only after he had completed all of his math homework and his mom had reviewed it with him. Yesterday, though, Vic really blew it. He forgot all about the math test and left his book at school. Instead of studying for the test, Vic was over at his friend's house playing touch football.

When he brings home his test today—a D minus—Vic knows that he is in trouble. He waits until after dinner to show his mom and dad the test paper. They are both upset with Vic even though he keeps apologizing and telling them it will never happen again. After a brief discussion, Vic's parents decide that he will lose his after-school privileges until his math grades improve. He also is grounded for the weekend. Vic is fuming about his punishment. He can't believe how unreasonable his parents are being about his schoolwork. It's just a stupid test! Vic is so mad that he doesn't know what he should do.

Should he . . .

A. Make plans to run away? After all, if his parents really loved him, they wouldn't punish him.

B. Stomp around his room, slam the door, and let his parents know how miserable he is?

C. Sulk around the house and refuse to talk to anybody until his parents give in and let him go out this weekend?

D. Calm down, accept his punishment, and realize that his parents are only trying to make him a better person?

E. Picket his home, letting the entire neighborhood know that his parents are unfair to kids?

 Check out Hebrews 12:10-11 to learn God's view of discipline. Then decide how Vic should respond.

The Younger Sister

Donna can't stand her younger sister, Chloe. Where Donna is dark and quiet, Chloe is all blonde curly hair, blue eyes, and dimples. She's the darling of the house, and everyone pays attention to her. If Donna hears one more time about how cute her little sister is, she is going to scream. Not only that, Chloe gets away with everything. No one ever suspects her of doing anything bad. Donna always gets blamed if something goes wrong.

Donna doesn't know how she is going to live through today. It's Chloe's dance recital, and she has a big solo in one of the dance routines. All Donna's relatives are coming to see Chloe dance. Mom is planning a party after the recital. Donna is an absolute klutz when it comes to dancing. Although she has to admit that Chloe is good, Donna wonders why she has to suffer through another "Celebrate Chloe" day. What do you think Donna should do?

Should she . . .
   A.   Go to the recital and encourage Chloe to do her best?
   B.   Go to the recital but take a good book to read?
   C.   Absolutely refuse to go to the recital?
   D.   Go to the recital but make fun of Chloe throughout the performance?
   E.   Tell her mom she can't go to the recital because she has to wash her hair and do her nails?

 See 1 Peter 1:21-22 to see how God intends for us to love our brothers and sisters.

3

School's Out—Almost!

Today is the last day of school, and everyone is antsy for summer vacation to officially begin. In fact, some kids are so anxious to get vacation started that they are planning to ditch school and meet at the city swimming pool for an afternoon of swimming, volleyball, and sunning. There is an awards ceremony and some other stuff going on that Riley doesn't want to attend. Mom, however, has told her to go to school.

When her friend calls to see if Riley is planning to meet her at the pool, she has to break the bad news to her. "Look," her friend says, "your mom will be at your sister's class picnic all day. All you have to do is put your swimsuit on underneath your clothes, walk down to the bus stop, and then ditch out at my house. It's so simple. Your mom will never know." It does sound like a good plan. And Riley can't stand the thought of spending one more minute in that dump of a school unless she absolutely has to. What do you think Riley should do?

Should she . . .
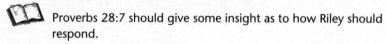
   A. Go to school and the awards ceremony and meet up with her friends later?

   B. Have her friend call in with an excuse for her absence, so it won't look like she's ditching?

   C. Who cares about the last day of school anyway? Everyone knows kids are supposed to ditch.

   D. Tell her mom she's not feeling well and needs to stay home—or at least until her mom leaves for the class picnic?

   E. Tell her mom that only students who will receive awards need to go to the ceremony?

Proverbs 28:7 should give some insight as to how Riley should respond.

Lazy Days of Summer

Tiffany stretches out in bed, lazily watching the breeze rustle the leaves outside her window. A warm breeze stirs the curtain. *Ah*, she thinks, *wonderful freedom from school, homework, teachers, and projects.* It's summer vacation, and Tiffany believes she has earned a long three months of doing nothing. She notes with satisfaction the blank spots on the calendar. "Nothing," she sighs blissfully, "absolutely nothing!" Of course, there will be some power sunning at the pool, and maybe a few cookouts with the gang, but certainly nothing taxing or strenuous.

Later that day Tiffany runs into a friend. Leah looks like she's in a hurry, but Tiffany stops her. "So what's up this summer for you?" she asks. "Taking it easy? I am!"

Leah looks at her and answers, "Didn't you sign up for the day-care center with the youth group? We're all volunteering down at the center a couple of hours each morning to help the children of homeless people. I'm on my way to the meeting now. Why don't you come?"

Tiffany waves her off with a look that says, *Do I look like I'm crazy?* But she begins to wonder about her summer plans. What do you think Tiffany should do?

Should she . . .
A. Apply more suntan lotion—getting a tan is the hardest work she wants to do this summer?
B. Pretend to be a homeless child so she can get free day-care help?
C. Forget it? Hey—she earned this summer vacation!
D. Find out more about the volunteering and donate a portion of her summer to the project?
E. Maybe saunter down to the day-care center when she gets bored at the pool?

 Read Hebrews 13:16 to see how the Lord wants Tiffany to use her free time.

5

Making a Good Impression

This is Janie's first experience at camp. She and her mom have spent weeks gathering all the right supplies and clothes. It took her two days to get everything packed.

At camp, as she waited for her other three tentmates to show up, Janie unpacked her things slowly. By the time she finished, two of the girls had arrived. They seemed pretty nice, and Janie felt encouraged. The last girl, Hope, finally arrived, and she seemed the nicest of all. The two hit it off right away, and Janie offered to help Hope unpack.

While she was helping Hope, Janie couldn't help but notice that she had really nice things. Her sleeping bag was the best, and her gym shoes were the latest style and most expensive ones on the market. All her clothes had her name sewn in, not written in permanent marker like Janie's. Obviously Hope's family is well off. Later that night as the girls crawl into their sleeping bags, they begin talking about their families. It soon becomes clear that Hope and the other two girls come from the same part of town—the wealthier side. They swap stories about the places their families have vacationed—places Janie has only heard about on TV. Finally the conversation shifts around to Janie. The girls want to know about Janie's family. Janie wants to fit in with these girls and make a good impression, but, honestly, her family isn't very impressive. *Average* would be a good word to describe them. What should she say?

Should Janie . . .

A. Make up a story about her family to impress the girls?

B. Shrug and let the girls form their own opinion about her?

C. Tell the truth about her family and not worry about what her friends think of her?

D. Shift the conversation to something else—like the great camp food?

E. Pretend she's asleep?

 Find out what happened in Genesis 12:10-20 when Abraham thought he had to make up a story to be well treated.

Scared Silly

Several months ago, the church choir director asked Alysse if she would sing a solo on one verse of a song in the choir anthem. Alysse has a beautiful voice, but this is the first time she has been asked to sing a solo. She agreed and since then has practiced regularly with the choir. In addition, the choir director has been helping her with intonation and rhythms after practice. Last week the director told Alysse that she was doing a wonderful job. Alysse knows she has worked hard on the part. She feels ready to sing. . . .

That is until several days before the performance. Alysse has come down with a good case of nerves. Every time she thinks about singing in front of the congregation, she gets a knot in her stomach. She's having trouble sleeping. Her concentration in school has been horrible. Today her teacher even called Alysse aside and asked what was bothering her. Alysse mumbled, "Nothing," but she knows better. Every time she thinks about Sunday, she wishes she never had agreed to sing. With only a few days before the performance what should she do?

Should Alysse . . .
A. Call the choir director and say that her family has an emergency and is leaving town Saturday?
B. Have her doctor write her a medical excuse forbidding her to sing?
C. Ask a friend to step in and take her part?
D. Have faith that God is with her and will see her through the performance?
E. Pretend she has selective amnesia and has forgotten all the words to the song?

 To know how Moses encouraged Joshua before he faced an even greater task, read Deuteronomy 31:6.

Special Delivery

It's the first day of summer vacation, but before Dean can even get comfortable in front of the TV, his mom informs him that she has signed him up for a "small job." Dean knows that can only mean one thing—hard work! Actually the job—delivering the new phone books around the neighborhood for ten cents a book—doesn't sound too demanding. His mom has a stack of two hundred phone books to be delivered. If Dean delivers all of them, he will make twenty dollars. That doesn't sound very difficult. *This should be an easy twenty bucks,* he thinks.

Armed with a water bottle and his trusty wagon, Dean loads up and takes off. Two hours and one hundred phone books later, Dean is dejected. Hauling these books up and down the streets in the hot sun is no fun. He finished his water bottle an hour ago, has been chased by five dogs already, got lost looking for a home, and still has one hundred phone books to go. He's hot, tired, and disgusted. His friends just rode by on their way to the pool, and they asked Dean to come along. Dean wants to join them, but what about the phone books? He is supposed to deliver them today or he won't get paid. But he would rather be lying by the pool instead of hauling phone books around in the hot sun. What do you think Dean should do?

Should he . . .
   A. Finish making the deliveries as he promised his mom?
   B. Find the nearest Dumpster and pitch the phone books? His mom never said *where* to deliver the phone books.
   C. Go to the pool and finish delivering the phone books later?
   D. Find another kid to take over the job for him and promise to pay him five cents a phone book?
   E. Leave the phone books on the corner? People can pick up their own phone books.

 Read Ezekiel 45:9-11 to see what the Lord says about honesty in business transactions.

Birthday Shopping

This weekend is Lily's mother's birthday—she's turning forty. Lily and her dad are planning a big surprise party for Mom. Lily has also been doing some extra baby-sitting to save her money to buy her mother a special gift. Mom loves music boxes, and Lily has spotted the perfect one in a small shop in the mall. Dad has agreed to give Lily an advance on her allowance so that she can buy the music box for her mom. Dad is taking her to the mall tonight so she can shop for her mom.

Lily's dad drops her off, and she hurries toward the shop. On her way, she passes her favorite clothing store. There in the window is the perfect jean shirt! Lily has been wanting to buy one. It would be a great addition to her wardrobe. She goes into the store and checks out the selection. There is only one shirt left in her size. Lily does some fast calculating. If she buys the shirt, she won't have enough money for the music box. But if she doesn't buy the shirt now, it might not be there when she has the money. What do you think Lily should do?

Should she . . .
   A.   Beg her dad to buy the shirt for her?
   B.   Buy the music box for her mom as she planned and wait to shop for a jeans shirt later?
   C.   Get one of her older sisters to pay half the cost of the music box so she'll have enough money left over for the shirt?
   D.   Buy the shirt and get her mom a mood ring?
   E.   Buy the shirt and the cool sunglasses with her money, and make her mom a card?

 Check out Philippians 2:4 for some good advice on what Lily should do.

9

Member of the Club

Max's family just moved into a new neighborhood. School ended a few days ago, and a dreary summer looms ahead. He doesn't know anyone, and it will be a long time before school begins. His mom is encouraging him to join the swim team or play baseball with the park district, but Max is not interested. It just wouldn't be the same as his old swim team, so why bother? Max has been spending a lot of time reading or just loafing around the house. In despair, his mom finally orders him to go outside and do something.

Max notices a group of boys at the end of the street. They look about his age, and when he looks over at them, they wave to him and say hello. Max goes over to talk with the boys and finds out that they are in the same grade as he is. They ask him to play some ball with them, and Max really enjoys himself. The next day Max goes out and joins them again to play ball. After the game, the boys lay in the shade. One of the boy asks Max if he wants to join their club. Max eagerly nods his head. "Sure," he says. "That sounds great." Then the boys tell Max that in order to join the club, he has to deflate the tires of a car on the street. They assure Max that everyone in the so-called club had to go through this initiation rite. Max is not so sure. He wants to keep these boys as his friends, but he has never done anything like that. Is now the time to start? What should Max do?

Should he . . .
A. Refuse and walk away?
B. Say, "Is that all?" and ask what else he can do to become president?
C. Agree and let the air out of an old man's tires that night?
D. Bargain with the boys and ask if he can join if he just tee-pees someone's house?
E. Say, "I want to be your friend but not at someone else's expense"?

 To know what Max should do in this situation, read Matthew 5:14-16.

10

Walking the Rails

Jamal and his friends have spent Saturday afternoon playing roller hockey at a newly built outdoor rink. After a couple of hours, the boys decide to quit. They grabbed some sodas and french fries at the burger place before getting ready to go home. All of the boys live a few miles from the roller rink, but none of them have any money left over to call a parent to come pick them up. Several rode bikes, so they take off. Jamal and his friends, however, have to walk.

On their way home, they have to walk over the railroad tracks that go right through the town. A train passes underneath them, and the boys stop to watch. Afterward, one of Jamal's friends suggests that they walk home on the railroad tracks. Since the train just went by, another won't be through for another couple of hours. Plus, the tracks are a good shortcut. Jamal is tired, and the thought of walking all that way isn't very appealing. But walking on the railroad tracks is dangerous and something his parents probably wouldn't approve of. What do you think Jamal should do?

Should he . . .
- A. Tell his friends it's too dangerous to walk on the tracks and continue his way home on the safer route?
- B. Suggest hitchhiking home instead?
- C. Call the railroad to see when the next train will come through?
- D. Go down to the tracks and put his ear to the rails to see if he can hear a train coming?
- E. Figure his friends must be right and go along with them?

 For help in knowing what Jamal should do, read Proverbs 22:17-18.

11

Whose Money?

Gerald's parents give him a weekly allowance. In addition, he makes extra money mowing lawns, shoveling snow, and doing odd jobs for the elderly couple across the street. Gerald and his parents have agreed that, whatever he makes, he will set a certain amount aside for savings and can keep a certain amount as spending money. They also agreed that he will set aside a tenth of his earnings as a tithe to the church. Gerald doesn't mind this at all. In fact, it makes him feel good to know he is giving something back to the Lord.

Gerald just received a check from his grandparents for $75 for his birthday coming up next week. They wrote in the card that he should use the money to buy himself whatever he wants. Gerald has been eyeing some new Rollerblades. The check would pay for the pair he has wanted. After dinner, his dad asks him about giving some of his birthday money in the offering on Sunday. Gerald is confused. This isn't the same as the money he has earned, is it? After all, 10 percent would be $7.50, and that's a lot of money to give. Gerald considers the check *his* money. What do you think Gerald should do?

Should he . . .

  A. Run out before Sunday and buy the Rollerblades before he has to give any of it to the church?

  B. Give a portion of his birthday money to the church, but less than $7.50?

  C. Realize that a tenth of all his money—wherever it comes from—belongs to the Lord?

  D. Pretend to put the $7.50 (really just green paper and fifty cents) in an envelope and then put the envelope in the offering plate on Sunday?

  E. Argue with his parents that the birthday money is a gift to him, not to the Lord?

 For insight on how Gerald should handle this situation, read Nehemiah 10:35-39, a story of how the Israelites answered a similar question.

12

Storm Clouds

Gary's baseball team just won the game. As Gary gathers his belongings, he looks at the sky and thinks it's a good thing they finished the game. Already huge storm clouds are building up in the west, and a breeze has picked up. Gary rides his bike home from the game, watching as the clouds continue to mushroom in the sky. *Boy,* he thinks, *we could be in for a big storm tonight.*

While Mom cooks dinner, Gary sits down with the rest of the family to watch TV. The western sky is getting darker by the minute. Gary's younger brother and sister are starting to ask questions. "Is it going to rain, Mommy?" "I don't like this." While his mom tries to calm them down, a "severe thunderstorm warning" is issued on the television. Gary's little sister starts to cry, and his brother is hanging on his mother. What should Gary do?

Should he . . .

A. Tell scary stories to really frighten his brother and sister?

B. Run around the house, yelling, "We're gonna die"?

C. Help his parents by calming the younger children and going to a safe place in the house?

D. Start building an ark?

E. Get a kite to try out an experiment on electricity?

For help in knowing what Gary should do, read Joshua 1:9.

Doggone It!

Don is in charge of his two younger brothers and the family dog, Pierre, while his mom is out running errands for the afternoon. All three boys and Pierre are playing ball in the backyard when a friend comes to the gate. Don's younger brother Bob opens the gate, and Pierre makes a run for it.

Don and his brothers take off in search of Pierre, but the dog is fast. By the time they catch up to him, Pierre is happily digging up the begonias in Mrs. Henderson's garden. Don quickly looks around and realizes that Mrs. Henderson isn't home. What should he do?

Should Don . . .

A. Try to fix the garden so it looks all right before Mrs. Henderson gets home?

B. Go back later when Mrs. Henderson returns, tell her what happened, and offer to fix the garden and pay for any repairs?

C. Quickly get Pierre home and pretend that nothing happened?

D. Put a disguise on Pierre so that no one will recognize him?

E. Start a rumor that there are large squirrels running amok in the neighborhood, tearing up people's gardens?

 For help in knowing what Don should do, read Proverbs 19:9.

Summertime Blues

Gary's parents have said that he can buy a new twenty-speed bike if he can earn half the amount, about two hundred dollars. Gary already has about one hundred dollars saved from birthday and Christmas checks from his grandparents and a few extra jobs here and there, but he really could use some steady pay. Now that it's summer, Gary has more time to devote to finding work. He has passed out leaflets throughout the neighborhood, advertising his availability to cut lawns, wash cars, walk pets, etc.

A week goes by without any calls. Today, however, an older neighbor down the street calls and asks if Gary would be willing to cut her grass once a week during the summer. Gary excitedly says yes and promises to come down the next day to work out a schedule and to discuss pay. The following day, Gary goes over all the equipment with his neighbor and agrees to a schedule. Everything is settled except the pay. His neighbor tells Gary how much she pays. Gary can hardly believe his ears. It will hardly make a dent in saving up for his bike. How's he going to save enough money for a bike with those earnings? What should Gary do?

Should he . . .
   A. Figure he'll give his neighbor "her money's worth" and not do a good job?
   B. Faithfully cut the neighbor's lawn but tell everyone how cheap she is?
   C. Do his very best because that's what he promised to do, regardless of the pay?
   D. Tell her it's not enough and ask for a higher amount?
   E. Look for a better-paying job and quit as soon as he can find one?

 For help in knowing how Gary should react, read Philippians 4:5.

"Oh, Brother!"

Chet is going on his first weekend retreat with his church's youth group. It's going to be a great weekend with canoeing, hiking, and swimming. The youth group leaders have planned some great activities, too. Chet can hardly wait. The only drawback is that his older brother and some of his friends have been asked to come along and help supervise. Chet doesn't mind too much. He and his brother usually get along pretty well, but he doesn't want it to look like his brother is baby-sitting him.

When the group arrives at the retreat center, the leader assigns the group to a teen helper. As it turns out, Chet and a few of his buddies are assigned to Chet's older brother. His brother tells the boys to get their gear and follow him, but the other boys want to see the lake first. They look at Chet and say, "Come on. It's only your brother telling us what to do. We don't have to listen to him. Let's go down to the lake." Chet is really confused. He doesn't want to make trouble for his brother, but he sure doesn't want to look like a wimp in front of his friends. What do you think Chet should do?

Should he . . .

A. Ask to be assigned to another group—immediately!?
B. Tell his brother that the boys want to find the bathroom and then go down to the lake?
C. Tell his buddies that since his brother is their supervisor, they'd better do what he requested first—then they can ask to go down to the lake?
D. Show off in front of his friends and tell his brother, "You can't boss me around"?
E. Take off with his friends and deal with his brother later?

For help in knowing what Chet should do, read 1 Peter 5:5.

The New Baby

Dominique can't believe her mother is serious. She's having a baby—at her age! Her mom looks so happy about the whole thing. Dominique doesn't understand it. How can her mom be happy when babies are nothing but trouble? One of her friends' mothers recently had a baby, and from what Dominique can tell all they do is cry. Doesn't she have enough trouble dealing with her younger brother and sister? And now her mother wants to add another one to the family? She must be crazy.

And who do you suppose will have to watch the baby, feed the baby, and, oh no, change the baby? Dominique is so angry at her mom, she feels like she is going to burst. What will all her friends say? It is too embarrassing to have her mom walk around pregnant. Dominique doesn't know how she is going to survive the next nine months—or however long her mom said it would be. Dominique spends the rest of the evening in her room. At bedtime, Mom comes in and asks if there is something Dominique wants to talk about. What do you think Dominique should do?

Should she . . .

A. Give her mom a long list of things she wants done before the baby comes, such as repainting her room, because they won't get done afterward?

B. Tell her mom that under no circumstances will she change the baby's diaper?

C. Tell her mom that she thinks having a baby at her age is a stupid idea?

D. Say, "Nothing's wrong" and continue to stew about it for nine months?

E. Talk with her mom honestly about her feelings and ask for help to work through them?

 Read Psalm 42, written by someone who was feeling depressed, to see where Dominique can find comfort as she struggles with her feelings.

17

The Long, Hot Summer

Rodney and his friends are bummed. They recently heard the bad news that the neighborhood pool would be closed this summer because cracks had been discovered in the foundation. The families of several of Rodney's friends have joined the newly opened country club, but Rodney knows that is not an option for his family. He and most of his friends are facing a long, hot summer. Every day he rides by the pool to check the progress on the repairs. He's hoping that somehow the pool will be fixed before the summer is over.

Today as Rodney is walking his dog and thinking about how he's going to stay cool, he sees two of his friends riding by on their bikes with their swimsuits on. "Where ya going? Did you guys join the country club or something," he asks. No, they tell Rodney. They are heading over to a classmate's house for the afternoon. Now, this classmate is a guy whom nobody can stand. He's a real brain-nerd, one of the smartest students in the entire school, but clueless when it comes to anything fun. In fact, Rodney and his friends usually make fun of him. When Rodney asks his friends about it, one of them says, "Look, the guy has a pool. Now if you'll just wise up and pretend you're his friend, you'll be swimming all summer—for free!" What do you think Rodney should do?

Should he . . .
   A. Go along with his friends' plan. It's better than sweating all summer?
   B. Tell his friends he doesn't think it's right to use this guy for his pool?
   C. Pray that his neighborhood pool will get repaired soon?
   D. Invite the guy over a couple of times to his house and hope he invites him over to swim?
   E. Get out his little sister's wading pool?

 Check out Psalm 28:3 for help in knowing what Rodney should do.

18

The Perfect Example

Logan's mom signed him up as a vacation Bible school helper. Logan was not exactly thrilled about the prospect of playing games with thirty little kids. His enthusiasm was dimmed further when he attended the training session. That's when he learned that he has to be at the church thirty minutes ahead of time to help set up. Then he has to stay afterward to help put everything away. This will mean getting up early when he could sleep in. Not only that, but the VBS leaders lectured the volunteers about the importance of setting good examples for the children. Logan rolled his eyes. *Sure, a bunch of five-year-olds are really going to look up to me,* he thought. *Fat chance!*

The week is about half over, and Logan has to admit it hasn't been all that bad. He really enjoys playing games with the kids. He even has a small following of little boys who gather around him when they see him coming. Logan's favorite is a shy, little boy who won't talk to anyone but him. Logan feels pretty good about helping the boy become part of the group. Today, as a reward for participating, each child receives an ice-cream treat. Logan only grabbed a piece of fruit for breakfast. He's really hungry and sure would like an extra ice-cream treat or two. All the children are told they may have only one. But surely that doesn't apply to Logan? No one's going to notice if he takes another one, will they? What do you think Logan should do?

Should he . . .
   A. Remember that he is the role model for these kids and not take another treat?
   B. Take two, but tell the kids he's going to give one to a friend?
   C. See if one of the kids doesn't like his ice cream and offer to take care of it for him?
   D. Tell the kids, "Look, there's Superman!" and scarf down an extra ice-cream treat while they're not looking?
   E. Look really pathetic so that one of the kids will give up his treat to him?

 To know how Logan should respond, read Titus 2:7.

19

The Sunday School Lesson

Dexter is one of twelve students chosen from the junior high youth group to serve as a youth ministry trainee. He has undergone six weeks of intensive training to prepare him for being an assistant Sunday school teacher. Dexter is assigned to help in the second grade classroom. There are twenty-four children each Sunday, and Mr. Watson is an excellent teacher. Dexter has learned a lot about teaching, being creative with lessons, and having fun in class. Usually, he will pass out supplies, help students find passages in the Bible, and generally do whatever tasks Mr. Watson gives him.

After two months, Mr. Watson asks Dexter if he would like to plan a small part of the lesson for next Sunday. It's a big responsibility, but Dexter is pleased that Mr. Watson thinks he can do it. Mr. Watson hands him some materials and gives him some ideas on planning the lesson. Dexter also has to prepare the craft, which will take some time. He is really excited. When he gets home, he decides he will start planning the lesson while it is fresh in his mind. He knows he has a busy week ahead with activities and homework, and he might run out of time.

Before Dexter gets started, his best friend calls up and asks him to go to a movie. It's one that Dexter has been anxious to see, and after all, he still will have a week to get his lesson planned. Why not go now? What do you think Dexter should do?

Should he . . .

A. Briefly leaf through the materials before he goes to the movie and save the planning and preparation for later?

B. Go to the movie now and hope he can squeeze in the planning between homework and activities during the week?

C. Decide that he really wants to do a good job for Mr. Watson and spend the time to outline his lesson today so he can work on it throughout the week?

D. Go to the movie and forget all about the lesson until Saturday night because more important things keep cropping up?

E. Go to the movie and then get his mom to help him later when he begins to panic?

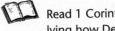 Read 1 Corinthians 14:33, 40 to see the biblical principle underlying how Dexter should respond.

20

Teamwork

Jackson wanted to earn some extra money for the summer. After reviewing his options, he decided to hand out flyers around the neighborhood advertising a pet care service for people going on vacation. It's a perfect job for Jackson because he likes all different kinds of animals. It's something he could do in his spare time, too, and wouldn't involve a whole lot of work. Plus, he could do it by himself. Or so he thought.

The first week, Jackson received two phone calls. One person needed him to take care of her two guinea pigs for five days; another wanted his dog walked and fed for a week. No problem. Things were going well. The next week, however, Jackson received eight calls for a variety of pet needs. He spent the next week running himself ragged as he tried to take care of everything. Still more calls pour in. Jackson doesn't want to answer the phone anymore! His best friend offers to help him, but Jackson is not sure. If he brings his friend in, he'll have to share the money. That will mean less for Jackson, and this is his business, after all. What do you think Jackson should do?

Should Jackson . . .

A. Turn down the business he can't handle (and lose money that way!)?

B. Keep accepting the new business and spend all day (and night) taking care of pets?

C. Call people back and tell them he's not in the business anymore?

D. Let his friend help but give him only 10 percent of their earnings?

E. Take his friend in as a partner because together they can handle more business more efficiently, and with less wear and tear on both of them?

 To check out the biblical principle underlying Jackson's actions, read Ecclesiastes 4:9-10.

21

Rainy Day Blues

Ted looks out the window, disgusted. It's raining, and on a Saturday! There go his plans for fishing down at the creek with Joe. How can things get much worse? After making a couple of phone calls, Ted decides it can get worse. There is absolutely no one who can do anything.

A long, boring rainy day looms ahead of Ted. What should he do?

Should he . . .

   A. Offer to help his parents with jobs around the house?

   B. Lie on the couch and watch TV?

   C. Practice the piano and work on his stamp collection?

   D. Walk around the house whining, "There's nothing to do"?

   E. Go back to bed and hope that when he gets up again it will be sunny?

For help in knowing what Ted should do, read Proverbs 12:11.

22

Real Worries

Erica turns off the television with a great sigh. The news is just not good. Planes explode in the air. Young children shoot each other with guns. Floods and other natural disasters destroy people's homes and communities. People continue to kill each other in the name of religion. What is going on anymore?

Erica gets depressed thinking about it. The world is really a scary place. What's worse is that no one seems to be doing anything to make things better. She wonders what kind of a future today's young people have. What should Erica do to cope with the prospect of growing up in a world that is seemingly out of control?

Should she . . .

    A. Worry about all the terrible things that could happen to her?

    B. Decide to never go outside her home again so she'll always be safe?

    C. Realize that God is in control and decide to trust him for the future?

    D. Start carrying a rabbit's foot for good luck?

    E. Start wearing rose-colored glasses so at least the world will look better?

 For help in knowing what Erica should do, read Matthew 6:34.

The Rock Concert

Brooke is confused. Her best friend from youth group recently won some tickets to a rock concert from the local radio station. Her friend's mom and dad agreed to take her, and she wants Brooke to come. All their friends are so envious that they have tickets to the concert. It's one of the hottest groups in the country right now. But Brooke isn't so sure that as Christians they should go.

Most of the group's songs promote drugs and use all sorts of gross language and images. Then there's the group itself. At one concert, the lead singer pulled the ears off a rabbit. And the group prides itself on being "party animals," with the emphasis on "animals." The group is known for its anti-Christian lyrics as well, making fun of anyone who believes in God. Brooke asks her friends about these things. Her friend seems unconcerned. "Hey, he only pulled the ears off a rabbit once—and he apologized later anyway. I mean what's the big deal? I just like their music. It's only a concert, after all." What do you think Brooke should do?

Should she . . .
    A. Go to the concert and walk out if anything gross happens?
    B. Go to the concert but put cotton balls in her ears?
    C. Tell her friend she is not going to go to a concert that mocks Christian values and beliefs?
    D. Tell her friend that only a really bad person would consider going to such a concert?
    E. Burn all her CDs and tapes to protest rock music?

 Read 2 Timothy 3:1-5 to find out how Christians should regard popular music—whether it's rock, metal, rap, country, etc.—that opposes biblical values.

24

The Voice of Experience

For the youth group meeting, Mr. Willard had invited a young man from a nearby Christian college to speak—to warn everyone not to make the same mistakes that he had made as a teenager. Corey listened intently as the speaker described how empty he felt as a teen. "I came from a broken home. I hated myself and everyone else," the young man related. He told the group that he had filled his emptiness with partying, alcohol, and drugs. All the time, he told them, he was trying to convince himself that he was having a good time. But all the partying did nothing to get rid of the hurt and the inner loneliness. "The only way to find true peace and acceptance is coming to know Jesus Christ," he said.

After the meeting, Corey and his friends discuss the speaker's message. Most are really impressed by his sincerity and his desire to save them the heartache of making serious mistakes like getting involved with drugs and alcohol. Corey keeps silent. He is not so sure. After all, this guy had his fun. Why shouldn't he? There is plenty of time for Jesus—later. Or is there? How do you think Corey should respond to the message?

Should he . . .
- A. Listen to the voice of experience and dedicate his life to Jesus and avoid making those same mistakes?
- B. Find out for himself? Just because this guy made a few bad mistakes when he was growing up doesn't mean that Corey can't handle the party life.
- C. Decide to go out and have his own fun? Jesus can wait.
- D. Decide that this guy is a party pooper? There's nothing wrong with having fun, is there?
- E. Make no decisions now—see what life brings and roll with the punches?

 To help understand what Corey should do, read Ecclesiastes 2 to see how Solomon described his frantic search for satisfaction, and read Ecclesiastes 12:13-14 to see how Solomon concluded his search.

25

Hard Times

The Nelson family at church has been through some incredibly difficult times. Mrs. Nelson is still recovering from a serious car accident. The older daughter recently was diagnosed with lupus. A year ago, Mr. Nelson lost his job, and he still has not found full-time employment. The younger son, who is in Stuart's grade, recently was suspended from school for pulling the fire alarm. He is continually in trouble at school. Stuart honestly doesn't know how the mother and father cope with him.

Yet, what Stuart doesn't understand is that despite all these difficulties, the family is in church every Sunday. The mom and dad, particularly, really seem to be worshiping and praising God. Stuart doesn't understand why. He's not so sure that he could praise God if his dad lost his job or if his mom was in a serious car accident. Why does God allow such awful things to happen in one family? Where is he anyway? How do you think Stuart needs to respond to his doubts about God?

Should he . . .
- A. Quit going to church because it is obvious that God doesn't care about people?
- B. Decide that God cares but is unable to do anything about his problems?
- C. Talk to his pastor and his parents about his doubts and questions as he looks for answers?
- D. Remember that God is in control—in good times and in bad?
- E. Decide that the Nelsons probably did something to deserve all these bad things happening to them?

 For words that give hope to all who hurt or experience difficult situations, read Habakkuk 3:17-19 to decide how Stuart should deal with his doubts.

Summer Help

Hannah is volunteering this summer at her town's safety program for preschoolers. Each summer, children going into kindergarten are taught safety rules about riding their bikes, crossing the street, and watching out for strangers. Older students, like Hannah, volunteer to help lead the groups. She got up early one morning to sign up for the program and then spent a half day in orientation. Today is the beginning of her session, and Hannah is ready to go.

When she arrives at the school where the program is being offered, there is a crush of children and parents. Hannah sees several other student volunteers and goes over to find out what she needs to do. There is a sign-in table with a list of all the assigned leaders and their groups. Hannah quickly scans the list and can't find her name. She spies one of the adult supervisors and tells her the situation. The supervisor informs Hannah that she is assigned as a floater for the session and doesn't have a group. She will be asked to fill in wherever needed. Hannah is very disappointed. This is not what she wanted to do when she signed up. She wanted to lead a group. What do you think she should do now?

Should Hannah . . .

    A. Quit because she's not a group leader?

    B. Try and swap places with another student?

    C. Throw a fit right in front of the supervisor and keep it up until the supervisor gives her a group?

    D. Do the very best job she can with whatever they ask her to do?

    E. Keep her assignment but complain about it the entire time?

 Check out Galatians 6:9 to know how Hannah should respond.

Going Shopping

All of Harriet's friends are talking about the new shop in town. It's really cool, with lots of candles, minerals, crystals, incense, and jewelry. Her friends encouraged her to come down and check it out with them. "The lady who runs the store is great," said Denise. "You're going to like her. She treats us just like adults." Sure enough, there were a lot of interesting things in the store. And the woman who runs the shop was very nice. She knew most of Harriet's friends by name, and she asked about their schoolwork and whatever else was going on. She seemed genuinely pleased to see Harriet come in.

Harriet has been back several times to browse, but there's something about the shop that bothers her. The woman is still pleased to see them, but lately she has been asking about more spiritual matters. When the girls say they are Christians, the woman tells them that they really don't need Jesus because God is everywhere and in everybody. "Salvation," she says, "is a matter of coming back to life [reincarnation] until you get it right." Harriet has some real problems with what the store owner is saying. Unfortunately, many of her friends are starting to believe this woman. What should Harriet do?

Should she . . .
  A. Follow her friends, even though she feels uncomfortable?
  B. Start screaming at her friends not to go back to the shop because the woman is evil?
  C. Run and tell her pastor that her friends are visiting this shop?
  D. Believe what the woman has told her because she is so nice to them and wouldn't lie?
  E. Explain to her friends that Jesus is God, the only one who can offer true salvation. Then decide not to return to the shop and try to encourage her friends to stay away too?

 For help in knowing how Harriet should react, read 3 John 1:11.

28

The Memory Game

Casey's Sunday school teacher is having a contest. For every Scripture verse a student memorizes, that student receives a huge candy bar. Then there's a big prize at the end of the Sunday school term for the student who has memorized the most verses. All of Casey's friends are very involved in the contest. One of them has earned five candy bars so far. Casey can't get into the contest, however. Memorizing Scripture is not his thing.

When Casey's Sunday school teacher asked him why he wasn't participating, Casey mumbled something about not having enough time. His teacher explained how valuable it is to memorize Scripture. "It can be a real source of encouragement in difficult times," he said. "It can help prevent you from doing the wrong thing when faced with temptation." But Casey thinks that memorizing Bible verses is just hard work and a waste of time. His teacher encourages him to memorize at least one verse. What do you think Casey should do?

Should he . . .

    A. Memorize the verse simply to get the candy bar?

    B. Think about what his Sunday school teacher told him and look for Scripture to memorize that will help him know how to live to please God?

    C. Tell his Sunday school teacher that he is too busy with other things to take the time to memorize some stupid verses?

    D. Make a halfhearted attempt to learn a verse but quit after five minutes the first day?

    E. Not even bother? He can hardly remember what he did in school last week—and that's the stuff that he gets graded on.

 For the biblical principle that should guide how Casey responds, read Psalm 119:9-11.

29

The Piano Player

Vince is a talented piano player. He started taking lessons when he was four and is quite good now, at age twelve. He has won several statewide piano competitions and is hoping to audition for a highly regarded summer music camp. Vince enjoys music, but what drives him is the challenge of tackling a new piece. He will spend hours working on a particular segment, perfecting his technique, until he has mastered it. He spends several hours each day practicing and takes lessons from an accomplished pianist in the city. Vince is truly on his way to becoming a fine pianist in his own right.

At church this week, Vince's mother noticed that the young children's choir needed a piano accompanist to help them with rehearsals and in performances. Vince has never played in church before because he has always been too busy, but his mom thinks this may be the perfect opportunity for him to use his gift for music as a ministry. She approaches Vince about it after supper. It would only involve one afternoon a week and several Sundays during the year when the children sing. Vince is not so sure. He has never played to accompany anybody, let alone a group of wiggly four-year-olds who can't sing anyway. It sure doesn't sound like much fun. What do you think Vince should do?

Should he . . .
- A. Whine, cry, and stamp his feet to emphasize how he really feels?
- B. Agree to help, but only when it fits into his practice schedule?
- C. Tell his mom there's no challenge in playing simple songs like "Jesus Loves Me" for a bunch of little kids?
- D. Tell her he would be glad to be able to use his gifts in serving others?
- E. Pretend to hurt his hand so he won't be able to play?

 Read 1 Peter 4:10 to see how Vince should "manage" his special gift for music.

30

The Graffiti Gang

Colin is riding his bike home from piano lessons. As he rounds the corner by the school, he sees a group of kids standing around the back of the school. He notices one of the kids has something in his hands that looks like a can of spray paint. As Colin gets closer to the school, he sees some graffiti spray painted onto the school wall. The kids move away as Colin passes by, but Colin sees the one boy quickly hide something behind his back. What should Colin do?

Should he . . .
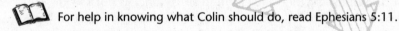
    A.   Get his own spray paint and join the group?
    B.   Tell his parents, who call the police?
    C.   Ride away and do nothing?
    D.   Ride up to the kids and point out a misspelled word?
    E.   Yell "Police!" so the kids will scatter?

For help in knowing what Colin should do, read Ephesians 5:11.

Split Decision

Every year, Ozzie's youth group decides upon a service project for the community. Last year, Ozzie came up with a great idea for the project. His idea was adopted, and Ozzie organized the project. He enjoyed it and felt really good when his pastor acknowledged his work in front of the congregation. Ozzie has been thinking about the service project for this year, and he thinks he has another great idea. He's confident the other kids will go along with his idea because he is one of the leaders in the group.

Sunday night is the vote. Ozzie has been talking up his idea among his friends, and they all agree it's a winner. He figures that even if all the girls vote against it, his idea will still win. When the youth leader asks for suggestions, Ozzie is the first one up. He explains his idea in great detail, handing out lists of contacts, a schedule of when things need to be done, etc. It is obvious to everyone that he has spent a lot of time thinking this through. A new boy, who recently joined the group, gets up next and offers his suggestion. It's simple but will truly reach a large segment of the community. He sits down, and the idea catches fire as the group discusses it. It's really a great idea. Ozzie senses that he is losing support for his plan, and he's not happy about it. Who does this guy think he is anyway? Ozzie's not going to let this happen without a fight! But what do you think he should do?

Should Ozzie . . .

A. Argue with the group about the merits of the new boy's plan. After all, this guy has never organized a service project, has he?

B. Offer to help the new boy plan the project if it is adopted by the group?

C. Threaten to quit if the group doesn't go along with his idea?

D. Put down the new kid because he can't possibly organize the project as well as he can?

E. Refer to an obscure point in Robert's Rules of Order and get the proposal dismissed on a technicality?

 To know how God regards quarrels among his people (and for help in knowing how Ozzie should respond), read 1 Corinthians 3:3.

2

Playing by the Rules

Meredith has attended a Bible study at her school for the past two years. There is a core of about twenty students and five teachers who meet once a week before school begins to sing praise songs and do a lesson. Meredith enjoys it, not only because she has made some good Christian friends, but also because she has gotten to know the teachers. This year, as one of the older students, Meredith is one of the group's leaders. She helps decide what study they will do, and she organizes the meeting time.

Meredith received a letter during the summer from the new principal at school. He is making some changes in the fall schedule, so every activity that meets before school must have a building request form filled out and be approved by the administration. Meredith doesn't know if the principal is a Christian, but she fears that if he isn't, he might not let the group meet. She calls a few of her friends from the study group to express her fears. They are angry about the new rules. "This is such a stupid rule! I can't believe he's doing this to us," says one. "We've been at the school all this time, and we've never caused any problems." The group discusses it some more, and one of her friends suggests that they ignore the letter and meet as usual. The group agrees. Now it's up to Meredith to express her opinion. She doesn't like the new changes, but is it really right to ignore the principal? What do you think Meredith should do?

Should she . . .
A. Agree with her friends and ignore the principal's letter?
B. Write a nasty letter back to the principal complaining that his rules are unfair and discriminatory?
C. Tell her group that they should fill out the building request form and see what happens?
D. Picket outside of the school with signs proclaiming that the principal is "Unfair to Christians"?
E. Have their parents complain to the school board about the new principal and threaten to sue if he changes the policy?

 For a real eye-opener about how God says we should respond to authorities, even those at school, read Romans 13:1-5.

3

Slumber Party Fiasco

This is Tricia's first big slumber party. She has had as many as three friends spend the night at her house, but she has never been to a party with a dozen girls all getting together. She's really looking forward to the party. All through the early part of the evening, a couple of the girls teasingly warned the other girls not to be the first one to fall asleep. Although Tricia asked why, no one would tell her. They only laughed and said, "You'll see!"

Try as she might to stay awake, Tricia was really tired, so she made the terrible mistake of being the first one to fall asleep. A few hours later she was awakened by a funny smell and a damp feeling on her head. Staggering into the bathroom, she discovered that her so-called friends had given her the "royal shampoo"—Vaseline, shaving cream, eggs, honey, and flour. She is beside herself. How will she ever get all of this junk out of her hair? As she fusses about the state of her head, she hears giggles and whispers coming from the direction of the living room. "Yeah," she mutters to herself, close to tears. "Laugh now. I'll get you all!"

Tricia is angry beyond words. She can't believe that the girls she considers her friends did this to her. It would serve them right if she were to stomp out of there, grab her sleeping bag, and go home. Of course, it's two o'clock in the morning, and her parents probably won't appreciate being awakened by the phone. What is she going to do?

Should Tricia . . .

A. Go into the living room and tell her friends off?

B. Get back at the girls, putting shaving cream and all sorts of glop in their sleeping bags after they fall asleep?

C. Start crying?

D. After her anger subsides, pray and ask the Lord to give her the strength to love her friends despite what they have done?

E. Vow never to go to another slumber party again?

 Check out 1 John 4:7-11 to see the biblical principle underlying Tricia's response.

Boooring!

Lloyd turns over in bed and puts the pillow over his head—he knows what's coming. Sure enough, thirty seconds later, Lloyd hears his mom calling his name and telling him to get up and get ready for church. Lloyd punches the pillow disgustedly. Why does he have to go to church anyway? It's so boooring. All they do is sing, pray, and talk, talk, talk. And boy, can his pastor go on. The worst part, though, is the singing. Lloyd can't carry a tune to save his life, so he just stands there when the congregation sings song after song. Why do they have to sing all those verses anyway? Wouldn't one do?

It's not as if Lloyd doesn't believe in God and Jesus. He does, but he wonders why he can't just read his Bible and worship in his own way at home. Who needs to hear what the pastor has to say about a certain portion of Scripture? Lloyd figures he can read it for himself. The more Lloyd thinks about it, the more he likes the idea. Plus, he believes he can worship more efficiently at home—probably in about half the time as it takes in church. And he won't have to dress up in Sunday clothes, either. That would save his mom a lot of laundry time. It's a perfect plan—if only his parents will agree. What do you think Lloyd should do with his plan?

Should he . . .
A. Promise his parents he'll do all the outside chores the rest of his life if they agree to let him stay home?

B. Come down with a convenient illness every Sunday and hope his parents won't realize that he's faking it?

C. Present to his parents all the positive points about worshiping at home and hope his logic convinces them that he is right?

D. Study Scripture to see what God has to say about worshiping with other believers?

E. Go to church, as usual, but refuse to participate?

 To help Lloyd make his decision, read Hebrews 10:25 to see what God's Word says about worshiping together.

The Grunge Express

Stan has a natural gift for music. He has taken piano lessons since age six and recently began studying the cello. His parents both have a classical music background, and Stan has grown up listening to the master composers: Bach, Handel, Beethoven, Mozart, Chopin. He knows more about classical music than most adults and certainly more than his classmates. But when Stan's friends start talking about the music they listen to, Stan doesn't have a clue.

Today Stan's friends are discussing the hottest new group, The Grunge Express. The Express is going to be in concert at a university near their town. The father of one of his friends can get tickets to the concert, and his friend is taking orders. "OK, how many want tickets? Stan, how about you?" the friend asks. Stan doesn't know what to say. He doesn't want to admit that he has never heard of the Express. But considering what he has overheard about the group's antics onstage, and their lyrics, he's not sure that he wants to know anything more about them. What do you think Stan should say?

Should he . . .
   A. Say, "I don't listen to trash music like that" and win lots of friends?
   B. Tell his friend that he wants a ticket but then sell it to someone else at the last minute?
   C. Tell his friend that his great aunt from New Zealand is flying in to see him that night, and he couldn't possibly miss her visit?
   D. Politely decline, saying that he usually listens to other types of music?
   E. Pretend that he knows all about the group and brag that he has front-row seats?

 For help in knowing how Stan should respond, read 2 Timothy 2:22.

The Natural

Judson is a natural athlete. Whatever the sport, Judson can play it well and without a lot of practicing. Take lacrosse, for instance. It was offered last fall for the first time. About thirty boys came to see what the game was all about. It took most of them the entire first week to get the hang of throwing and catching the ball with the lacrosse stick. Not Judson. He picked it up the first day. But Judson's best sport is baseball—he's really good, with a strong arm and compact swing. He can play all the positions well.

Unfortunately, Judson knows he is good, and he expects the other guys to play as well as he does. If one of them messes up, they'll usually hear about it from Judson before they hear from the coach. But not everyone is overly impressed with Judson's natural abilities. One of the new assistant coaches, in particular, wants to work with Judson on his batting technique. When he asks Judson to stay after practice one day, Judson looks at the coach as though he were crazy. "You can't be serious," he says. What do you think Judson should do?

Should he . . .

A. Inform this coach that, as the team's star player, he can't be bothered with extra practice sessions?

B. Swallow his pride, stay after practice, and see what he can learn from this new assistant?

C. Tell the coach that he will catch him later that week?

D. Complain to the head coach that this guy is really bugging him?

E. Stay after practice, but let the assistant coach know, in no uncertain terms, that he really doesn't need any batting tips?

 For help in knowing how Judson should respond, read Luke 18:9-14 where Jesus talks about people who think highly of themselves.

Pass It On

Several months ago, Gloria broke her leg in a bad bicycle accident. Riding home from her soccer game, she was hit by a car. It was a horrifying experience. It was a bad break, also, taking the doctors several hours to set the bone right. Gloria had to stay in the hospital for a week; then it took more than six months for the bones to heal completely. She is slowly regaining the strength in her leg. The doctors are hopeful she will be up and playing soccer next spring.

Gloria was in a lot of pain for quite a while. During that time she wondered why God had allowed this to happen to her. At times, Gloria didn't think she would make it through the day. But she did—with a lot of prayers and support from her youth group. Gloria knew her friends were praying for her. They came to visit and shared encouraging words from the Bible with her. Gloria was grateful for all the comfort and support she received during that difficult time.

Now that she is recovering, Gloria tries not to think about the accident, but she still has nightmares about being hit by the car. Some days it is easier to forget than others, but today is not one of them. She just learned that one of her good friends was in a car accident and has some broken bones. Gloria knows exactly what this girl is going through. She ought to call or visit her friend, but thinking about her brings back too many painful memories for Gloria. What do you think she should do?

Should Gloria . . .
A. Send some flowers and a cheery "Get Well" card?
B. Pray for her friend—when she thinks about it?
C. Encourage, and pray for, her friend consistently, sharing what she learned from her trials, and the comfort she found in God's Word?
D. Forget about it—after all, Gloria has enough troubles of her own?
E. Visit the friend and describe all the gory details of her own accident?

 To know how Gloria should respond in this situation, read 2 Corinthians 1:3-7.

8

The Wicked Stepmother

Angelica's father recently remarried. Her new stepmother moved in this spring with her two children, both younger than Angelica. Ever since then, Angelica's life has been miserable. She can't stand her two new stepsisters. They are spoiled rotten and never do anything around the house. Angelica has to do all the work, and even then, her stepmother still yells at her. It doesn't matter what is going on—it's always Angelica's fault. Her stepmother is constantly picking on her.

Take today, for example. Angelica has finished her chores and is planning to meet a friend at the park. As she is about to leave, her stepmother yells at her to get back in the house and feed the dog. Angelica is steamed. Why can't one of her stepsisters feed the dog? Why does she always have to do all the work? She hesitates, thinking about what she should do. Her stepmother is really yelling now. Angelica can't take it anymore. How can she possibly learn to love her stepmother? What do you think she should do?

Should Angelica . . .

A. Call on her fairy godmother to get her out of her predicament?

B. Take off and let her stepsisters feed the dog?

C. Start yelling back at her stepmother to get off her case?

D. Go in the house, feed the dog, and, then, go meet her friend?

E. Start packing her bags to live somewhere else?

 For help in knowing how Angelica can handle her situation, read Romans 15:5.

Stranger Danger

Cyrus is walking home when a car pulls up beside him. He doesn't recognize the woman in the car. She looks very upset, and she motions for Cyrus to come over. Thinking it might be the mother of one of his friends, he stops and listens but does not move toward the car. The woman, who doesn't introduce herself, asks Cyrus if he has seen a little girl, about two years old, wearing a pink jacket and blue pants. The woman explains that her daughter wandered away from a friend's backyard while she was visiting, and she can't seem to find her anywhere. Cyrus tells the woman he hasn't seen her, but he will keep a lookout for her.

But the woman doesn't leave. As Cyrus continues walking, she drives the car alongside. "Please, I think she might have wandered over to the park. But I don't know this neighborhood. Maybe you can show me the way. Please get in and help me look for my little girl," she begs. Cyrus doesn't know what to do. He knows he should not get in a car with someone he doesn't know, but this is a mother who needs help. And she is so upset about her daughter. He truly wants to help her. What do you think Cyrus should do?

Should he . . .

A. Get into the car to help the woman look for her daughter?

B. Tell the woman that he will get his bike and meet her at the park to help her look?

C. Run from the car, screaming, "Kidnapper!"?

D. Give the woman directions to the park?

E. Immediately go home or to his nearest friend's house and ask an adult to call the police?

 Read Judges 16:16-19 to see what happened to Samson when he made a wrong decision, even though he knew better.

The Ballerina

Juliana is a talented dancer. She learned to dance when she was five years old, and she has been dancing ever since. Juliana takes ballet lessons three times a week at the best dance studio in her town. She practices at least an hour, if not more, every day. Her dad set up a mini-studio in her basement, with floor-to-ceiling mirrors and a practice barre. She dreams of one day joining the American Ballet Theater. During the school year Juliana somehow manages to squeeze her schoolwork in—between dance lessons, recitals, and practicing. But dance usually comes first. Often Juliana does her homework at breakfast before rushing out the door.

At church youth group last Sunday, the leader said something that made Juliana think. The leader talked about how certain things can become gods in our lives if we let them become more important than God. Juliana knows she has missed youth group on several occasions because of practices and recitals. Sometimes she has missed church because of out-of-town recitals. Does this mean that dancing has become an idol to her? She is unsure of what she should do about her dancing. What should Juliana do?

Should she . . .
  A. Tell herself that God understands how important dancing is to her?
  B. Vow to miss church only when absolutely necessary?
  C. Cut out dancing totally?
  D. Pray that God will show her if dancing has, indeed, become more important than him and help her to make whatever changes are necessary?
  E. Forget about it—the youth leader really wasn't talking about something harmless like dancing, right?

 Read Exodus 20:1-3 to see what God has to say about putting other things before him.

Thank You!

For his birthday, Toby received some very nice gifts from his grandparents and his uncle. His one set of grandparents sent him several books, a football jersey, and a video that he has wanted. He got a neat set of books on Egyptian history and a few CDs from his other grandparents. And his uncle sent a cool model airplane kit. Mom said he should write thank-you notes to everyone right away, and Toby assured her that he would.

More than two months have passed, and Toby still has not sent the thank-you notes. Today, Saturday morning, he comes down to breakfast wearing the football jersey his grandparents had given him. His mom looks at it and says, "That's a very nice jersey. Did you ever write those thank-you notes to your grandparents and uncle?" What do you think Toby should do?

Should he . . .

A. Tell his mom that the statutes of limitation for writing thank-yous has run out?

B. Tell his mom he plans to fax them all a thank-you later today?

C. Tell his mom that he called his grandparents and uncle to thank them; they don't need a note confirming it?

D. Tell his mom that he plans to include their thank-you notes with his thank-yous for Christmas?

E. Confess that he hasn't written the notes yet and then go upstairs to do it immediately?

Check out 1 Thessalonians 5:16-18 for the attitude God desires for Toby.

Soccer Camp

Allyssa volunteered this summer to work at her church's soccer camp. It's a great outreach to the neighborhood. Kids can come and learn soccer skills. Then, because of the relationships formed at the camp, perhaps many will come back to church to learn more about Jesus. Allyssa is good at soccer, but she's not so sure about sharing her faith with these kids. Maybe no one will ask, or if they do, she can send them over to the director.

During the week, Allyssa has a wonderful time at the camp. She has six boys and girls in her group, and they have had a great time together. Today is their last day. They will have a scrimmage and then an ice-cream social. The director plans to give her testimony during the ice-cream social and invite the boys and girls to come back and visit the church on Sunday. Allyssa is a bit nervous about it. She really likes these kids and believes that they got to know each other well this week, but she still feels shy about talking with them about Jesus.

After the director gives her talk, one of the boys, who has been listening intently, comes over to Allyssa. "Do you believe in Jesus?" he asks her. Allyssa can tell that her answer is important to this boy. If only she didn't feel so tongue-tied. What do you think Allyssa should do?

Should she . . .
  A. Tell the boy to talk with the director?
  B. Gently tell the boy that she does believe in Jesus and then tell him why?
  C. Shrug and say, "I guess so"?
  D. Change the subject and ask the boy to get her some more ice cream?
  E. Compliment the boy on his soccer skills?

 Read 1 Peter 3:15 for help in knowing how Allyssa should respond.

13

Pushing the Right Buttons

Seth baby-sat his younger brother—not because he wanted to, but because he owed his mom some baby-sitting time. It was a long afternoon. His brother whined about the lunch, the TV shows, going outside, and coming inside. Seth had had it by the time his mom returned. As soon as she walked in the door, the little brother began complaining about Seth. None of the complaints were true, but Seth got a lecture anyway. Seth was very angry! Storming off to his room, he vowed to get back at his brother big time.

Later in the afternoon, Seth is watching TV when his brother walks in with some kind of contraption he made over at a friend's house. He proudly shows it off to his mother who nods her head and says, "That's nice." Then he brings it in to show it to Seth. Seth realizes this is a perfect pay-back time. He knows that all he has to do is start laughing at his brother, and his brother will start screaming. Then Mom will yell at his brother and send him to his room. Perfect! As his brother shows off his newest invention to Seth, what do you think he should do?

Should Seth . . .

    A. Tell him it's great and go back to his TV show?

    B. Start laughing hysterically—and wait for the fireworks?

    C. Ignore his brother until he starts screaming at him—same result!?

    D. Tell his brother that his contraption is a piece of junk?

    E. Compliment his brother and offer to help him work on his next invention?

 To see how God views those who provoke others, read Proverbs 11:29.

14

The Garage Sale

Colton's family is going to have a garage sale this weekend. For weeks, his mom has been going through closets and drawers to sort things for the sale. She has asked Colton and his brother to sort through their old books, puzzles, games, and toys to see what they would like to sell at the sale. She has promised that whatever items they contribute, they will get the money earned from their sale. Colton and his brother have amassed a small pile of stuff for the sale already, but Colton is looking for some big-ticket items he can sell. He would like to make enough money to buy himself a new pair of Rollerblades.

One possibility is his old ten-speed bike. He could clean it up, shine up the handle bars, and it will look like new. The only problem is that the chain falls off after the bike is ridden several blocks. The brakes squeal a bit, too, after it is ridden, but they work. Colton figures that no one will take it out for a test spin. Or if they do, they won't ride far enough for the chain to fall off. He probably could get twenty dollars for the bike on appearances alone. That would help a lot toward his Rollerblade fund. What do you think Colton should do?

Should he . . .
A. Sell the bike at a reduced price and let the buyer know about the chain?
B. Try and fix the chain before he sells the bike?
C. Donate the bike to a charity organization that rehabs and fixes bikes for needy children?
D. Sell the bike as is for twenty dollars? After all, let the buyer beware!
E. Demonstrate how well the bike operates (before the chain falls off) and offer it to the highest bidder?

 Take a look at Proverbs 16:11 and Ezekiel 45:9-11 for guidance in knowing what Colton should do.

Finders Keepers, Part 2

Jerry is hanging out on the playground during recess. He doesn't feel like playing freeze tag or joining in the soccer game, so he's just kicking the stones and walking around. Suddenly, Jerry's foot strikes a hard object. He looks down, and much to his surprise, he discovers an expensive-looking hunting knife at his feet.

The knife is encased in a fancy leather holder. Jerry takes the knife out and can't believe his eyes. It looks like it has ivory inlay on the handle. Jerry doesn't see a name anywhere on the knife or the holder. He quickly looks around to see if anyone is watching. What a find! What should Jerry do?

Should he . . .

A. Immediately take the knife to the lost and found at school?

B. Take the knife home, tell no one about it, and keep it for himself?

C. Give the knife to his dad to make up for the one that he ruined chopping wood?

D. Leave the knife on the ground?

E. Try to sell the knife for one hundred dollars?

For help in knowing what Jerry should do, read Luke 12:15.

Just Desserts

Katie is having dinner at her friend Hillary's house. Katie is a frequent guest for dinner, and Hillary's mom knows that Katie loves her special double-chocolate fudge brownies. The girls help clear the dishes while Hillary's mom gets dessert ready.

Katie hopes there are brownies for dessert. Sure enough, Hillary's mom brings over a huge plate piled with freshly baked brownies and tells Katie to help herself. As Hillary's mom puts the plate down in front of Katie, what should Katie do?

Should she . . .
    A. Immediately grab a brownie and begin eating?
    B. Say thank you, take one, wait for everyone to be served, and then eat her brownie?
    C. Look for the biggest brownie and put it on her plate?
    D. Take two huge brownies—one for now, one for later?
    E. Take a brownie and stuff it down quickly so she can have another one before the brownies are gone?

 For help in knowing what Katie should do, read Proverbs 23:19-21.

Drinking Buddy?

Chase is one of the more popular boys in the youth group, but he has a bit of a wild side. He always seems to have a quick comeback for everything and everybody, including his teachers, the youth group leaders, and his parents. Chase's mouth tends to get him into trouble with adults, but his friends think he is hilarious. Chase probably has had more detentions at school than the rest of the youth group put together. But among the boys, Chase was the undisputed leader. Until last weekend, that is.

It seems that Chase was at a friend's house. The parents went out for the evening, leaving Chase and his friend in charge. After putting the younger children to bed, Chase and his friend helped themselves to the liquor cabinet. They got a little wild and broke some windows in the neighborhood. Everyone at youth group knows that Chase was grounded for a long time and has to pay for the damage he did to the windows.

Before youth group starts, the group is buzzing about Chase. When he walks in, the room goes silent. A few girls roll their eyes and move over to the other side of the room. As Chase finds a place to sit, a couple of the guys make snide remarks. "Hey, look, it's the party animal. Want another brewski?" Chase stares stonily ahead. How do you think the youth group should handle this situation?

Should they . . .
   A.   Kick Chase out until he has repented enough?
   B.   Treat Chase as though he has some rare, contagious disease?
   C.   Make fun of Chase like some of the boys are doing?
   D.   Ignore Chase—maybe he'll take the hint and leave?
   E.   Be supportive of Chase and show compassion for his situation?

 To see how Jesus responded in a similar situation, read John 8:1-7.

The Great Bargain

Melissa really wants a new CD player for her room. She's been saving her baby-sitting money and whatever else she has earned for chores around the house. Melissa knows which CD player she wants, and today she sees that it's on sale. The only problem is that she is short about thirty dollars. Melissa's next baby-sitting job isn't for several weeks, and the sale is only for the next two days. What should Melissa do?

Should she . . .

A. Take the money she needs from her mom's purse?

B. Plead with her parents to buy the CD player for her?

C. Relax and wait, knowing that it will be on sale again in the future?

D. Give up saving for a CD player and spend the money she already has saved on something else?

E. Apply for a credit card?

 For help in knowing what Melissa should do, read Galatians 5:22.

The Name above All Names

Dinah's new friend, Melina, is really funny. She always has a good joke to tell, and she has the best stories. Dinah is sure that Melina exaggerates a little bit every now and then, but it makes for a better story. Dinah's crowd has easily accepted Melina into the group, and she makes a great addition. There's only one small problem. Melina uses the Lord's name, or rather misuses it, in at least every other sentence. She can't seem to say anything without taking God's name in vain.

Dinah hasn't had much of a chance to talk to Melina about her faith. She doesn't feel she knows her well enough yet. From what Melina has said about her activities on Sunday, Dinah is sure that she doesn't go to church regularly, if at all. It doesn't seem to bother anyone else, and Dinah would hate to make a big production about it. Still, it bothers her because it's obvious that Melina simply doesn't know Jesus, or she wouldn't use his name in that fashion. Dinah has been praying about the best way to approach her new friend. What do you think Dinah should do?

Should she . . .

    A.   Roll her eyes every time Melina says God's name, so she'll get the hint?

    B.   Get up and leave the group when Melina gets on a roll?

    C.   Quietly take Melina aside someday and introduce her to Jesus?

    D.   Laugh when she uses God's name, like the rest of the crowd, so she doesn't cause a scene?

    E.   Figure nothing is happening to her friend, so she should talk like Melina does when she's with Melina?

 Read Philippians 2:9-11 for some bold words that would help Dinah in her situation.

20

The Farewell Bash

Leigh and her friend are planning a good-bye party for Joellen, who is moving overseas with her family. Everyone is sad to see Joellen leave. Leigh wants to make this a special occasion, so she and her friend have spent weeks planning the party. Leigh loves to cook and has planned an elaborate menu with many of Joellen's favorite foods. The night before the party, Leigh and her friend put up the decorations. Leigh goes to bed, satisfied that everything will go smoothly.

And everything does—at least for all the guests. Everyone is having a great time at the party. Joellen loves the decorations, and the food is terrific. Everyone is enjoying themselves, except for Leigh. She is in the kitchen trying to put the finishing touches on the main entree she has planned. She could use another pair of hands, but her friend is nowhere to be found. Leigh is getting more frustrated because the dish will be ruined if she doesn't hurry. She looks out the window and sees her friend laughing and talking with Joellen. What do you think Leigh should do?

Should she . . .

    A. Go to Plan B and order in some pizzas, so she can enjoy the party too?

    B. Drag her friend away from Joellen and order her to help out?

    C. Tell everyone that the party is over because the entree is ruined?

    D. Sulk and complain that she has to do all the work?

    E. Recruit some other friends to help out with kitchen duty?

 Read what Jesus had to say to Martha in Luke 10:38-42 when she found herself in a similar situation.

21

Make Up Your Mind!

Luis is excited, though a bit nervous, about the prospect of going to a new school in the fall. It's a great opportunity because he will be able to concentrate on his music. This school offers a unique fine arts program—the only one like it in the area. Luis really should learn a lot. The only drawback is that the school is located on the other side of town. It's much bigger than the one he now attends, and he will have to take a bus to get there. He won't be with any of his friends, so he will have to make new friends.

The biggest worry, however, is the students who attend this school. Luis has heard stories about the kids there. Many are very talented and believe in "free expression." Often that expression is anti-God and goes against much of what Luis believes. He knows the temptation will be great to give in to "peer pressure" and become like the other kids there in order to fit in.

Luis never really experienced much pressure from friends at his old school to do bad things. In fact, he was pretty much the acknowledged leader among his friends there, and he has been able to influence them positively. Luis is not so sure how he will handle this new situation. What do you think Luis should do?

Should he . . .
- A. Make up his mind now to stand firm for God and for what he knows is right?
- B. See how things go; if it's not really all that bad, maybe he can compromise a bit?
- C. Go along with the crowd until he feels comfortable and has made some friends?
- D. Walk around with a big black Bible on top of his books to ward off temptation?
- E. Tell his parents that he would rather stay at his old school?

 Read Daniel 1:8 to find out how Daniel withstood great pressure to do something he knew was wrong.

22

Video Role

For the last few weeks, Megan and Colleen have been almost inseparable—they seem to do everything together. In fact, just the other day, Megan told her mother that Colleen was the best friend she has ever had.

To celebrate Colleen's birthday, her mom said she could have a slumber party, so she invited eight of her close friends. Of course, Megan was included.

During the party Megan is having a great time. But later in the evening, Colleen pops a video in the VCR that Megan knows she shouldn't see (and that she knows her parents wouldn't allow her to see). What should Megan do?

Should she . . .

A. Call her parents and have them take her home?

B. Stand in front of the screen and say, "I cannot allow my friends to ruin themselves with garbage like this"?

C. Close her eyes and put her fingers in her ears till the movie is over?

D. Watch the movie anyway so she won't offend her friends?

E. Politely excuse herself and go to another room, explaining that her parents wouldn't want her to watch it?

Two verses to help Megan know what to do are Philippians 4:8 and Hebrews 4:13.

The Loyal Friend

Hank is worried about his best friend, Zeke. Zeke's parents are going through a messy divorce, and Zeke is caught up in the middle of it. Every so often, Hank will ask Zeke how things are going with this family, but he usually doesn't want to talk about it. So Hank lets the subject drop, but he knows his friend is hurting. Lately, Zeke is not much fun to be around. He's argumentative and never wants to do anything the rest of the group does. If the subject of parents comes up, Zeke leaves the room. Hank's other friends feel very uncomfortable when Zeke is around.

That's the problem. The boys are planning a camping trip for next weekend. Hank wants to go, but he wants to ask Zeke to come with them. The other guys are balking. "That jerk? No way. He's a real downer. I'm afraid he'll hit someone if they say the wrong thing," says one guy. And to Hank's dismay, the entire group agrees. He has already mentioned the camping trip to Zeke, so he has to say something to him about it. He doesn't want to abandon his friend right now when he needs him the most, but he does want to go on this camping trip. What do you think Hank should do?

Should he . . .

A. Tell his friends he's planning to go with Zeke, and they can decide if they want to come along or not?

B. Plan to go on a camping trip with Zeke another time?

C. Demand that his friends allow Zeke to come along?

D. Tell Zeke that the camping trip was canceled?

E. Refuse to go on the camping trip at all if his friends are going to behave that way?

 For help in knowing what Hank should do, read Proverbs 27:10.

The Good Neighbor

Sean is late for choir rehearsal. He grabs his jacket, tosses an apple into his pocket, and jumps on his bike. If he races through the park and takes the shortcut, he should only be five minutes late. But that's a big "if." Sean tears down the street and races toward the park. As he is approaching the park, he sees an elderly woman approaching him pushing a shopping cart filled to the brim with groceries. Sean is wondering how the woman managed to push a shopping cart this far, when, suddenly, she is broadsided by a kid on a skateboard.

Sean sees the woman crumple to the ground. Groceries go flying in different directions. Then to Sean's amazement, the boy on the skateboard never stops to see if the woman is all right. Sean quickly looks around. No one else has seen what happened. As he rides closer, he can see that the woman is badly shaken and may need some medical assistance. But does Sean have to be the one to help her? He's getting later by the minute. But if he takes the shortcut, he will have to ride right by this woman. If he goes the other way, he will be late, but at least he won't have to stop to help the woman out. What do you think Sean should do?

Should he . . .
- A. Stop immediately to help the woman and get her medical attention, if necessary?
- B. Ride quickly by the woman but look to see if she's all right?
- C. Take the other route to choir and call 911 to report the accident?
- D. Amuse his friends at choir with stories of how funny the old woman looked flying through the air?
- E. Go chasing after the skateboarder and make him come back to help the woman?

 Jesus had strong words about helping our neighbors. Read what he has to say in Luke 10:30-37.

25

The Cold War

Kay and Crystal are not speaking to each other. Actually, it has been that way for several weeks now. The girls had a huge fight. Some strong words were spoken: Kay accused Crystal of betraying a secret; Crystal accused Kay of being a liar. Their broken relationship is affecting all of their friends. Many have chosen sides. Others have tried to stay out of it but have been forced to act as go-betweens to pass along messages of more accusations. Everyone wishes that the two girls would resolve their differences so things would get back to the way they were. But that doesn't appear likely.

Lately, however, Kay has been missing her friend. When she hears a funny joke, she immediately wants to tell Crystal—until she remembers that they are not talking. The other day, she went shopping at the mall and saw a shirt she knew would be perfect for . . . Crystal. The youth group activity night is coming up on Friday, and Kay knows deep inside that it won't be as much fun if the two girls aren't talking. She has to face it: Life isn't nearly as interesting or fun if you're not sharing it with your best friend. Kay begins to question whether what they argued about is worth losing such a valuable friendship. She wonders what she should do?

Should Kay . . .
   A. Wait until Crystal calls her because, after all, she is the one who started the fight?
   B. Decide that it would look too wimpy to back down now and continue the cold war?
   C. Get a friend to call Crystal and see if she wants to apologize?
   D. Drop hints that she is willing to forget about the past?
   E. Call Crystal and admit that she allowed some silly stuff to come between them and that she is sorry and wants to work things out?

 For help in deciding what Kay should do, read 1 Peter 4:8.

26

Promises, Promises

Last month Devin got the scare of his life. In the middle of the night, his mom had been rushed to the hospital, seriously ill. Devin had spent several anxious hours at his neighbor's house waiting for his dad to come home. When his father returned, he had told the family that Mom wasn't in any danger, but the doctors didn't know what was wrong with her. They kept Devin's mother in the hospital for several weeks until they were able to determine what was causing her illness.

Those weeks were difficult for Devin and his dad. Every night before Devin went off to a troubled sleep, he prayed and promised that if God would help make his mom better, he would read his Bible every day.

Now his mom is back home. She still is weak but definitely on the mend. The doctors had determined that the illness had been caused by a virus she picked up on the family vacation. She needs to take it easy, but Devin is glad to have her back at home. While his mom is tucking him into bed tonight, she whispers, "Thank you for all your prayers, Devin. They helped me get through this. Our God is so good."

Devin smiles in the dark to himself. *Yes,* he thinks, *God is good to bring my mom back to me.* But then he remembers his promise to God about reading the Bible. He has to admit that he hasn't had the time lately because he has been helping out more around the house. What should he do about the vow he made to God?

Should Devin . . .

   A. Forget about it—surely God isn't going to hold him to a silly promise like that?

   B. Open his Bible and start reading wherever it falls open?

   C. Decide that his promise didn't mean anything because he had his fingers crossed when he made it?

   D. Ask his parents or Sunday school teacher to help him come up with a good plan to read through the Bible because he truly wants to know God better?

   E. Get a child's picture Bible to read—he didn't specify what kind of Bible, did he?

 For an eye-opening look at how God views Devin's promise, read Ecclesiastes 5:1-5.

27

The Long Haul

arilee loves nature and the outdoors. One of her favorite places to spend time is at her town's nature preserve. After much consideration, Marilee decides to be a junior volunteer at the preserve. She attends the training session, gets her volunteer's patch, and is ready to go. At first glance, the program doesn't appear that demanding. Marilee has to volunteer twice a month for an entire year, help during the big events, such as the maple syrup time in March and the harvesttime in the fall, and attend at least two of the lectures on the preserve. She is eager to start.

After two months, Marilee knows she has made a mistake. Instead of calling them junior volunteers, they should call them junior slaves, thinks Marilee. The juniors, as they are called, get to do all the dirty work. If someone needs materials carried out to a site, the juniors get to do it. If someone needs water, the juniors are called. And they have to pick up the trash left over from events. The fun Marilee anticipated from helping people learn about the preserve is nonexistent. Not only that, but spending a long January afternoon outside at the preserve is not her idea of a good time. Marilee is seriously considering quitting the program. What do you think she should do?

Should Marilee . . .
  A. Honor her commitment to the nature preserve and continue through the year?
  B. Call in sick every time she is scheduled to volunteer?
  C. Organize all the junior volunteers and go on strike?
  D. Turn in the volunteer director for violating child labor laws?
  E. Continue to show up for her scheduled volunteer times but take off for the nature trails instead of working?

 Read Acts 20:22-24 to see how Paul reacted under less-than-perfect working conditions.

Just Cruisin'

Ed's friend Nick has some great news. He and his family are going on a vacation cruise. Nick shows Ed all the brochures of the cruise ship and all the exotic islands they will visit while on the cruise. Ed's family usually goes to visit his grandparents in Ohio for a week during their family vacation. They have never been anywhere exotic like the places Nick will visit on the cruise.

Ed would love to go on a vacation cruise. He dreams about seeing the beautiful beaches in the Caribbean, not to mention all the cool things that Nick will get to do while on the cruise ship. Nick is so excited about the trip. What should Ed do?

Should he . . .
   A. Say he is happy and excited for Nick?
   B. Tell Nick that he's sure to get seasick, and he'll be bored looking at all that water?
   C. Be jealous and wish he were going instead?
   D. Get angry and complain, "All we ever get to do is go to Ohio. It's not fair! Everybody goes on cruises except me"?
   E. Make up an imaginary vacation cruise to the exotic Fiji Islands that is way cooler than Nick's old trip to the Bahamas?

 For help in knowing what Ed should do, read Romans 12:15.

Fun at the Water Park

Dorrie's church youth group is sponsoring a trip to a really cool water park today. About fifteen kids signed up to go on the all-day trip along with three adult leaders. They arrived at the water park around ten o'clock and lugged all their stuff until they found a spot to settle their stuff in. The youth group leader told the kids that they could do whatever they wanted, but they needed to meet back at this spot at 3:45 P.M. to get ready for the ride home. Dorrie and her friends grabbed a couple of tubes and raced off.

They are having an absolute blast. Before lunch (and before the lines get too long), the girls got in as much slide time as they could. After a quick lunch, they raced off to spend some time in the wave pool, riding some pretty cool waves. Then they floated down the "Lazy River" for a while. Now, before they know it, it's almost time to leave. One of Dorrie's friends yells, "Let's go on the tube slide one more time before we have to go." The girls race over to the slide only to discover a long line. Dorrie shrugs. "Well, that's it. We'd better turn in our tubes now. We'll never get through this line before 3:45." But her friends urge her to stay with them and wait.

"The others won't leave us here," they tell her. Dorrie is not sure this is a good idea. What do you think she should do?

Should Dorrie . . .

A. Stay with her friends in line, knowing that the group will wait for them?

B. Cut in the front of the line, explaining to everyone that they have to leave in five minutes?

C. Tell her friends that she is going to turn in her tube and rejoin the group at the designated time and spot?

D. Put on a life preserver and blow a whistle, pretending to be a lifeguard, and inform those in line that the slide is closed. Then, when everyone leaves, take off the preserver and go down the slide with her friends?

E. Leave her friends in line and tell the youth group leader she doesn't know where they are—they deserve to be left behind!?

 For help in knowing what Dorrie should do, read Exodus 23:2.

30

The Eldest Elder

At Edwin's church one of the elders, Mr. Turner, seems to be at least one hundred years old. Actually, he is only eighty, but he's the oldest member of the church. Mr. Turner has been going to First Church since he was a young boy. His family is one of the town's founding families and owned one of its original farms. Mr. Turner is a walking history book of Edwin's town, and he can relate the entire history of the town without blinking an eye. That's one reason Edwin avoids him. Once Mr. Turner starts talking, he doesn't stop! Besides that, Mr. Turner talks funny. When he prays in church, the boys roll their eyes and start to snicker. Mr. Turner still uses *thee, thou, whilst,* and *shouldest* in his prayers. He sounds so strange that the boys can't help but laugh.

Today before church, Edwin's mom gives him the horrifying news that Mr. Turner is coming over to their house for lunch after the service. Edwin can't believe his ears. He will have to spend the entire afternoon with this boring old man. If someone asks a question, Mr. Turner may never stop talking! And what if Dad asks Mr. Turner to say grace? How will Edwin stop from laughing? *This is going to be some afternoon,* Edwin thinks gloomily. What do you think he should do?

Should Edwin . . .

A. Tell his mom that he has made other plans for lunch?

B. Wolf down his lunch as quickly as he can and then tell his mom he has tons of homework to do?

C. Make fun of Mr. Turner in front of his younger brothers whenever Mr. Turner isn't looking?

D. Listen respectfully as Mr. Turner talks about "those days," and discover (to his amazement) that Mr. Turner has some interesting stories?

E. Sit at the lunch table but wear earphones plugged in to his portable CD player?

 Read Leviticus 19:32 to see what the Lord says regarding how Edwin should treat Mr. Turner.

31

Leader of the Pack

After a particularly rowdy Sunday school class, the teacher asks Gil if he could stay after for a few minutes. Gil wonders what his teacher wants. Gil wasn't the only one cutting up today in class, and besides, he wasn't one of the guys who crumpled his lesson paper and tried to make it stick on the ceiling. Although, he has to admit with a grin, he did suggest it. He didn't draw the picture of the Sunday school teacher on the white board, either, although he did make a few improvements.

Gil waits impatiently until the last student leaves the classroom. What his Sunday school teacher says surprises him. "Gil, you are one of the leaders in this classroom. Whatever you do or suggest, the others tend to go along with. Now you can either help me a great deal in this class or you can hurt me. I would like your help in being a positive leader for the other students," she says. Gil never thought of himself in that way before. He knows the boys all seem to listen to his suggestions and watch what he does. *This is pretty cool,* he thinks. What do you think Gil should do with this newfound source of power?

Should he . . .

   A. Stage a coup and take over the Sunday school class?

   B. Check out the extent of his leadership over the other boys by asking them to do some ridiculous things next Sunday?

   C. Think about what his Sunday school teacher said and try to be a positive leader for the class?

   D. Ignore what his teacher said—things are going well in class just as they are?

   E. Figure his influence includes other places—such as school, home, soccer field—and see what he can get away with?

 To see what Gil should do, read 2 Chronicles 19:4-7, King Jehoshaphat's instructions to the judges he appointed as leaders over the people.

1

The Chat Room

Griffin's family recently purchased a new computer for their home. It has all the latest technology—state of the art. His dad bought a color printer, too, so now Griffin can print color graphics for his papers and reports. He and his sister have spent hours trying out all the new programs. The neatest thing about the new computer, however, is that the family received one hundred free hours on the Internet. Griffin is allowed ten minutes each day to surf the Net, and he has discovered several sports Web sites and a kids' news page. What interests Griffin the most, however, are the kids' chat rooms. Griffin has found one that he has visited several times. He is beginning to recognize some of the regulars.

Mostly, Griffin has only observed the conversations that go on in the chat room. Today, he wants to be a participant. As he signs on and makes known he wants to be part of the conversation, he is quickly greeted by a number of the kids already in the room. They want to know about him—where he lives, what he likes to do, what his hobbies are, etc. Griffin is not completely comfortable sharing such information with kids he doesn't even know. Maybe he should make up some information to throw them off. These kids wouldn't know if he were telling the truth or not. And besides, it's not really lying if it's not face-to-face, is it? What do you think Griffin should do?

Should he . . .
   A. Tell the kids he's the president and wants to know their views on the big issues?
   B. Sign off and leave the chat room?
   C. Ignore the questions and ask the other kids information about them?
   D. Answer their questions truthfully, but generally, without giving out information such as his phone number and address?
   E. Make up a fake name and other false information to give them?

 Read Psalm 34:12-13 to discover God's unchanging word about telling the truth, regardless of technology.

2

Admit One

The county fair opens today. Tom and his friends look forward to the fair every summer, and they plan to go this afternoon. Tom has been saving his money so he can play the carnival games and win lots of prizes. He really wants to win one of those large stuffed animals for his mom.

When they get to the fair, Tom notices that there is a special child's admission price for children ten and under. Tom is eleven, but he looks young for his age. He probably could pass for being ten, no problem. And that would mean more money for playing the games and buying cotton candy. What should Tom do?

Should he . . .

    A. Say nothing and hope the person selling tickets will think he is a "child" and charge him the cheaper price?

    B. Lie, say he is ten, and ask for a child's ticket?

    C. Pay the adult price?

    D. Dress like a clown and hope the fair people will think Tom is part of the show and let him in for free?

    E. Have one of his taller friends say that Tom is his younger brother and pay for a child's ticket for Tom?

 For help in knowing what Tom should do, read Psalm 24:3-4.

That Wild and Crazy Guy

Martin is a wild man. Ask anyone at school. If a crazy prank has been pulled, look for Martin. He probably spends more time in the detention center than in the classroom. Once he put Vaseline on all the classroom doorknobs. Another time, he ordered a dozen pizzas to be delivered to the gym teacher. Last spring, on the last day of school, he released a greased pig in the hallways. Martin has a record a mile long and quite the reputation. If you're looking for trouble, Martin will help you find it.

The last place anyone would expect to find Martin was church, so imagine the surprise on everyone's face at youth group when Martin walked in and sat down. No one said anything to him at first because they were shocked. But the question on everyone's mind was the same: *What in the world is Martin doing at youth group?* As the night progresses, it becomes evident that Martin has changed. He still has a wacky sense of humor, but he seems more subdued. He actually listens to the youth group leader explain about being a follower of Christ. Martin couldn't possibly have become a Christian, could he? The group doesn't know what to think. How do you think the group should react to Martin?

Should they . . .
  A. Give Martin a few weeks before they decide whether this is for real or not?
  B. Decide this is one of Martin's more elaborate pranks and warn the youth leader about him?
  C. Corner Martin after the meeting and demand, "What are you doing here?"
  D. Pull a prank on Martin, like giving him a greased Bible?
  E. Accept Martin as a fellow believer and help him to grow in his faith?

 To know how the group should react to Martin, read Acts 10:34 to see how Peter responded when he heard that a Roman officer was seeking to receive Jesus as his Savior.

Cleanup Detail

I t's the last day at camp, and everyone is excited about going home. After a quick breakfast, the camp leader divides the girls into groups and gives each group a list of tasks that have to be completed before they can break camp. They have about an hour to get the work done, or they will miss the truck taking them back to the main camp where, hopefully, their parents will be waiting for them. The girls are anxious to get started with their jobs. Marissa is appointed leader of her group, which is given the cleanup detail. Marissa gets her group together and explains what they have to do: sweep the cabins, pick up the trash around the campsite, take the garbage down to the dump, and clean the latrines.

A chorus of protest goes up. "No way are we going to clean the latrines," says one girl. "That's not fair! We're not going to do that!" Time is wasting as the girls argue over who is going to take that dirty job. As group leader, Marissa knows that she had better do something fast or else they all will be walking the two miles back to the campgrounds. What do you think Marissa should do?

Should she . . .
   A. Order the two youngest girls to clean the latrines?
   B. Have everyone draw straws—the two short straws lose?
   C. Skip the latrines; maybe no one will check them until later?
   D. Step forward and volunteer to clean the latrines herself?
   E. Tell the group that no one is leaving until two girls (other than herself) volunteer to clean the latrines?

 For help in knowing what Marissa should do, read the example Jesus sets in Matthew 20:26-27.

Roughing It

Eileen is going with her youth group to a church-based work camp. During the week, the kids will be assisting some families in a neighboring town that had been hard hit by floods earlier in the summer. The group will be based at the camp, and then they will be bused to work sites in the community. Camping is really not Eileen's thing, and she enjoys cleaning up even less. But her parents both agreed that the experience would be good for Eileen. As she waves good-bye to her parents, Eileen still is not convinced that she needs this kind of experience.

After two days at the camp, Eileen is absolutely sure she does not need the experience. It is worse than she expected. She is exhausted. They get up every morning at five-thirty and work until five o'clock that evening. It's hot, the bugs are awful, the beds are lumpy, and the food is terrible. Eileen can't remember ever feeling so tired, hungry, and dirty—all at the same time. She doesn't think she can last another day. How will Eileen make it through the next five days?

Should she . . .
- A. Refuse to get out of bed until "working conditions" improve?
- B. While in town, escape, find the nearest phone, and call for help?
- C. Resolve that, through the strength of God, she will make the best of a difficult situation?
- D. Tell her counselors that she can't work anymore because she has a broken nail?
- E. Instigate a camp revolt and hold the counselors hostage until the parents come and pick their kids up?

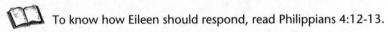 To know how Eileen should respond, read Philippians 4:12-13.

6

Movie Madness

Mark is not allowed to see PG-13 movies. On Friday night, he and his friends decide to see the latest G-rated movie playing at the local theater. Mark's parents give the OK and drive them to the theater. Once they get to the theater, Mark's friends have a change of plans. They all head to the nearest PG-13 movie, leaving Mark standing in the middle of the lobby. What should Mark do?

Should he . . .
A. Hide in the bathroom?
B. Politely explain that he doesn't want to see a PG-13 movie and go into the G one, whether anyone joins him or not?
C. Go to the PG-13 movie but keep his eyes closed?
D. Excitedly agree and lead his friends into the worst movie showing?
E. Pretend he has a sudden stomachache and tell his friends he has to go home?

 For help in knowing what Mark should do, read Romans 12:2.

Learning to Ride

Becky's little brother is finally learning to ride his bike. He has been thinking about it all summer and now feels ready to try. Becky's dad buys him a new helmet and sets out early Saturday morning to start the lesson. After about an hour, Dad comes in to catch his breath. His arms and legs are bruised. The lessons, he says, are progressing, but her brother hasn't mastered it quite yet. Finally, her brother comes running in to tell his sister to come see him ride his bike.

Becky and her friend, who spent the night, dutifully go outside to watch her brother's first solo attempt. Becky nudges her friend, "This ought to be good." Becky knows her brother is sensitive about trying new things. She also knows that he hates being laughed at—especially by his older sister. So when he first wobbles off, she stifles a giggle. He looks so funny weaving down the street. But when he doesn't quite make the turn at the corner and goes wobbling straight into the bushes, Becky is about to explode with laughter. What do you think she should do?

Should Becky . . .

   A. Split her sides right there?

   B. Tell her brother that he would make a good stunt man?

   C. Run inside the house so she and her friend can share a good laugh?

   D. Run up to her brother and help him up, telling him he's doing a good job?

   E. Tell her dad that she wants to get the video camera so she can tape this for "America's Funniest Home Videos"?

 For help in knowing what Becky should do, read Ephesians 4:32.

Put on a Happy Face!

No way," Stella protests, looking out the window. The rain is coming down in sheets. The team's final softball game probably will be canceled if this keeps up. She kicks off her covers and takes a look in the mirror. Oh no! What happened to her hair? It's sticking out all over the place. Stella can tell it's going to be one of those days. She scours her room for her favorite black T-shirt only to discover it wadded up in a corner. Her mom will never let her leave the house wearing a wrinkly (not to mention dirty) T-shirt. She throws it back into the corner and grabs something else to wear.

Grumpily she comes down to the breakfast table. Her mom cheerily calls out, "Good morning, dear. Having a bad hair day?" Stella feels like screaming. Her little brother, already on his third bowl of cereal, points out through a mouthful of cereal that he got the prize in the cereal box. Stella looks at it (actually, *she* wanted the prize) and pronounces it a piece of junk. Her brother breaks into tears, and now her mom is on her case. Can things get much worse? As Stella stomps around the house, throwing things into her backpack, her mother looks at her. "You had better adjust your attitude before you leave this house or you truly will have a miserable day." What do you think Stella should do?

Should she . . .
  A. Kick the dog on her way out the door?
  B. Take her mom's advice and try to look on the bright side of things? (Maybe the rain delay will give her team extra time for practice.)
  C. Complain to her friends about the bad day she is having?
  D. Snap at everybody to make it the absolute worst day ever?
  E. Shave her head and wear wigs so she will never have another bad hair day again?

 Read Proverbs 15:13 to see what Stella should do.

Worship Time

Travis and his family have been going to the same church for about six years. Travis has become good friends with a number of boys that attend church and Sunday school. Today one of his friends asks him to sit with a group from Sunday school during the worship service. Travis usually sits with his family, but this would be great fun. Travis asks his dad, who, after a quick consultation with his mom, agrees. Dad's parting words echo in his ear, "But no monkey business."

The boys find a spot toward the back of the church. The church is crowded today, so the seats fill up quickly around the boys. As the service begins, Travis can see his family ahead of him. Boy, does he feel grown up, sitting with his friends at church. This is really cool. As the service progresses, however, Travis begins to feel a bit uneasy. His friends begin to pass notes and whisper jokes. People around them are looking, and some even seem a bit annoyed. Travis glances at his family. Has his father noticed the boys' disturbance? Uh-oh, here comes another note. What should Travis do?

Should he . . .
- A. Write a very funny joke he heard last week and try to get his friends to laugh out loud?
- B. Make faces at the people around them so they will stop staring?
- C. Ignore his friends' actions and decide to sit with his family next Sunday?
- D. During prayer, try to sneak out and find another place to sit?
- E. Ask his friends to be quiet so he can worship?

 For help in knowing what Travis should do, read Psalm 29:1-2 and Hebrews 12:28.

It's a Dog's Life

Dara loves animals, any kind of animals. She is always bringing home a stray dog or cat to feed. She makes sure that there is plenty of food for the squirrels and birds in her backyard. If there is an injured animal, Dara's the one to take it in or find it some proper care. That's why it pains her so much to see the poor dog down at the corner house. Dara walks by the dog every day. The dog appears malnourished and dirty. He is chained in the yard but doesn't seem to belong to anyone. Dara can't understand why people have pets they don't care about.

Although the dog barks at most people walking by, Dara has made friends with him. Every day she finds time to spend a few minutes with the dog, giving him a treat and petting him. She has even made up a name for the dog. Whenever Dara comes by, she sees no signs of life around the house. Today, however, as Dara is petting and feeding the dog, an old man with unkempt hair and torn clothing comes out and yells at her to get away from his dog. Dara is startled. She wants to say something to the man, but he quickly calls the dog to him and goes back inside the house. Now Dara is afraid that the man won't let the dog out in the yard anymore. She needs to do something about this situation. What do you think she should do?

Should Dara . . .
- A. Report the man to the humane society?
- B. Steal the dog and care for him herself since the man obviously doesn't care about him?
- C. Pray for the right opportunity to approach the man and ask if she can help care for the dog when he is away?
- D. Go back to the house when the man is there and demand that he take proper care of the dog?
- E. When no one is around, let the dog out and then put up a sign that reads, "Doggone!"?

 To see what Dara should do in this situation read Proverbs 3:5-6.

No Big Deal?

Alec and his friend Gus spent the afternoon working on Alec's go-cart. It's nearly finished, and it's a beauty. The boys spent two hours on the project. Alec figured that they would need another hour to paint it and put on the final touches. Then the go-cart would be ready for the race on Saturday. Glancing at his watch, however, Gus suddenly said he really had to go. His mom was expecting him home to mow the lawn. After Gus took off for home, Alec went back to finishing his work.

That night Gus calls. Alec senses something is up because Gus sounds funny on the phone. Quickly Gus explains that he didn't exactly go home right after he left Alec's house that afternoon. Instead, he went over to another friend's, and it seems they got into some trouble there. Could Alec be a real sport and tell his mom that Gus was at his house for the entire afternoon? Alec tells Gus he would rather not because it would be lying, but Gus insists, "It's no big deal. It's only a little lie. It won't hurt anyone. I don't want to get into trouble with my mom and miss the race." Alec sure doesn't want to lose Gus as his partner for the race, but is that true? Is telling a small lie "no big deal?" What do you think Alec should do?

Should he . . .
  A. Go ahead and tell a "small lie" to Gus's mom because he wants to be in the race?
  B. Tell Gus he's sorry, but he's not going to lie for him?
  C. Tell Gus's mom the truth, but only after the race on Saturday?
  D. Get angry at Gus for doing such a dumb thing in the first place and refuse to talk to him?
  E. Tell Gus's mom he forgot how long the two of them were together that afternoon?

 Read Ezra 9:5-15 to see how Ezra felt about "small" sin and to find out what Alec should do.

12

The Ketchup Caper

Dennis's mom has left him in charge of his younger brother while she runs out to do a few errands. Dennis is supposed to get lunch for his brother and then take him to the park. Lunch is no big deal. All Dennis has to do is microwave a couple of hot dogs, make chocolate milk, and put out some carrots and chips. But Dennis's brother is being a real pest. He doesn't want his chocolate milk in the yellow cup; he wants the blue cup. And when Dennis gets out the potato chips, his brother screams because he wants pretzels.

Finally, Dennis manages to get lunch on the table and his younger brother seated in his chair. Before he forgets, Dennis grabs the yellow mustard from the fridge. That's when the trouble begins. Dennis's brother starts crying and carrying on because he doesn't like mustard on his hot dogs. Totally frustrated by now, Dennis goes back to the fridge and gets out the ketchup. Pointing it at his brother, Dennis tells him to calm down and quit crying. Dennis doesn't realize the bottle's top is open, and when he squeezes the bottle in frustration, ketchup squirts on his brother and on the wall. Dennis's brother screams louder.

Just then, Dennis's mother walks in. She takes one look at the ketchup on the wall and the screaming child, and immediately blames the younger brother for the mess. She is about to punish him. Everything is happening so quickly, Dennis doesn't know what to do. How should he react?

Should Dennis . . .

A. Say nothing—after all, his brother has been a real pest and deserves to be punished for something?

B. Encourage his mother to be merciless? (See answer A)

C. Suggest a lighter punishment? ("After all, Mom, red isn't such a bad color," he could say.)

D. Say that the dog had grabbed the ketchup, squirting it on the wall?

E. Admit to being the one who accidentally squirted the ketchup, saying he didn't know the bottle was open?

 To know how Dennis should respond, read Exodus 20:16.

13

Cashing In

Danielle is buying a few school supplies at the drugstore. She makes her selections and takes them to the cashier. The total is $8.50, and Danielle pays the cashier with a ten-dollar bill. The cashier gives Danielle her change. As Danielle walks out the door, she notices that the cashier has mistakenly given her $5.50 in change instead of $1.50.

The cashier is already ringing up the next customer. What should Danielle do?

Should she . . .
   A. Go back and tell the cashier about the mistake and return the extra money?
   B. Run out the door and pocket the money?
   C. Buy something else with the money to see if the cashier will make an even bigger mistake?
   D. Figure it must be God's will and give the money to charity?
   E. Tell all her friends about the "stupid" cashier at the drugstore?

 For help in knowing what Danielle should do, read Proverbs 11:3.

Holding a Grudge

Clarissa still can't believe it. She and her best friend, Dawn, just had a terrible fight. It really was all Dawn's fault. The two of them had made plans to go shopping for school supplies last week. They had arranged to meet at the mall at 11:30, shop, and then to go get something to eat at the food court. Well, Clarissa was there, but Dawn wasn't. Clarissa waited over an hour, until she finally called her mom to come get her. Not only did she not get her school supplies, but she got good and angry as well. Then to make it worse, Dawn didn't even call her until the next day. She had completely forgotten about it and, in the meantime, had gone out and bought her school supplies.

The misunderstanding grew into a big fight. Clarissa and Dawn exchanged angry words. The conversation ended with both girls vowing never to see one another again.

It has been three days since the fight, and Clarissa hasn't heard a word. She promises herself that she will not call until Dawn apologizes. But she misses Dawn. They have been friends since third grade. It just doesn't seem the same without her around. Just then the phone rings. It's Dawn, and this time she starts off with, "I'm really sorry. I feel really bad about what happened. I was helping my mom at home and completely forgot about going to the mall. Will you please forgive me?"

Now that Dawn finally has apologized, what should Clarissa do?

Should she . . .
  A. Accept Dawn's apology but tell all her friends that Dawn is unreliable?
  B. Accept Dawn's apology but constantly remind Dawn about the time she stood her up?
  C. Refuse to accept Dawn's apology until Dawn goes out and buys school supplies for her?
  D. Get mad all over again about the incident and hang up on Dawn?
  E. Accept Dawn's apology, offer her own, and then forget about it?

 To know how Clarissa should respond, read Matthew 18:21-22.

15

Just a Little Sin

Chad's best friend has what he calls a "tiny" problem. He can't seem to utter a sentence without swearing. Although he manages to control his speech at school and at youth group, he doesn't seem to notice the string of four-letter words that comes out of his mouth on the playground or at home. To Chad's best friend, swearing is second nature. Profanity is used all the time at his house. As he explains, "It's our way of expressing ourselves."

Although on several occasions Chad has tried to point out that using such language offends God, his friend doesn't appear too concerned. "I'm reading my Bible and going to church and to youth group. Why should God care about my language? I'm not doing anything to hurt anyone. It's just my way of talking. This isn't anything major. It's only a little thing," his friend argues. Chad is stumped. Maybe it is only a little sin. His friend is faithful about coming to church, reading his Bible, and going to Bible study every week. He is considerate of others and genuinely seems to love the Lord. Maybe Chad is making too much of his friend's language. What do you think he should do?

Should Chad . . .

A. Ask his youth group leader for help in letting his friend know that God doesn't ignore "little sins"?

B. Forget about it and let his friend talk however he wants?

C. Continue to harp at his friend about cleaning up his mouth?

D. Figure if it's OK for his friend to talk that way, why not do it himself?

E. Dump his friend because he's not "good" enough?

 Read James 3:7-10 to see how God feels about cursing.

The Right Choice

It's the last week of softball. There are three more practices, and then the final game is on Wednesday. This is Carlie's first year on the team. She is not one of the star players, but she has worked hard throughout the season to improve. The coach has appreciated her dedication and faithfulness in coming to practices. But now Carlie has a choice to make. One of her good friends who has moved away is back in town for a visit. This friend is spending the weekend at another friend's house, and they are making plans for the weekend.

The girls want to go to a movie on Friday. Carlie's friends decide to go to the early show because it is cheaper, but Carlie won't finish softball practice until 5:00 P.M. The movie starts at 4:45 P.M. Carlie's friends are urging her to skip practice and come to the movie with them. Carlie is unsure what to do. It *is* the last week of practice, and she isn't that important to the team. It wouldn't hurt to miss one practice, would it? And besides, it's not often that she gets to see her friend. Would do you think Carlie should do?

Should she . . .
   A.   Tell her softball coach that she has a doctor's appointment and skip practice?
   B.   Go to practice, and tell her friends that she will catch up with them later, after the movie?
   C.   Suggest that her friends go to a later movie so she can go?
   D.   Get mad at her friends for making plans without considering her schedule?
   E.   Go to practice, get hit in the head with a ball, act woozy, go the locker room, and leave early?

 For help in knowing what Carlie should do, read Acts 24:16.

The Big Celebration

Dana's parents are planning a fiftieth wedding anniversary celebration for her grandparents. It's a surprise, so for the past three months, her mom has spent hours on the phone with out-of-town relatives making travel arrangements and accommodations. It has been a major undertaking for her parents. Dana and her sisters have been involved in some of the planning as well. Everyone in the family is very excited as the day approaches. Dana's cousins will stay with them during the week-long festivities—a huge family reunion is being planned as well. There are many details to take care of before the main event.

As the day approaches, Dana's mom enlists her sisters and her for some major housecleaning. Each girl is responsible for her room—cleaning out the closet, washing the windows, and giving the entire room a good dusting. The day before their company is to arrive, each girl is handed a list of tasks to be accomplished that day. Working orders in hand, the girls get down to business. By evening, everything on her mom's list has been checked off. The entire house is sparkling. As the family sits down for a dinner of pizza and soda pop, Dana waits expectantly. Surely there must be some kind of reward for all the work they just did. Dana has never worked so hard in her entire life. And she wonders how she can let her mom know it's time to pay up. What should Dana do?

Should she . . .

A. Hand her mom a bill for services rendered?

B. Make broad hints about a new bike that she has seen in the bike shop downtown?

C. Go on strike, refusing to do any more chores until she is paid properly for all the work she has done?

D. Realize that she has only done her part to help out the entire family?

E. Whenever she wants something, remind her mom of all the hard work she did for her grandparents' party?

 For help in knowing what Dana's attitude should be, read Luke 17:7-10.

18

The Competition

Gavin, the youngest of four brothers, has plenty of role models. He also has plenty of competition. All of his older brothers excel in sports. They all play baseball, basketball, and soccer. But for all three older brothers, their best sport by far is soccer. Since they were in grade school, each boy has made the traveling soccer team. The oldest brother's team won the state championship three years in a row. His older brother is now the star player on the varsity soccer team at the high school. The other two are making their names known on their respective teams.

Now it's Gavin's turn. Everyone in the family, at school, and especially on his soccer team expects Gavin to excel as well. Gavin has all the natural ability to play the game well—he's fast and is well coordinated. He certainly knows the skills because he has played with his brothers for years. But whenever Gavin gets out on the field, he freezes. It's as if he has never seen a soccer ball before. The coach is beginning to grumble at him. Even his brothers are making small jokes about it. Gavin doesn't believe he can compete with his brothers. He's not so sure he even wants to play soccer. What do you think he should do?

Should Gavin . . .
- A. Find another sport to play and do well?
- B. Practice even harder than his brothers so he can outdo them?
- C. Realize that all he needs to do is his best—and forget about his brothers?
- D. Quit sports and take up music?
- E. Tell everyone that his brothers really aren't that good?

 To know how Gavin should respond in this situation, read Colossians 3:17.

Family Devotions

Ever since Tina's mom and dad went to the family conference at church, things have been different around their home. Some of it, in Tina's opinion, has been for the good. For instance, her mom and dad are making a real effort not to yell as much. They have set some definite guidelines about bedtimes, homework, and having friends over that Tina can easily understand. But Tina is reserving her opinion about this family devotions thing. Now, every day after dinner, the entire family has to sit around the kitchen table and listen to her father read from the Bible. Then her mom asks them some questions about how the passage applies to them today. *That's dumb,* thinks Tina. *All that stuff happened ages ago.*

But the other night, the entire family got caught up in a discussion of a problem one of Tina's sister was having at school. To Tina's amazement, the Bible passage they read that night had something to say about how her sister should handle her problem. *Maybe there is something to this family devotion thing after all,* she thinks. How do you think Tina should respond to this new family devotion time?

Should she . . .
  A. Sneak comic books to the table to read?
  B. Interrupt the family discussion to talk about what happened on her favorite TV show?
  C. Pay attention to the Bible passage and see what she can learn from it?
  D. Tell her parents she has a ton of homework and doesn't have time for family devotions?
  E. Pretend to be very interested so that everyone will think she is super spiritual?

 Check out Matthew 7:24-27 to learn how a wise person would respond in this situation.

The Pool Party

About thirty members of Mason's church youth group are attending a youth conference in another state. The group is spending the night in a hotel by the conference center. Mason and three of his friends are rooming together, and they plan to have a good time! The hotel has a game room and a pool that the boys want to try out. During the first day of the conference, however, there's not much time for anything else other than attending the sessions and breaking for lunch and dinner. After dinner the entire group of about 250 kids gather for singing praise songs and watching some skits performed by a Christian comedy troupe.

By the time Mason and his friends get up to their room, it's 10:30 P.M. They have a 7:30 A.M. breakfast call before the final session, and then it's time to go home. All the kids have been told that they need to stay in their rooms and have lights out by 11:00 P.M. When Mason gets upstairs, he begins to get ready for bed. One of his friends sees him, and says, "What are ya doing? It's time to get crazy and party! Let's go down to the pool for a while and get rowdy." The pool does look inviting, and Mason did want to get some swimming in. It couldn't hurt to take a quick dip. There's already a party going on at the pool. Certainly no one will notice if Mason and his friends joined them. What do you think Mason should do?

Should he . . .
- A. Tell his friends that they should stay in the room as they have been told to do?
- B. Take the plunge and join the party at the pool?
- C. Stay in the room and throw ice cubes over the balcony instead?
- D. Invite some of the other groups into their room for a "lights-out party"—that way they would be following the instructions!?
- E. Pretend he's asleep and let his friends get into trouble?

 To know how Mason should respond in this situation, read Exodus 18:19-20.

The Church Choir Clown

Chet loves to goof around and make people laugh. At times, his natural quick wit is funny. At other times, especially during choir rehearsals, his comedic talent causes nothing but trouble. Chet seems to enjoy disrupting choir practice. He doesn't want to be in choir, but his mom makes him come. So Chet amuses himself the best way he knows how—by entertaining everyone else. Last week, Chet had the choir in stitches as he kept up a steady stream of snappy comments while the choir director was trying to teach them a song. Finally, the choir director stopped the rehearsal and told Chet to leave.

Chet's back this week, and this time, he has revenge on his mind. He has a bag full of pranks to pull on the choir director. He shows them off to a couple of his friends before practice begins. Several of them can't wait to see the choir director explode when Chet gets going. But one of his friends stops him: "Hey, why are you doing this to her? She's in charge and is trying to help us learn these songs. I think you ought to put those things away and shape up." Chet is momentarily lost for words. *It's not like this is school or anything,* he thinks. What do you think Chet should do?

Should he . . .
 A. Listen to his friend's advice and show the choir director some respect?
 B. Put a whoopee cushion on the choir director's chair for starters?
 C. Forget the tricks but find other ways to disrupt practice?
 D. Ignore his friend. He's just a spoilsport?
 E. Decide to play the pranks on this friend instead?

 Check out 1 Timothy 2:1-2 to see how Chet should respond.

The Bonus Offer

Sheldon's dad recently got him a small job working for his friend at the paint store. Once a week Sheldon goes to the shop and helps clean up the back room where the paint is mixed. He picks up any trash lying around, throws out the old paint sticks, and makes sure that all the paint can lids are on tightly and the cans put back on the shelves. It usually takes Sheldon about two hours to finish, and his dad's friend gives him five dollars for the afternoon. The money is enough for Sheldon to buy himself a couple of those scary spook stories that are popular right now.

Today Sheldon hears about a new double-bonus scary story set that just came out. Anyone who buys it at the local drugstore before Friday will get a free set of trading cards. Sheldon sure would love to get the bonus set. He has a little money left over from his job, and if he could make his five dollars for this week, he would have enough money. The only trouble is that Sheldon is not supposed to work until Saturday. Sheldon knows his dad's friend isn't there today. If Sheldon shows up, the guy in charge will never know that he's not scheduled to work today. What do you think Sheldon should do?

Should he . . .
   A. "Borrow" the money from his mom by slipping a few extra dollars from her purse and paying her back on Saturday?
   B. Go in and tell the guy in charge at the paint store that he was asked to come in for an extra time this week and hope the guy doesn't tell the boss?
   C. Wait until Saturday and the next bonus special?
   D. Ask the guy at the drugstore if he will accept a down payment on the bonus set?
   E. Ask his dad's friend for an advance on his salary?

 Read Proverbs 11:28 for help in knowing what Sheldon should do.

23

Love Your Enemies

Jenna can't believe that Peggy is in her class again this year. Last year, Peggy, a popular athlete, decided, for whatever reason, that Jenna would be her target. Peggy tried to turn all the other girls in the classroom against Jenna and continually made snide, cutting remarks about her. Fortunately, not all the girls thought Peggy was cool, so Jenna didn't have a completely miserable year. Still, she could have used a break from Peggy this school year. Maybe, just maybe, Peggy has forgotten about her, she hopes.

No such luck. The first day back, Peggy appears absolutely delighted to see her "favorite" target back in class. Jenna has tried to steer clear of Peggy. To make matters worse, however, Jenna's teacher has assigned them to the same science group for lab. Today, the group has its first lab. Peggy is absent because of a dentist appointment. Jenna doesn't give it much thought until the phone rings after school. Much to her absolute amazement, it's Peggy. She wants to know if she can get the lab notes from her. Jenna is dumbfounded. What should she do?

Should Jenna . . .

A. Scream, "Forget it!" into the phone and hang up?

B. Say yes and then give Peggy all the wrong notes so that she will flunk the lab?

C. Agree to give Peggy the notes if she will quit bothering her?

D. Tell Peggy it will cost her five dollars for the notes?

E. Not only give Peggy the notes but go over the lab work with her so that she will understand it?

 The biblical principle on how Jenna should respond can be found in Luke 6:27.

At Your Service

T racy loves children. She baby-sits her younger brother frequently, and she has even started to sit for the neighbors. Recently, Tracy completed the Red Cross babysitting class, and she is preparing fliers to hand out around the neighborhood. The pocket money is nice, but what Tracy truly enjoys is caring for the babies and toddlers. Children are just her thing. She is beginning to think about becoming a teacher someday, or perhaps opening a day-care center for working moms.

So when the director of Christian Education calls her home one night, Tracy isn't too surprised. There are lots of children, especially toddlers, at her church. And there just never seem to be enough helpers. From time to time, Tracy has worked in the nursery or the toddler room, but it means giving up her youth group or worship time. Now the Christian Education director is asking if Tracy will serve full-time in the nursery during the eight o'clock service. Tracy told her she would have to talk it over with her mom and dad.

It certainly would be a great opportunity. Tracy feels honored that the director would consider her. She knows she would be good with the children, but it would mean going to church at eight o'clock and staying until at least noon because her parents want her to go to worship and to her Sunday school class. Tracy is not sure what to do.

Should she . . .
    A. Thank the director for thinking of her but offer to work in the nursery just on special occasions?
    B. Tell the director she would be honored to serve in the children's ministry in this way?
    C. Go occasionally, when she can get up in time for the eight o'clock service?
    D. Recommend another one of her friends?
    E. Refuse because it's too early?

 For help in knowing how Tracy should handle this situation, read 1 Corinthians 15:58.

25

Follow the Leader

At the edge of town, there is an old abandoned house where no one has lived for at least fifteen years. The windows are boarded up; the grounds overgrown. No Trespassing signs are posted all over the property. It's an eyesore, but a legal battle is preventing the town from tearing it down. Trent and his friends go past the house every day on their way to the ballpark and usually think nothing about it. But a new boy has joined their group, and the house has caught his interest.

The new boy has boasted to the group that he has spent the night in the house. He claims that the house is haunted and that he has seen several ghosts there. Trent laughs and responds, "That house has been there for years. Everyone knows it isn't haunted!"

The new boy, angry, dares Trent to go into the house and see for himself. The other boys, sensing a challenge, back away. Trent is the acknowledged leader of the group, and he knows the other boys are watching to see what he will do. He doesn't want to appear to be a wimp, and there is no one around who would see him if he dashed in. What do you think Trent should do?

Should he . . .

A. Accept the challenge and dash in and out of the house?

B. Tell the new guy he has to get right home and then leave?

C. Let the new guy know he is not about to break the law on a silly dare?

D. Tell the new boy that he will go into the house only if he sees him go in first?

E. Take a vote and see how many of his friends want him to do it—and hope for a favorable outcome?

 Look up Philippians 2:12-13 to see how Trent can make the right decision.

His Brother's Keeper

Duane's younger brother absolutely idolizes him. He follows Duane around wherever he goes. When Duane has friends over, his brother wants to be included. He wants to do all the same things as Duane. He even wears his baseball cap at the same angle as Duane. Mom thinks it's cute that the little brother does this, but Duane has a different opinion. To him, his brother is just a major pest. Duane tries to avoid him unless it's absolutely necessary. And today it appears necessary.

Duane's mom and dad are going out for the day. They asked Duane if he would mind watching his younger brother. Of course, he would mind! He wanted to get together this afternoon with the guys to play football. "Oh, that's OK. You can still do that as long as you bring your brother along," Mom says on her way out. Duane is stuck. He has to spend the entire afternoon with his pest of a brother. This is not the way he wanted to spend Saturday afternoon. What do you think Duane should do?

Should he . . .

A. Lock his brother in his room and take off to meet his friends?

B. Take his brother along with him but not let him play?

C. Ditch his brother at another friend's house and pick him up after the game is over?

D. Take his brother along and include him, teaching him how to play football?

E. Stay home and ignore his brother for the entire afternoon?

 Read Psalm 133:1 for a quick lesson in how God says brothers should live.

27

Sweet Rewards

Vance's Sunday school teacher, Mrs. Solcumb, likes to reward her class with sweet treats. If they remember to bring their Bibles, they get a candy treat. If they behave in class, they get another candy treat. If they bring their assignment from the previous week, they can earn as many as five candy treats. Remembering a Bible verse earns another five treats. It has become a contest to see how many candy treats a person can collect during one Sunday school class. And to the boys' shame, the record is held—and continues to be held—by a girl.

Today, Vance and his buddy are early for Sunday school. As they walk into the classroom, their teacher greets them and asks if they can help her put away some supplies. Unpacking one of her bags, the boys come across a whole new stash of treats. She tells the boys to finish putting the supplies away while she runs to get more pencils for class. As soon as she leaves, Vance's buddy suggests they get a headstart on the candy count and help themselves to a few extra treats. Won't the girls be surprised when he and Vance have at least twenty candies apiece! What do you think Vance should do with this golden opportunity?

Should he . . .
  A. Tell his friend he doesn't think they should take the candies because that would be wrong?
  B. Take only a few so Mrs. Solcumb won't notice?
  C. Take the whole bag! Mrs. Solcumb might think she forgot to bring them this morning?
  D. Take the candies and sell them to their friends for a nickel apiece?
  E. Report his friend to the Sunday school superintendent?

 Read 1 Timothy 1:18-19 to know how Vance can make the right decision.

The New Kid on the Block

Cassandra and her family recently moved to a new town over the summer. Cassandra has met a few kids in the neighborhood, but most of them are younger than she is. As school approaches, Cassandra has mixed feelings. She is bored sitting around at home and wants to get back to school, but she is really anxious about walking into a new school. What will the kids be like? Will they like her? Will she make some new friends quickly?

The first day arrives, and Cassandra changes her outfit about four times before she decides what to wear. Since the school is close to her home, Cassandra walks to school. On her way, she notices the various groups of kids walking together, what they are wearing, and who is walking with whom. Suddenly the school looms in front of her. Part of Cassandra wants to turn around and run right home. But she takes a deep breath and walks inside. The other students are greeting each other after the long summer, laughing and joking. Cassandra wonders, *How will I ever get to know anybody here?* What should she do?

Should Cassandra . . .

A. Dress really wild and talk big so others will notice her?

B. Find out who the "cool" kids are and hang around only with them?

C. Try to be nice to others and just be herself?

D. Hold a big party after school one day and invite a lot of kids to show off her TV, video games, and pet snake?

E. Stand in the hallway and scream, "I'm heeeere!"?

 For help in knowing what Cassandra should do, read Philippians 2:3-4.

29

Brotherly Love?

Jim's dad has been out of town on business for the past several weeks. He has promised Jim and his brother, Dave, that he will spend Saturday with them and do a special activity of their choosing. Jim really wants to try out the latest video game at the arcade in the mall. He can't wait until the weekend.

Saturday comes, and when his dad asks what the boys want to do, Jim shouts, "Let's go to the mall!" But his brother quickly disagrees, "No, let's go to the basketball game." Jim stares in disbelief at his brother. How could he not want to play that new video game? Their father awaits the decision. What should Jim do?

Should he . . .

A. Present an airtight case for why they should go to the mall and play the game?

B. Whine and nag until his father says, "Forget the whole thing—we're staying home"?

C. Go to the basketball game but refuse to have fun and have a rotten attitude the entire day?

D. Suggest an activity that both he and Dave would like to do?

E. Flip a coin?

 For help in knowing what Jim should do, read 1 Corinthians 13:5.

The Competitor

Ike is one of the best athletes in the school. Off the field, he is one of the nicest guys—considerate, kind to others, with a great sense of humor. But when Ike takes the field—no matter what sport or level of competition—it's like he's a different person. Ike is an intense competitor. He wants to win, and he wants his teammates to want to win. Nothing frustrates Ike more than when he sees a teammate not trying his best. Ike expects the same level of concentration and determination from his teammates that he expects of himself.

Today in gym class, Ike's team is losing in a volleyball game, and he is getting more and more frustrated with one of his teammates. This particular boy doesn't appreciate Ike's level of intensity and, on a couple of volleys, deliberately lets the ball fall to the ground. Ike doesn't like to lose, even if this is only a game in gym class. He's getting close to the breaking point with this guy. What do you think Ike should do?

Should he . . .
    A. Control his temper and concentrate on doing his best?
    B. Spike the ball off this guy's head?
    C. Get his other teammates to gang up on this boy?
    D. Complain to the gym teacher that this boy is losing the game on purpose?
    E. Tell the gym teacher that he refuses to play on a team with this boy?

 To know the best course of action for Ike, read Proverbs 16:32.

A Good Steward

A couple of weeks ago, Ariel borrowed some CDs from her friend. She was interested in hearing some of the music from this new group before deciding whether to buy their CD or not. After listening to the music for a while, Ariel decided that the group wasn't for her. She set aside the CDs in her room and forgot about them. A few days later, her older brother asked if he could listen to the CDs before she returned them to her friend. Ariel didn't see any problem with that and agreed on the condition that he bring them right back. "No problem," assured her brother.

Today, her friend asked if Ariel was done with the CDs. Ariel promised to bring them back to school the next day and even made herself a note so that she wouldn't forget. When Ariel gets home, she scours her bedroom looking for the CDs. Then she remembers that her brother borrowed them. When she asks him, however, he claims that he already returned them to her room that same day. They must be in her room somewhere. Ariel has turned her room upside down looking for the missing CDs but can't find them anywhere. What is she going to tell her friend?

Should Ariel . . .

A. Tell her friend the CDs are missing and offer to replace them?

B. Avoid her friend for several weeks and hope she forgets about the CDs?

C. Blame her brother for misplacing the CDs?

D. Go out and buy two new CDs and don't tell her friend what happened?

E. Tell her friend that she forgot to bring the CDs and keep stalling until, hopefully, she can find them?

 To find out what Jesus has to say about being responsible with worldly wealth, read Luke 16:11-12.

1

The New Job

After her divorce, Lana's mom went back to work full-time as a teacher. Her mom gets home soon after Lana and her brother arrive from school, so afternoons are pretty much the same routine. But mornings are horrible. Mom is nearly frantic trying to get herself ready for work and Lana and her brother ready for school. Lana is finding herself having to make her own lunch, help her brother get his backpack together, and make sure she has everything. Frankly, Lana does not like this new arrangement at all.

There are other inconveniences as well. The laundry gets washed and dried, but often doesn't get folded and put away. Lana constantly finds her T-shirts for school still in the laundry basket. If she wants something ironed, she has to do that herself. Mom told Lana that she doesn't have time in the morning to iron for her. And the other day, Lana had to go back to school with her gym clothes unwashed because her mom forgot to take them out of the bag and wash them. Lana knows her mom is having a hard time adjusting to the new schedule as well, but this is not working out. Lana thinks it's time to have a talk with her mom. What do you think Lana should do?

Should she . . .
A. Demand that her mom quit her job and go back to being a mom?
B. Give her mom a detailed list of things that have to be done to help her keep track?
C. Ask her mom how she and her brother can pitch in and help out?
D. Surprise her mom and fold the laundry once?
E. Suggest that now that her mom is working they should get a maid to do all these things?

 Take a look at Hebrews 10:24 to see what Lana might do to help her mom.

2

Stick of Gum

Andrew finishes his lunch and pulls out a pack of his extra-special, absolutely most favorite gum. There are two pieces left, one for now and one for after school. Andrew takes out one stick and puts the other back in his pocket. As he looks up, Andrew sees that his friend has been watching him. What should Andrew do?

Should he . . .
A. Pretend there is nothing in his mouth?
B. Pretend that the stick of gum in his mouth is his last and offer to split it with his friend?
C. Offer his friend the last stick of gum?
D. Act like his friend is invisible and say, "See you later"?
E. Promise his friend a piece of gum the next time he gets a new pack?

 For help in knowing what Andrew should do, read 2 Corinthians 9:6.

3

The Missing Bike

Joel finishes his last math problem for homework and slams the book shut. Finally he can join his friends for a couple of innings of baseball. They told Joel to meet them at the ball field near the school. Joel figures that if he rides his bike really fast, he will only miss the first two innings. Joel runs into the garage to grab his bike and get going . . . only to discover that his bike is missing! Joel knows that he put his bike away last night. He's sure of it. But a thorough search of the garage yields no bike. He looks frantically outside, but his bike is not there. Someone must have stolen it!

Joel is about to inform his mom about the bad news when he spots some kid on a bike down the street that looks suspiciously like his. He looks closer, and sure enough, it's his brother riding his bike! He should have known. Joel has probably missed half of the game already. He stands in the driveway, arms folded, ready to unload on his brother. What he doesn't know is that his brother's bike is broken. Joel's mom asked his brother to quickly run some groceries down to a neighbor who is housebound with sick children. She told him to use Joel's bike—since Joel was busy doing homework—and to come back right away. Joel's brother can tell as he approaches the driveway that Joel is angry.

Joel knows his brother is trying to tell him something as he approaches. He's waving his arms and shouting something. But Joel is hopping mad, and rightfully so, he believes. What do you think Joel should do?

Should he . . .
  A. Listen to his brother's explanation and then yell at his mom for allowing his brother to ride his bike?
  B. Let his brother have it without giving him a chance to explain?
  C. Tell his brother that he should have walked to deliver the groceries?
  D. Tell his brother, "What do I care about some stupid neighbor—I'm missing my game"?
  E. After listening to his brother, ask him to let him know *before* the next time he borrows his bike?

 For help in knowing how Joel should handle this situation, read James 1:19-20.

4

The Friend

Jerome is a good kid. He is nice looking, polite, athletic, and a good student, and he has a great personality. But Jerome isn't very popular. That's because he just moved to the area last spring, so he doesn't know too many people. During the summer, however, Jerome met Jason, a boy in the same grade who lives a few blocks away. He and Jason became pretty good friends. They spent sunny afternoons shooting baskets in the park and rainy days surfing the Internet.

But now the boys are back in school. Jerome still doesn't have many friends besides Jason. He certainly would like to be popular, especially with the athletes and cheerleaders.

Earlier today, Ted, the football quarterback, and Justine, a cheerleader, were very friendly to Jerome in English class. That made him feel really good about himself. Then, after practice, they called him over to their circle of friends as he began to walk home. Right now, Jerome stands with that circle of popular kids on the field near the locker room. They're talking and laughing, and he loves it. Then one of the kids sees Jason leaving school by another door, and he makes a joke about the "computer geek." Some of the others laugh and make cutting comments about him. Jerome wants to be accepted by this group, but Jason is his friend.

Should he . . .

A. Keep quiet and hope that someone changes the subject?

B. Abruptly change the subject himself by cutting down another kid leaving the building?

C. Agree with everyone and tell a very funny story about Jason and his computer?

D. Fall on the ground and pretend to have a seizure, complete with foaming at the mouth, and then jump up and say, "Just kidding"?

E. Come to Jason's defense by telling everyone what a great guy he is?

 For help in knowing how Jerome should react, look at what God says in Proverbs 17:17 and 1 Corinthians 13:7.

5

Forgive and Forget

For many years Lydia has been close friends with Carmen. Ever since Lydia began attending church and going to a neighborhood Bible study, however, Carmen has dropped her like a bad habit. Not only did Carmen sever their friendship, but she also made fun of Lydia's faith whenever she could. The worst thing Carmen did was to spread totally false and hateful rumors about Lydia being caught drinking at the school dance. Lydia was deeply hurt by her friend's actions. Whenever she thinks about those awful days trying to defend herself against the false accusations, she still wells up with anger.

At lunch today, another one of her friends greets her with some startling news: "Guess what? Carmen became a Christian at a church camp this summer." Lydia doesn't believe it. *After all the ribbing and hard time Carmen gave me, there is no way she is a Christian,* Lydia thinks. That night, however, Lydia receives a phone call from Carmen. She tells Lydia that she is terribly sorry for the hurt and suffering she caused her. She wants to become friends again. Will Lydia forgive her? Lydia still can't forget how her former friend treated her. Now Carmen wants Lydia to forgive her? What do you think Lydia should do?

Should she . . .
A. Demand a written apology from Carmen?
B. Tell Carmen it's too late; she can never be friends with her again?
C. Tell Carmen she'll forgive her if she promises never to do anything like that again?
D. Demand that Carmen print a retraction in the school newspaper of all the unfounded rumors she started about her?
E. Forgive Carmen and pray that the Lord will help her forget it?

 Consider Jesus' words on forgiveness in Matthew 6:14-15 to know how Lydia should respond.

6

The Teacher's Kid

Gus's mom teaches English at his school. It's not so bad, for the most part, having his mom at the same school. When he forgets his lunch money, all he has to do is run down to his mom's room and get it. If he wants to go home with a friend after school, he can quickly ask his mom. And if he has a load of books to carry home, he can get a ride home from school. But there are also disadvantages. All the other teachers, especially in English, expect Gus to be a star pupil. He doesn't get away with much, and when he does goof up, his mom knows immediately.

This year Gus's English teacher seems to enjoy giving him a hard time. Every time there is a difficult question, Mr. Blackwell says, "Well, let's ask the expert. Gus, what do you have to say about that?" If Gus doesn't know the answer, he hears about it from Mr. Blackwell. Gus also is certain that he is graded harder than the other kids. Gus is a decent writer, but he received the only D in the class on a recent paper. Sometimes Gus doesn't know how he is going to get through the year. He's tired of Mr. Blackwell picking on him. What do you think Gus should do?

Should he . . .

    A. Patiently endure the class with Mr. Blackwell and do nothing?

    B. Tell his mom to get Mr. Blackwell off his case?

    C. Ask for a transfer to his mom's class? After all, what mother would give her own son a bad grade?

    D. Start acting up in class to give Mr. Blackwell something to talk about?

    E. Write mean things about Mr. Blackwell on the school walls?

 Take a look at Proverbs 25:15 and Ecclesaistes 10:4 for insight into how Gus should handle the situation.

Vote for Me!

Today at school, June's class is voting for class president. There are three different students running for president, including June's friend Cleo. Each of the students has devoted a lot of time and energy to the campaign. All of the students are eager to vote and see who the winner is. Except June, that is. During the campaign, June has carefully listened to each candidate speak about their ideas and how they plan to organize class activities. Although Cleo has some good points, June finds that she agrees more with one of the other candidates. But as Cleo's friend, she is expected to vote for her.

Reluctantly, June accepts her ballot and thinks long and hard about her vote. She knows Cleo is watching and is probably wondering what is taking her so long. Finally, June knows she has to vote for the most qualified person—and that is not her friend. Quickly she fills out her ballot and drops it in the box. Later that day, her friend finally catches up with her. "Hey, what took you so long to fill out your ballot? What did you do, vote for someone else?" Cleo jokes. When June doesn't say anything, Cleo takes a hard look at her. "Well, who did you vote for?" she demands. June doesn't know what to say.

Should she . . .
    A. Tell Cleo she has to get to class and run off?
    B. Say, "Come on. Who do you think I voted for?" and leave it at that?
    C. Lie and say she voted for Cleo?
    D. Say, "Mickey Mouse!"?
    E. Tell Cleo she voted for another candidate whose ideas she admired?

 Read Psalm 51:6 and Proverbs 23:23 for help in knowing what June should do.

Braggin' Rights

Since making the football team, Darnell has been hanging out with the guys from the team. It's not that he doesn't want to be with his old friends, but he enjoys talking about the games and the practices with all the guys. They're good guys, clean cut, and OK students, and they all live and breathe football. The older guys on the team in particular have been really nice to Darnell, helping him through the summer camp and the practices.

Today after practice, a group of guys decide to grab some burgers at the fast-food joint near the school. They ask Darnell to go, and he readily agrees. As they wash down their food with some soda pop, one of the guys begins bragging about how well he played last year. He won some awards and set some team records that he doesn't think can be beat. Soon the conversation develops into a "can you top this" session, and each guy can hardly wait for the other to finish before he can proclaim his accomplishment. Darnell knows he's a pretty good player for his first year, and he has many accomplishments in school and other areas. But he doesn't like the idea of bragging. What do you think Darnell should do?

Should he . . .

A. Come up with the most outlandish accomplishment that no one can top?

B. Keep quiet, knowing his best "accomplishment" is trusting the Lord?

C. Toss in a few of his accomplishments so he's not really bragging too much?

D. Play down his achievements as if they were nothing?

E. Go find his old friends—at least they like him for who he is, not for what he has done?

 To find out how Darnell should respond, read 1 Corinthians 1:31.

Passing Notes

Elly was totally bored in geography class today. It was thirty minutes until lunch, and she was tired of hearing about longitude and latitude. What she had was a bad attitude. To pass the time, Elly decided to write a note to her best friend three seats ahead of her and tell her about the snobby new girl in her class. She wrote with relish about how this girl snubbed one of their good friends. She threw in a few nasty comments about the girl's appearance for good measure. Folding the note, Elly tapped the boy in front of her and asked him to pass it on.

The note made it to the second person when Miss Herold snatched it. To Elly's horror, she read the note aloud. The new girl turned crimson red. Elly wanted to disappear under her chair. Then the most unbelievable thing happened. Miss Herold assumed that the girl holding the note had written it, and she gave her an after-school detention. Elly had escaped! When the class is over, Elly rushes to meet her friends. They discuss the mean girl who wrote that nasty note. "What a cruel thing to do! Who would want to be her friend," says one. Elly feels awful. Should she tell them that she was the one who wrote the note? What do you think she should do?

Should Elly . . .
  A. Thank her lucky stars that she was not given an after-school detention?
  B. Admit to her friends, and to Miss Herold, that she wrote the note?
  C. Agree loudly with her friends that the girl who wrote this note is a real creep?
  D. Say she didn't think the note was that nasty—after all, the new girl *is* a snob?
  E. Say nothing but vow to herself to never write another note in class again?

 Check out Proverbs 21:3 and Micah 6:8 to see what Elly should do in this situation.

Finding Time for God

Lorraine is one busy girl. On Monday and Wednesday mornings, she leaves the house at six-thirty to attend honor band rehearsal. On Tuesdays and Thursdays, she has a school newspaper meeting before school. After school, she has cross-country practice five days a week. Once a week she has swim practice after dinner, and she's in the jazz band. Of course, there's also the matter of homework, saxophone practice, and sleep—if her schedule allows for that!

Lorraine also manages to volunteer at the local hospital twice a month. She likes to work in the church nursery at least once a month. Sometimes, she will even go over and help during special events. She sings in the church choir and attends youth group on Sunday evenings. There's not a spare minute in her schedule. No one is going to find Lorraine sitting around doing nothing.

Lately, however, Lorraine has this nagging feeling that something is missing. Her best friend is going through a difficult time at home with her parents. She asked Lorraine to pray for her because she knows Lorraine is a Christian. But, quite frankly, Lorraine hasn't had time to meet with God. She wants to be a good witness to her friend, but there's no time between the track meet and band rehearsal. Lorraine feels guilty, but what can she do? She enjoys all of her activities—and they are all worthwhile. What do you think Lorraine should do?

Should she . . .
   A. Give up some of the activities on her schedule so she can spend time with God and her friends?
   B. Get up at three in the morning to have some quality time with God?
   C. Pencil God in three weeks from now—when cross country ends and before volleyball begins?
   D. Pray about her schedule and ask God's guidance for those activities she should be involved in—that is, if she can find time to pray?
   E. Wait until things calm down (whenever that might be)—then she can spend more time in prayer and Bible reading?

 Read Daniel 6:10-23 to find out what Daniel risked to spend time with God and to help determine what Lorraine should do.

11

Going the Distance

Simon and Evan have decided to join the cross-country team this fall. Evan really wants to do it and has been doing some training over the summer. Simon is not so sure about it, but he thinks it would be good exercise and a good excuse for putting off his homework. Besides, the cross-country team gets some cool uniforms, and everyone makes the team.

After a week of practice Evan is feeling really good about his effort. He has been making some good times and can keep up with the fastest group of boys. He really is enjoying himself. It's a different story for Simon. He's really struggling. Simon walks a good bit of that first week, and his legs hurt. Still, he decides to stick it out.

Today is the first cross-country meet. Simon and Evan line up with the rest of their age group. The race is on! Evan gets a quick start. He's right behind three of the fastest boys as he makes the first loop around the course. Simon, well, he's hanging toward the back of the pack. Evan completes the second loop and heads toward the finishing gate. With a last-minute surge, he is able to finish third. Evan grabs a cup of water and watches for Simon.

Several groups of boys come in, but no Simon. Suddenly, Evan spots Simon. He is dead last and is part running, part walking. A couple of the boys are snickering as Simon makes the final bend and heads toward the finishing gate. What do you think Evan should do?

Should he . . .

   A. Yell as loud as he can to cheer Simon on and be the first to congratulate him on finishing the race?

   B. Walk away and pretend he doesn't know that Simon is last?

   C. Make fun of the other boys because they finished behind him too?

   D. Run up to Simon and let him know how well he (Evan) did?

   E. Join the boys and make fun of Simon too?

 Read 1 Thessalonians 5:11 for help in knowing how Evan should respond.

12

Four-Eyes!

Maggie has been having trouble seeing the blackboard in school. Finally, after missing a few math problems because she couldn't see them correctly, Maggie's teacher asked if she was having trouble with her eyesight. When Maggie admitted she was, the teacher wrote her mom a note. The next thing Maggie knew she was at the eye doctor being fitted for a pair of glasses. It wouldn't have been so bad except her mom insisted that Maggie get a practical pair of glasses—brown, sturdy frames that make Maggie look like the biggest nerd on the planet.

Maggie looks at herself in the mirror. No way is she ever going to walk into school again. Just wait until the kids see her with her new glasses! She will never hear the end of it! *No way,* thinks Maggie, close to tears. If only she could have talked her mom into a pair of cool frames. But the kids in her class—especially the boys—will take one look at these glasses . . . Maggie's life is over. What do you think she should do?

Should Maggie . . .

A. Make fun of the other kids before they make fun of her?

B. Tell her mom she "accidentally" broke her glasses in gym?

C. Don't wear her glasses, continue to squint at the board, and hope she gets everything right?

D. Stay in her room and refuse to go to school until her mom allows her to buy a new pair of glasses?

E. Realize that the glasses will help her see and that they won't change the person God created her to be?

Read 1 Samuel 16:1-13 to see what is most important to God—a person's appearance or heart. Decide what the key verse is for Maggie to know.

A Bad Attitude

Haley's Girl Scout troop is helping to host Mystery Night at camp for all the younger girls. Each troop is assigned a station, where the younger girls will do a variety of activities. As each group of girls goes through the various stations, they will attempt to resolve the "mystery." At the end of the night, everyone will gather for hot chocolate and roasted marshmallows.

For Haley, this will be the fifth time she has participated in a Mystery Night, and quite frankly, she's bored. She would rather be going to the movies with her other friends than spend the night freezing outside, helping a bunch of dumb Brownies. Her attitude doesn't improve when she discovers that her group is in charge of the night walk. At this station, the girls have to walk down a path without flashlights and see if they can spot the fake animals hidden along the trail. *This is so hokey,* Haley thinks, as she hangs a bat upside down in a nearby tree.

As the first group of Brownies comes along, they are not very eager to walk along this path without any flashlights. One girl in particular is quite scared and looks as though she is about to cry. It's Haley's turn to walk with these girls down the path. What do you think she should do?

Should Haley . . .
  A. Start making creepy noises to really scare the younger girls?
  B. Take the one girl aside and reassure her that there is nothing to fear and that she will be walking right beside her?
  C. Tell the younger girl to grow up—after all, she is a Girl Scout?
  D. Make fun of the girls and call them "fraidy cats"?
  E. Grudgingly help the girls but complain about how silly they are to be scared of some dumb, fake animals?

 For help in knowing what Haley should do, read Galatians 6:3.

14

The New Teacher

Ever since school began, Kirk and his friends have been talking about the new P.E. teacher. Mr. Hamilton is as strict as they come. Even though they have been in school for less than a month, Mr. Hamilton has made his presence known. Already Kirk has had to run five extra laps for dogging it during gym class. Another one of his friends received a detention for not washing his gym clothes over the weekend. And today, Kirk had to stay after class and get chewed out because he had forgotten his gym shoes.

Kirk is still grumbling when he sits down to lunch with his friends. Immediately the topic switches to Mr. Hamilton. Each boy has his own horror story to contribute. In the retelling, of course, the stories seem to get a bit more exaggerated than before. Now the boys all want to know what happened to Kirk. Kirk knows that he deserved what he got because it was careless of him to forget his shoes, and Mr. Hamilton really didn't yell all that much. Mr. Hamilton actually smiled at Kirk when he left his office. But Kirk doesn't want to disappoint his friends. How should he answer them?

Should Kirk . . .
A. Tell his friends that Mr. Hamilton is making him wash the locker room floor after school?
B. Tell his friends that Mr. Hamilton yelled at him so loud that the glass clock on the wall broke?
C. Shrug and say nothing?
D. Tell his friends that it was so bad he would rather not talk about it?
E. Tell his friends the truth and let them know that Mr. Hamilton is not so bad?

 For help in knowing what Kirk should do, read Colossians 3:8-9.

The Newspaper Staff

This is Lucy's first effort at putting out the school newspaper. At the end of last year, the faculty advisor asked Lucy if she would like to be editor. Lucy, who has dreams of becoming a journalist, was ecstatic. "You bet I would," she told the advisor. Now it's time to get the first paper out. Several weeks ago, the newspaper staff met to discuss the first issue, and Lucy handed out the assignments. Today the group is to turn in their articles. Lucy is a bit worried because this year's staff includes a number of younger students. She hopes they can write well.

Staff members straggle in and toss their articles into the bin. Lucy takes a look at the first couple of stories. *Oh, no! This is terrible!* she thinks. It seems as though none of the new staff members have done anything right. They didn't follow the right format. They didn't even do the story assigned to them and just wrote whatever came into their head. Lucy is steaming. Now what is she going to do? How will she ever get the newspaper out? How should Lucy react?

Should she . . .
   A. Scream at the new staff members and fire them?
   B. Write all the articles herself and turn the newspaper into a one-student production?
   C. Tell the advisor what a terrible staff she has and resign?
   D. Work patiently with the new members of the staff, instructing them on the right way to turn in articles—delaying publication of the first issue if necessary?
   E. Recruit some of her friends, who are good writers, to replace the younger students and tell the younger students to come back next year—when she will be gone?

 Check out 2 Timothy 4:2 to know how Lucy should respond.

16

The Matchmaker

Deanna's best friend is a born matchmaker—or at least she thinks she is. Before every school dance, her friend is burning the phone lines, trying to fix up all her friends with boys. She even has girls from other classes ask her to find them boys they can "go with" for a day or two. Deanna's friend is only too happy to help. So far, Deanna has been able to escape her friend's notice. But with the first dance coming up this weekend, Deanna may not be so fortunate.

Sure enough, the day before the dance, Deanna's friend grabs her before lunch and points to a tall boy standing in the lunch line. "See that guy! He's perfect for you. He's tall enough, and he wears nice clothes. How about him?" she says excitedly. Deanna protests, "But I don't even know that guy. How can I go with someone whose name I don't even know?" That doesn't stop her friend. By the next day, she has all the information, and she urges Deanna to make this perfect match. "You don't want to go to the first dance without a boyfriend, do you? Everyone will have someone to dance with except you," she warns. Her friend is pretty convincing. What do you think Deanna should do?

Should she . . .
- A. Tell her friend that she already has a date and show up with her brother?
- B. Take up her friend's offer—and then dump this guy at the dance?
- C. Tell her friend to buzz off—she's not interested in the perfect match!?
- D. Explain she doesn't need a "date" to enjoy herself at the dance?
- E. Get mad at her friend and refuse to speak to her until she forgets this whole silly mess?

 For a look at God's guidelines for relationships, read Romans 12:10 and 1 Corinthians 16:13-14.

17

The Older Sister

Libby's older sister, Natalie, is perfect. Or so it seems to Libby. Natalie does everything effortlessly. She is a talented musician and plays in the school's honor band and jazz band. She is a natural athlete and participates in volleyball, soccer, and softball during the school year. Those aren't even her best sports, however. Natalie is an outstanding swimmer. She holds the records for the swim club in three different events. Everybody likes Natalie. She is pretty, smart, and outgoing. In short, Natalie is a tough act to follow.

Libby is, basically, everything that Natalie is not. She is quiet and enjoys being by herself, reading, or writing in her journal. Libby doesn't really enjoy sports; she's not terribly coordinated. She goes out for the swim team every summer and does OK. But she doesn't even come close to Natalie. Mom and Dad are encouraging Libby to join the band and play an instrument like Natalie. Libby likes music, but she would rather listen to it than play. Instead of band, she would rather join the Literary Club or the newspaper staff. What do you think Libby should do?

Should she . . .
- A. Do everything exactly like Natalie?
- B. Strive to do those things that she enjoys and is good at?
- C. Agree to play an instrument to please her parents?
- D. Start telling stories about how mean Natalie is at home so that people won't like her as much?
- E. Keep trying to compete with Natalie until she finally beats her at something?

 To know how Libby should respond, check out Galatians 6:4.

The Recycling Rap

Maggie is the new president of her school's Ecology Club. Each year the club sponsors events during Earth Day and conducts a littering awareness campaign. This year Maggie has big plans. Concerned about the paper wasted each school day in the classrooms, she wants to start a school-wide recycling program. She plans to propose it to the club at its first meeting.

When Maggie unveils her idea, she is surprised by the club members' reactions. A few students think it is a good idea, but most think it will involve too much work. They don't want to be responsible for collecting paper all the time. Even her advisor is lukewarm, suggesting that Maggie discuss the idea with the principal.

After talking with the principal for more than an hour, Maggie was dejected. The principal was not very supportive either and asked about many details that Maggie hadn't even considered. Where will she get bins to collect the paper? What kinds of paper will be accepted? Who will collect the paper and how often? Who will take the paper away? How much money will this cost? The list of questions goes on and on. Maggie doesn't know what to do first. She begins to think that maybe this wasn't such a hot idea after all. Maggie is tempted to dump the whole project. What do you think she should do?

Should Maggie . . .

A. Enlist the support of those members who back the idea, research answers to the questions posed by the principal, and formulate a master plan?

B. Tell club members that the principal posed too many objections to the project and to forget about recycling?

C. Quit the club in disgust—obviously they don't really care about ecology?

D. Suggest to the club that they do the project next year, after she has graduated?

E. Dump the project—it's too hard to get anything done at this school?

 Read Nehemiah 4 to find out how Nehemiah handled opposition to his plans to rebuild the wall.

19

Earning Trust

For the past four years, George has gone to a baby-sitter's house after school until his mom gets off work. He hasn't minded it up until now, but recently George thinks he has outgrown the baby-sitter. He wants to come home by himself, let himself in the house, get his own snack, and start his homework. Before school starts, George outlines his plan to his mom and dad. He promises that he will come home immediately after school, call his mom first thing, have a snack, and get started on his homework. Any changes in plans he will clear with his parents ahead of time.

They agree to a trial period of a month and will then evaluate how things are going. George is hopeful that if he can prove himself, his parents might allow him to fly out to visit his best friend who recently moved to another state. Things go well for the first two weeks. George gets home right after school. He calls his mom, fixes a snack, and then digs into his homework. By the third week, he is fully comfortable with the routine.

Today, after school, his friend asks George to stop by and check out his new twenty-speed bike. The friend says that George can even take the bike for a spin. George has been considering buying a bike like this. *What would it hurt to stop in a few minutes?* he thinks. He figures that he could take a quick ride and then run home and still get everything done. His mom would never know that he didn't go right home. What do you think George should do?

Should he . . .

A. Call his mom from his friend's house and act as if he's at home?

B. Stop just for a quick look—a few minutes isn't a big deal?

C. Take the bike for a spin? If his mom asks why he didn't call sooner, he can tell her he forgot.

D. Ask if he can come by tomorrow after he has cleared it with his mom?

E. Spend the afternoon at his friend's house and then rush home right before his mom is expected to arrive?

 For the biblical principle underlying how George should respond, read Luke 16:10.

20

Making a Quick Profit

Jeremy is always thinking about the fastest, easiest way to pick up some extra cash. Now he has an idea that can't fail. He can hardly wait to tell his friends his latest scheme. Jeremy was in the city over the weekend, visiting his aunt and uncle. While they were at the zoo, he came across some guys on the street selling "designer" sunglasses. Jeremy knew, of course, that these sunglasses were knockoffs, but they had the designer labels on them. Some kids in school would be fooled. The guys on the street were selling the sunglasses for five dollars a pair when the real things cost about thirty-five in the stores.

Jeremy uses all his spending money to buy ten pairs of the phony sunglasses. Now, he wants his friend to sell the sunglasses to kids at school for twenty dollars each. His friend will get to keep five dollars, and Jeremy will get fifteen from each sale. (Hey, he made the initial investment, and it was his idea!) What do you think his friend should do about Jeremy's latest scheme?

Should he . . .

A. Report Jeremy to the Better Business Bureau?

B. Tell Jeremy that he should be honest when selling them and tell his customers that the sunglasses are knockoffs?

C. Suggest that Jeremy raise the price so that the profits are bigger for both of them?

D. Sell all the sunglasses and get Jeremy to look around for other "products" to market?

E. Tell Jeremy that he's not interested in sunglasses, but he does have a nice designer watch that Jeremy might want to buy?

 Read Proverbs 19:1 to see what God thinks of Jeremy's "get rich quick" scheme.

The Handicapped Student

This fall a new student with Down's Syndrome has joined Monica's class. She is smaller than most of her classmates, looks and speaks differently than everyone, and is slower intellectually than the other students. Before this new girl joined the class, Monica's teacher had informed the class of the girl's disabilities to help them understand her better and also to discuss ways that they could help her adjust to being in their classroom. Monica is curious about the new girl but also wants to do what she can to welcome the girl into the classroom.

During the first few weeks of school, Monica has invited the girl to eat lunch with her and her friends. She has also included the girl in their activities during recess. Monica has discovered that this girl is friendly and funny and enjoys being with the other kids. Unfortunately, not all the students in her class feel the same way about the new girl as she does. Today at lunch Monica overhears some of the other kids talking about "that retard" and making fun of the way the girl talks. Monica turns red with anger. What do you think she should do?

Should Monica . . .
A. Ignore those kids?

B. Tell the lunchroom aide that the kids are being mean?

C. Yell at the kids and tell them that they are the retards?

D. Find ways for these kids to get to know the new girl and see what she is like for themselves?

E. Pray that something terrible will happen to those kids so they will know what it's like to be different?

 Read Matthew 20:29-34 to know how Jesus treated people with disabilities.

22

The Right Friends?

Bethany and her family recently moved to a new town in mid-June, shortly after school got out. She spent a long, miserable summer without meeting a single friend. All the kids in her new neighborhood are either older or way younger than herself. She tried to get on the neighborhood swim team, but the season was half over by the time they moved in. She thought she would meet some new kids in school, but the first couple of weeks were awful. No one even seemed to notice she was there.

Lately, however, Bethany has become friends with a few kids who hang out at the school playground. They have been really friendly to Bethany. She feels good to finally know someone who actually greets her by name and seems happy to see her. The only problem is that the kids are a little rough. They swear sometimes and wear T-shirts with crude slogans on them. None of them attend church, and sometimes they even make fun of church. Still, these are the only kids who seem to know that Bethany even exists. Are these friends OK? What do you think Bethany should do?

Should she . . .
- A. Get herself a crude T-shirt and join the gang?
- B. Hang out with these kids but let them know she doesn't approve of them?
- C. Be nice to these kids but look for some new friends whose values are closer to hers?
- D. Give up on meeting any friends, anywhere, and stay in her room?
- E. Try to convert her newfound friends by bringing her Bible to the playground and preaching to them?

 To know how Bethany should respond, read Psalm 1:1.

Class Elections

As editor of the school newspaper, Brandon will decide whom the paper endorses for class president. It's an awesome responsibility, and Brandon is not taking it lightly. He plans to interview the two candidates and then make his decision based on their qualifications and views. Or so he thinks. The first candidate he interviews is Chelsea. She's a bright, serious girl who has already served in student government for two years. Chelsea is not particularly pretty, and, consequently, she is not very popular. But as Brandon interviews her, he appreciates her thoughtfulness and her views.

Josh comes next. Josh has everything going for him. He is good-looking and athletic, and he comes from a wealthy family. Josh is known for the great parties he throws for every organization he belongs to. He's one of the most popular kids at school. The only things he lacks are experience in student government—he never had an interest in serving before—and any good ideas for why he wants to be class president.

Brandon faces a real dilemma. The popular choice would be to endorse Josh and leave it at that. He's the favorite in the race and most likely will win. But Brandon is bothered by Josh's lack of ideas. Chelsea really has some good ideas, but endorsing her would be an unpopular stand to take. The endorsement is due tomorrow. What do you think Brandon should do?

Should he . . .
A. Go with the flow and endorse Josh—it could be worth a few party invitations?
B. Endorse Chelsea because she is the most qualified candidate and has the best ideas?
C. Decide the newspaper will not endorse any candidate this year?
D. Begin a write-in campaign for himself?
E. Flip a coin to decide who will get the endorsement?

 Read James 2:1-4 for the biblical principle that should guide Brandon's decision.

The Litterbugs

Football practice ended early, and some of the boys' parents won't pick them up for another half hour. Shane and his friends decide to grab some burgers and pops at a nearby fast-food joint. It is a warm fall afternoon, one of those glorious Indian summer days, so the boys decide to take their food outside to the park. They goof around for a while at the park until it is time to go back to school. Because Shane is walking home, he stays at the park for a few more minutes.

When Shane gets ready to leave, he notices that none of the boys—including himself—have thrown away their trash. There are papers, crushed cups and bags littering the ground. Shane looks around for a garbage can. The nearest one is clear across the park in the opposite direction of Shane's walk home. He doesn't feel like hauling trash across the park. Besides it's getting late, and his mom will wonder where he is. What do you think Shane should do?

Should he . . .
A. Shove all the litter in a tree and hope that the squirrels eat it?

B. Leave the litter and get home before his mom gets mad?

C. Pick up his own trash and yell at his friends the next day for not throwing away theirs?

D. Scatter the litter around as he walks home so it doesn't look as bad?

E. Carry the litter to the garbage can and then go home. His mom will understand if he's a little late?

 Read Genesis 1:27-30 to see who God put in charge of caring for the environment.

25

The Guilt Trip

Several months ago, Catherine had taken an unclaimed beach towel from the pool. It was a really nice towel—oversized, plush, and practically new. It had been lying there for several days without anyone claiming it. No one had seen Catherine take it, and Catherine never told anyone that she had taken it. Catherine never heard anyone talk about losing a towel when the pool season ended.

But now Catherine is feeling guilty about taking the towel. She knows she should have turned it in to the lost and found or put up a note on the pool bulletin board about finding it. She did neither. Catherine knows she was wrong. She keeps thinking about it and doesn't know what to do.

Should Catherine . . .
- A. Try not to think about it?
- B. Keep smiling and act as though nothing were wrong?
- C. Take out her guilty feelings on everyone else, getting mad over every little thing?
- D. Confess her sin to God and accept his forgiveness?
- E. Vow to buy an even nicer towel and "leave" it at the pool for someone to find next swim season?

 For help in knowing what Catherine should do, read 1 John 1:9.

Great Performances

Barbara was recently chosen for the lead female role in the school musical. She is thrilled. This will be the first time she has performed in a big production. Barb wants to do a great job, so she is taking extra singing lessons to help her prepare for the part. Rehearsals are after school until five o'clock, so Barbara has scheduled her lessons with the music teacher before school. She barely has time for her homework after dinner because she usually has another activity in the evening. Some nights she stays up until midnight to get her homework done.

Barb's mom is beginning to get worried about her. Barbara is not getting enough sleep, and it's starting to show. Some mornings she can barely get out of bed; when she does, watch out! She's a real grouch. Mom is afraid that if Barb doesn't get her rest, she'll end up sick by the time of the show. Mom suggests that Barbara drop one or two of her night activities and take extra singing lessons on Saturday afternoons so she can get more rest. Barb doesn't want to mess up her part, though. She thinks she can keep up the grueling pace until the show is over. What do you think Barbara should do?

Should she . . .
- A. Increase her extra singing lessons as she gets closer to the performance?
- B. Drop one or two of her night activities but keep the before-school lessons?
- C. Sit down and work out a reasonable schedule with her mom so that she does get her proper rest?
- D. Ignore her mom? Who needs sleep anyway?
- E. Load up on vitamins and plenty of OJ?

 For some interesting insights on what Barbara should do read Genesis 2:2-3, Psalm 127:2, and Mark 6:30-31.

Loyal Friends

Lois and Camille are part of a big circle of about ten friends who all hang out together. They sit at the same table for lunch, go to the basketball and football games together, and plan parties together. Lately, however, Lois has noticed that three or four of the other girls in the gang are distancing themselves from Camille. When they have parties at their homes, Camille often is not invited. The other day, Lois heard these girls making fun of Camille's clothes. Lois feels bad for her friend. But since the others haven't said anything, she decides not to make a big deal about it.

Today Camille is taking a makeup test in math during lunch, so she isn't at the table. Lois reminds the girls that she is having everyone over after the football game Friday night. One of the other girls rolls her eyes and says, "Well, I sure hope you're not including Camille. I can't stand the cheap outfits she always wears. I think it's time to drop her from the party list, don't you?" The other girls quickly agree. No one speaks up for Camille. Lois stares at her friends and wonders how to react. Standing up for Camille may mean losing her other friends. What do you think she should do?

Should Lois . . .

A. Tell the girls that she definitely plans to invite Camille—they can come if they want?

B. Tell Camille that the party has been canceled?

C. Take Camille shopping for some nicer clothes so that the girls will like her?

D. Go along with the crowd and drop Camille as a friend?

E. Be friendly to Camille, but only when the other girls aren't around?

 Read Proverbs 17:17 for help in knowing what Lois should do.

The Detour

Les is one of the best cross-country runners at his school. He has a good chance to be crowned district champ at the meet today. Les also has a reputation among the racers of being a fair competitor. He doesn't trash-talk his opponents or boast when he wins. He is well liked among his team members and coaches as well as among the competing runners. For the district championship, Les's school is hosting the meet. He feels confident about running on his home turf. He knows the route through the forest preserve, where he should conserve his energy, and where to make his final sprint. As long as the weather holds, it should be a good race for Les.

Several hours before the race, it begins raining. If there is no thunder or lightning, the race will be held, but it will mean a more difficult course. At race time, the rain ends, but the course is muddy and slippery. It's unlikely that any meet records will be broken during this district championship. Les lines up with the other runners. At the sound of the gun, they're off. Les gets off to a quick start, but he can feel the others right behind him. As he rounds the first corner, Les slips and tumbles several times. He gets up and stumbles a bit before he can get in stride again. He has fallen well behind his closest competitors. Glancing behind, he sees that the next group of runners are fairly well behind him. Les knows about a path up ahead that would allow him to cut off a portion of the course and get him right back to the leaders—where he would be if he had not slipped. No one would suspect him of taking a shortcut, so why not? What do you think Les should do?

Should he . . .
A. Give up and walk the rest of the way in because the course is too muddy?
B. Take the shortcut—after all, he is expected to win?
C. Continue to run the course and do the best he can?
D. File a complaint with the judges that the course was too slippery?
E. Accuse one of the other runners of pushing him down?

 Check out 2 Corinthians 8:21 to know what Les's top priority in finishing this race should be.

Losing Effort

Sam kicks the ground in disgust. His soccer team, previously undefeated, played the neighborhood rivals today and lost 14-1. Many of Sam's friends are on the team, and Sam really wanted to win this game. To add insult to injury, Sam also played poorly. He didn't score any goals, and when the ball was passed to him, he frequently overplayed the pass. His other teammates didn't do so well, either.

As Sam is getting his gear together, his coach calls him over. *Oh, no,* thinks Sam. *now I'm going to get a lecture.* Sam doesn't want to hear about how poorly he played, but the coach merely wants to talk the game over with him. The coach tells Sam what he did right, what he did wrong, and areas where he could improve. What should Sam do?

Should he . . .
- A. Listen and then say, "What do *you* know? If you'd let me play forward, we'd win"?
- B. Listen carefully, ask questions, and determine to work hard to improve?
- C. Think about the mistakes his teammates made and point these out to the coach?
- D. Halfheartedly listen, grunt three or four times, and say, "Whatever"?
- E. Make an excuse for his poor performance by saying that he didn't get enough sleep?

 For help in knowing what Sam should do, read Proverbs 15:31.

Forbidden Fruit

I t's a cold, brisk fall afternoon. The wind whips up the leaves in a whirl in front of Grant as he walks home from school along the wooded path. At this secluded spot Grant always enjoys the brief moments of quiet it provides him. It offers a welcome break from the hectic pace at school before he has to tackle his homework. And what homework. *Boy,* thinks Grant, *the teachers really are piling it on now that it's October.*

Grant turns up his collar to the wind as another brisk breeze comes up behind him. It rifles the pages of a magazine that lies abandoned along the side of the path. Grant stops to pick it up and immediately notices that it's a dirty magazine, the kind typically found behind the counter at the local drugstore. Grant looks around. No one has seen him pick up the magazine. He has never looked at one before, and now here it is right here in his hands. What should Grant do?

Should he . . .

A. Throw the magazine into the first trash can he finds?

B. Take the magazine home and hide it so he can look at it later in his room where it's warmer?

C. Take the magazine and show it to his friends?

D. Take the magazine to school for show and tell?

E. Quickly leaf through the magazine to see for himself what's so bad about magazines like this so he can warn his friends about them?

 To see how Grant should react, look up Matthew 5:28.

The Editor

Stacy puts the finishing touches on her story. It's her first article for the school newspaper, and she has spent a lot of time on getting it just right. Stacy is proud of her effort. She interviewed the school principal, who is new this year, and she wants to make sure that every fact is correct. This is an important story. Stacy thinks it might even be put on the front page. Wow! Wait until her friends see her name on the front page of the school paper!

At newspaper club that afternoon, Stacy waits nervously while the advisor works with each student on the articles. Finally, the advisor calls up Stacy and hands Stacy her article. What are those red marks all over her story? Stacy stares in disbelief. Her advisor begins, "This is a good start, Stacy, but I have a few suggestions for making it even better." The advisor begins to point out the various corrections, but Stacy hardly hears anything. How can the teacher do this to her article? It was perfect—or at least she thought so. Stacy walks back to her desk, stunned. What is she supposed to do now with her story?

Should Stacy . . .

A. Tear up the article and tell her advisor, "Forget it! I'm not writing anything else for you"?

B. Listen to her advisor's corrections and learn how she can improve her story?

C. Argue with the advisor that the story is perfect as written and doesn't need to be changed?

D. Look over the corrections but only include a few that won't change it too much?

E. Make the corrections but complain to the other students on the newspaper staff that their advisor is unfair and just wants to do things her way?

 Check out Proverbs 18:15 to see how Stacy should respond.

Gang Turf

At Sanford's school, certain gangs rule. There are two major gangs—the Hoods and the Bad Dudes. The gangs run the halls and the playground. Belonging to a gang is the only way to win respect in the school—and protection. Most of the kids younger than Sanford have joined gangs simply to be able to go to and from school without being hassled. Those who don't belong run the risk of being beat up every day or losing their lunch money to gang members. For kids like Sanford, who are not athletic or strong, the gang seems to be the only way to go.

Sanford and his friend have vowed not to join a gang. But this year, his friend finally gave in to the pressure and joined the Hoods. His friend is trying to convince Sanford to join as well. They don't have to actually do anything too bad, he says, and they will be protected from the older kids who go to the nearby high school. Sanford's friend advises him that it's the smartest thing to do. Sanford is tempted to join. What do you think he should do?

Should Sanford . . .

A. Pay off the gang leaders every month so they won't hassle him?

B. Carry a wooden bat for protection?

C. Join his friend's gang for protection?

D. Refuse to join and seek help from an adult if he runs into problems?

E. Form his own gang and arm everyone with slingshots, taking a lesson from David?

 Read 1 Corinthians 10:13 for help in knowing how Sanford can handle this difficult situation.

The Progress Report

Torrie is having fun at school. She's a member of the pep band and the yearbook staff. She's on the student council and is trying out for volleyball this fall. In fact the only thing interfering with Torrie having an absolutely fabulous time at school is, well, school. When it comes to her classes and studying, Torrie doesn't have the time. She would rather spend two hours after school trying to sell ads for the yearbook than hit her books. Consequently, she hasn't been doing very well in her classes. Lately, her parents have been asking when the progress report will be coming home. Torrie hopes that hers will get lost in the mail.

Today, Torrie is the first to arrive home. She flips through the mail and sees a letter addressed to her parents from the school. It's her progress report. Torrie knows that this can only be bad news. She tries to look through the envelope to see how bad the report is, and she considers steaming it open. But that won't solve her problem because Mom and Dad will still see the report. If her parents see how poorly Torrie is doing in school, they will make her give up some activities—and she doesn't want to do that. What do you think Torrie should do with the letter?

Should she . . .

A. Open up the envelope and try to change her grades with a black pen?

B. Pitch the letter—if her parents ask her about the report, say it must have gotten lost in the mail?

C. Give her parents the report and explain her poor grades by saying that the teachers grade low to scare students into working harder?

D. Give the report to her parents and agree to drop a few activities until her grades improve?

E. Laugh when she gives them the report and say, "These things are such a joke!"?

 Check out Proverbs 12:13 for guidance in knowing what action Torrie should take.

4

Blowing Smoke

I t's Friday night, and Beth and her friends go to the party following the football game. A lot of friends from school are there. There's plenty of good food and dancing. Everyone is having a great time when one of the boys brings out a pack of cigarettes. To Beth's dismay, everybody—including her friends—takes one and lights up. Beth watches while the pack is passed around the room. Inevitably, the pack ends up in Beth's hands. What should Beth do?

Should she . . .
- A. Take a cigarette, light it, and try to look cool?
- B. Tell her friends that they are stupid to smoke?
- C. Turn down the offer, explaining that she doesn't want to smoke?
- D. Pretend to be sick and go to the bathroom?
- E. Say she only smokes menthol?

 For help in knowing what Beth should do, read 1 Corinthians 6:19-20.

The Food Drive

Bruce's church is having a food drive on Saturday. The church sponsors this event every fall. Food donations come to the church, and then members deliver the food to the homeless and to various shelters around the area. This year, the youth group has agreed to help with the drive by being at the church to accept donations and to bag the food for delivery. Each member has signed up for a three-hour time slot to help out. Bruce has written the event on his calendar at home.

Later that week, Bruce's friend asks if he wants to go the big college football game that weekend. His father got the tickets from one of his business clients, and they have great seats on the fifty-yard line. Bruce is really excited. The team has a couple of All-Americans playing, and he would love to see them in action. When Bruce gets home, he realizes that the football game is the same day as the food drive. What do you think Bruce should do?

Should he . . .

A. Call his church youth group director and see if he can come another time?

B. Tell his friend he can't make it that Saturday because he's helping out at the food drive?

C. Go with his friend, figuring there are enough kids in the youth group to cover the food drive, and later say, "I forgot"?

D. Go for about a half hour to the food drive then sneak out the backdoor to meet his friend for the game?

E. Get his brother to substitute for him at the food drive?

 The biblical principle that tells how Bruce should respond can be found in Titus 3:14.

Keeping Secrets

Bonnie is planning a big weekend. She is having one of her friends spend the night Friday after the hayride with the youth group. Then she and her friend will be going to the big college football game on Saturday. Bonnie is so excited. But she's also a little bit nervous. The problem is not what she will be doing this weekend, but with whom. Bonnie has two very good friends—one of whom she has known since the first grade. They do a lot of things together, and Bonnie usually asks her when she has something special planned—like this weekend.

But Bonnie wants to ask someone else this time. This girl recently moved in and is in Bonnie's classes this fall. Ever since they first met, the two girls have gotten along very well. Bonnie has never invited this girl over to her house, and she thinks this will be the perfect time to ask her. But Bonnie is worried that her other friend's feelings will be hurt if she finds out. After much thought, Bonnie decides to ask her new friend, who enthusiastically accepts. On Friday, however, Bonnie's other friend calls and asks if she is taking the new girl to the football game. Bonnie is surprised. She doesn't know how her friend found out, but she can hear the hurt in her voice. What should Bonnie say?

Should she . . .

    A. Tell her the truth and say, "Yes, I wanted a chance to get to know her better"?

    B. Say, "What football game?" and hang up?

    C. Say, "No, I wasn't planning to go anywhere this weekend"?

    D. Answer, "Speaking of football, how about that quarterback! Speaking of quarterback, did you ever get your quarter back from the candy machine"?

    E. Say, "That's none of your business"?

 For help in knowing how Bonnie should respond, take a look at Zechariah 8:16 and Ephesians 4:25.

High Standards

Pierce knew he was in trouble when he hooked Mr. Turner as his social studies teacher. Mr. Turner has one of the worst reputations in school for being a hard grader. Very few students earn an A from him. Worse yet for Pierce, social studies is not one of his strongest subjects. Since the beginning of the school year, he has tried to keep a low profile, work hard, and do his best. Their first paper was due last week, and Pierce worked hard on it. He spent at least a week researching the topic and then another week writing and rewriting it. He was proud of his final paper. Pierce feels that it was one of the best papers he has ever written.

Today Mr. Turner hands back the papers. Pierce anxiously awaits his. He's confident that he has earned at least a B on it, maybe even an A. Pierce is stunned when he looks at his paper. It is filled with red marks and has C minus on top and the message "See me after class" scrawled across the top. Pierce feels sick to his stomach. All that work and only a C minus. What will he do now? He approaches Mr. Turner after class. Mr. Turner informs Pierce that he has the beginnings of a good paper, but he didn't quite hit the mark. If he wants, he can redo the paper and turn it in next week. If he makes the necessary improvements, he will receive a higher grade. Pierce is upset. How can he do any better than this? What do you think he should do.

Should Pierce . . .
  A. Accept the C minus; why waste his time?
  B. Fold his paper into an airplane and sail it at Mr. Turner as his answer?
  C. Take the paper home and redo it, following Mr. Turner's suggested improvements?
  D. Turn in the same paper the following week?
  E. Talk to his guidance counselor about getting out of Mr. Turner's class?

 Check out Ephesians 6:5-7 to see the biblical principle that should guide Pierce's response.

The Birthday Sweater

Lorna's grandmother from New York recently sent her a sweater for her birthday. Unfortunately for Lorna, it's absolutely horrible. It's pink and has bows on it—perfect if Lorna were turning four, but she is twelve. She couldn't possibly wear it to school, or anywhere else for that matter. Lorna stuffs the sweater in her bottom drawer, dutifully writes a thank-you note to her grandmother, and forgets about it.

Until last week . . . That's when her grandmother arrived for an extended visit with her family. Lorna loves her grandmother. She is fun to be with and always has interesting stories about her travels. (Not to mention fun gifts from her many travels as well!) The last day of her visit, Lorna's grandmother promises to take Lorna and her sisters out for tea. The girls are supposed to dress nicely. They are busy planning what they will wear when Lorna's grandmother walks in. "Why don't you wear that nice sweater I sent you for your birthday," she asks. "You wrote how much you liked it in your thank-you note." Lorna is stuck. What will she do now?

Should Lorna . . .

A. Tell her grandmother that the sweater is at the cleaners?

B. Explain that she would rather wear something not so nice because she's afraid of spilling tea on her sweater?

C. Tell her grandmother that her mother accidentally washed the sweater and shrunk it?

D. Put on the sweater and hope that she doesn't run into any of her friends?

E. Gently tell her grandmother that her taste in clothes has moved on from bows and the color pink?

 Read Ephesians 4:15 to see what Lorna should do in this situation.

The Missing Brother

Francie has been dreading this day for years—the day when she would have to walk to school with her younger brother. Her brother is in kindergarten, and now, after the first several weeks when her mom walked him to school, it has become Francie's job. Her mom gives her strict instructions: walk him to the line where the students wait; make sure he gets there on time; make sure he doesn't goof off on his way to school. Francie assures her mom that she will take care of her brother, despite the fact that he is a major pest.

The first several weeks go fine. Lately, however, Francie has been more interested in meeting her friends and talking than in watching her brother. She knows he's behind her, and she usually waits until she sees him round the corner and walk up to the kindergarten door. Her mom didn't say she had to lead him by the hand! But today, Francie became so engrossed in her conversation with a friend that she forgot to watch for her brother. When the bell rings, she runs to see if he is in the kindergarten line. To her surprise, her brother hasn't made it to school yet. Francie doesn't want to be late for school herself, but she is (she admits) a bit worried about her brother. What do you think Francie should do?

Should she . . .

A. Report him missing to the principal?

B. Assume that he's goofing off and deserves to be marked late?

C. Call her mom and alert her—but at the risk of getting into trouble herself?

D. Go to class because she knows her brother eventually will make it?

E. Start walking back to find out where her brother is and make sure he does get to school, even if both of them will be late?

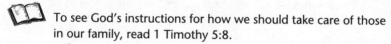 To see God's instructions for how we should take care of those in our family, read 1 Timothy 5:8.

10

The Egghead

Nora is one of a handful of students selected for an accelerated math class. The class has been very challenging. Nora has studied hard every night to master each concept. Yesterday was the big test on everything covered since the beginning of school. Nora stayed up late to study for the test. She thinks she did pretty well on it and is eager to get her test back today.

When the class walks in, the teacher does not looked pleased. It appears that the majority of the class did not do very well, the teacher announces as she hands back the tests. Nora is almost afraid to look at hers. When she turns it over, however, to her immense relief, Nora sees she has earned an A.

The teacher informs the class that there was only one A in the entire class and that the rest of the class did poorly. A retest is scheduled for Friday.

As Nora leaves class, she sees a couple of her classmates comparing their test answers. She overhears them discussing who got the A and how they would like to get back at that person for making them look bad. When they see Nora, they call out, "Hey, Nora, what did you get?" Nora is proud of her effort, but she doesn't want to look like the class egghead. What should she tell her classmates?

Should Nora . . .

A. Lie and tell them she flunked the test?

B. Tell them she did OK and get out of there as quickly as possible before they ask anymore questions?

C. Tell them she got lucky and got an A?

D. Say it's none of their business and walk off?

E. Tell them the truth—that she studied very hard and got an A?

 Read Psalm 64 to learn, from David's example, how to face opposition.

11

The Cookie Caper

Carolyn wearily closes the book and eyes the clock. Nine o'clock—she finally finished all her homework and now it's time for bed. Still, Carolyn feels satisfied that she did a good job on her math problems and on her English essay. With a yawn, she stretches and starts getting her things ready for tomorrow.

Carolyn smiles as she thinks about the newspaper staff meeting after school the next day. They're going to plan the next issue, and Carolyn has some interesting story ideas. As she gets into bed, she suddenly remembers that she promised to bake cookies for the staff meeting. Oh no! What should Carolyn do?

Should she . . .

A. Get up, talk to her mom, and stay up late to make the cookies?

B. Ask her dad to run to the store and buy some cookies?

C. Lie in bed thinking up excuses she can give for not bringing the refreshments?

D. Think, *They won't miss my cookies. I always bring cookies. This time I'll just bring prunes.* Then go back to sleep?

E. Pretend that she has forgotten about making cookies and act shocked when her friends ask where the refreshments are?

 For help in knowing what Carolyn should do, read Proverbs 12:22.

"I Told You So"

Drew's youth group was planning a fall festival as one of its big outreach activities. The group decided to have a hayride, a hot dog and marshmallow roast, a fall scavenger hunt in the neighborhood, and some other games as part of the festival. They hoped to invite friends and to attract kids from the nearby neighborhoods to attend. The only remaining issue was the date. After discussion, the group decided on the first weekend in October before the weather got too cold.

Drew knew that a dance for one of the local junior highs was scheduled for that weekend, as well as the football game for the big crosstown rivalry. He suggested to the group that they move their festival to another weekend, but everyone was convinced that the weekend they picked would be the best time. Well, the weekend came and, sure enough, not many kids showed up. So now the group is stuck with thirty packs of hot dogs, twenty bags of marshmallows, and not much to show for all their efforts.

Afterwards, Drew meets with one of the festival planners. What do you think Drew should say to him?

Should he . . .
- A. Say, "I'm sorry things didn't work out. Maybe we can plan better next time"?
- B. Say, "I told you so"?
- C. Make a sarcastic joke about all the "hot dogs" in the group?
- D. Criticize the group for overbuying?
- E. Suggest that the group sell hot dogs after the next worship service?

 Read Acts 27:10-25 to see how Paul handled a life-threatening situation when those in charge didn't listen to his advice.

The Party Animals

Winston likes a certain girl in his English class. The only problem is that she is one of the most popular girls in school. He did a class project with her once, and they got along well. Since then, however, Winston hasn't had much opportunity to talk with her. She hangs out with a different group of kids than Winston—the football players and cheerleaders. Winston sees her briefly in class and in the hallways, but that's only for a quick hello and wave. Winston has been racking his brains to come up with a way to spend some time with her outside of school.

Today, Winston is given the perfect opportunity. He has been invited to a party Friday night after the football game. He knows the girl will be there since her crowd always goes to the parties. The only trouble is, Winston knows what this party will be like. This crowd can get wild, and Winston is pretty sure that there will be drinking and smoking and maybe even some drugs. When Winston confides about the party invitation to one of his friends from youth group, his friend warns him about going. Winston thinks he can handle the pressure to get involved in these activities. Besides, he wants a chance to talk with this girl. What do you think Winston should do?

Should he . . .
A. Ignore his friend's warning—he can handle the peer pressure to drink and smoke?
B. Go, but stay in a corner the entire night wearing a big cross and clutching his Bible, and hope the girl will see him?
C. Decline the invitation and ask the girl to one of his parties with the youth group?
D. Go and have a wild time, hoping this will attract the girl's attention?
E. Tell his parents about the party and let them decide this one for him?

 See what God has to say about wild parties in 1 Peter 4:3-5 to decide what Winston should do.

14

Cinderella, Cinderella!

I n Wendy's family, everyone has jobs to do around the house, including her little brother. As the oldest, Wendy has the longest list. Not only does she have more chores to do than anyone else, but she also has the dirtiest and most difficult ones. It doesn't seem fair to Wendy.

Today, for example, her parents and her younger brothers are driving to her aunt's house. Wendy wants to stay home so she can go to the football game in the afternoon. Her parents have agreed, but her mom gave her a list of jobs that she has to do before she can go to the game. Wendy is positively steaming when her parents pull out of the driveway. The list is a mile long! She has to clean and dust her room, fold the laundry, and then iron a stack of clothes. Considering the list, Wendy knows there is no way she will finish all this before her friends come to pick her up. She feels like Cinderella. Unfortunately, no fairy godmother will come and rescue her. What do you think Wendy should do?

Should she . . .
A. Pitch right in and get as many of the chores done as possible before the game—and then leave the rest until later?

B. Take a halfhearted sweep through her room, toss the clothes in the closet, and hide the ironing—then she will have time to polish her nails before the game?

C. Finish all her chores and catch up with her friends later if necessary?

D. Forget about the list? After all, she isn't the maid!

E. Go to the game and hurry home so she can get everything done before her parents get home?

 For help in knowing how Wendy should respond, check out Colossians 3:20.

15

The Soccer Tournament

This weekend is the big soccer tournament, and Juan's team is favored to take the state title. They practiced hard all week to prepare for the tournament. It's single elimination, so the teams have to win to move on.

Because Juan's team was seeded number one, they were matched up with the lowest-seeded team in the first round. Juan was confident that his team could easily put this team away. No problem! The night before the tournament, however, it poured. When the teams arrived to play the first game at eight o'clock, the field was soaked. Unfortunately, the water and mud gave Juan's opponents an edge. The conditions made it more difficult for Juan's team to play their type of game: a precise passing and quick striking attack relying on excellent skills and speed.

The two teams battled to a zero-zero tie at halftime. Juan's teammates were exhausted from slogging through the mud. Juan could sense that his teammates were worried. Their worst dreams were realized when their opponents won on a fluke play. Juan and his friends were finished. Dejectedly, they watched the other team celebrate. All they could do, then, was watch the other games from the sidelines.

As it turns out, the team that beat them got crushed ten-zip. Not only did they get humiliated, but one of their players broke his arm in the game. Juan took grim satisfaction that at least this team didn't win the title. Later that weekend, Juan sees the boy who broke his arm in the game. The boy recognizes Juan and is coming over to talk to him. What should Juan say?

Should he . . .
  A. Compliment the boy on the good game he played and say that he is sorry to hear about the boy's broken arm?
  B. Laugh and say, "Heard you got wiped out"?
  C. Tell the boy that he deserved to get his arm broken because his team is so bad?
  D. Ignore the boy and walk away?
  E. Tell the boy that his team will get them back next year?

 Read Obadiah 1:12 and Proverbs 24:17-18 to see what the Bible says about gloating over other's misfortune.

16

The Shopping Spree

Mimi and her friends are going shopping at the mall today. Mimi isn't going to buy anything in particular; all she plans to do is window-shop. Maybe she can check out a few items to possibly buy for her dad's birthday next month. When they get to the mall, her mother and friends decide they will go to the jeans store first. There the girls discover that the designer jeans everybody at school wears are on sale. There are some cool sweatshirts on sale as well. Each of the girls grabs a couple of pairs of jeans and sweatshirts to try on.

While Mimi is standing around, one of her friends asks her if she is going to try on the jeans. "You just have to. You'll look great in them, and besides, you don't want to be the only one at school that doesn't have a pair," her friend says. Mimi hesitates. She doesn't need a new pair of jeans. Her mom bought her a pair before school started, and they are still in good condition. Yet she doesn't want to be the only one in her crowd without the latest style. What do you think Mimi should do?

Should she . . .

A. Tell her friend that she doesn't need the jeans right now?

B. Grab a pair of jeans and try them on but pretend she doesn't have enough money to buy them?

C. Tell her friends that she doesn't like that particular style of jeans?

D. Using a marker, draw the designer logo on a piece of paper and tape it to her jeans?

E. Go along with her friends and buy the jeans?

 Read Psalm 16:8 and Romans 12:2 to know how Mimi can withstand pressure from her friends.

17

Dating Dilemma

All of Heidi's friends have a crush on a boy in her social studies class. He's on the football team, is tall and cute, and has a great smile. The boy is rather shy, however, and he tends to hang out with one friend. For the most part, he acts as if girls don't even exist. Lately, though, he has been stopping to talk with Heidi at lunch or after school at her locker. All her friends are beside themselves. They can't believe he is actually talking to a girl. Heidi's friends spend the entire lunch hour discussing whether this guy wants to "go out" with Heidi. She dismisses their talk as a bunch of nonsense.

Tonight, however, the boy calls Heidi to ask her "go out" with him. Heidi is so surprised that she doesn't know what to say. She stammers something like, "I'll think about it and let you know tomorrow" before hanging up in a hurry. Heidi is confused. She thinks this boy is nice, but she doesn't know him very well. Besides, what does "going out" mean? Are they supposed to go out on a date, or does it mean talking together after school? She isn't sure what her parents would say, but she sure knows what her friends would tell her. Heidi wants to make up her own mind before she gets to school tomorrow. What do you think she should do?

Should Heidi . . .

A. Draw up a pre–going out contract so she knows exactly what is expected of her?

B. Tell the boy no way but let him know that other girls are interested in going out with him?

C. Agree to go out with the boy but then dump him after a day?

D. Tell the boy that she would feel more comfortable just being friends?

E. Ignore the boy the next day and hope he forgets about this going out business?

 Read Ephesians 5:15-17 for some good advice to guide Heidi in this situation.

18

The Geeky Stepbrother

Neal's mom recently remarried. His new stepdad is OK. He travels a lot, so he's not around much. When he's home, he and Neal play catch with the football. The real problem is Neal's new stepbrother, Hubie. This boy, to put it bluntly, is a real geek. He's a year younger than Neal, wears big thick glasses, and has to be one of the shortest kids in the school. When Neal has tried to play baseball or basketball with Hubie, it has been a disaster. The kid is totally uncoordinated and couldn't hit a barn with a beachball if he tried.

Neal does his best to ignore Hubie at school. Fortunately, they have different lunchtimes and recesses. Unfortunately, Hubie waits for Neal after school each day to walk home with him. Neal has been successful in ditching him a couple of times. Today, Neal comes out of school and sees Hubie waiting for him. What Hubie doesn't see is a group of older kids who are look like they are up to no good. It appears to Neal that they are planning to gang up on Hubie and give him a hard time—a real hard time. What do you think Neal should do?

Should he . . .
   A.   Walk back into the school and go out the other door. Hubie can handle those guys himself?

   B.   Wait and see exactly what the boys have in mind. Maybe they just want to talk with Hubie?

   C.   Go over and join Hubie and tell the boys to pick on someone else?

   D.   Tell Hubie to run home and hope he's faster than the other kids?

   E.   Go home and tell his mom that Hubie is in trouble?

 For a look at how God cares for the weak, read Psalm 72:12-14.

The Substitute Horn

T he first concert of the year is tonight. The band from each grade will perform, including a performance by the honors band. Hallie, who plays French horn in the seventh grade band and in the honors band, is looking forward to the performance. She has worked long hours on perfecting her parts, and she knows that her band instructor is pleased with her progress. The band director gives final instructions and dismisses the group.

Hallie is sticking around after school for her weekly French horn lesson when Mr. Brady frantically comes into the library, where she is finishing her homework. "I've been looking for you everywhere Hallie," he says. Mr. Brady informs Hallie that he received a call from the mother of the French horn player from the eighth grade band. The boy broke his arm playing soccer this afternoon and won't be able to make the concert. He needs at least two horn players for the concert and now only has one. "Will you be willing to step in and play the parts?" Mr. Brady asks her. It will mean spending the rest of the day at school, working on music she has never seen before. She would rather spend the time before the concert relaxing. What do you think Hallie should do?

Should she . . .
   A. Tell Mr. Brady she thinks one French horn should be enough?
   B. Tell him she has to go home and shine her horn for the performance?
   C. Tell Mr. Brady she would be glad to step in and work on the parts until the concert?
   D. Suggest that Mr. Brady hire a professional horn player?
   E. Give him a look that clearly says, "You must be joking! Learn all new parts by this evening? That's a good one, Mr. Brady"?

 Read Romans 8:5 to learn how Hallie should respond in this situation.

20

Smoke Signals

Edy's best friend has started to smoke. She gets her older brother to buy her cigarettes, and she heads back to the woods for a smoke after school. As far as Edy can tell, her friend hasn't shown up at school with her smokes. Edy has tried talking to her about the dangers to her health from smoking, but she won't listen. Whenever her friend offers her a cigarette, Edy refuses and dramatically coughs and chokes to make her point. Needless to say, her friend doesn't ask anymore if Edy wants to smoke with her.

Today, however, her friend comes running up to her after school. "I've got my cigarettes in my purse, and my mom is picking me up to go to the doctor's. I don't want to have them on me in case they fall out. Please, please, can you put them in your backpack? I'll come over as soon as I can to pick them up." Edy doesn't want to do it, but her friend looks desperate. She puts the cigarettes in her backpack and forgets about them.

That night her mother comes into her room, holding the pack of cigarettes. "I found these in your backpack while I was looking for your permission slip I have to sign. What do you have to say for yourself?" Edy can't believe she got herself into this mess. If she tells her mom the truth, her mom will call her friend's mother. Then her mom, her friend's mom, and her friend will be mad at her. What do you think Edy should do?

Should she . . .
  A. Say, "What cigarettes"?
  B. Look really innocent and say, "I don't know. I never saw them before"?
  C. Tell her mom that it's an experiment the church youth group is conducting on temptation?
  D. Tell her mom that she must have picked up the wrong backpack today and that those cigarettes belong to someone else?
  E. Tell her mom that the cigarettes really belong to her friend?

 Check out Proverbs 13:5 for help in knowing what Edy should do.

21

Be True to Your School

Woody is sitting with a group of his friends at the local burger joint in town after the football game. For what seems like the zillionth time, the cross-town high school has beaten Woody's school. It's a long-standing rivalry, and the other school usually wins. Woody is tired of hearing about his school's wimpy football team. He's proud of his school. The school offers many fine programs, and, academically, it is one of the top in the state. But that doesn't cut it on the football field.

As they are finishing up their sodas, a group of boys from the rival school come in. Woody wants to get out of there before they can spot them, but it's too late. The group comes over and starts razzing Woody and his friends. "Hey, next time you come to play us, why don't you bring your team." "Our girls could beat your football team." The taunts continue as Woody does a slow burn. These guys are so obnoxious. He truly would love to show them up, but is it worth it? What do you think Woody should do?

Should he . . .
    A. Smile and congratulate the boys on a good game?
    B. Ask the boys how many of their football players know how to add?
    C. Hurl french fries at the guys?
    D. Challenge the guys to a fight outside the burger joint?
    E. Say, "Wait till next year"?

 Check out Proverbs 25:21-22 and Romans 12:20-21 for the biblical principles that should guide Woody's response.

Just Listen!

Larry's friend Earl is going through a really difficult time at home. Earl's dad recently lost his job, and his parents seem to fight all the time about money. Earl worries a lot about what will happen to his family. Larry notices that whenever the subject of buying the latest CD, or the new school sweatshirt comes up, Earl gets very quiet. He also notices that Earl brings a lot of peanut-butter-and-jelly sandwiches to school. Some of the kids are even beginning to tease Earl about his lunch "selections."

Earlier today, between classes, Earl told Larry that things are getting pretty tense at his house. He's afraid that they may lose their home or worse—that the family may split up until his dad can get back on his feet again. Earl wants to talk things over. Larry agrees to get together with Earl after school, but he's nervous about it. All afternoon, he thinks about what he should say to Earl. Larry wants to help, but he's afraid of saying the wrong thing. Maybe he's not the right person to talk to Earl. What do you think Larry should do?

Should he . . .

A. Tell Earl he forgot that he had a dentist appointment and skip their meeting?

B. Go home another way and call Earl later to tell him he forgot they were getting together?

C. Make up a long list of suggestions for Earl and his family?

D. Quietly listen and offer his friendship to Earl?

E. Tell Earl he should see a psychiatrist who can really help him with his problems?

 Read Job 2:13 to see how Job's friends responded when he was wiped out by tragedy.

Fixing the Blame

A boy in Michelle's homeroom is really different. He hangs around with rough kids from another school and doesn't have many friends at this school. He always dresses in a black T-shirt, baggy dirty jeans, and unlaced gym shoes. He never says much, and he tends to stay by himself. Rumor has it that he's been in trouble with the police already for knocking down mailboxes in the neighborhood. A couple of weeks ago, a bike was stolen from school, and Michelle knows for a fact that this boy was questioned about it.

When Michelle gets home from school, she discovers that her wallet is missing. She is really upset. She had about thirty dollars in it, which she had planned to spend at the bookstore. The last time she remembers seeing the wallet is when she took out her calendar to look up something—and that was in homeroom. Michelle immediately thinks of this boy. He has to be the one who took it! She doesn't have any evidence—as a matter of fact, she can't remember being near him during homeroom. But he has to be the one. He's the only one who would do such a thing. What do you think Michelle should do at school tomorrow?

Should she . . .

A. Make an announcement in homeroom about her lost wallet and see if anyone found it?

B. Make a scene in class, in front of everybody, and accuse the boy of stealing her wallet?

C. Quietly confront the boy and ask that he return her wallet?

D. Set up a trap by announcing, within the boy's earshot, that she has a new wallet with fifty dollars in it. Then she can wait and catch the boy when he comes to steal it?

E. Report the stolen wallet and her suspicions to her homeroom teacher?

 Check out Proverbs 3:30 to see how Michelle should respond.

Great Job!

Today the results of the science project contest will be announced. Every student could submit a project, either with a partner or alone. The project had to deal with the subject of nutrition and include a written report. Projects were judged on topic, appearance, research, and content. Celina put in many hours working on her project. Science is her favorite subject, and she is one of the better science students in the school. But the best science student is Norbert. He has won the science fair two years in a row.

Celina is confident that this year will be different. She is determined to beat out Norbert and win the contest—at least, she hopes she will. Celina is nervous all morning waiting for the results. Finally, at lunchtime, the winners are announced. The principal announces the honorable mentions and then moves on to the second and first place awards. "And second place goes to Celina . . . ," the voice intones. Celina feels her stomach drop. Again, she lost to Norbert. She is so disappointed that she doesn't even hear the congratulations being offered her.

After school, she goes to pick up her project and sees Norbert's project. It is good, she has to admit. As she is reading it, Norbert walks up. It's too late to get away. Celina will have to say something. What do you think she should say?

Should Celina . . .
    A.   Tell Norbert he was lucky again this year?
    B.   Say, "Wait until next year. I'll beat you for sure!"?
    C.   Point out a few errors in his project?
    D.   Tell Norbert, "Great job. I really enjoyed your project"?
    E.   Stick out her tongue and walk away?

 Romans 15:2 will help you decide how Celina should respond.

Losing a Friend

Conan can tell immediately when he walks in the house that something is terribly wrong. His mom is sitting at the kitchen table, head in hands, with swollen eyes. Softly and gently, she tells Conan that Digger, their golden retriever, was hit and killed by a car today. She opened the garage door for their morning walk, and before she could react, Digger ran out into the street and was hit broadside by a passing car. Conan is dumbfounded. He can't believe the dog he has loved for ten years is no longer with them.

Conan needs to be alone. He grabs his coat and walks for what seems like hours. He ends up at the park. Sitting on the swing, with nobody around, Conan breaks down and weeps. While he is at the park, his friend Jip comes by. Jip is obviously embarrassed to discover Conan crying, but he asks what's wrong. Conan tells him. Jip feels bad for his friend but is clearly uncomfortable to see his friend crying. What should Jip do?

Should he . . .

A. Sit with his friend and let him cry?

B. Tell him to stop being such a crybaby?

C. Tell him, "You can always get a new dog. Don't worry about it"?

D. Say, "Gee, that's too bad" and cut out of there as fast as he can?

E. Say, "Only girls cry. Come on, it was only a dog"?

 Read John 11:30-36 to see how Jesus reacted when his friends lost a loved one.

Sloppy Homework

Carlin dumps his books on his bed. He has homework in every single subject tonight. How is he ever going to get his work done? After a quick dinner, Carlin gets down to the books. The first few subjects aren't too difficult—some definitions in geography, two pages of math problems, and five questions in science. Carlin gets through it pretty quickly. He decides to take a break and ends up watching two TV shows before he gets back to work.

His mom calls to tell him to get ready for bed in ten minutes. Yikes! Carlin just started his English homework, and he knows his teacher is very particular about how homework is turned in. If he takes the time to do it neatly, he'll never get it done. Carlin glances at the clock. Should he tell his mom he needs some extra time for homework? Then she'll know he was goofing off. What do you think Carlin should do?

Should he . . .

A. Do his homework neatly and finish as much as he can before bedtime?

B. Carelessly whip right through it—it's only homework?

C. Plead with his mom for some extra time to do his homework—and promise he'll never goof off again?

D. Tell his teacher he did his homework on the computer and the system crashed (Or maybe the dog ate the computer)?

E. Do his English homework on the bus. It will look great after a few bumps?

 Check out Ecclesiastes 9:10 and Colossians 3:23-24 for a clue as to what Carlin should do.

A Hairy Experience!

Cassie is spending the weekend with her friend while her parents are out of town. She's been looking forward to this for weeks. Her friend goes to a different school, and they usually don't have much time to see each other during the week. In fact, she hasn't seen her friend for over a month since volleyball practice started. They will need the entire weekend to catch up with each other on all the latest news. Cassie gets her last minute instructions from her parents, and then she's off.

When her friend comes to the door, it's apparent what she has been up to. Her hair is pink! Not just a mellow kind of strawberry pink, but a shocking, hot, neon pink. Cassie tries to keep from staring, but she can't help it. Her friend laughs at her, "Do you like my hair? All my friends at school are dying their hair. Don't worry—we can do yours while you're here." That's exactly what Cassie is worried about! She doesn't want to dye her hair any color, let alone hot pink. But it's going to take a lot of stamina to withstand her friend's pressure. She's not sure she will be able to handle it. What do you think Cassie should do?

Should she . . .
- A. Tell her friend she has a change in plans and is staying with another friend?
- B. Let her friend dye her hair so she won't have to listen to her all weekend?
- C. Tell her friend that she doesn't want to dye her hair—and resolve to stand by her decision?
- D. Tell her friend that hot pink is not her color?
- E. Tell her friend that she has head lice and can't dye her hair right now?

 Take a look at Ephesians 6:13-15 to see how Cassie can withstand her friend's pressure.

28

Home Sweet Home?

Brenda's family does not have a lot of money. They live in a small, modest home in the less wealthy part of town. The family works hard to keep the home neat and clean, but everything in the house is old and worn. The entire house could use a new paint job. The carpeting is beginning to fray, and the furniture in the living room is threadbare. Brenda has been over to some of her friends' homes, and there is a world of difference. Some of them live in brand-new homes with huge kitchens and great rooms. One friend even has a loft in her bedroom. Brenda has never invited her friends over to her house. After being in their homes, she is ashamed of where she lives. Brenda doesn't want her friends to think she's not good enough because she lives in a dumpy house.

Today at school, Brenda and her friends are planning the float that they will build for the Hometown Days parade. Each class at school builds one, and Brenda and her friends are on the float committee. They need some chicken wire, and Brenda knows she has some in the garage. She offers to bring it over to them, but one of the girls says, "Why don't we build the float at your house? It would be so much easier." Brenda is horrified. She doesn't want them to see her house. What do you think she should do?

Should Brenda . . .

A. Give her friends a fake address?

B. Tell her friends that she will bring the chicken wire to them?

C. Tell her friends that she is quitting the committee because it's interfering with her schoolwork?

D. Invite the friends over and not worry about what they think of her house?

E. Suggest to the friends that they build a float with ice cream and root beer?

 For help in knowing what Brenda should do, read James 3:13-16.

The Presidential Debate

For the past three weeks, Kenton's class has been discussing the U.S. government, how it works, the different branches, and the election process. Kenton's family visited Washington, D.C., this summer, so it's been interesting to connect all the places they visited with the class discussion. As the culminating activity for the unit, the class staged a mock election. The class selected two candidates and their parties, developed issues, and conducted a campaign. Each student was assigned a role—media advisor, reporter, campaign manager, political strategist, and so forth. Kenton learned a lot through the process.

At lunch today, the kids are talking about their mock election. The topic switches to the real political arena, and students begin talking about which political party they favor. One student begins cutting down the current president. "Oh, he's a real idiot. I can't stand the way he talks. He's so boooring!" Other kids chime in with their opinions. A couple even have jokes to share about the president. Kenton wants to say something to his friends, but he doesn't want to look like a goody-goody. What do you think Kenton should do?

Should he . . .

A. Put down the other political party leaders to be fair about it?

B. Not say anything. After all, adults do the same thing all the time?

C. Offer a few jokes that he has heard about the president?

D. Tell the other kids they don't know what they are talking about?

E. Say he believes that the president deserves respect—not put-downs?

 Take a look at Exodus 22:28 to see how seriously God regards showing respect to leaders.

30

The Club Treasurer

Penny was appointed treasurer for the school's Spanish Club. Each quarter, the club collects dues from its members and then holds a party or special event. For the first event, the club wants to put on a Spanish fiesta. Penny is in charge of shopping for the party, buying a piñata, some salsa and chips, and other goodies for the party. Her dad agrees to take her to the store after school so she can make her purchases.

Penny picks out a cool looking bull piñata from a party store and buys some inexpensive candy to put in the piñata. She buys napkins and some plates that go along with their fiesta theme. At the grocery store, she buys the food and drinks. After completing her shopping, Penny still has about ten dollars left. She notices one of the new Trapper notebooks on sale in the grocery store. It's less than ten dollars, and she could easily spend the club money without anyone noticing. How will they ever know she didn't spend it all? She's the one who keeps track of the spending, after all. What do you think she should do?

Should Penny . . .

A. Use her own money to buy the notebook?

B. Use the club's money and "fix it" to look like she spent more on the party goods?

C. "Borrow" the club's money and repay it later—sometime?

D. Increase the club dues next quarter so she can get some CDs she has wanted?

E. Spend every penny of the money by buying the Trapper notebook *and* colored pencils.

 Look at Psalm 37:21 and Psalm 112:5-6 to see how Penny should respond in this situation.

31

Center of Attention

Stephanie can hardly wait. Basketball practice begins today, and this promises to be a great year. Stephanie went to basketball camp this summer and has spent long hours at home practicing her shooting. She is a sure bet to make the starting lineup as the center. She can't wait to try out some of the new moves she learned at camp.

As Stephanie walks into the gym, a number of girls are already shooting baskets and warming up. Over by the coach is a girl Stephanie hasn't seen before. The coach whistles for the team to come over. The coach introduces the new girl, who recently moved into town from out of state. The coach mentions that Ellen played center for her old basketball team and will be trying out for that position. Stephanie can hardly believe her ears.

Practice begins. Stephanie keeps an eye on the new girl. Ellen drives to the hoop and makes an easy basket. The coach shouts her encouragement. Stephanie gets a hollow feeling in the pit of her stomach. *This girl is good,* she thinks. *What am I going to do now?* What should she do?

Should Stephanie . . .

A. Try to make the new girl look bad in practice?

B. Try to get the other team members to turn against the new girl?

C. Steal the new girl's shoes?

D. Realize that competition will improve her game, making the team better and vow to do her best?

E. Complain to the coach that she was there first and should get the starting position?

 For help in knowing what Stephanie should do, look up Philippians 2:3.

On Top of the World

Reed is in a great mood. It's a glorious fall day, the sun is shining, and the temperature is cool. It's a great day for football. Not only that, but Reed's favorite football team is on a winning streak. Reed is feeling good about life in general. Things have been going very well this fall. He has a great teacher—the best in the school and the one he wanted. His best friends are in class with him. He is breezing through his subjects at school—nothing has been too hard yet. He has a good chance of making the basketball team. And he and his friend are planning a camp-out—just the two of them—next weekend. Life couldn't be better.

When he comes down to breakfast, his dad asks if he plans to go on the youth retreat next weekend. Reed would rather go on the camp-out that he and his friend have been planning. The only weekend they both have free is next week. Besides, Reed thinks, who needs that God stuff now anyway? Things couldn't be going better. Church is only for when you're in trouble, right? What do you think Reed should do?

Should he . . .

A. Tell his dad that he will think about it?

B. Wise up and realize that God has blessed him greatly this fall?

C. Take his friend on the church retreat with him?

D. Go camping with his friend as he has planned?

E. Tell his dad that he's on a roll and doesn't need to go to church activities right now?

 Take a look at Nehemiah 9:35 and Psalm 119:65-66 to see how Reed should respond.

Piecrust Promises

Lamont is in a hurry to finish his work around the house so he can get to the park to play basketball. His younger brother already has finished his jobs and is about to leave to meet his friends. Lamont pleads with his brother to help him finish the chores. "If you do, I promise that I will take you to the fun fair at your school next Saturday," Lamont begs. This is a good deal for his brother because their parents are both busy next Saturday, and he had no way of going—until now. His brother agrees. The boys finish the chores and run off to meet their friends.

During the week, Lamont forgets all about his promise to his brother. He and his friend are planning to go to the local bookstore for a book signing with their favorite coach. On Friday night, Lamont calls his friend to make the final arrangements, and his younger brother overhears him. As soon as Lamont gets off the phone, his brother starts yelling: "You promised to take me to the fun fair. I helped you with your chores. Now you have to take me!" Lamont doesn't want to miss the book signing, but he did make a promise. What do you think he should do?

Should Lamont . . .

A. Drag his brother to the book signing instead of the fun fair?

B. Laugh and say, "You thought I was serious about that fun fair? I was only kidding"?

C. Take his brother to the fun fair and go to the book signing later?

D. Offer to do all of his brother's chores for two weekends if he doesn't have to go to the fun fair?

E. Tell his brother to buzz off—he's not going to any fun fair?

 Take a look at John 6:38 to see Jesus' example in serving others, not self.

The Inferiority Complex

Wes gathers up his gym stuff and shuffles out of the school, head down, eyes focused on the ground. It hasn't been a good day. He has been practicing hours for the basketball tryouts today, but he knows he didn't make the team. The tryout was a total disaster. He couldn't make a shot to save his life. When the coach passed him the ball, he dropped it. Then he dribbled off his foot. Next, his pass hit the other guy in the head. Worse yet, Wes flunked his history test because he didn't study enough—he had spent all his free time practicing basketball.

Now, he thinks, *it's a total bust. No team. Flunked test. A total zero of a day.* Wes can't think of anything he can do well. He's not big enough to play football. He's not fast enough for soccer or track. And he sure isn't coordinated enough to play basketball. Wes can't play a musical instrument or even pass a simple history test. He doesn't have many friends. And the one or two boys he considers friends probably only hang around him because they feel sorry for him. It's hard to imagine why anyone would want to pay attention to someone like him—a big failure.

Wes is feeling pretty low, and he needs help in pulling out of his funk. What do you think Wes should do?

Should he . . .
    A. Enroll immediately in a self-improvement course?
    B. Send away for a muscle-building program to build up his body?
    C. Hang around with someone who is worse off than he is to help him look better?
    D. Realize that he has value and immeasurable worth in God's eyes?
    E. Cry really hard and run away from home?

 Read Luke 12:6-7 to see how much Wes (and you) are valued in God's eyes.

The Basketball Shoes

Brady recently made the basketball team, and he was elated. All those months of hard work finally paid off. Brady was new in school, so he was eager to become part of a team and get to know some more guys. But after the first day of practice, Brady wasn't too sure. All the guys wore the latest basketball shoes—some of which Brady knows cost over $150. They all have the latest practice gear and carry it around in fancy gym bags. Brady knows that stuff costs a ton of money. Brady also knows his family doesn't have extra money to spend on gym gear and basketball shoes, especially ones that cost $150 a pair.

Today, after practice, he overhears one of his teammates bragging that he owns three pairs of the shoes. He has a pair for games, a pair for practice, and another pair for home. He tells his friend that he gets to buy new shoes every three months so they don't wear out. Brady can hardly believe it. He quickly puts his gear into his gym bag and gets ready to leave. Brady notices that the boy left his basketball shoes on the bench. No one is around, and Brady is tempted to take the shoes and stuff them into his bag. This guy can certainly afford to "lose" a pair of gym shoes, after all. What do you think Brady should do?

Should he . . .
A. Take the shoes and quickly try to find the boy who left them?
B. Hide the shoes for a few days and see what happens. If the boy doesn't say anything about losing his shoes, keep them and wear them? (They're the right size.)
C. Take the shoes to the lost and found?
D. Leave the shoes there?
E. Take the shoes, sell them, and buy a different brand-name pair that the boy won't notice him wearing?

 Look up Ephesians 4:28 for help in knowing what Brady should do.

5

The Problem with Math

Martha is struggling in math this year. She was placed in the advanced class, and it is proving to be more difficult than she thought it would be. Martha likes math, and usually does well, but these new concepts are tough. To keep up with the other students in her class, she has stayed after school for tutoring with her teacher. Mom and Dad work with Martha every night to help her with the homework, but she still struggles. It seems that the other kids in her class seem to catch on so much quicker than she does. Martha feels as though she is the only one who doesn't get it.

Today there is a big test in math. Martha studied about three hours with her parents last night, going over different problems. When she walks into class, she feels confident that she knows the material and should do well. Martha quickly looks over the test when her teacher hands it to her. Her heart sinks. This stuff doesn't look like what she studied last night. She does the best she can, but she knows that she didn't do well. Before she leaves for home, her math teacher catches her in the hall. "I'm afraid you flunked the test today," she tells Martha. "Why don't you stay after tomorrow. We'll review this chapter, and I'll give you the test again. I know you are working very hard, and I know you'll get it." Martha doesn't want to take a retest. She wants to quit. She doesn't think she will ever get it. What do you think Martha should do?

Should she . . .
  A. Work with her teacher and take the retest?
  B. Ask to transfer back into the regular math class?
  C. Tell her teacher that she's too stupid to be in the class?
  D. Start running down the hall screaming, "No! No! No! I hate math!"?
  E. Tell her teacher she has math anxiety and can't take a math class ever again?

 See James 1:2-4 to see how we can overcome the trials in our lives.

6

Science Says . . .

Wade's science class is studying the origin of the earth. The class takes a field trip to the natural history museum to see the newest dinosaur exhibit. The exhibit is extremely interesting and well done, but it is confusing to Wade as well because God and creation are not mentioned at all. According to the exhibit, life started on Earth as a single cell, which eventually evolved over millions of years into dinosaurs, the animal kingdom as we know it today, and then human beings. That is not what Wade has been taught to believe or what he has read in the Bible.

When the class gets back to school, they discuss the field trip. One student Wade knows from Bible study asks about evolution and how that fits into creationist belief. The other students start to laugh at this student. "Don't tell us you believe the earth was created in one day. Come on. That's for little kids to believe," the other students say. Even the teacher dismisses the student's question as unscientific. Wade wants to disagree with the others, but he knows he will be shouted down. What do you think Wade should do?

Should he . . .
 A. Politely point out that evolution is only a theory and hasn't been conclusively proven?
 B. Run around the classroom acting like a monkey and tell his teacher he hasn't evolved yet?
 C. Tell the other students that they are too stupid to realize the truth about creation? (That should win the argument right there.)
 D. Say nothing and act like he agrees with the majority. What's the point anyway; they'll never agree with him?
 E. Bring his pastor in to debate the science teacher?

 Read Isaiah 42:5 and Colossians 2:8 to know the truth about evolution. And read 1 Peter 3:15 to see how Wade should respond.

7

Mad Money

Every year for Jocelyn's birthday, her grandfather encloses money in her birthday card. When she gets home from school, Jocelyn runs straight to the pile of mail and digs through it until she finds his card. Opening it, she gasps as a crisp, new fifty-dollar bill falls out. Wow! Her mom advises her to put it away and says she will deposit it in the bank for her tomorrow. Jocelyn, though, wants to bring the bill to school and show it to all her friends. She bets they never saw a fifty-dollar bill before. Her mother says under no circumstances can she take it to school, but she can keep it in her room until they take it to the bank.

The next morning, Jocelyn decides that she has to take the money to school. She tucks it into her math book and runs out to the bus. During lunch, she pulls the fifty-dollar bill out of her books and shows it off to all her friends. They all pass it around, and Jocelyn makes sure she gets it back. Suddenly, a commotion breaks out in the lunchroom, and food starts flying everywhere. The girls all giggle and scream as they run for cover.

Later that day, Jocelyn remembers her fifty dollars and looks for it in her math book. Flipping through the pages, she can't seem to find it. She flips through again, it's gone! She anxiously rummages through all of her other books. No sign of it. Then she remembers the lunchroom! What if she dropped it when she grabbed her books to run during the fight? Or worse, what if she threw it away with her lunch garbage? Now what will she do?

Should Jocelyn . . .

A. Get a group of friends to help her go through the garbage Dumpsters to find the money?

B. Tell her mom she lost the bill because she foolishly took it to school with her?

C. Tell her mom she decided to bury the bill in the back yard to save it for a rainy day?

D. Tell her mom she donated the money to charity?

E. Ask the principal to make an announcement that she lost the money?

 Proverbs 1:8-9 will give you a clue as to what Jocelyn should have done in the first place.

8

The Pity Party

Paige's school recently held a writing contest. Anyone could enter a piece of creative writing—an essay, a short story, or a poem. The winners would receive a trip to New York City for a young writers' conference and have their entry published in a national magazine. It's a fantastic opportunity. Paige has worked really hard on her piece. She has spent many hours writing and revising her poem until it is perfect. Paige thinks that some day she would like to be a writer. Attending the writers' conference would be a wonderful experience for her. Paige has her heart set on winning the contest.

Today the winners are announced. To Paige's deep disappointment, her entry is not a winner. In fact, it is not even an honorable mention. But a girl in her English class wins the poetry division. Paige is seething. The girl is not one of the better students in English. Paige can't imagine how she ever won. All the way home, Paige can't stop thinking about the contest. Maybe she's not such a good writer after all. Paige is near tears by the time she gets home. The more she thinks about it, the sorrier she feels for herself. *It's no use,* Paige thinks, *I'm not any good.* How do you think Paige should handle her disappointment?

Should she . . .
   A. Give up all hope of ever becoming a writer?
   B. Spend the entire weekend in her room, sulking about losing?
   C. Complain to anyone who will listen about the unfair judging?
   D. Tell her friends that this contest really wasn't all that important anyway?
   E. Be thankful for the writing talent God has given her and resolve to try again next year?

 Read 1 Samuel 12:24 for help in knowing what Paige should do.

9

Lazybones

Before Caleb and his mom entered the classroom, Caleb already knew what his teacher would say: "Caleb is a very smart boy, but he doesn't apply himself." It's the same thing every year. Even Caleb has to admit his teachers are right. He is lazy, but he likes being lazy. If the teacher hands out an assignment with extra credit points, Caleb won't waste his time doing any extra credit. If volunteers are needed to help around the classroom, you won't catch Caleb raising his hand. Oh no—that would be way too much work.

But Caleb's laziness may be catching up with him. His class is going on a trip to Washington, D.C., in the spring. But only students who achieve a certain grade level are eligible to go. Caleb hasn't worked hard all fall—until he heard about the trip. Now it may be too late. He and his mom are hoping to work out a plan today with his homeroom teacher that will allow Caleb to earn—groan—extra credit to make up for his poor grades.

Caleb's teacher outlines a weekly plan that Caleb must follow if he wants to earn the grades to go on the trip. Caleb looks at the list. Can he really get this all done before the trip? Does he want to do it? Caleb is not so sure. What do you think he should do?

Should Caleb . . .
- A. Forget about it? Who wants to go to Washington, D.C., anyway?
- B. Make a major attitude adjustment and work as hard as he can to earn the extra credit?
- C. Pay one of his friends to do the work for him?
- D. Negotiate with his teacher to whittle down the list by, say, half?
- E. Start out following the plan but give up halfway through because it is too much work?

 To find out how God views lazy people, read Proverbs 6:6-11.

10

The Phone Fib

By the time Spencer's dad walks in the door, it's eight o'clock at night. Their mom takes a warmed-up plate of food and sticks it in front of their father. "Boy, it was a lousy day at the office. My project is running over budget, and the boss is mad," his dad complains. Spencer's mom listens sympathetically and then mentions that the pastor called earlier to discuss a budget issue with him. Spencer's father shakes his head. "It can wait until tomorrow. I'm too tired to think about numbers right now. All I want to do is watch the game on TV and read the paper."

As soon as Spencer's dad sits down in front of the TV, the phone rings. Spencer jumps up to get it. Before he can answer, however, his dad instructs him, "If it's the pastor, I'm not home, got it?" Spencer picks up the phone, "Well, hello, Pastor Ted. How are you tonight?" In the background, Spencer can see his dad shaking his head no. "My dad, well, let me see . . ." Spencer doesn't know what to do. He sure doesn't want to lie to the pastor of all people, but he doesn't want to get his dad upset with him either. What do you think Spencer should do?

Should he . . .

A.   Start to talk and in the middle of the sentence, press the button to disconnect to give the impression that they had been cut off. Then, before the pastor can call back, leave the house?

B.   Tell the pastor, "I cannot tell a lie. My dad is sitting right here. Let me get him." Then duck as his dad gets the phone!?

C.   Say, "My dad is resting right now. Can he call you back tomorrow"?

D.   Say, "I think I see his headlights turning into the driveway right now. He'll call you back in a few minutes"? (Wow! A double lie!)

E.   Say, "My mom is here. Do you want to talk with her? Maybe she knows where my dad is"?

 The pastor may never know if Spencer is telling a lie or not, but read Acts 5:29 and Hebrews 4:13 for help in knowing how Spencer should react and to see who knows everything about what Spencer does.

11

Activity Overload

Bev loves to be busy. The more on her schedule, the happier she is. The worst thing in the world to Bev would be an afternoon with nothing to do. She will make plans with one friend for the early afternoon, come home, and then want to call another friend later to make plans to do something else. When it comes to clubs and activities, if Bev can join it, she will. She's on the yearbook club, the debate club, the French club, and the radio club. She plays an instrument, sings in the choir, and plays volleyball.

Bev doesn't know how to say no! In addition to all of her activities, if someone needs a volunteer, the first person they call is Bev. Today, the youth group leader calls and asks if she can help hand out flyers on Saturday about an upcoming concert at the church. Without looking at her calendar, she agrees. Later in the day, Bev realizes that she has a radio club activity that morning, a volleyball practice in the afternoon, and baby-sitting in the evening. Only if she gets up at 6 A.M. will she be able to hand out flyers to some pretty sleepy people. Even Bev feels overwhelmed by keeping up with that schedule. What do you think she should do?

Should Bev . . .
A. Call the youth leader back and say she can't make it because of other obligations?
B. Squeeze in handing out flyers while eating her lunch between activities?
C. Get up at 6 A.M. and blanket the neighborhood with flyers?
D. Cancel one of her other activities?
E. Collapse in a heap and not leave the house for three days?

 Take a look at Psalm 69:13-17 to see how David coped with an overwhelming situation.

Best Friends

Jay and Arnie have been best friends since their preschool days. Their moms met at the park, and they have been together ever since. The boys have been through Cub Scouts, mini-soccer, traveling soccer, swim team, T-ball, and Little League together. The two have been inseparable. All of their friends know that if they want to find Arnie, they should look for Jay. And if they are looking for Jay, they should find Arnie.

When the boys started middle school this fall, they signed up for many of the same activities. They both made the sixth grade football team, so it looked like business as usual. Lately, however, Jay seems to be drifting apart from Arnie. Jay has always gone to church with his family, and recently he committed his life to Jesus. He has some new friends at his church youth group, and the leader has been encouraging the group to grow in their faith though prayer and Bible study. Jay wants to get involved in the Bible study group at school, but he is afraid of what Arnie will say. Church has never been high on Arnie's list. But now it matters very much to Jay. He knows that if he allows his friendship with Arnie to determine his actions, he will never grow in his faith. What should Jay do?

Should he . . .

A. Do nothing and ride out the year to see where his friendship with Arnie will go?

B. Tell Arnie he doesn't want to be friends anymore?

C. Go to the Bible study but not say anything to Arnie and slowly let the friendship dissolve?

D. Ask Arnie for his advice?

E. Go to the Bible study and invite Arnie to attend?

 To find the biblical principle underlying what Jay should do, read 2 Peter 1:5-8.

13

Better Business

Recently, Buzz was selected to help run the school's concession stand at the basketball games. Along with a teacher advisor, Buzz chooses the brands of candy and snacks that they will sell, keeps the inventory, and marks the prices. He also is supposed to set up the concessions before the games and put everything away afterward. It is quite a responsibility, but he is eagerly looking forward to the challenge. Buzz wants to pursue a career in business someday, so he figures that this will be good experience.

Today is Buzz's first day on the job. He got to school an hour before the game and helped haul out the supplies, arrange the candy, get the money box ready, and put out the signs with the prices. During halftime Buzz is doing a brisk business. It seems that he made all the right choices because the candy and snacks are selling well. After the first rush dies down, a couple of his friends come by to see him. They chat for a while, hanging around the concession table. One of the boys picks up a giant-sized candy bar and says, "Hey, how about this? These are great!" Buzz tells him the price, but his friend doesn't have any money. Neither do the others. The boys look at Buzz pleadingly. "Come on, Buzz, just give us one. No one will ever know. You're in charge." These are Buzz's friends—what do you think he should do?

Should he . . .
- A. Call for the police?
- B. Slip them the candy—after all, it is only one measly bar?
- C. Tell them, "Sorry. Better bring some money to the game next time"?
- D. Yell, "Look over there!" and while they are looking, take all the candy, put it in the boxes, and run away?
- E. Tell them that the stand is closed and put everything away?

 Read Proverbs 16:11 to know how Buzz should respond.

Just Say No!

At the dance tonight, Rusty hears that his friend has something big planned that will grab everybody's attention. Rusty is not so sure he wants to know about it. His friend has a reputation for practical jokes—some of which can get out of hand. Last year, his friend was banned from the school dances after he released mice on the dance floor. He's back this year but on strict probation. Rusty doesn't think that planning another prank is a very good idea.

When Rusty finally hears what his friend has planned, he *knows* it's not a good idea. His friend wants Rusty and a couple of other guys to table-top the assistant principal. Table-topping is one of the biggest pranks going at school these days. Basically, one guy gets down on all fours, right behind a person. Then several others come up and bump the person over the "table." Rusty's friend thinks it will be hilarious to see the assistant principal go flying. Rusty is pretty sure his friend will be the one to go flying. When he tries to bow out of the prank, his friend gets mad. "You can't back out now. You know all about it, and you'll tell. I won't let you back out," he tells Rusty. What do you think Rusty should do?

Should he . . .
- A. Not show up at the dance at all?
- B. Write an anonymous note to the assistant principal and tell him he's on the "table-top" hit list?
- C. Report his friend to the assistant principal?
- D. Refuse to participate and try to talk his friend out of this harebrained prank?
- E. Agree that it will be hilarious and do his part to pull off the prank?

 Isaiah 50:7 will help you determine what Rusty should do.

15

Pet Care

Trey had begged his parents for months to get a pet. He promised that he would feed the pet and do whatever he had to do to take care of it. Because his mom is allergic to dogs and he doesn't want a cat, Trey and his parents agreed on buying a guinea pig. Trey checked out several books from the library on caring for guinea pigs. He and his dad bought a suitable cage, the bedding for the cage, and the right food. Everything was finally ready. So Trey and his dad went to the local pet shop and selected a brown-and-white guinea pig.

For the first several weeks, Trey spent hours every day with his new pet, grooming him, playing with him, and caring for him. As school activities began to crowd the schedule, however, Trey began to spend less time playing with his guinea pig. He still managed to feed it and to keep its cage clean. Today, after school, his mom wants to talk with Trey. She tells him she went into his room to clean, and the poor guinea pig was squealing because it had no food or water, and its cage was dirty. She warns Trey that if he can't take care of his pet, they will have to give it to someone who can. What do you think Trey should do?

Should he . . .
  A. Agree that they need to give the guinea pig away?
  B. Vow that he will be more serious about caring for his pet?
  C. Pay a friend to take care of the guinea pig for him?
  D. Put an ad in the school paper to sell his guinea pig?
  E. Say, "Mom, you don't understand guinea pig language. My beloved pet wasn't hungry and thirsty; it was singing"?

 Read Matthew 25:14-29 where Jesus offers some strong words about taking care of what has been given to us.

Lost and Found

Tyrone likes to take the shortcut through the woods on his way home from school. He always finds some interesting bug or rock to inspect along the way. He watches the chipmunks and squirrels scurrying. Once, he even surprised a deer on the way. The other kids don't get to see *that* walking along the sidewalk. Sometimes his friends will join him, but usually Tyrone walks home by himself.

Today, Tyrone stayed after school to finish a project for the teacher. He hurries home now through the woods. He doesn't stop to look around because he doesn't want to be late for his piano lesson. But he can't help shuffling through the leaves—it makes such a wonderful sound. As he shuffles along, he kicks up something that clatters along the path. Stopping to pick it up, he sees that it is an expensive gold pen, similar to the one his friend recently bought. *What luck!* Tyrone thinks (he needs a new pen). What do you think Tyrone should do?

Should he . . .
A. Take the pen to the school lost and found?
B. Keep the pen and see if his friend mentions anything about losing his?
C. Take the pen to his friend to see if he lost it?
D. Leave the pen in the woods, hidden behind a tree. If no one finds it in a few weeks, keep it?
E. Keep the pen and sell it?

For help in knowing how Tyrone should handle this situation, look at Proverbs 3:27-28.

17

Future Plans

Archie's friend is one of those rare youths who knows from a young age exactly what he plans to do with his future. His friend's father is a doctor at the local hospital, and Archie's friend plans to follow in his father's footsteps. Archie is amazed at his friend's confidence. He has planned out the courses he must take in order to get into a good college. Every activity and class is calculated to help him get into the best medical school possible.

Every once in a while Archie's friend will ask him what he plans to do with his future. Archie doesn't have a clue. He enjoys a variety of subjects and activities. Some days he wants to be a teacher; at other times a professional athlete. He doesn't know yet, and it bothers him that he doesn't have a goal or driving ambition like his friend. He thinks that maybe he should begin planning for his future before it is too late. What do you think Archie should do?

Should he . . .
    A. Take a professional aptitude test and use that to determine his future career?
    B. Relax and trust that God has a plan for his life that will be fulfilled?
    C. Write a number of possible careers on slips of paper, put them in a hat, and then pick one out?
    D. Talk to his guidance counselor before it's too late?
    E. Panic and decide to work at a gas station?

 Psalm 25:4-5 will help Archie decide where to find the best direction for his future.

18

Something Borrowed, Something New

Gwen's mother is close friends with a woman at church who is a single mom raising three daughters. Mom is constantly loaning them things and sending Dad over to help fix their car when it breaks down (frequently). She also sends over clothes that Gwen has outgrown for the daughters. One of the woman's daughters is Gwen's age and attends her school. Gwen has tried to be friendly toward this girl, but the girl will have none of it. She tries to act as though her family has more money than they do so the kids will accept her.

Gwen feels sorry for the girl and usually tries to stay out of her way. She never mentions everything her family does to help out to any of the other kids. Today, however, Gwen overhears this girl talking about a new sweater she is wearing. It happens to be one of the sweaters Gwen's mother gave to the family. Gwen outgrew it last year, but it was one of her favorites. The girl is saying, "Oh this old thing . . . I hate it, but my mom makes me wear it. I can't wait until we go shopping this weekend for some new things." Gwen is burning. What do you think she should do?

Should Gwen . . .

A. Let the other girls know that those are her old clothes the girl is wearing?

B. Forget about the incident and walk away?

C. Tell her mom not to give away any of her clothes to this girl again?

D. Inform the girl that this was her favorite sweater when she wore it?

E. Take up a collection for the girl so she'll have better clothes to wear?

 Read Ruth 2:15-16 and Matthew 25:31-40 to see how God wants us to treat the needy.

19

Share and Share Alike

Sadie takes great pride in her wardrobe. She baby-sits a lot, and saves most of her money for buying new clothes. She loves nothing better than to flip through fashion magazines and check out the hottest fashion trends. Her younger sister, Callie, on the other hand, is a T-shirt-and-jeans girl. She wouldn't be caught dead in half the stuff her sister wears. But right now she is in a pinch.

Today is the awards ceremony for the basketball team, and Callie is expecting to receive the most valuable player award. The coach has told the girls to wear something nice. Callie has a jean skirt that will do, but nothing to wear with it. She runs upstairs to her sister's room and asks if she can borrow one of Sadie's new sweaters. Sadie isn't planning to wear the sweater, but she doesn't want to lend it to her sister, either. Callie is not known for taking the best care of her clothes. Certainly not like Sadie! Her sister is looking desperate at this point. What do you think Sadie should do?

Should she . . .
A. Charge her sister ten dollars for the dry-cleaning bill she is expecting after Callie wears the sweater?
B. Suddenly decide to wear her sweater after all?
C. Hide the sweater and say that it is at the dry cleaners?
D. Keep stalling until her mother yells at her to help out her sister?
E. Let Callie wear the sweater and hope that she wins the award?

 Take a look at Luke 12:32-34 to see how Jesus describes what our attitude should be toward sharing with others.

Get a Whiff of That

Garth meets with his friend at the park. "What do you want to do today?" Garth says as he greets his friend. "Want to play baseball or shoot a few hoops?" But his friend has another idea. "Let's take a walk," says Byron, "I want to show you something special." His friend usually isn't this secretive. Garth's curiosity is up. Byron heads toward an isolated part of the park. When the boys are well off the path and fairly secluded from any intrusions, Byron turns to Garth and takes a small bottle out of his pocket.

Garth takes a closer look. Byron has some Wite-Out fluid for correcting mistakes. "Here," he says. "Take a whiff of this. It gives you a great high. It makes you feel awesome." Garth heard some of the boys in gym class talking about sniffing Wite-Out and the feeling they get. He knows that a lot of kids at school are doing it. He's a bit curious about what can be so great about smelling a bottle of correction fluid. What do you think Garth should do?

Should he . . .
A. Take a small sniff just to say he has tried it?
B. Report Byron to Officer D.A.R.E?
C. Tell Bryon he's not interested in doing that kind of stuff?
D. Grab the bottle and say, "Great! I need this for when I make mistakes"?
E. Tell Byron maybe another day; he has a cold today?

 For help in knowing what Garth should do, read Romans 13:11-14.

Keeps on Ticking

For his birthday, Luis received a beautiful, expensive new watch. It's a waterproof sports watch with a dial that illuminates in the dark. Luis thinks it's the coolest gift he has ever received, and he takes great pride in showing it to all his friends. Luis has been careful to take it off each night and leave it on his nightstand beside his bed. He wants to take good care of his watch because he knows that if he doesn't, it will be a long time before he gets another watch as neat as this one.

Today, he and his friends are hanging out at the playground. Luis and his friend start wrestling and rolling around on the ground. His friend gets him in a half nelson and twists Luis around. Luis's arm goes flailing and slams onto a rock. Luis can hear the impact of his watch on the rock before he sees it. With a sickening feeling in his stomach, Luis looks at his watch. Although the watch is still ticking, the face is shattered. His friends gather around. "Oh no, your new watch! What will your father say?" his friend asks. Luis doesn't know, and he's not so sure he wants to find out. What do you think he should do?

Should Luis . . .

A. Get some Saran Wrap and make it look as though his watch still has its cover?

B. Play with his younger brother and make it look as though his brother broke the watch while they were messing around?

C. Get a toy watch that looks like the broken one and wear it so his parents won't ask where his new watch is?

D. Stop wearing the watch and tell his parents it hurt his wrist?

E. Take the watch to his parents and let them know what happened?

 Read Genesis 27:1-12 to find out about a Bible character who was more afraid of being caught than doing what was right.

The Knife Fight

On his way to school today, Keenan walked behind a group of boys who have a tough reputation at school. These boys get into fights at the school dances and like to intimidate the younger students. Keenan had a run-in with one of the boys earlier this year, so he usually tries to stay out of their way. As he was walking, Keenan slowed down because he didn't want to attract the boys' attention. Then he caught a glint of something that one of the boys was holding in his hands. Keenan couldn't be sure what it was because the boy quickly stuffed it back into his pocket.

Keenan forgot about the incident until later that day. As he is getting dressed in gym class, he overhears two boys talking about a knife fight that will take place after school. One of the boys mentioned is the one that Keenan saw that morning with the shiny object. It had to be a knife, Keenan thinks. What do you think he should do?

Should Keenan . . .
   A. Sell tickets to the fight?
   B. Help spread the rumor around the school?
   C. Tell the principal what he saw and let the principal take care of the situation?
   D. Don't say anything because he doesn't want this boy coming after him?
   E. See if the boy will sell the knife to him?

 Check out Esther 4:13-14 to see how Mordecai advised Queen Esther when she had to handle a difficult situation threatening her people.

A Call for Help

Reba has it all figured out. If she can finish her math by 7:30, then she can get in her piano practicing, take a shower, and still have time to work on her craft before bed. Reba and her mom are making a quilt that they plan to donate to the nursing home for Christmas. Her mom is an expert quilter and is teaching Reba. It has occupied every spare minute of Reba's time, and she is quite proud of her handiwork. Maybe someday she can become a master quilter like her mom.

As Reba sits down to open her math book, the phone rings. Mom calls up to her and says that the call is for her—it's Nan. Reba knows Nan from school, although she wouldn't call Nan one of her best friends. Nan has been sitting with Reba and her friends at lunch for the past several weeks. What Reba does know about Nan is that she is a gabber. Once she gets talking, she doesn't stop. Reba also knows that Nan is going through a particularly hard time. Her dad recently died of cancer, and she doesn't have many friends at school. Reba feels sorry for Nan, but she doesn't have the time to spare right now to spend a half hour on the phone with her. What do you think Reba should do?

Should she . . .
   A. Ask her mom to say that she had to go out (as she runs out of the house)?
   B. Tell Nan that she is only allowed to talk on the phone for five minutes?
   C. Tell Nan that she's busy and will talk with her at school in the morning?
   D. Take the time to talk with Nan and plan to work on the quilt another time?
   E. Give Nan the phone number of another friend she can call?

 For help in knowing what Reba should do, read 1 Thessalonians 4:18.

Dirty Politics

Leo is running for class president against a very popular boy, Nelson Brown. Although Leo has conducted a solid campaign and has good ideas to offer on organizing after-school activities and service projects, this boy has a definite edge because of one thing—his looks! All the girls have a crush on Nelson, and from what Leo can tell, they are planning to vote for him. The election is just a few days away—Leo knows he has to do something drastic, or he will lose the election.

Leo is telling his friends about his worries when one of his buddies comes up. "I've got the solution to your problem," he announces. "I overheard Nelson talking to some of his friends, and he said the girls are stupid to like the Flaming Tar Pits band. All you have to do is let the girls know that Nelson thinks they're stupid, and you're in. No girl is going to stand for that!" Leo agrees that the girls would definitely be mad at Nelson and probably wouldn't vote for him if they heard about what he said. This could be the key to the election. After all, it's just twisting Nelson's words a bit. What do you think Leo should do?

Should he . . .

A. Direct his campaign staff to print up posters that read Nelson Brown thinks girls are stupid?

B. Tell his friend he wants to win—or lose—this election fairly?

C. Have one of his friends start the rumor that Nelson thinks girls are stupid?

D. Call the school newspaper anonymously and leave them a tip on Nelson's antigirl platform?

E. Offer free homework passes to anyone who will vote for him?

 Read Leviticus 19:16 and Proverbs 25:18 for insight as to how Leo should handle this situation.

25

What's for Lunch?

Roy's mom usually packs him a bag lunch for school each day. She makes sure he has fruit, a healthy snack, a low-fat dessert, and two sandwiches. Today, however, she has a meeting to go to, so she tells Roy that he has to buy his lunch. Before she leaves the house, she encourages him to get a piece of fruit and something else nutritious for his lunch. Roy assures her he will eat well and not to worry about it.

By the time lunch rolls around, Roy is starving. The line is unusually long. He plans on buying one of the hot lunch offerings, but by the time he gets to the front of the line, the one selection he wanted is sold out. The other two alternatives look pretty frightening. The only other options are junk food. It's getting late, and Roy has to make a decision quickly. What do you think he should do?

Should he . . .

A. Try one of the alternatives, even if it does look like fish eyes and glue?

B. Select something nutritious from the á la carte menu, such as cheese and crackers, an apple, and a bagel?

C. Grab for the french fries, brownies, and soda pop—and throw in an apple to make it look good for his mom?

D. Decide that this is a good day to start his high-fat diet and load up on junk food?

E. Offer to buy a bag lunch from one of his friends?

 Check out the importance of eating right in Daniel 1:8-16.

Line Up!

All three children's choirs are singing this Sunday, including the youngest singers who range in age from three to five. In total, nearly sixty children are involved. The children arrive and get ready to enter the sanctuary about fifteen minutes before the service begins. The choir director and her assistants get the children lined up properly in the order they should march into church and then tell everyone to stay in line. About five minutes before they are to enter, however, the director is called away to solve a minor last-minute problem.

As soon as she leaves the hallway, the children start to get antsy. The younger ones start to wander away. A few of the older boys begin tussling with one another. Several other children decide this is a good time to switch places so they can stand next to their friends. As one of the older choir members, and with no adult around, Simone feels as though she should do something to restore order. What do you think Simone should do?

Should she . . .

A. Scream at the top of her lungs, "Get in line now—or else!"?

B. Run and try to find the choir director to take care of matters?

C. Quietly go down the line and try to restore order?

D. Take down the names of all the troublemakers in the choir so she can report them later?

E. Figure it looks like fun and help switch the kids around?

 Proverbs 27:18 and Titus 2:1 will give insight into how Simone should respond in this situation.

27

The Saturday Couch Potato

Saturday is finally here, and Addie is looking forward to some rest and relaxation. For the first time in what seems like months, she doesn't have a game, a scout activity, or a church program. Only pure blissful freedom from school and the hectic schedule of activities during the week. Addie quickly helps out with the Saturday chores in the morning and is free to do what she wants by 11 A.M. The only decision she needs to make is what she will do for the rest of the day.

Addie has a whole stack of books that she had checked out from the library the other day. There's a sewing project she could finish. It's a beautiful day outside, perfect for a bike ride along the river with her family. Or she could be a couch potato and sit in front of the tube watching the Saturday cartoon lineup. After a demanding week at school, sitting in front of the TV and vegging out doesn't sound like such a bad option. What do you think Addie should do?

Should she . . .

- A. Get the remote, park herself on the sofa, and plug in?
- B. Play solitaire?
- C. Read some trendy teen magazines that have all the latest dirt on teen heartthrobs?
- D. Polish her nails and toenails?
- E. Take a bike ride with her family and enjoy some family time together?

 The biblical principles in Ephesians 5:15-17 and 6:2-3 will help you decide what Addie should do.

Practice Time

Georgette recently began playing the trombone at school. She and her parents went to the band organizational meeting, rented the instrument, and even arranged to have Georgette take some private lessons on the side. Her parents agreed to buy her an instrument when they see she has made a commitment to continue playing. As part of their agreement, Georgette must practice at least twenty minutes each day.

The first several weeks, Georgette was excited to get her instrument home and try to make a sound on it. She has progressed since then to playing simple tunes such as "Hot Cross Buns" and "Old MacDonald." Usually her mom asks her after dinner if she has practiced, and Georgette goes up to her room to practice. Tonight, her mom is in a hurry to get to a meeting at school, so she doesn't check with Georgette to see if she has practiced. Georgette finishes her homework and is about to head downstairs to watch TV when she spies the horn standing in a corner of her room. She knows she should practice, but her mom didn't say anything about it before she left. What do you think Georgette should do?

Should she . . .
   A. Practice as she usually does?
   B. Go watch the TV show. Her mom would have mentioned it if she wanted her to practice, right?
   C. Blow a few notes to say she practiced and then go down to watch TV?
   D. Look blankly at her mom if she asks about practicing when she comes home and say, "I forgot"?
   E. Ask her mom right before bedtime, "Did you want me to practice tonight?"

 Read 1 Samuel 15:1-11 to see what happened to King Saul when he selectively obeyed God's command.

All Alone

Troy is a transfer student. Although he still lives in the same town, it's as if he has entered a different world. Troy and his family made the decision to switch schools because of the advanced math courses offered at his new school. Troy dreams one day of becoming a doctor, and he thought the more challenging classes would help him toward that goal. Troy knew that the academics would be difficult, but he never dreamed the social aspect of transferring schools would be so tough.

The majority of kids at his new school live in a wealthier part of town. They are into wearing designer label clothes, comparing vacation spots, and seeing who has the most "toys." Troy's family is less wealthy, and, frankly, those kinds of material possessions don't appeal much to Troy. He's more interested in a friend who appreciates a good touch-football game, going fishing in the river, or relaxing after school listening to some good music. Troy is beginning to think that no one shares his interests and values. Right now Troy is feeling very much alone and discouraged. What do you think he should do?

Should Troy . . .

A. Put an ad in the school newspaper and advertise for friends?

B. Ask his parents if he can transfer back to his old school?

C. Start wearing designer clothes so he can fit in with the new crowd?

D. Trust that God is with him and will help him through this difficult transition?

E. Give up on ever meeting friends at his new school?

 Read Genesis 28:15 to see how the Lord comforted Jacob when he was alone.

Those Lucky Laces

Trevor has noticed that one of his teammates on the basketball squad goes through the same ritual before every game. He lays out his uniform on the bench exactly the same way each week. He always puts his left shoe on first and then his right. But the shoelaces are particularly strange: One is white, and the other is black. Finally, after watching this guy do this for several weeks, Trevor can't contain his curiosity any longer. "Why do you have two differently colored shoelaces?" he asks.

The teammate matter-of-factly explains that these are his lucky laces. "I always buy one pair of laces for the season. I say a few incantations over them before I wear them, and then they are lucky. So far, every time I have worn them, we have won the game," he says. Trevor has to admit the team has been very successful this season. They have only lost one game, and come to think of it, that was the game his teammate missed. Trevor looks at his teammate to see if he's laughing—but he's not. Trevor can tell that the boy takes this ritual very seriously. Maybe, thinks Trevor, there is something to these lucky laces after all. Maybe he should check it out further. What do you think Trevor should do?

Should he . . .
   A.   Buy his own pair of lucky laces and ask the boy to say a few words over them?
   B.   When the boy isn't watching, take the laces and see what happens to the team?
   C.   Tell his teammate, "Boy, you must be really stupid to believe in lucky shoelaces"?
   D.   Tell his teammate, "I don't believe in superstitions. The Lord is in control of all things, not some shoelaces"?
   E.   Get a rabbit's foot, lucky charm, and four-leaf clover and start carrying them around?

 Check out Hebrews 13:9 to see how Trevor should respond.

1

Gaining an In-Sight

The big choral competition is going to be held next week. All students entering the competition must prepare a solo with an accompanist and then read a piece of music they have never seen before. Ferguson is entering the competition for the first time this year. He has prepared what he thinks is an excellent solo to showcase his tenor voice. What he is worried about, however, is the sight-reading—it counts for about 40 percent of the final rating. He has not had a lot of practice with sight-reading.

After finishing his practice session with the choral director, Ferguson remembers that he didn't ask her about warm-up times. He hurries back into the choral room, but the director isn't there. He happens to glance at her desk and sees a piece of music laying there. Taking a closer look to see if this is something the choir will be singing this winter, he realizes that this *is* the sight-reading selection for the competition. Ferguson can't believe his good fortune. If he learns this, he will be selected for the state choral group—a goal he has set for himself since joining chorus. The opportunity is there, but should he take it? What do you think Ferguson should do?

Should he . . .
A. Tell the choral director he accidentally saw the sight-reading selection and request a new one for himself?
B. Quickly run out and copy the music before the choral director discovers it missing?
C. Scan the piece of music to note any difficult intervals and key changes?
D. Charge his friends for the name of the sight-reading selection?
E. Find a copy of the selection at the local music store to prepare for it ahead of time?

Listen to the warning in Proverbs 10:9 to know what Ferguson should do.

2

The Scary Flick Fest

Fiona's friends are into scary movies big time. The more monsters in the flick, the better. Scary movies are not exactly Fiona's preference. Every time she watches one, *she* is a horror the next day because she was too scared to sleep. Usually when her friends get together for a scary flick fest, Fiona takes a pass. But it has been several months since their last horror movie gathering, so when they ask Fiona to join them, she agrees. She's growing out of that phase, she believes, and can handle a few monsters now.

The girls plan to make it an all-night affair, with scary movies and popcorn. Fiona thinks it sounds like fun, but when she checks it out with her parents, they are skeptical. "Are you sure you want to do this?" they ask, advising her that it may be wiser to avoid the movies. But Fiona assures them that she will be all right and will get enough sleep so she'll be fresh for her grandmother's birthday party the next day. Five minutes into the first movie, however, Fiona realizes that she has made a terrible mistake. She is scared silly and doesn't know what to do. She doesn't want to wimp out in front of her friends, but she is frightened! What do you think Fiona should do?

Should she . . .
A. Watch the movies with the girls and show up like a zombie at her grandmother's party?
B. Hide under the bed and tell her friends she's looking for dust bunnies?
C. Pretend that she has to take a bath and hide out in the bathroom for a couple of hours?
D. Tell her friends that she is going to read upstairs while they watch the movies?
E. Call her dad to come and get her—before the monsters do?

 Read Proverbs 3:21-24 and Proverbs 4:3-4 to see what Fiona should do.

The Christmas Pageant

All the kids in the children's choir have been talking about the Christmas pageant. Tryouts were last week, and today everyone will receive their part. April is especially excited. She is finally old enough to try out for a good part, and she did pretty well during the auditions. Sure enough, April is selected for one of the leading roles. She can't wait to get home and tell her parents. Before she leaves rehearsal, the director asks April to stay after a few minutes so she can explain a few things about her part. "You see, April, this is an important role. We gave you this part because we think you can do the best job with this character. She has to be funny, yet not too overdone. We think you are the perfect one for the part," the director tells April.

Riding her bike home, April considers what the director said. *Wow,* she thinks, *this is a big responsibility.* Bigger, to be honest, than April expected. The more she thinks about the part, the less confident she feels about it. *What if I can't do it? What if I can't be funny? What if the director doesn't like the way I act? What if . . .* The "what ifs" keep running through April's mind. By the time she gets home, she isn't so sure she wants to take the part. She doesn't want to be the biggest flop of the whole performance. What do you think April should do?

Should she . . .
- A. Call back the choir director as soon as she gets home and tell her she's having second thoughts, not to mention pre-stage fright?
- B. Hire an acting coach to get her through the part?
- C. Trust that God will enable her to do the part—and give her peace of mind?
- D. Go to the bookstore and buy a joke book so she can be *really* funny?
- E. Suggest another choir member for the part?

 Read Joshua 1:5-9 for Scripture that can give April some much needed encouragement.

4

Come Clean!

Albert has been lying in his bed, eyes wide open, mulling over his conversation this evening with his best friend, Rusty. He can't stop thinking about it. Albert had finished his homework when the phone rang. It was Rusty. Albert had listened in almost disbelief as Rusty poured out his recent problems and struggles. Albert mostly listened and tried to understand his friend's situation, but it wasn't easy. To make things more difficult, his dad interrupted in the middle of the conversation and told Albert that he needed to get off the phone.

The biggest problem is that Rusty confessed to doing something terribly wrong. He admitted that he was the one who stole the expensive piece of equipment from the band room. The band director had talked to the entire band today about it and had said that they would have to cancel their next performance if they couldn't replace it. Rusty admitted to Albert that he did it on a dare, but now he feels terribly guilty about it and doesn't know what to do.

Albert knows that he will see Rusty tomorrow. He wants to help Rusty, but what should he do?

Should Albert . . .
   A.   Go directly to the band director and report Rusty?
   B.   Tell his father about Rusty and ask him what to do?
   C.   Start yelling at Rusty and ask him how he could do such a thing?
   D.   Talk with Rusty gently and encourage him to confess what he did, letting him know that God forgives him and loves him?
   E.   Tell his other friends what Rusty has done?

 To know how Albert should respond, read God's wonderful promise in Joel 2:12-13 to all who are guilty of sin.

5

The Naysayer

The church youth group is discussing plans for the upcoming year. One of the goals is to involve as many kids as possible. The group is discussing ways to accomplish this goal. One of the suggestions is to give rewards to the member who brings the most friends to meetings during the year. Another is to plan at least one major activity each season that will attract lots of kids. The group decides that the second idea is the best way to go. Now all they need are some ideas for what activities to plan. The group begins brainstorming, and they start a list: hayride, game night, roller-skating, spring carnival.

Talbot looks at the list in disgust. *None of these ideas are any good,* he thinks. Every youth group has a hayride. It's so boring, and besides he has hay fever. Carnivals are for little kids, and Talbot hates to play games. Roller-skating is for geeks. He can't believe they are even considering these ideas. It's useless anyway because the same old kids always come to youth group and always run the meetings—it never changes. Talbot is disgusted. When it is his turn to voice his opinion, he is ready to let them have it. What do you think Talbot should do?

Should he . . .
- A. Tell the group that their plans stink?
- B. Suggest they hire D.C. Talk to perform at the church— that would attract attention?
- C. Tell the group that they will never get any new kids to come because youth group is boring?
- D. Offer some constructive criticism and alternatives to the proposed plans?
- E. Shrug his shoulders and say, "Whatever"?

 Read Deuteronomy 1:22-28 to see the effects of listening to negative opinions.

My Grandmother

Rhoda loves her grandmother dearly. They have a wonderful relationship and share many of the same interests. Like Rhoda, her grandmother likes to read. She has hundreds of books at her house, which she shares with Rhoda. Rhoda likes nothing more than to ride her bike over to her grandmother's house and pick out a few of her grandmother's favorites from when she was a girl. Rhoda has read all of Louisa May Allcott's stories and Charles Dickens's books because of her grandmother. Often when Rhoda was about to start a new book, her grandmother would sit and read to her. They would spend many pleasurable afternoons reading together.

Now her grandmother is dying of cancer. They discovered the cancer in her liver about two months ago. Her grandmother was put on chemotherapy, which only made her feel more ill. Today the doctors released her grandmother from the hospital, saying they could do nothing more for her. Rhoda is angry. She is angry at the doctors. She is angry at her grandmother for getting sick. Most of all, she is angry at God for allowing this to happen. She feels confused as well. Her parents keep telling Rhoda to pray for her grandmother, but she doesn't see the point. What do you think Rhoda should do?

Should she . . .

   A. Tell her parents she refuses to pray anymore because it's hopeless?

   B. Express her anger to God because he knows how she feels?

   C. Lock herself in her room and refuse to come out?

   D. Throw a tantrum because she can't understand what's happening?

   E. Pretend that everything is OK and refuse to accept the fact that her grandmother is dying?

 Read Psalm 13 to see how David expressed, with honesty, his anguish and anger toward God.

7

The Houseguest

Millie is spending a week at her cousin's house while her parents are away. Millie and her cousin, Coretta, are the same age. During the year, they exchange letters, so they know that they share many of the same interests. Since Coretta and Millie live in different parts of the country, however, they have not spent much time together. This is the first time Millie will spend a lot of time with Coretta. She is looking forward to the visit. Her cousin lives near the mountains, and Millie is eager to go hiking and exploring.

After the first day, Millie knows she is in for a long week. She and her cousin may share the same interests, but not in the same manner! Her cousin is a grouch! Coretta is constantly complaining and arguing with her mother and brother. She never wants to do anything that Millie suggests, yet she never has any suggestions as to what she wants to do. Coretta never seems to enjoy anything but watching TV. Millie can do that at home. Millie doesn't know how she is going to make it through the next five days. What do you think she should do?

Should Millie . . .
   A. Write and ask her parents to cut their trip short and come get her?
   B. Complain to Coretta's mother about her?
   C. Stay in her room the entire visit? At least she won't have to listen to Coretta.
   D. Make the best of the situation and pray that God will help her through the week?
   E. Tell Coretta to snap out of it!?

 Take a look at Romans 5:3-5 to see how Millie can survive the week.

A Judgment Call

Jonah's lab partner is a quiet girl who recently moved into his community. Vera is very good at science and is a great to have as a lab partner. Jonah, who struggles in science, appreciates her quiet way of explaining things to him without making him feel stupid. He actually has learned a lot about setting up a lab experiment from watching her. He would like to know Vera better, but she tends to keep to herself. She doesn't come to any of the school social activities. As far as Jonah can tell, she comes to school and then goes home.

Today in the lab, Jonah notices that Vera's arms are bruised, and there is a small cut above her right eye. He takes a look at her and says, "Hey, what happened to you? Did you run into a door or something?" Vera quickly averts her eyes and mumbles, "Oh nothing. I tripped or something." But Jonah knows something else is wrong because Vera's hands are shaking, and she won't look at him. This is not the first time Vera has come to school with a cut or a bruise. What if someone in her family is beating her up? Jonah is concerned about Vera, but he doesn't know what to do about it. What do you think he should do?

Should Jonah . . .

  A. Follow Vera home and see if he can find out anything?

  B. Ask Vera if she is on a Roller Derby team?

  C. Call the police and report Vera's family?

  D. Ignore the situation—if things were bad at her home, Vera would surely say something?

  E. Confide his suspicions to either his parents or a guidance counselor at school?

 Read Galatians 6:2-3 to see how Jonah should respond in this situation.

Math Buddies

Ethan is the math whiz in his class. Give him any problem, and he can rattle off the answer in ten seconds or less. It doesn't matter what the class is studying—fractions, decimals, multiplication, long division—it's a snap for Ethan. Today, the class is starting a unit on measurements using the metric system. The teacher pairs the students off and gives them a workbook to complete by the end of the week. Students must participate in doing it and can work on the project in class or after school if they want.

Ethan flips through the workbook. No problem, he thinks. Then he hears who his math partner will be—Lennie, the worst math student in the class. Ethan is not so sure this guy knows how to read a metric ruler, never mind converting to the metric system. This will be a long week. The two boys sit down to tackle the first page of the workbook during class. As Ethan expects, Lennie is beyond hope. He doesn't even know that there's a difference between meters and yards. Ethan can't believe his bad luck in getting Lennie as his partner. What do you think Ethan should do?

Should he . . .
   A. Demand a new partner?
   B. Work with Lennie a little bit each day until he understands the metric system?
   C. Take the workbook home and do all the math himself?
   D. Let Lennie know that he is a real mess-up in math, and he doesn't want him as a partner?
   E. Give Lennie a crash course in "Metrics for Dummies"?

 To find out what Jesus has to say about our pride and what our attitude towards others should be, read Mark 9:33-35.

Bus Stop

The kids on Bernie's bus are a bit rowdy—to put it mildly. Already they have had two bus drivers since school began. Today is the first day for their new bus driver.

Mrs. Nelson is an older, grandmotherly type. Already, Bernie feels sorry for her because he knows that the older boys will make her life miserable. Sure enough, as soon as the boys get on the bus, they start calling the driver "Granny" and carrying on in the back of the bus.

As the situation worsens, Mrs. Nelson stops the bus and refuses to go farther until all the boys in the back sit down. She yells at the entire busload of kids and lets them know that the next time she has to stop for bad behavior, she is writing down every student's name and turning it in to the principal. Bernie believes that she will do it, too.

The next day at the bus stop, one of Bernie's friends gives him a piece of paper. "What's this?" he asks. "It's a petition to the school to fire Mrs. Nelson. She has no right to yell at us the way she did. We want to get rid of her," his friend explains. This friend wants Bernie to sign the petition. Bernie can see that more than half the kids on his bus have already signed the petition, but he doesn't know what to do. It seems to him that they all deserved what happened yesterday because no one was cooperating. What do you think Bernie should do?

Should he . . .
 A. Politely say no and explain that he believes Mrs. Nelson is trying to do her job and maintain safety on the bus?
 B. Sign the petition because most of the other kids have signed it?
 C. Sign the petition and then offer to get more signatures?
 D. Get his mom to drive him to school so he can avoid more trouble on the bus?
 E. Start a smear campaign against Mrs. Nelson so she will definitely be fired?

 To know how Bernie should respond, check out 1 Peter 2:17.

The Tutor

Newt is having trouble in his English class. He struggles writing a complete sentence, and now he is expected to write a term paper for the end of the semester. Newt and his parents have had several conferences with his teacher already. She has recommended that Newt have a tutor to help him with his term paper. She gives his parents several names, and his mom has made arrangements for Miss Birdwell to come and tutor him on Monday afternoons. Newt is not so sure about this arrangement. What he would like is for someone to come and write the paper for him—not tell him how to do it!

Today, Miss Birdwell is expected to show up after school. Newt drags home—he is not looking forward to this meeting at all. Promptly at four o'clock the doorbell rings and in walks Miss Birdwell. Newt nearly gasps when he first meets her. She has a huge, red birthmark that extends from her neck up the left side of her face. He can hardly take his eyes off it. It seems to dominate her entire face. Newt doesn't know how he is going to concentrate on his lesson. What do you think Newt should do?

Should he . . .
- A. Blurt out, "What's that thing on your face"?
- B. Keep his eyes on the floor and not look at her for an entire hour?
- C. Make fun of her behind her back and call her Splotch-Face?
- D. Ask his mom to get him another tutor because Miss Birdwell is too distracting?
- E. Realize that Miss Birdwell's appearance has nothing to do with the knowledge she can share with him and ignore the mark?

 Take a look at the biblical principle expressed in Proverbs 31:30-31 to know how Newt should respond to his new tutor.

The Pastor's Daughter

It's not easy being the daughter of a pastor—just ask Kendra. Not only is her dad the pastor of one of the largest churches in town, but he is also highly visible in the community. He has been in the local paper several times; on one occasion, the photographer took a picture of the entire family. Kendra was so embarrassed that she considered changing her name until everyone forgot about it. She took a lot of kidding from her friends about that picture. Kendra is proud of her dad and is committed to serving the Lord, but she wishes the kids in school would leave her alone.

Kendra doesn't try to preach at her friends or convert them. Sure, if they ask her a serious question, she is prepared and willing to answer. But most of the kids call her "Holy Roller" and "the Rev." Some of the boys start thumping on their books and call her "Bible-thumper." Other kids at school are Christians, too, but they don't get mocked like she does. Sometimes it is really difficult to ignore. Like today. One boy taunts her the entire way home: "Hey, I bet you think you're better than everyone else, huh, Preacher Girl? Think you're pretty good, huh!" Kendra is near tears and near the breaking point. What do you think she should do?

Should Kendra . . .
A. Turn around and pop this guy good?
B. Say, "Look, loser, I'm certainly better than you are"?
C. Pray hard that God will give her the strength to overlook these insults and allow her to be kind to her tormentors?
D. Wear heavy makeup, weird clothes, and get in trouble at school to show that she doesn't take this Christian thing very seriously?
E. Plan a series of subtle attacks—writing notes, spreading rumors, etc.—on this boy and the others?

 Read 1 Peter 3:9 to know how Kendra should respond.

13

Double Trouble

Gretchen is baby-sitting the Thompson twins tonight—the two-year-old terrors of the neighborhood. In the span of two hours, the twins have taken out every toy they own and have deposited them throughout the house. One has run through the downstairs trailing a roll of toilet paper. The other has removed all the books from the bookshelves in the family room. There are cookie crumbs everywhere—a sure sign of Gretchen trying to bribe the boys to stop whatever they were doing.

Bedtime was a nightmare. Gretchen succeeded in getting one boy into his bed when the other decided he needed a drink of water. Finally after forty-five minutes of the boys popping in and out of bed, the house is quiet. Gretchen is exhausted, and it is only nine o'clock. The Thompsons aren't expected back until eleven-thirty, so Gretchen is looking forward to a quiet two-and-a-half hours. The house is a total wreck, however. Mrs. Thompson gave her instructions about taking care of the twins, but she never mentioned the house. Gretchen knows her mom wouldn't want the house looking like that, but hey, they hired a baby-sitter, not a maid. What do you think Gretchen should do?

Should she . . .
  A. Pick up the worst of the damage and leave the rest for Mrs. Thompson?
  B. Grab a bowl of ice cream, plug in a video, sit back, and relax?
  C. Call the Merry Maid Service and bill it to Mrs. Thompson?
  D. Clean up the entire mess, but charge Mrs. Thompson twenty dollars extra?
  E. Get going and clean up the mess before the Thompsons come home?

 Look at Ruth's example in Ruth 2:1-7 to see what Gretchen should do.

14

The Blizzard

Last night it snowed about ten inches in Davis's town. School is canceled, and it feels like a holiday. The sun is shining brightly, and although it is cold, it's going to be a great day for sledding! Davis can't wait. First, however, he knows he has to help his dad shovel the driveway. By the time he gets downstairs for breakfast, Davis discovers that Dad has already shoveled the driveway so he can get to work. Davis can't believe his good fortune until Mom tells him he needs to go down the street and shovel out the driveway of his elderly neighbor, Mrs. Bates. Davis is still stuck shoveling, but it shouldn't take him long.

Davis rings Mrs. Bates' doorbell to let her know he's there to shovel her driveway. Mrs. Bates is so appreciative that Davis has a hard time getting away. It takes about forty-five minutes for Davis to clear her driveway. He still has time to get in some sledding this morning, he thinks. He looks up at Mrs. Bates' house and realizes that the front walk is not shoveled, nor is there a path shoveled to her backdoor. Davis knows his dad always shovels that for Mrs. Bates, but his mom only mentioned doing the driveway. He wants to get going. Mrs. Bates probably isn't going out anyway today and doesn't need her walkways shoveled. What do you think Davis should do?

Should he . . .

A. Figure that the sun will melt the snow—eventually?

B. Promise to come back later, after his sledding, to finish shoveling the walks?

C. Let his dad shovel the walks when he comes home from work?

D. Go ahead and finish the job by shoveling the walks for Mrs. Bates?

E. Figure he has done enough shoveling for one day and go sledding?

 For help in knowing what Davis should do, read Hebrews 13:16.

15

The New Outfit

Noelle and her best friend, Joyce, are shopping today for a new outfit for the upcoming school dance. Joyce is going to help Noelle pick out something that will wow the guys. Joyce is popular with the boys, and she thinks she can give Noelle some good advice on what kind of clothes attract the boys. Noelle is a bit skeptical. She likes Joyce as a friend but is not so sure about her as a fashion consultant. Joyce has a different style than she does. Joyce is bold. She wears the latest styles and doesn't mind if she stands out in a crowd. In fact, the more attention she gets, the better.

Noelle is the exact opposite. She is quiet and reserved. A nice pair of jeans and a sweater suit her fine. But Joyce was so insistent that, in the end, Noelle agreed to the shopping excursion. Now she's in the dressing room, looking at herself in the mirror. Joyce has selected a black leather miniskirt with a red top and vest with neon colors in geometric patterns. She brings Noelle a pair of gaudy earrings that are perfect for the outfit. Noelle has to admit she does look good in the outfit, but it just isn't her. Joyce nods approvingly and tells her it's perfect. Noelle is not so sure. What do you think she should do?

Should Noelle . . .
- A. Tell Joyce she wouldn't be caught dead in this outfit?
- B. Tell Joyce her father absolutely forbids her to wear black miniskirts?
- C. Thank Joyce for her help but stick with her jeans?
- D. Buy the outfit but throw it in the back of her closet?
- E. Wear the outfit to the dance but stay in the girls' bathroom the entire night?

 Check out 1 Timothy 2:9-10 to see how Noelle should handle this situation.

The Grandparent Dilemma

Abe and his friends are planning to attend a rock concert at a local Christian college next Saturday night. Several new groups are scheduled to play, including a band that Abe has heard a lot about. This is the band's first appearance in the area. Abe plans to get tickets on Saturday afternoon and ride to the college with one of his friends' brothers who attends the school. This will be Abe's first rock concert, and he is excited about it.

At the dinner table tonight, however, Abe's dad tells him that his grandparents are coming for a visit. Abe and his family haven't seen them since the last holiday. Grandma and Grandpa plan to arrive next Friday night, and they want to take Abe and his two sisters to the circus. Abe thinks that's great until he hears the time—Saturday night, the same night as the rock concert. Abe's grandparents don't come to town very often, and he enjoys visiting with them. But this is an important night for Abe. When he explains the situation, his dad says, "It's up to you to decide what you want to do." What do you think Abe should do?

Should he . . .
- A. Flip a coin?
- B. Tell his grandparents that he's too old for the circus?
- C. Spend Friday night and all day Saturday with his grandparents and then head for the concert on Saturday night?
- D. Tell his friends there will be other concerts and spend the time with his grandparents?
- E. Invite his grandparents to the rock concert?

 Read Psalm 39:4 and James 4:13-15 for the biblical principles that should guide Abe's decision.

17

Youth Group Rap

Faye has decided to invite one of her school friends to her church youth group. She has been praying about this for some time. Jasmine is new to the school and doesn't know many people. On the quiet side, she is easily overlooked in a large crowd. But if any group will welcome Jasmine, Faye knows it's her youth group. The kids are friendly and easy to talk to. Faye believes this could help Jasmine make some new friends.

Faye has a hard time convincing Jasmine to come to the youth group, but after several weeks of gentle nudging, Jasmine agrees to attend tonight's meeting. Faye is eager to help her friend become acquainted with the group. After the introductions, however, the kids in the youth group move toward their own friends and leave Faye and Jasmine standing alone. Faye can't believe how rude everyone is behaving. She is angry at her friends. After all it took for her to get Jasmine here, and now no one is talking to her. What do you think Faye should do?

Should she . . .

   A. Scream at the group at the top of her lungs to meet her new friend?

   B. Say nothing at the meeting but tell off a few of them after the meeting?

   C. Quietly take Jasmine and join one of the small conversation circles?

   D. Apologize to Jasmine for the rude kids in the group?

   E. Tell the youth group leaders about these rotten, self-centered kids?

 Check out Proverbs 12:16 to see how Faye should react.

Trading Cards

Bud is an avid baseball card collector. He attends shows and keeps up with all the latest dealings. He has a fairly extensive collection that he and his dad have put together over the years. Today, he plans to trade one of his best cards for several cards of lesser value, but ones that he needs to complete some team rosters from the mid 70s. It was a difficult decision, but Bud decides that he wants to complete as many team rosters as he can.

Bud meets his friend at the burger joint to make the trade. The boys make the swap. Before Bud can pick up the cards to put them away, his friend accidentally spills his milkshake on the table. The cards that Bud just traded for are covered with gooey, chocolate shake. Bud stares in dismay. His new cards are ruined. What do you think he should do?

Should Bud . . .
- A. Say the deal is off because his cards are ruined?
- B. Spill his milkshake on his friend's card?
- C. A deal is a deal—wipe off the cards and keep them?
- D. Cry over spilled milkshakes?
- E. Demand more cards from his friend as replacements for the damaged ones?

 Check out Judges 15:7-11 and Luke 11:4 to see what Bud should do.

Meet My Brother

Raquel and her family moved in during the fall. Raquel likes her new school and has met lots of people. She has been making friends, especially with girls in chorus—Raquel loves to sing. She has been working hard at learning the music for the winter program and is one of the few younger students to have a solo.

Tonight is the performance, and Raquel's entire family is coming to hear her. Raquel is anxious for her parents to meet some of her new friends from chorus. She also wants her friends to meet her younger brother, Ellis. Raquel loves her brother, although he is different from other children. Ellis was born with a nerve disorder that causes him to make sudden loud noises and move jerkily. He is a lovable little boy with a terrific sense of humor. Raquel is sure her friends will love him too.

Before she has a chance to introduce her family, the chorus is lining up, getting ready to make their entrance. Just before going on stage, Raquel can hear her brother making noises. A few of the students look out at the audience and giggle. Raquel notices her friends whispering and giggling, too, as his loud noises continue. "Hey, who brought the dorky little kid. What a weirdo," Raquel overhears the girls talking. She can feel her face turning bright red with embarrassment. What do you think she should do?

Should Raquel . . .

A. Join in the giggling and pretend that she doesn't know the little boy?

B. Explain to her friends about her brother so they will understand why he makes those noises?

C. Get mad and tell her friends they are a bunch of inconsiderate creeps?

D. Skip out right after the concert so her friends won't know that the boy is her brother?

E. Ask her parents not to bring her brother to any more concerts?

 Raquel can find guidance in this situation in Psalm 139:13-14, a wonderful testament to God's amazing design for each person.

20

The Honors Classes

Carlton and his dad are planning to meet with the guidance counselor today. Carlton has an opportunity to get into honors science and honors math because of his good grades. He is worried about the meeting because he and his dad have wrestled with the decision. Carlton's dad believes that the honors classes will help prepare Carlton for college and will challenge him in those areas. Carlton agrees, but he still doesn't want to take those classes.

Right now, Carlton doesn't have to work very hard to do well in school. That has given him time to explore other activities without getting stressed out about homework. Carlton knows that if he takes the honors classes, he may have to drop some activities that he enjoys. He also knows that he will have to work hard to get good grades. Carlton is not very excited at that prospect. He figures that college will come soon enough, and he can work hard then. His dad says that Carlton can make the final decision. Now it's time to decide. What do you think he should do?

Should Carlton . . .

A. Agree to take the honors classes because they are the best preparation for college?

B. Compromise and take one honors class to see how it goes. If he doesn't have to work too hard, then fine?

C. Tell his dad that he's doing fine in his classes now and doesn't want to make any changes? Why mess up a good thing?

D. Tell his dad that if he takes the honors classes and flunks, then he won't get into college at all?

E. Ask the counselor if he can sit in during the classes to see how bad it might get and then decide?

 Take a look at Proverbs 6:6-8 for insight into what Carlton should do.

The Party Poopers

Following their basketball game, Alvin and his buddies are at a party thrown by a girl he knows. About thirty friends from school are there, and everyone is having a good time eating pizza and listening to music. Alvin and some of his friends, however, decide that they want to liven things up a bit, so they start messing around downstairs. They decide that it would be a good idea to play football. They start tossing a football around the room, nearly breaking a lamp. The boys dart in and out of the crowded room, almost knocking people over. Kids start screaming, and the entire room is in a frenzy.

Finally, the girl's father comes downstairs. He grabs Alvin, who is carrying the football, and a couple of other boys, and says they have to leave, *now*. As they walk out of the room, a couple of boys make comments about what a jerk Alvin was to start the football game. Alvin is totally humiliated. He is angry about being tossed from the party. What do you think Alvin should do?

Should he . . .
   A. Tell everyone at school what crummy parties this girl throws?
   B. Sit down and write an apology to the girl and her parents for his rude behavior?
   C. Go back that night and toilet paper the house?
   D. Plan to crash the girl's next party and make an even worse scene?
   E. Make sure to humiliate the girl in school on Monday?

 Read Numbers 22:21-34 to see what Balaam did when confronted by God after reacting angrily because of his wounded pride.

Talk of the School

Everybody at school is talking about Edwin's best friend. Actually, it's his best friend's older brother. The other day, a story appeared in the local newspaper that his friend's brother, a star player on the high school football team, was suspended from school for undisclosed reasons. No one knows why, and no one on the team is talking, including the coach. It's a huge blow to the team and could hurt their chances in the state tournament. Edwin knows that his friend's family is quite upset about the entire incident. He also knows the story behind the suspension because his friend confided in him.

At lunch today, the boys are talking about his friend's brother. The rumor mill is working overtime, and there are some pretty weird rumors flying around: The guy hit the coach; the coach hit him for mouthing off; the guy sold drugs; he bought drugs; he was caught cheating on a test. Then the boys start saying untrue things about Edwin's friend. Edwin is getting mad now. He knows the true story, and it doesn't have anything to do with what these boys are saying. Edwin wants to set the record straight about his friend's brother and his friend, but he doesn't want to break a confidence. What do you think he should do?

Should Edwin . . .
- A. Tell the boys only a portion of what he knows so they will shut up?
- B. Tell the boys the whole story so they will get it right?
- C. Keep quiet and say nothing?
- D. Make up an even more outrageous story to keep the boys off track?
- E. Tell the boys that he knows the truth but is not going to tell them?

 To know what Edwin should do, read David's words in Psalm 57:1-7 about his feelings concerning those who were spreading rumors about him.

23

Working behind the Scenery

Rena is a very talented artist, one of the best in the school. About two months ago, the director of the school musical asked Rena if she would help them design the scenery for this year's production. Rena had never tackled a project that big, but she agreed. Since then, Rena has devoted long hours to coming up with set designs and working with the director to create the right atmosphere for each scene. It's a huge project, but Rena has diligently worked to get the job done.

It's opening night. Rena spent several hours before the show to make sure that everything was in the right place. When the curtain opens, Rena is pleased to see how well the scenery works with each scene. She is proud that her hard work paid off. After the show, Rena is waiting for a friend in the lobby. She overhears people raving about the music, the singing, and the acting, but no one is talking about the scenery. After all those long hours, Rena feels that she deserves some recognition. What do you think she should do?

Should Rena . . .
 A. Offer to take these folks backstage to see the scenery close up?
 B. Take quiet satisfaction in a job well done?
 C. Go up to everyone in the lobby and ask them how they liked the scenery?
 D. Ask the director to make a special announcement about all her hard work?
 E. Brag to anyone who will listen about the great job she did on the scenery?

 Check out 2 Corinthians 10:17-18 for the biblical principle that should guide Rena's response.

Roommates

Jayna has to share her room with her younger sister. For a while, Jayna had her own room. But when the family moved, and her brother was born, Jayna's sister moved right in. Her sister is a real mess. She never picks up her clothes or puts away any of her games or books. Jayna fights an ongoing battle just so she can get to her side of the closet! Whenever Jayna wants to listen to one of her CDs or put on the radio, her sister constantly argues about what she wants to hear. Even though both girls have a desk, Jayna's sister is constantly rummaging through her things to find a pencil or a piece of paper.

The most difficult thing, however, is privacy. Jayna never has time to be alone. Whenever she wants to be by herself, her sister is always there, pestering her about something. When friends come over, Jayna practically has to lock her sister out of the room so they can have time to talk. Jayna is reaching the boiling point on this issue. She wants her own room, but she knows that won't happen. What do you think Jayna should do?

Should she . . .

A. Ask Dad to build a wall in the room to divide her side from her sister's side?

B. Move into the garage?

C. Work out a plan with her mother and her sister so she can have some private time? (Also work out a cleaning schedule!)

D. Move in with another friend's family that has a spare room?

E. Ask to trade her sister for a pet hamster?

 For help in knowing what Jayna should do, read Jesus' words in Matthew 5:25.

25

Go Ask Mom

Otis has been bugging his mother all morning to see if she can take him to the new toy store that recently opened at the mall. This isn't just any toy store. It has all the latest computer games, model airplanes, and science kits that Otis is anxious to check out. His friends have already been to the store and have told him about all the cool stuff there. So far, however, his mom hasn't been too agreeable. She is having company tonight and has a list a mile long of things she has to do before her guests arrive.

Still, Otis has not given up hope. But he knows that the last time he went in to ask her about going to the store he was on dangerous ground. He could almost see the steam coming out of Mom's ears. She had warned him that if he asked again, he would be sent to his room for the rest of the day. Otis has beaten a hasty retreat and is now trying to figure out his next move. Just then his younger brother walks in the room. It dawns on Otis that he could send his brother to ask his mom. His brother hasn't been pestering her, and besides, she hasn't issued the same threat to him. Otis knows that if he mentions the words "toy store" to his younger brother, his brother won't quit asking until his mom gives in. What do you think Otis should do?

Should he . . .

    A. Casually tell his brother about the new toy store and leave it up to him?

    B. Tell his brother to ask Mom about going to the toy store?

    C. Wait until his mom has time to take them to the toy store?

    D. Promise his mom that he'll never ask her to take them again if they can only go today?

    E. Use a tag-team approach to keep pestering his mom until she loses it totally?

 Check out Proverbs 24:8-9 for a lesson about scheming.

26

The Killer Cat

Lina and her mom are avid bird lovers. In their backyard they have six different types of feeders designed to attract a variety of birds. They even have a special feeder for squirrels so they won't bother the bird feeders as much. Lina likes to keep track of the different birds that stop at the feeders when they migrate in the spring and fall. She and her mom are becoming experts in identifying the birds at their feeders.

The only problem is the neighbor's cat. The cat spends most of its day outside, and because of all the delicious-looking birds in Lina's yard, it spends quite a bit of time there. Sometimes Lina will come home to see the cat sitting underneath the birdbath waiting and watching. On more than one occasion, Lina has chased the cat from their yard. She has even discovered a dead bird that obviously had fallen prey to the cat. The cat has become quite a nuisance and is spoiling their hobby. What do you think Lina should do?

Should she . . .
  A. Wait outside with a BB gun?
  B. Borrow her other neighbor's Rottweiler to take care of the cat?
  C. Tie a big cowbell around the cat's neck as a hint to the neighbor?
  D. Write an anonymous nasty note to the neighbor complaining about their killer cat?
  E. Talk to her neighbor about keeping the cat inside more?

 Read Romans 13:8-10 for the biblical principle that should guide Lina's response to her neighbor.

Off-Limits!

Jed's mom works at home. She has an office set up in the family's den off the kitchen. There's a computer, a printer, a fax machine, and other office supplies that she uses for work. The room is off-limits to Jed and his sisters when Mom is working. If Jed needs to do some homework on the computer, he usually can use it after dinner. It is clearly understood that no one may go into Mom's office without her permission.

After school, Jed invites a couple of his friends over to his house. While they are eating their snack, Jed's mom tells the boys she has to run out for a quick errand. The boys are to keep an eye on Jed's younger sisters until she gets home. Soon after Jed's mom leaves, one of the boys notices the closed door to the den and wants to know what's behind it. Jed explains that it's his mom's office, and it is off-limits because of all the expensive equipment. One of his friends says, "Hey, cool! Let's go and fax something to the school. We're not going to break anything. Your mom will never know!" The other friends eagerly agree, and Jed is stuck. It probably wouldn't hurt anything, and his mom would never know. But he's not sure. What do you think Jed should do?

Should he . . .
- A. Try to distract his friends by offering them huge bowls of ice cream?
- B. Say that the office is strictly, and he means strictly, off-limits to kids, and they are not allowed in there?
- C. Go ahead and let his friends in his mom's office—and pray that she won't ever find out?
- D. Only let one friend at a time go in the office and look around?
- E. Let his friends into the office, but tell his mom, when she gets home, that they forced him to do it?

 For help in knowing how Jed should react, read James 1:12. Also check out Genesis 3:1-7, the story of a young woman who was tempted to disobey her Father's instructions.

It's Just a Joke

Bryce's aunt and uncle have come over for dinner. Everyone has finished eating, and the adults are drinking their coffee and talking. Bryce's uncle likes to tell stories, and he is a good storyteller. Bryce enjoys the stories, but often his uncle's jokes are off-color or contain insulting remarks about different ethnic groups. Bryce's parents tell him to ignore what his uncle says. Sure enough, while they are sitting at the table, Bryce's uncle relates a funny story about something that had happened at work that week. The story includes a racial slur. It is a funny story, however, and all the adults laugh.

Later that week, Bryce and his friends are sitting around, shooting the breeze. They start telling jokes, and Bryce remembers the story his uncle recently told at his house. Bryce knows that his friends would enjoy it, but he's not so sure about repeating the racial comment. He wonders if it is wrong to repeat one that someone else has said? After all, Bryce did not say it first, and it is part of the story. What do you think he should do?

Should Bryce . . .

A. Repeat the story, but use a slur about an obscure group of people that couldn't possibly offend anyone?

B. Tell the story but leave out the reference to race?

C. Figure that if it's OK for his uncle to tell the story, then it's OK for him, too?

D. Tell the story, and next time his uncle comes, write down some of his other stories and jokes for his friends?

E. Don't tell any of his uncle's stories?

 Check out Ephesians 5:4 and Colossians 4:6 to see what Bryce should do in this situation.

TV Trauma

Arden's best friend is staying with her family for several days while her friend's parents are away on a business/pleasure trip. Arden is eager to spend the time with her friend. She plans to go to her favorite restaurant, go to the movies, and visit a museum while her friend is staying with her. She wishes her friend could stay longer so they could fit more in. There's no fear of getting bored at Arden's house!

The only thing Arden is concerned about is the TV. Her friend's parents don't allow her to watch television on school nights and are very strict about the type of shows she watches. One of Arden's favorite TV shows is on tonight. She never misses an episode, and this is supposed to be a good one. She and her friends have been talking about it for days. When her friend arrives, they stow all her stuff in Arden's room. "Come on," says Arden. "It's time for my TV show." Her friend hesitates. She tells Arden that she is not allowed to watch that show. Arden can't believe it. This is the one episode she can't possibly miss. What do you think Arden should do?

Should she . . .

A. Make her friend stay up in her room until the TV show is over?

B. Look at her friend and say, "You've got to be kidding. There's nothing wrong with that show!"?

C. Convince her friend that it would be OK to watch the show this one time?

D. Tell her friend they can skip the show and do something else—summer reruns will be here soon enough?

E. Get her dad to run out and buy a videotape to tape the show?

 The biblical principle that should guide Arden's response can be found in 1 Corinthians 10:23-24.

30

Mind Your Own Business

Manny and his friend Coop are having a quick snack before shooting baskets at Coop's house. Coop grabs some cookies and pours some milk for them when the phone rings. Coop asks Manny to put the milk away while he answers the phone. As Manny is shutting the refrigerator door, he sees a note stuck on the door with a magnet. The note has their reading teacher's name and phone number. He can't imagine why Coop would have her name on his refrigerator. Their reading teacher is one of the strictest teachers in the school—definitely not someone you would want to hang around with outside the classroom.

When Coop comes back, Manny points to the paper and jokes, "Hey, what are you doing with Miss Whiteside's name and phone number? Asking her for a date?" Coop turns bright red. He mumbles, "Oh, that's nothing." Manny can tell that there is something to this. Now his curiosity is peaked. He wants to know why her number is there, so he presses Coop. Finally, Coop turns to him and angrily says, "Look, it's because I'm having trouble in reading. She's my tutor." Manny doesn't know what to say. He didn't know Coop was having any trouble. What do you think Manny should do?

Should he . . .
  A. Start laughing and say, "Hey I bet my little sister can read better than you"?
  B. Run out the door so he can tell the rest of the gang that Coop is hanging out with Miss Whiteside?
  C. Realize that Coop is embarrassed and not say anything?
  D. Suggest he try one of the remedial reading programs on TV?
  E. Say, "Gee, I didn't know you were so stupid in reading"?

 Take a look at Proverbs 13:3 for help in knowing what Manny should do.

Answer Key

The Ring   *The correct answer is B.*

DISCUSSION QUESTIONS:
1. Why do you think Julie has become so frustrated with Debbie? Who is really at fault in this situation?
2. Why do you think answer D would not be a good solution for Julie? Is it addressing the real issue in this situation?
3. Have you ever envied a friend for something he or she had that you wanted? What, if anything, did you do about it?

Envy and jealousy are such strong emotions that God specifically mentions them in the Ten Commandments—"Do not covet desire anything your neighbor owns." Love, God tells us, does not envy and is not jealous. We should not allow another person's possessions to become more important to us than the person.

Getting Even   *The correct answer is C.*

DISCUSSION QUESTIONS:
1. Why isn't just leaving the jacket on the floor a good solution?
2. Doesn't Wade "deserve" to have his jacket trashed by Tony? After all, he has been very mean to Tony.
3. When have you been so mad at someone that you wanted to get even with him or her? What did you do? Why?

Jesus' teachings often fly in the face of the world's wisdom. The world tells us to get even with those who wrong us. Jesus, however, tells us not only are we to *love* our enemies, but we are also to do good to them. Loving our enemies, as Jesus taught, means acting in their best interest—even when we might not like them.

The Star Player   *The correct answer is A.*

DISCUSSION QUESTIONS:
1. From where does a believer's strength come? How does knowing that keep a believer from becoming too cocky?
2. How do you react to teammates or classmates who think they know it all?
3. How should you act towards others when you are obviously more talented or smarter than they are?

God alone is the source of our strength, our gifts, and our confidence. When you are tempted to boast about your achievements and abilities, take a few minutes to reflect on where you got your strength and confidence. Then rest in God and wait in "quietness and trust" for him to provide what you need instead of relying on your own resources.

We're Here to Praise Him! *The correct answer is C.*

DISCUSSION QUESTIONS:
1. What usually prevents you from fully praising God?
2. When you have had a particularly tough week, why do you find it difficult to worship on Sunday? How can you change that?
3. Why do you think it's important to worship God despite what you may be experiencing or feeling at the time?

David wrote Psalm 70 during a very difficult time in his life. He pleads with God to come and rescue him. Even in his difficulties, however, David doesn't forget to praise God. Praise is important because it helps you remember who God is. Even when things look bleak, don't forget to thank God for all he *already* has done and to worship him for who he is.

Pressed for Time *The correct answer is D.*

DISCUSSION QUESTIONS:
1. What rules do you have about homework? How well do you follow them?
2. Why does it really matter if Mike goofs off while his mother is gone, particularly if she won't ever find out?
3. When did you try to get away with something that you knew your parents wouldn't know about? (Be honest!) What happened?

We may not always be happy with the rules set by Mom and Dad. And we might not understand the reason for all these rules. But God says to children, "Always obey your parents," because this pleases him.

Found Treasure *The correct answer is C.*

DISCUSSION QUESTIONS:
1. When have you found something valuable? What did you do with it?
2. Why wouldn't it be right for Amber to take the money and consider it her reward for finding the wallet?
3. Why might it be considered stealing to keep the money, even though Amber just found it?

God tells us to be honest with him, with ourselves, and with others. To keep something that we know doesn't belong to us is dishonest. Only when we are obedient can God teach us more of his wisdom.

My Hero? *The correct answer is A.*

DISCUSSION QUESTIONS:
1. What qualities do you admire in a hero?
2. Who are your heroes—and why?
3. Who are your friends' heroes? Do you agree with their choices? Why or why not?
4. How would you rate today's heroes according to David's standards in Psalm 101:5-6?

David sets some pretty high standards for the people he would choose as models and friends—the godly and the truthful. Look at who doesn't make the grade:

those who are proud, deceitful, and dishonest. Make sure your role models hold up to David's standards, not the world's.

The Bike   *The correct answer is C.*

DISCUSSION QUESTIONS:
1. When have you received something new that you just couldn't wait to show your friends? What did you do?
2. If bragging isn't OK, why wouldn't it be a good solution for Greg to get the bike dirty so it doesn't look so new?
3. How do you feel when someone brags about something new?

Everyone enjoys receiving new things. It's how we handle those things that concerns God. When we receive something new, God doesn't want us to brag about it. Nor does he want us to not use it or abuse it. Rather, God wants us to have the right attitude—to enjoy and be thankful for the things we have and to use them correctly and without a lot of fanfare.

Secret Notes   *The correct answer is B.*

DISCUSSION QUESTIONS:
1. What do you think is the best way to get to know someone you like?
2. Why do you think Maddie should tell Joe what was in the note? How do you think Maddie would feel in telling Joe the truth? What about Joe?
3. Why is being honest in this situation so important?

Maddie probably shouldn't have written the note in the first place. More than likely she embarrassed Joe, not to mention herself. But that is not an excuse for lying. God wants us to be honest with others—no matter how embarrassing it may be for us!

A Double Life   *The best answers are B and C.*

DISCUSSION QUESTIONS:
1. Why should Olivia tell her friends at school that she is a Christian?
2. In addition to telling her friends about her faith, why should Olivia also change her lifestyle?
3. How do your friends outside your church group know you are a Christian? What changes might you need to make to let them know?

Make no mistake. God doesn't just watch our behavior on Sunday. He sees wherever we are and whatever we are doing. He will judge us—maybe not today, or the next day, but no one will escape that final encounter with God. Thus, people who love God should try to always obey him and do what he wants.

The Locker   *The correct answer is C.*

DISCUSSION QUESTIONS:
1. Why wouldn't it be OK for Steve to walk past the locker and do nothing?
2. If someone got you into trouble at school, what would you do?
3. When your friend wanted to get back at someone, what did you advise him or her to do?

4. Does Chris deserve to be punished for his actions? By whom?
   When someone gets us into trouble, it is almost overwhelming to want to get back at that person. Paul says, however, that a Christian acts differently. Even when someone has hurt us, instead of giving that person what he or she deserves, we are to befriend our "enemy" and act kindly toward him or her.

The "In" Crowd   *The correct answer is C.*

DISCUSSION QUESTIONS:
1. Is it all right for Meg to want to be popular? How should she handle her newfound popularity?
2. Why is being popular so important to kids? How important is being popular to you?
3. What do you think should be Meg's most important consideration?

Popularity contests don't mean much to God. While it is very tempting to run with the "in" crowd, it is more important from God's perspective to treat everyone with equal respect and kindness—not just the "important" people.

Just a Minute   *The correct answer is E or B.*

DISCUSSION QUESTIONS:
1. How do you typically respond when your parents ask you to do something?
2. Do you think asking her mom to wait until the show was over was a good solution? Why or why not?
3. When you ask someone to do something, how do you expect them to respond?

If our faith in Jesus is real, it will usually prove itself at home, in the relationships with those who know us best. God has uniquely placed us in our families, where children and parents have a responsibility to each other. God requires that children obey their parents "because you belong to the Lord, for this is the right thing to do."

The Invitation   *The correct answer is D.*

DISCUSSION QUESTIONS:
1. What children in your class, or at Sunday school, are like Jeff? How do you usually treat them?
2. Why do you suppose Tim might be reluctant to accept Jeff's invitation?
3. How do you think someone like Jeff, who doesn't have many friends, feels about that?

Love, as God defines it, is not a feeling of affection for another person. Love is a choice that involves action. It means choosing to act in another's best interest, even if we don't feel like it or don't know that person very well. Love should always be our highest goal.

JANUARY 15

A Friend in Need   *The correct answer is D.*

DISCUSSION QUESTIONS:
1. Why wouldn't it be enough for Vanessa just to ask God to give Shirley some helpers?
2. How do you react when you see someone in need?
3. Why do you think what a person "does" with God's Word is important?

Christians need to study God's Word, and they need to pray for one another. But it is also important to *obey* God's Word by *doing* what it says. When you see someone in need and are able to help in that situation, God expects you to act!

JANUARY 16

The Sunday Matinee   *The correct answer is B.*

DISCUSSION QUESTIONS:
1. Why should Lucas get his homework done early?
2. When you are tempted to put off your homework until later, what usually happens?
3. What might help Lucas become more disciplined in getting his work done?

God wants his people to live disciplined lives. It may seem like a minor matter, going to the movies instead of finishing homework, but compromise there makes it easier to make excuses on the bigger issues. Training yourself now to be disciplined may not seem pleasant, but it will pay off later!

JANUARY 17

The Final Exam   *The correct answer is C.*

DISCUSSION QUESTIONS:
1. When were you tempted to cheat on a test? What did you do?
2. What would you advise Jodie to do differently in studying for her next exam?
3. Can you think of a situation where cheating would be OK?

In this situation it would be far better for Jodie to accept the consequences of cramming for the test the night before than taking a shortcut by cheating. In Psalm 101, David writes about how he plans to live a blameless life—with God's help. One thing he—and God—will not tolerate is lying and deceitfulness. Don't lower your standards in those areas, either, for yourself or for others.

JANUARY 18

The Substitute   *The correct answer is C.*

DISCUSSION QUESTIONS:
1. Why do you think that ignoring what is going on in the classroom is not a good solution for Matt?
2. How do you think Matt should handle the situation with his classmates?
3. How do you think the substitute teacher feels?

When we see something wrong going on, God does not want us to look the other way or ignore it. Instead, he wants us to act. God wants us to take whatever steps we can to correct an injustice or wrongdoing.

What a Week!   *The correct answer is E.*

DISCUSSION QUESTIONS:
1. When you have a difficult week ahead of you, how do you handle it?
2. How can knowing Jesus help a person get through the tough times?
3. How can you rely on Jesus more to help you through tough times?

Jesus wants to help us with our daily problems. We can draw "nourishment" from Jesus and the strength to complete our daily work by being obedient to him and seeking to learn from his life and his teachings. Let Jesus be your guide and he will see you through every situation.

The Comic Book King   *The correct answer is A.*

DISCUSSION QUESTIONS:
1. What harm is there in collecting comic books?
2. What occupies your time? Does it occupy more of your time than God does? What changes might you need to make?
3. What do you think are the keys to disciplining yourself?

The Christian faith is not a passive activity—sitting around, waiting for God to act in our lives. God does act, but we also have a responsibility to respond and act on our faith. Paul uses strong words to describe the Christian life: *run, follow, pursue, fight, hold tightly.* Christians are called to an active faith. So when you are tempted to fall back, like Milt, take courage and keep walking!

The Loan   *The correct answer is A.*

DISCUSSION QUESTIONS:
1. Do you think it would be OK for Elizabeth to gently remind Lindsey about the dollar? Why, or why not?
2. When you loan someone something, what do you expect about being paid back?
3. What is more important here—for Elizabeth to forgive Lindsey or for Lindsey to repay Elizabeth her dollar? Why?

In situations where we feel we are wronged, it is important to remember that God has freely forgiven us for the things we do wrong, and that we are to show that same forgiveness to others. Having received God's forgiveness, we will want to pass it on.

Lights Out!   *The best answers are C and D.*

DISCUSSION QUESTIONS:
1. Jean is in a hurry and knows her mom is waiting for her. Why would it be good for her to stop?
2. When you were in a hurry and noticed someone who needed help, what did you do?

In Matthew 7:12, we find a rule Jesus gives that covers everything. Commonly called the Golden Rule, Jesus tells us to treat others as we would like them to treat us. It is not enough to refrain from harming others. Rather, we are to take the first step in doing good for others. We should never be in such a hurry that we can't be kind and good to others, showing the same kind of love God showers on us each day.

All the Right Moves   *The correct answer is E.*

DISCUSSION QUESTIONS:
1. What would prevent Malcolm from accepting this new boy's help?
2. In what areas of school or activities do you excel? Can you still learn more in these areas?

Acts 18:24-28 tells about Apollos. He was a well-educated, gifted speaker, who spoke eloquently about John the Baptist and the Old Testament prophets. But he didn't know the entire story. Fortunately for the early church, Apollos was willing to learn. Although he could have been proud of his natural abilities and giftedness, Apollos was a willing student of the Gospel. And because he was willing to learn, he became an even more effective teacher. How willing are you to learn so that you can become all God wants you to be?

The Sick Classmate   *The correct answer is C.*

DISCUSSION QUESTIONS:
1. Lauren doesn't really know Emily. Why do you think she should offer to bring home Emily's schoolwork?
2. If Lauren does nothing, do you think she would be guilty of sinning? Why, or why not?
3. If you are not doing something wrong, can you still sin by *not* doing something right? When has this happened to you or a friend?

Usually, we think of a sin as doing something wrong. But the Bible tells us that we can also sin by not doing something right. When we know we can do a kind act or offer a service to someone in need, then we should do it. We should be willing to help as God gives us the opportunities.

Doubting Ray   *The correct answer is A.*

DISCUSSION QUESTIONS:
1. When one of your friends expressed doubts about God, how did you respond?
2. What are some ways Ray can help his friend "find the answers"?

The Bible tells us to show mercy to those whose faith is shaky. Responding in shock to a friend's doubts, or calling a friend's questions about God "dumb" will do little to help that friend. As ambassadors of Christ, the best way we can help someone who has doubts about God is to listen without judging that person and treat him or her with the love of Jesus.

Shooting Hoops   *The correct answer is C.*

DISCUSSION QUESTIONS:
1. Why would Brian be more honest in simply refusing Ross's invitation?
2. How do you usually deal with obnoxious classmates?
3. How can Brian be a true friend to Ross?

Paul challenges us to live up to being Jesus' representatives here on earth. This includes being gentle, humble, patient, understanding, and peaceful, "making allowances for each other's faults because of your love." Think of the people like Ross in your life, and how you can represent Jesus to them.

JANUARY 27

Guess Who's Coming to Dinner?   *The correct answer is B.*

DISCUSSION QUESTIONS:
1. When you have guests over, particularly younger ones, do you withhold certain possessions, or do you share everything?
2. Why is it so difficult to share possessions with others?
3. Read 1 Peter 4:9. What are some ways you can practice hospitality without grumbling?

The things we own—right down to the coolest remote control truck—will have no meaning in heaven. We will not spend eternity with possessions, but with other people. What matters most in heaven—and on earth—is people and how we treat them. Invest your energy and time on the things that matter the most.

JANUARY 28

Early Edition   *The best answers are A and D.*

DISCUSSION QUESTIONS:
1. In what ways do you think answer D would be an appropriate response? In what ways is answer A better?
2. How do you react if a friend drags you into something without first asking you? Do you do it, or argue about it?
3. Why do you think Tyler should go ahead and help Lou?

If we belong to Jesus, our lives should reflect his character of peace, patience, and gentleness so that we "shine like stars" in a dark world. Grumbling and complaining will only serve to cloud our witness. Make sure you shine for God!

JANUARY 29

Egg-spectations   *The answer is C.*

DISCUSSION QUESTIONS:
1. What do you think Brendan's primary consideration should be in making a decision on what to do?
2. What might the consequences be if Brendan goes along with Garrett? And if he doesn't?
3. Are you willing to risk a friendship if it means doing something wrong?

Doing something we know is wrong can be tempting, particularly if it makes us feel like one of the crowd. But God wants us to make choices, not based on the flashy appeal of a friendship, but on the long-range consequences of the act. Sometimes that means steering clear of people who want to tempt us to do something we know is wrong.

JANUARY 30

Stolen Goods   *The correct answer is A.*

DISCUSSION QUESTIONS:
1. Why should Jared go to the principal and tell what he saw?
2. Is it such a big deal that the boy only took candy bars and cookies?
3. When you knew that kids were stealing, what did you do?

Whether it's candy bars from the cafeteria or pencils from the supply closet, taking things that don't belong to you is stealing. God makes it very clear that stealing is wrong—it's sin.

Show a Little Respect   *The correct answer is D.*

DISCUSSION QUESTIONS:
1. What's the best way to present your views when they are opposite of a teacher's, parent's, or other authority's?
2. Read 1 Peter 2:13. Why do you think Christians should obey people in authority over them?
3. How is answer D in keeping with Peter's instruction to cooperate with authorities?

Whenever possible, Christians are to live according to the laws of those in authority over them. Those who disagree should do so respectfully, and not in anger. This is to be done, as Peter says, "for the Lord's sake," so that the Good News and God's people will be respected.

The Terminator   *The best answers are C and D.*

DISCUSSION QUESTIONS:
1. If Ben is becoming increasingly more aggressive, shouldn't Jonathan learn to defend himself?
2. Do you think someone who doesn't fight back is a wimp? Why, or why not?
3. What would you do in Jonathan's situation?
4. How can Jonathan truly love someone who picks on him all the time?

We gain much in the eyes of God, and others, when we learn to walk away from a fight and not give in to our anger. Christians are to go one step further, and "Love your enemies, do good to those who hate you, bless those who curse you, pray for those who mistreat you." It takes a conscious effort to do something kind to someone who is hurting us. But when we do, with the help of the Holy Spirit, Jesus tells us that our reward will be great.

The Sweater Swap   *The correct answer is E.*

DISCUSSION QUESTIONS:
1. What would you do in Paula's situation?
2. Why isn't B a good solution to this problem?
3. How would you feel if you ruined something you borrowed from someone? Would you be fearful of their response?
4. How do you expect your things to be returned?

When we are more fearful of a person's *response* to something we did, rather than God, we can be easily swayed into doing what is wrong. God tells us to trust him instead. Do what is right, and let God take care of the rest.

Heard It through the Grapevine   *The correct answer is B.*

DISCUSSION QUESTIONS:
1. Do you think C would be a good solution to Susan's situation? Why or why not?
2. Why do you think it isn't enough not to pass along untrue stories?
3. What do you think is the best way to handle gossip among your friends?

Knowing the latest rumor in the school is very tempting. In fact, Proverbs says that listening to gossip is like eating candy—taking one piece usually results in wanting more. God says that the best way to handle gossip is not to listen. But when we do hear gossip, particularly when we know it's untrue, we have a responsibility to set the record straight.

The Challenge   *The correct answer is B.*

DISCUSSION QUESTIONS:
1. What might Kurt say to Eric to avoid a fight?
2. What are some possible consequences if Kurt decides to fight Eric? What about if he doesn't?
3. What could Kurt have done to avoid this entire situation?
4. How do you handle the kid in your class who is a know-it-all?

Backing down from a fight, particularly in front of classmates, can be difficult. There is the fear of being called a coward or a wimp. God's Word, however, teaches that a wise person works to calm the anger of those around him or her. Indeed, Jesus, in his most famous sermon, the Sermon on the Mount, tells his followers that those who are the peacemakers will be "called sons of God."

The Tough Guy   *The correct answer is B.*

DISCUSSION QUESTIONS:
1. Why do you think Sam would want to be like Adam?
2. What do you think are some other ways Sam can win his friends back?
3. What would you do in Sam's situation?

It's difficult to watch our friends choose another person as the "leader," particularly when that person is the class bully. The temptation to "fight fire with fire," and try to beat that person at his or her own game, is great. But God tells us not to envy a "violent person or choose any of his ways." God will honor those who honor him by doing what is right.

Don't Believe It   *The correct answer is A.*

DISCUSSION QUESTIONS:
1. Why is Charlotte so quick to defend her friend? Shouldn't she at least check out the rumor first?
2. When you hear gossip about your friends, how do you respond?
3. What is the best way to handle gossip?

When you love as Jesus loves, you will not take delight in hearing or passing along bad news about a friend. The Bible teaches that unselfish and outward seeking love will rejoice over truth, never give up or lose faith in a friend, is always hopeful, and will endure through all circumstances. Does that describe the type of love you have for your friends? Find out what you need to do to love your friends the way that Jesus does.

FEBRUARY 7

Spilled Beans   *The correct answer is A.*

DISCUSSION QUESTIONS:
1. Why is it difficult to admit to a friend (or family member) that you did something wrong?
2. What happens when you respond in anger to someone who is angry with you?
3. What might happen if Joy quietly answers Darcy? Do you think Darcy will continue to blast her?

It's hard to argue in a whisper. And it's equally hard to argue with someone who insists on answering gently and quietly. On the other hand, answering with a rising voice and angry tone almost always makes a fight worse. Choose gentle words to turn away from anger and a fight.

FEBRUARY 8

The Good Old Days   *The correct answer is A.*

DISCUSSION QUESTIONS:
1. Why do you think Dustin doesn't want to get advice from his dad?
2. How do you feel about getting advice from your parents? Your teachers? Your Sunday school teachers?
3. Why do you think it is so difficult to accept advice from another person?

Proverbs spends much time talking about wise and foolish learners. Wise learners listen carefully to the advice of others and learn from others' mistakes. We can avoid a lot of heartaches and possible disasters by listening to good advice—especially from those who want the best for us.

FEBRUARY 9

Channel Surfing   *The best answer is B.*

DISCUSSION QUESTIONS:
1. Why shouldn't Jenny demand that her brother turn back her program? After all, she was there first.
2. What might be some possible outcomes if Jenny politely asks her brother to switch back to her show?
3. Why do you think getting up and leaving the room is the best solution?
4. What might happen if Jenny insists on getting her way?

When we begin thinking we "deserve it because we were there first," the temptation to fight back is strong. Sometimes the best, and only, way to avoid an argument is to walk away, regardless of who was there first. Once a fight begins, it tends to get worse quickly, far beyond the original issue. Proverbs tells us it is best to "drop a matter before a dispute breaks out."

FEBRUARY 10

The Windfall   *The correct answer is E.*

DISCUSSION QUESTIONS:
1. Would saving Rick's money for something worthwhile like a computer be a good idea? Why or why not?
2. What do you usually do with money you receive as a gift?

3. What's wrong with Rick spending the money on what he enjoys—like baseball cards and candy?

Proverbs gives much practical advice on using our money wisely. Sometimes it's not the type of advice we want, particularly when we are eager to spend our money on the first thing we see. The Bible warns us not to waste our money on foolish things, but to put it to good use.

FEBRUARY 11

Looking for Answers   *The correct answer is A.*

DISCUSSION QUESTIONS:
1. What do you think is preventing Tucker from telling the teacher he doesn't know how to multiply fractions?
2. What does this phrase mean: "With humility comes wisdom"? What is humility?
3. What kind of attitude does someone need in order to learn?

Pride often prevents people from admitting that they don't know something. They don't want to appear stupid in front of friends or the teacher, so they don't say anything. Then when it comes time to show what they know, they're in big trouble. Don't let your pride prevent you from getting wisdom.

FEBRUARY 12

Facing Unjust Criticism   *The correct answer is D.*

DISCUSSION QUESTIONS:
1. What would be the benefits of Carson staying in the band and working through his problem with Mr. Parke?
2. When you encounter a constant barrage of criticism from somebody, how do you feel? How do you handle it?
3. What else do you think Carson can do, with prayer, to help him through this situation?

Carson has every reason to be discouraged. He has been ridiculed, humiliated, and misunderstood—just like Hannah in the passages from 1 Samuel 1. We can learn from Hannah's experience, however, that honest prayer and leaving the problem with God can help immensely. Then we can rely on the support of good friends and counselors.

FEBRUARY 13

Math Problem   *The correct answer is C.*

DISCUSSION QUESTIONS:
1. How do you feel when someone breaks a promise to you?
2. Why doesn't Randy make arrangements to study with Pat another day? Do you think that's a good solution? Why, or why not?
3. How good are you at following through on what you say you are going to do?

We make promises every day—promises to clean our room, do our homework, take our sister to the park. What's important to God is what we do *after* we make a promise—do we follow through and do what we said we would? Proverbs clearly teaches that God delights in those who keep their word.

The Group Project   *The correct answer is D.*

DISCUSSION QUESTIONS:
1. Why is it is important for Dalton to encourage this boy, rather than kick him off the project? What might be some reasons this boy isn't participating?
2. When you have someone on your team not doing his or her job, how do you react?
3. In what ways does encouraging this boy help him? How does it help the group?

In 1 Thessalonians 5:14, Paul says to warn the lazy and encourage the timid. Our first responsibility is to determine whether a person is not working because he or she is lazy or just doesn't know what to do and is afraid to ask. Be sensitive to the needs of each person and respond with the proper warning or words of encouragement.

Practice Makes Perfect   *The correct answer is B.*

DISCUSSION QUESTIONS:
1. Why isn't A an appropriate answer to Amanda's mother's question? After all, she *did* practice some.
2. What might happen if Amanda told her mom yes and then later her mother discovered the truth?
3. When did you try to hide something you did wrong? What happened?

It is human nature to want to hide our sins or mistakes. But hiding often makes everything worse when the truth is finally discovered. We run the risk not only of not learning from our errors, but also of breaking down the trust between us and others. Confessing our sins, on the other hand, is the first step toward forgiveness and mercy.

Hoop Dreams   *The correct answer is A.*

DISCUSSION QUESTIONS:
1. How do you respond to someone who brags about himself or herself all the time? Do you enjoy being around that person?
2. Kyle had a great game. Why shouldn't he bask in the glory?
3. How do think Kyle should handle all the attention?

No one likes to be around a person whose favorite topic is himself or herself. Every person has God-given gifts and talents. God wants us to use those talents and gifts wisely for his glory, not our own. If we do a good job in the process, we should let others do the talking, not ourselves!

The Slumber Party   *The correct answer is E.*

DISCUSSION QUESTIONS:
1. What would you do if an uninvited guest came to your party?
2. When you were excluded from a party, how did you feel?

We all probably have a favorite group of friends whose company we particularly enjoy. But the Bible tells us we are not to show favoritism to only a few select people. Paul reminds us to be gentle and show kindness and respect to everyone.

FEBRUARY 18

The Clique   *The correct answer is C.*

DISCUSSION QUESTIONS:
1. When you were in a situation like Jackie's, how did you respond?
2. How do you think Jackie should treat Catherine and Jamie if they continue to cut down Christina?
3. How can Jackie show her loyalty to Christina?

Proverbs 3:3-4 is a call to action! We are never to get tired of *being* loyal and kind. More than just attitudes, loyalty and kindness involve action. Then, says Proverbs, we will earn a good reputation among our friends and, more importantly, with God.

FEBRUARY 19

The Stock Boy   *The correct answer is C.*

DISCUSSION QUESTIONS:
1. When working with others, how do you feel when someone doesn't do his or her share of the workload?
2. What would you do if you were Lance's partner?
3. Why do you think it is important for Lance to do his share—even if he is tired?

Paul teaches that when it is time to work, Christians should jump right in. We should make the most of our time and talent to carry the workload. Make sure you follow this principle at school, at home, or in working for someone else.

FEBRUARY 20

The Baby-sitting Blues   *The correct answer is E.*

DISCUSSION QUESTIONS:
1. Why wouldn't C be a good solution to Scott's situation?
2. How would you describe Scott's attitude towards Mrs. Johnson's request for help?
3. What is your attitude when someone asks you for help?

Instead of looking at a request as a nuisance, we should view it as an opportunity to help others. Paul tells us we are to share each other's problems and burdens because "in this way we obey the law of Christ." No one should consider himself or herself too important to take time to help out another person.

FEBRUARY 21

Spreading the Word   *The correct answer is D.*

DISCUSSION QUESTIONS:
1. How do you respond when spiritual matters come up in a conversation?
2. How do your friends know you are a Christian?
3. What else could Kim do in this situation?
4. Why do you think Kim's friend is asking so many questions?

Think about why we are embarrassed when talking about our faith. Is it because we are afraid we'll lose friends or that our friends will make fun of us? Jesus gives us a sobering warning in Luke 9:26. He says that if we are ashamed of him and his message, then "I . . . will be ashamed of you. . . ." Whose opinion do you value more?

FEBRUARY 22

Fire! *The correct answer is E.*

DISCUSSION QUESTIONS:
1. What would you do in Peter's situation?
2. What might be some reasons people wouldn't stop to help in an emergency like this?
3. What should Peter do if he doesn't know those particular neighbors?

Jesus tells us that one of the two greatest commands God gives us is to love our neighbors as ourselves. It doesn't matter if we know them personally, or if we even like them. We can show we love our neighbors by *actively* helping to meet their needs. In God's eyes, there is no excuse for refusing to help.

FEBRUARY 23

Pet Peeves *The correct answer is B.*

DISCUSSION QUESTIONS:
1. Why can't Anne Marie take care of the dog after the party?
2. Would A be a good solution to this situation? Why, or why not?
3. What would you do in a similar situation?

Since creation, God has given humankind the responsibility to take care of all his living creatures. When we take a pet into our home we must be willing to care for it—and not just at our own convenience. As Proverbs says, "The godly are concerned for the welfare of their animals."

FEBRUARY 24

And Today's Topic Is . . . *The correct answer is B.*

DISCUSSION QUESTIONS:
1. How many of your classmates know about Jesus? How do you know?
2. How would you explain the Christian faith to a class in school?
3. Why would Stephanie feel embarrassed to explain what she believes?

Some Christians think their faith is a personal matter that should be kept private. But Peter clearly teaches that we should *always* be ready to explain what we believe. Instead of hiding our faith, we should always be looking for opportunities to talk about Jesus.

FEBRUARY 25

The Birthday Gift *The correct answer is E.*

DISCUSSION QUESTIONS:
1. What did you do when you "wandered" into an area you knew was off-limits?
2. Why would it be important for Hunter to tell his friend they should leave—and do it?
3. Are you a follower or a leader? In what ways can you lead the way for your friends as a good example?

Even very young people can set a good example for others in the way they speak and live. Regardless of age, believers should live so that others see Christ in us in all areas of their lives.

FEBRUARY 26

The Big Hurt   *The correct answer is C.*

DISCUSSION QUESTIONS:

1. Why do you think E is not a good solution?
2. When you see someone in trouble, how do you typically respond? Do you want to stick around and help, or do you feel someone else should do it?
3. Think of a time that you helped someone you didn't know. How did you feel afterward?

It is often easy to convince ourselves that we shouldn't take the time to help someone else—we're in a hurry; we have someplace we have to be; we really don't know first aid; we don't know the person. But as Jesus relates in the familiar parable, "The Good Samaritan," there is no excuse for not helping a person in need.

FEBRUARY 27

Making Fun   *The best answer is A.*

DISCUSSION QUESTIONS:

1. Why do you think D is not the best solution to Lisa's situation? If Lisa just walks away from her friends, is she helping the girl?
2. When your friends cut down others, how do you respond?
3. What other steps could Lisa take to help this girl?
4. Who in your school could use someone to stick up for them?

Everyone knows the kids in school who get picked on and cut down on a daily basis. Maybe we don't join our friends in cutting others down. Maybe we walk away. The Bible tells us, however, that we have a greater responsibility to "rescue the poor and helpless and deliver them from the grasp of evil people." Think of what you could do to "deliver" that person in your school.

FEBRUARY 28

The Woodcutter   *The correct answer is C.*

DISCUSSION QUESTIONS:

1. When you were caught in the act of doing something you knew was wrong, how did you respond?
2. What will be the consequences if Nathan tells his father the truth?
3. What will be the consequences if Nathan tries to cover up his mistake and lies to his father?

Sometimes, when we are caught doing something wrong, we try to hide our mistake by lying about what we were doing. We often discover, too late, that as Proverbs said, "lies are soon exposed." When faced with a choice of covering up or confessing, telling the truth is always the best course to follow.

MARCH 1

On Time   *The correct answer is E.*

DISCUSSION QUESTIONS:

1. How do you feel when someone constantly nags you about something? How do you typically respond?
2. Do you think nagging helps or hinders a situation?
3. What do you say to a friend who is usually late or unprepared?

Nagging almost never helps. In fact, a constant stream of "reminders" can feel like torture. If you resort to nagging to get through to somebody, you need to ask yourself if you are more concerned about yourself or in helping the person you are nagging. If you truly want to help, use words of patience and love, and see what happens!

On the Air   *The correct answer is D.*

DISCUSSION QUESTIONS:
1. Why do you think C is not a good solution to Lizzie's situation?
2. What do you do when your friends listen to music or DJs that you know are off-limits for you?
3. Why do you think Lizzie should explain her reasons for not listening to that station?

Have you ever heard the statement "garbage in, garbage out"? It usually refers to computers. If we don't put the right information in the computer, we can't possibly get good information out. That's true for our minds, too. What we put into our minds determines what comes out in our words and actions. Paul says that believers should fill their minds with things that are true, noble, pure, lovely, and excellent.

The Shortcut   *The correct answer is D.*

DISCUSSION QUESTIONS:
1. Why do you think Greg was wrong to take the shortcut through his neighbor's yard? After all, he was hurrying for a good reason, wasn't he?
2. When you were in a hurry and took a shortcut, what happened?
3. What do you think concerns God most in Greg's situation?

People can find excuses for doing almost everything—but God looks right through those excuses to see the person's true motives. Often it is difficult to know what is the right action to take. But we can help determine the right choice if we ask, "Will God be pleased with my real reason for doing this?"

The Cutting Edge   *The correct answer is A.*

DISCUSSION QUESTIONS:
1. How would you feel if the kids in your class were making up jokes about you?
2. Why is telling jokes about other people harmful, even if they never hear the jokes?
3. When kids start making fun of another classmate, how do you respond?

Jesus taught that people should love one another, not judge each other or make jokes about others. If we treat others generously, graciously, and compassionately, we will receive these same qualities back. But if we are critical, rather than compassionate, we can expect to receive criticism in return.

You've Got a Friend   *The correct answer is A.*

DISCUSSION QUESTIONS:
1. How would you confront a friend who was doing something that you knew to be wrong?
2. Why do you think Julie should say something to Grace?
3. Why do you think that avoiding Grace or finding a new friend would not be a good solution?
4. Why is how Grace responds to Julie important?

God gave Ezekiel the job of confronting a nation with the truth of what they were doing wrong. God told him—three times—not to be afraid, but to be obedient and speak the truth. Sometimes being a good friend means speaking the truth in love. It might not always be fun; it might not be well received; but if you are obedient to God's truth, he will honor you.

Setbacks   *The correct answer is C.*

DISCUSSION QUESTIONS:
1. Why would it be best for Tamara to accept the situation? What can she do now to change it? What will be accomplished by getting angry and blaming her partner?
2. How do *you* react when things don't go exactly as you planned?

Joseph woke up one day and found himself falsely accused of trying to steal his master's wife. The next thing he knew, he was thrown into prison. Now Joseph certainly could have seen his situation as hopeless. He could have gotten angry at his master's wife, his master, even at God. But Joseph did none of those things. Instead, he did his best with each small task he was given. Joseph's diligence and positive attitude were noticed—and rewarded. The next time you find things going wrong, follow Joseph's example. Do the best with what you have, and remember that God was able to turn Joseph's situation completely around.

Room Service   *The correct answer is C.*

DISCUSSION QUESTIONS:
1. How do you respond when you want to go out but have work around the house to do first?
2. What do you think are the possible consequences of Leslie doing a quick, but poor, job of cleaning her room? Why wouldn't this be a good solution to her situation?
3. Why do you think it is so important that Leslie do her chores first?

God desires that we live wise, disciplined lives, and Proverbs makes it clear that working hard is a vital part of wise living. It takes discipline to put jobs first, before fun. But God promises that the person who works hard will enjoy success and be satisfied.

The New Girl   *The correct answer is C.*

DISCUSSION QUESTIONS:
1. How do you let someone know you want to be his or her friend?

2. Why isn't talking to this girl's best friend a good solution?
3. What would you advise Justin to do?

When Jesus wanted to know people, he spent time with them talking and listening. Ephesians 5:1-2 teaches that believers are to follow Jesus' example in loving others as he did. The best way to make friends (even those of the opposite sex) is to show an interest in them by talking and listening to them—just like Jesus did!

Finders Keepers, Part 1   *The best answers are A and B.*

DISCUSSION QUESTIONS:
1. Why do you think B is a good solution? What might be the consequences if Mack's friend refuses to split the money?
2. What should Mack do if his friend refuses to split the money with him?
3. How do you react when a friend claims something you believed rightfully belongs to you?

When someone claims something that we feel belongs to us, our human tendency is to lash out in anger and fight for what is "ours." Proverbs teaches, however, that rather than arguing, we should keep our cool and offer a solution that is acceptable to both parties. "Good people will enjoy the positive results of their words."

Great Expectations   *The best answers are A and C.*

DISCUSSION QUESTIONS:
1. If you were Emmet's friend, what would you advise Emmet to do first? Why would it be important for Emmet to both talk to his dad and remain obedient at this time?
2. What might happen if Emmet tries out for the production without telling his dad or if he rebels?
3. When you are hoping to explore new ventures your parents may not be keen about, how do you approach them?

Lydia was a wealthy business woman in Philippi whose heart already was open to God. As a Gentile and a woman, however, she probably was not allowed to do much in terms of worship. But Lydia had an open and willing heart. When Barnabas and Paul sat down beside her and began talking about Jesus, Lydia responded personally and practically. We, too, need to have an open and willing heart to God's plan for us and for his timing. While we are waiting, we need to be obedient to where God has placed us.

Partners in Prayer   *The correct answer is A.*

DISCUSSION QUESTIONS:
1. For what types of things do you pray?
2. When you shared a prayer request with another friend, what were your expectations about your prayer request?
3. Do you feel, like Elliott, that praying for something that big is only for grown-ups?

God's people have the responsibility to pray for each other. It doesn't matter how big the problem is. God is bigger than any problem. The important thing is to bring *all* of your prayers and requests to God. He will take care of the rest.

Truth and Consequences   *The correct answer is C.*

DISCUSSION QUESTIONS:

1. How could Betsy have handled this situation better? What could she have told her friend?
2. Why do you think it is best for Betsy to admit what she did wrong?
3. What do you usually do when you are caught doing something wrong? Do you find it better to confess or to hide what you've done?
4. What happened to you when you tried to hide your sin from your parents? From God?

When we know we have done something wrong, we are tempted to hide what we have done. But lying only makes matters worse. God already has forgiven our sins, but we still have to accept the consequences for our actions. Do as David did—confess, and enjoy God's forgiveness!

Going to Church   *The correct answer is D.*

DISCUSSION QUESTIONS:

1. What would you tell your friend about why you go to church?
2. Why do you think Ned would be afraid to answer his friend?
3. Read 2 Timothy 1:8. What do you think it means to suffer "for the proclamation of the Good News"?

Paul is quite clear when he says that believers should never be ashamed to share their faith and tell others about Jesus. But he is equally clear that believers may "suffer" when they tell others about Christ. The good news, however, is that we can call on the Holy Spirit to give us the strength and courage to be truthful witnesses for our Lord.

The Birthday Present   *The correct answer is B.*

DISCUSSION QUESTIONS:

1. Why do you think Angela's parents say this gift will become one of her most treasured possessions?
2. How often do you read your Bible? Where is it right now?
3. How can you be a "good worker" who "correctly explains the word of truth"?

In 2 Timothy 2:15, Paul teaches that believers should work hard so that God will approve their work. By building our lives on God's Word—and building God's Word into our lives—we can ensure that we will know how to live for God and serve him. Those who ignore the Bible will certainly be ashamed when they stand before God.

Surfing the Net   *The correct answer is C.*

DISCUSSION QUESTIONS:

1. What would you do if you were to stumble across material on the Internet that you knew was off-limits?
2. What would you say to a friend who is passing along the address for the hottest Web site—and you know it is X-rated?

3. Why do you think Henry shouldn't pass along the information about the Web site to his friends?

The technology may change, but the temptations remain the same. Our faith should not be passive, but active. When we confront a temptation, Paul says—whether it's on the movie screen, in a book or magazine, or on the computer—we need to *run* from it and chase after "a godly life."

M A R C H   1 6

Decisions, Decisions   *The correct answer is C.*

DISCUSSION QUESTIONS:
1. With whom do you talk to help you make difficult decisions?
2. Why do you think prayer can be an important part of decision making?
3. How do you advise a friend who has to make a difficult decision?

James says that those who need wisdom for making difficult decisions should ask God. He generously will give what is needed to make the right decisions. You can consult your parents. You can ask your friends for advice. But don't forget to ask God for his wisdom. He won't fail you!

M A R C H   1 7

The Talent Show   *The correct answer is A.*

DISCUSSION QUESTIONS:
1. When you are complimented for doing a good job, how do you respond?
2. Why do you think answers C or E would not be good responses to doing a good job?
3. What makes you worth something? (See Romans 12:3 for a hint.)

Feeling good about ourselves is important because too often we think too little of ourselves. (See answer E.) On the other hand, we can think too highly of ourselves as well. (Answer D.) The key to a honest—and accurate—self-evaluation is knowing who we are in Jesus. Without him, we aren't capable of anything by God's standards. Our true value lies in our relationship with Christ and what God thinks of us.

M A R C H   1 8

The New Pastor   *The correct answer is E.*

DISCUSSION QUESTIONS:
1. When your friends make fun of someone in authority—a pastor, teacher, principal, or coach—how do you react? Do you join in? Or do you try to stop your friends?
2. What's the harm in telling a few jokes at someone else's expense?
3. Imagine if the pastor walked in while the boys were doing their imitation. How would the pastor feel? How would the boys feel?

Paul tells us we are to respect and honor those who are our leaders because "they work hard among you and warn you against all that is wrong." We may not like everything about our leaders, their actions or their personalities, but we are commanded to hold them in "highest regard" because of their work.

The Gross Joke   *The correct answer is C.*

DISCUSSION QUESTIONS:

1. What do you do when your friends tell a gross joke?
2. Why do you think God doesn't want his people to take part in that kind of joke telling?
3. Why would changing the subject be the best action to take?

God wants us to fill our minds with the right books, music, movies, magazines, and conversations. To do this we need to replace harmful input with wholesome and "excellent" material. Above all, we need to pray that God will help us to continually focus on what is good and pure. It takes practice, but it can be done!

We're Number One!   *The correct answer is D.*

DISCUSSION QUESTIONS:

1. How do you feel when you have lost a close game? How about when you have won?
2. When you see a team really show off after a win, how do you feel?
3. When your team has a *big* win, how do you and your teammates usually act?

Nobody likes a poor loser. But nobody likes a poor winner, either. Showing off after a win, or putting down another team, not only shows a lack of good sportsmanship but also a lack of being humble. James says that God opposes the proud but "shows favor to the humble." Remember that the next time your team wins.

Standing Firm   *The correct answer is C.*

DISCUSSION QUESTIONS:

1. When kids start making fun of you for your faith, what do you do?
2. How do you feel toward kids who make fun of you or others?
3. How can you be nice to those kids?

No one appreciates being ridiculed or mocked. If we're honest, we probably want to call those who make fun of us a name or two back. Paul says, however, that we should "bless those who persecute us; bless and do not curse." We can't do this on our own power. Instead, we must trust that the Holy Spirit will help us *show* love to those for whom we may not *feel* love.

Exposed!   *The correct answer is C.*

DISCUSSION QUESTIONS:

1. What would you do if you found some money lying on the floor? How about if you found out later it belonged to someone else?
2. What would you do if you knew a good friend of yours had picked up something and had not returned it to its rightful owner? Would you confront that friend like Jeremy's friend did?
3. Read Psalm 51:4. David wrote this psalm after his sin was exposed by Nathan. Why do you think David says he has sinned against God?

It is not easy to hear the truth, particularly when we are in the wrong. But when confronted, follow David's example. Confess your sin, and seek God's forgiveness. Remember that sin not only hurts us and others; it ultimately offends God.

True Confessions *The correct answer is D.*

DISCUSSION QUESTIONS:
1. Why should Missy confront the girl with what she is doing?
2. When a friend confesses to you something that he or she did wrong, what advice do you give?
3. What should be your motive in confronting another person with something that he or she did wrong?

If your motivation in confronting another about a wrongdoing is to embarrass that person or to make him or her feel bad, then you should keep quiet. The Bible teaches that believers should do nothing out of hatred for another person. When confronting someone about a personal issue, do it privately and directly, so you won't share in his or her guilt.

Reckless Words *The correct answer is C.*

DISCUSSION QUESTIONS:
1. How did you feel when you overheard a nasty remark about yourself?
2. In James 3:6, why does James compares the tongue to fire? How can words be like fire?
3. Rate your speech: Are you careless with your words—or careful?

Words can have a tremendous impact on others—for good and for bad. In Proverbs, reckless words are compared to a piercing sword; in James, to a raging fire. We cannot afford to be careless with the things we say—the consequences can be terribly damaging. No one can stop the results of our words once they are spoken.

The Fashion Patrol *The correct answer is D.*

DISCUSSION QUESTIONS:
1. How do you think Valerie feels? What do you think she feels like doing?
2. When you were mocked by a group of friends, how did you feel? What did you do?
3. What are the possible outcomes of Valerie simply walking away from Mary's taunts?

It hurts to be the object of a group's taunts and mocking. It's human nature to want to lash out in anger towards our tormentors. But God's Word tells us that a wise person will control his or her anger. By overlooking wrongs done to us, we will earn the respect of others.

Just One Drink *The correct answer is D.*

DISCUSSION QUESTIONS:
1. What would you say to friends who want to experiment with drinking?
2. Looking at Proverbs 23:20-21, why do you think God doesn't want us to join those who drink too much?
3. In what ways might even taking a small drink be harmful?

The misuse of wine—or any type of alcohol—can lead to many dangerous consequences. It can lead to physical and mental "poverty" by dulling the senses and limiting clear judgment and self-control. Clearly, the best policy is to stay away from drinking—and those who drink.

MARCH 27

Singing the Blues   *The correct answer is B.*

DISCUSSION QUESTIONS:
1. What would you do in Felicia's situation?
2. How do you handle competition? Do you welcome it or shy away from it?
3. When you are competing against someone as equally (or more) talented as you, what do you feel toward that person? Do you want to beat him or her? Help him? Hope she gets sick?

Paul says that believers are to "take delight in honoring others." Sometimes we "honor" our teachers so we'll get a good grade. Or we will "honor" our coach so we can play the best position. But as Christians, we are to honor people because they, too, are made in God's image and have a unique contribution to make as well.

MARCH 28

The Perfect Pen   *The correct answer is A.*

DISCUSSION QUESTIONS:
1. How do you respond when you find out that your friend has shoplifted?
2. Do you think it would be OK to steal the pen for a good cause—like getting a favorite teacher a really great gift?
3. Do you think Dan's teacher cares about the price of the pen?

God is very clear in his commandment: Do not steal. No ifs, ands, or buts. While the end result may be for good—a gift for someone you care for or helping another person—stealing is never the right solution. Remember, stealing is not only a sin against a store or a neighbor, but a sin against God.

MARCH 29

The English Test   *The correct answer is C.*

DISCUSSION QUESTIONS:
1. When friends want information about a test you've already taken, what do you tell them?
2. Why do you think it is wrong to tell them what is on a test?
3. How would you feel if you knew that someone got all the questions for a test from another student?
4. What do you think might happen to Freddie if Mrs. Todd finds out? How about Jason?

Cheating is a difficult sin to avoid, particularly if it is in the guise of helping out a friend. But once a person gets involved in cheating, it can have far-reaching effects. Then it becomes very difficult to trust that person. Never take cheating lightly.

The Real Race   *The correct answer is D.*

DISCUSSION QUESTIONS:

1. How can Theo break through the invisible barriers that divide the different races at his school?
2. How do you relate to kids from different ethnic backgrounds? Do you mingle, or do you tend to stay with kids who are just like you?
3. In John 4: 4-30, what can we learn from Jesus' example?

In Jesus' time, there was a long-standing hatred between the Jews and the Samaritans. Jews did not associate with Samaritans to the point that they did whatever they could to avoid traveling through the region where Samaritans lived. Jesus broke through that barrier in order to share the good news of God's plan of salvation with the Samaritan woman. Believers today should break down artificial barriers and share God's Good News with all kinds of people.

Benched!   *The correct answer is C.*

DISCUSSION QUESTIONS:

1. When situations arise that don't go the way you would like, how do you typically react?
2. Which of the answers listed do you think come most naturally? What would you predict most people would do in Pamela's situation?
3. What do you think Pamela is feeling in this situation? What would help her overcome her disappointment?

In Romans 8:28, Paul teaches that God will work everything together "for the good of those who love God." Notice that this does not say that everything that happens will be good, or that God is working to make his people happy. It does say, however, that God is able to turn every circumstance around for our long-range good according to *his* purpose. Remember that the next time things don't go your way. God has a better plan for you!

Pop Quiz!   *The correct answer is C.*

DISCUSSION QUESTIONS:

1. When you have been caught unprepared for a test, what did you do?
2. What do you say to friends who have cheated on tests?
3. What are the consequences for a person who is caught cheating? What about if the person isn't caught?

Proverbs 11:1 couldn't say it any plainer: God hates cheating. Dishonesty, in whatever form, only serves to work against us—others will no longer trust us (including our teachers and parents), and we can't even enjoy what we have achieved through cheating. The next time you may be tempted to cheat remember that God "delights in honesty."

A Full Recovery   *The correct answer is D.*

DISCUSSION QUESTIONS:

1. Think of a time when God answered your prayer. How did you respond? Who did you tell about it?

2. When you are worried about something, what do you usually do?
3. Why do you think it is important to thank God for what he has done?

Taking time to thank God acknowledges his work in our lives and how dependent we are on him. Philippians 4:6 says that we don't have to worry about *anything*, but we can bring all our prayers and concerns to God who will give us what we need. Then our natural response will be to thank him for all he has done.

APRIL 3

To Tell the Truth   *The correct answer is E.*

DISCUSSION QUESTION:
1. What would you do if a friend gave you some unwanted, but truthful, advice?
2. What might happen if Gemma refuses to listen to her friend? What about if she does listen?
3. What happened when you confronted a friend who was doing something wrong?

From whom would you rather hear unpleasant advice—a friend who has your best interest at heart or an enemy who wishes to tear you down? Everyone receives unpleasant advice at times. When that happens to you, consider the source. A friend's advice, no matter how painful, can be good.

APRIL 4

The Last-Minute Report   *The correct answer is D.*

DISCUSSION QUESTIONS:
1. Why should Blake accept the consequences of his actions?
2. When you do something wrong, are you always willing to accept the consequences of your actions? Why or why not?
3. Why do you think it may be easier for a Christian than a non-Christian to accept the consequences of doing something wrong?

First Chronicles 21:8 tells about David realizing that he had made a foolish mistake. Rather than hiding it or making excuses for himself, David recognized his sin, took full responsibility for it, admitted he was wrong, and asked God to forgive him. Like David, you also need to take responsibility for your actions, admit when you are wrong, and ask God's forgiveness.

APRIL 5

The Job   *The correct answer is A.*

DISCUSSION QUESTIONS:
1. Kris has proven herself to be a hard, reliable worker in her job. What would be the harm in slacking off just once and working twice as hard the following week?
2. Why do you think it is so important that Kris does the best job she can?
3. When have you been in a situation like Kris's? What did you do?

God has given us work to do—whether it is schoolwork, an after-school job, or doing chores at home. No matter what the setting, God wants us to view our "work" as an act of worship or service to him. Having that attitude about daily chores would eliminate a lot of complaining and resentment.

The Party Invitations   *The correct answer is E.*

DISCUSSION QUESTIONS:
1. When you have made a promise to a friend, what do you do if something better comes along?
2. Why don't you think answer D is a good solution to Melanie's problem?
3. How do you feel when someone breaks a promise to you—for whatever reason?

There are two powerful forces that the writer of Psalm 25:21 desires: honesty and integrity. Honesty will keep us on the path to right living according to God's rules; and integrity—being what we say we are—will make sure we walk consistently in God's way. God delights in those who have integrity!

Money in the Bank?   *The correct answer is C.*

DISCUSSION QUESTIONS:
1. Why would it be unwise for Phoebe to spend money from her college fund for the computer?
2. Why is wise for young people to save for the future, such as college?
3. Why isn't asking her parents to buy the computer, promising to repay them, a good idea?

God approves of foresight and restraint. Saving and planning for the future shows that we are wise and responsible stewards of the resources God has entrusted to us. We need to examine whether our spending is God-pleasing or merely self-pleasing.

The Bible Study   *The correct answer is D.*

DISCUSSION QUESTIONS:
1. Why should Brent admit that the Bible is his?
2. Why do you sometimes hide your faith from others?
3. When kids start making fun of you for believing in God, what do you tell them?

When kids start to make fun of you because of your faith, remember three facts: (1) The Good News is the message of salvation; (2) the Good News has life-changing power; (3) the Good News is for everyone. The next time you find yourself being mocked, focus on God and what he is doing in the world, rather than yourself. Then you won't be ashamed or embarrassed.

Overtime!   *The correct answer is B.*

DISCUSSION QUESTIONS:
1. When you have broken curfew, what do you do?
2. Why wouldn't answer A be a good solution? After all, Curtis is already late.
3. In what ways do you "listen to your father (or mother)"?

We show respect to our parents when we listen to them. By admitting our mistakes, rather than covering them up, we show our parents that we respect their wisdom and guidance. Then Mom and Dad learn, as Proverbs says, "What a pleasure it is to have wise children. So give your parents joy!"

Common Ground *The correct answer is C.*

DISCUSSION QUESTIONS:
1. How do you respond when you meet someone who is different from you—in race, color, background, or language?
2. How do you think Sherry and this new girl can become friends?
3. In what ways can you reach out to others who are "different" from you?

In 1 Corinthians 9:22, Paul wrote that he tries to find the "common ground" between himself and others so he can bring them the Good News. In the same way, we can make friends by looking for those interests and bonds we share with others, rather than looking at the things that make us different.

The Accused *The correct answer is B.*

DISCUSSION QUESTIONS:
1. What would you do in Marilyn's situation?
2. How would you feel toward someone who accused you of something you didn't do?
3. What are some ways Marilyn can *show* that she is not the thief?

We may not always be able to prevent others from accusing us, but we can act in such a way that they have no "evidence" upon which to base those accusations. As long as we do what is right, their accusations will be empty and will only serve to embarrass them.

Unlocked Secrets *The correct answer is A.*

DISCUSSION QUESTIONS:
1. Why do you think Erin should simply close the locker and relock it?
2. What did you do when you accidentally opened someone's private belongings—whether it's a locker, backpack, notebook, diary, or purse?
3. How do you want others to treat your personal belongings?

Paul says that followers of Jesus should make every effort to do good in all situations. The right thing to do here would be to respect the other person's personal, private belongings. When we are careful to do "good deeds all the time," everyone benefits.

And the Answer Is . . . *The correct answer is C.*

DISCUSSION QUESTIONS:
1. Why shouldn't Marcus let Roger look at his test?
2. How do you respond when a classmate asks to copy your homework or look at your test answers?
3. Why would Marcus be a better friend to Roger by not allowing him to cheat?

God wants his people to act wisely in all areas of their lives. Proverbs 8:1-8 portrays wisdom as a woman who guides us and makes us succeed if we will listen to her. Listen to Wisdom—she has the right words, and she hates every kind of deception.

Behind the Scenes   *The correct answer is E.*

DISCUSSION QUESTIONS:
1. When you didn't get a part you wanted in a play, or in orchestra, or on a sports team, how did you react? Did you feel like quitting?
2. Why should Alice take on the job as stage manager?
3. If you have a particular gift or talent, do you think that makes you more important than others? Why or why not?

God gives each person different abilities and talents that they are to use for the good of everyone. To use our gifts effectively, we need to realize that they all come from God. We need to dedicate our gifts to God's service, not our own personal successes.

The Great Debate   *The correct answer is B.*

DISCUSSION QUESTIONS:
1. How do you handle the kid at school who knows it all?
2. Why do you think it's not worth arguing with kids like that or trying to prove them wrong?
3. When you are involved in an argument, how important is it that you get the last word in? Why?

The temptation to show up a "know-it-all" or to prove your point of view during an argument can be strong. But Paul says we should avoid any type of foolish debate that leads only to a fight. When tempted to join an argument, ask yourself whether proving your point will turn people to God—or away from him.

The Grass Looks Greener   *The correct answer is E.*

DISCUSSION QUESTIONS:
1. How do you feel when you are at a friend's house that is bigger than yours?
2. Read Luke 12:15. What do you think it means to be on guard against all kinds of greed? Do you think Mickey is being greedy?
3. What do you think is most important to God—the things we have in our homes, or the things that go on in our homes? In what ways do you think Zachary might be "poor"?

The message of the world is that the more things people have, the better those people will feel about themselves, the more comfortable they will be, and the happier they will be. Jesus warns, however, that the "good life" has nothing to do with being wealthy. He teaches that his people should guard against wanting what they don't have. The truly "good life," Jesus says, can be found in living in a relationship with him and doing his work.

Sharing   *The correct answer is B.*

DISCUSSION QUESTIONS:
1. How do you respond when your friends make fun of a classmate who doesn't dress well?

2. Why do you think it's a good idea for Shannon to know the girl before giving her the clothes?
3. What are some ways you can practice hospitality among your friends?

The world is filled with needy people. Paul says that as God's people, we should do what we can to help them out—whether it's inviting them over for dinner, sharing out of our abundance, or just being a friend. Be on the lookout for how you can reach out to those in need.

APRIL 18

The Class Picnic   *The correct answer is C.*

DISCUSSION QUESTIONS:
1. Why do you think Claire should give Rachel an opportunity to share when it's obvious that Brett has the best suggestion? Or does he?
2. As the leader, do you think Claire should let the group dictate how to run things?
3. How do you feel when you are involved in a group where the leader favors only certain members?
4. How does a good leader act?

Good leaders will show understanding and respect to everyone—not just a favored few. As good leaders, we should treat each person fairly and not make decisions based on popularity.

APRIL 19

That's No Excuse   *The correct answer is C.*

DISCUSSION QUESTIONS:
1. What are the advantages to the statement "everyone is doing it"? What are the drawbacks?
2. What are the most important factors you consider in making a decision?
3. On what should Hugh base his decision?

The argument that "everybody is doing it" didn't carry much weight with God when he punished the Israelites for copying the evil customs and worship of the surrounding nations. It may not always be easy to do the right thing and obey God but consider the alternatives. When facing a tough decision where you are tempted to go along with the crowd, determine to be God's person and do what he says regardless of the cost and who's doing it.

APRIL 20

The Hospital   *The correct answer is E.*

DISCUSSION QUESTIONS:
1. When you feel lonely, scared, or confused, what do you do?
2. Read Psalm 62:8. What does it mean to "pour out your heart" to God? Is it all right to tell God that you are angry? afraid? confused?
3. How can you help a friend who is going through a difficult situation?

When you are feeling stressed out, prayer—pouring out your heart to God—can help release the inner turmoil. Tell God your thoughts and feelings. You can't shock him. He already knows what's going on. Allow God to be your refuge. When you rest in his strength, nothing will be able to shake you.

After-School Activity   *The correct answer is A.*

DISCUSSION QUESTIONS:
1. Why should Brock continue to follow the rules in this situation?
2. What might be the consequences if Brock were to go to the bookstore?
3. What is the source of Brock's temptation?

When tempted to do wrong, we should remember, as James said, that our own sinful desires tempt us. When you feel tempted to do something you know is against the rules, take a look at why you want to do it. You can resist the temptation when you turn to God for strength and choose to obey.

APRIL 22

Third Chair   *The correct answer is D.*

DISCUSSION QUESTIONS:
1. How do you handle disappointment, especially after working so hard?
2. Where do you think Ian's thoughts are focused in this situation—on his situation and himself, or on God?
3. Read Psalm 42:5-6. How can thinking about God help you when you are discouraged?

People become discouraged when they think about their difficult situations and how helpless they are to make any changes. According to this psalm, the way to counter discouragement is to think about God's goodness and *his* ability to help.

APRIL 23

In the Middle   *The best answers are C and E.*

DISCUSSION QUESTIONS:
1. What do you do when you are caught in the middle of your friends' fight?
2. How do you feel about being in the middle? Do you avoid your friends until they work out their problem? Or do you try to help patch things up?
3. Why do you think answers C and E would be all right? What do you think Kristen should do first?

God loves peacemakers! The next time you find yourself in the middle of your friends' fight, ask God for his wisdom—which is pure, peace loving, and gentle. Choose your words carefully and lovingly, using them to "plant seeds of peace." Then you will "reap a harvest of goodness."

APRIL 24

The Sick Mom   *The correct answer is B.*

DISCUSSION QUESTIONS:
1. How do you help your mom or dad when they aren't feeling well?
2. Read 1 John 3:18. How can we *show* love to those we care about? What can Barrett do in this situation to show his love?
3. When you aren't feeling well, how do you like to be treated?

John says that it is not good enough to merely say we love each other. As Jesus' followers, we are called to show our love through our actions. How clearly do your actions say that you really love others?

Moving On   *The correct answer is D.*

DISCUSSION QUESTIONS:

1. How did you react when your family had to move? How did you feel about it? What were some of your concerns?
2. What advice would you give to a friend, like Darren, who was worried about moving to a new town?
3. How does knowing God help at a time like that?

The Bible promises that God will meet all of our needs. That doesn't mean, however, that God will always give us what we *want*. There's a difference between *needs* and *wants*. By trusting God, we can change our attitude from *wanting* everything our way, to thanking God for what he has provided. Trust God to take care of your worries about new situations and to provide for your every *need*.

Taught to Pray   *The correct answer is E.*

DISCUSSION QUESTIONS:

1. Why isn't answer B a good solution? What about answer C? Why do you think answer E is the best solution?
2. How would you describe your prayer habits? What goal would you set for yourself?
3. Read Psalm 5:3. Why do you think morning is a good time for prayer?

The secret of a close relationship with God is having a regular time when we can talk to him. As with any friendship, regular communication is important for building a strong relationship. (Imagine not talking to your best friend for a week!) The morning is a good time because your mind will be free from the day's problems, and you can commit that day to God in prayer.

Personal Best   *The correct answer is A.*

DISCUSSION QUESTIONS:

1. How did you feel when you finally did better in some activity than your competitive friend? How did you react?
2. How do you handle a friend who always wants to do better than you?
3. Read Jeremiah 9:23-24. What is the only thing that anyone should boast about?

Competition is a fact of life. There will always be someone better than us, along with others who don't do as well. But while we tend to admire those who are stronger, faster, and more athletic, God puts the highest priority on knowing him personally and living a life that reflects his godly character.

New and Unusual   *The correct answer is A.*

DISCUSSION QUESTIONS:

1. How do you and your friends react to kids who look different? Do you ignore them or try to invite them into your group?
2. How can you tell from a person's appearance if that person is a Christian or not?
3. Read Romans 15:7. How does Jesus want us to act towards others?

If Jesus is Lord of our life, then we will begin to look at things—and people—differently. We are to have his attitude of love toward other Christians and accept them as he accepts us. As we grow in faith and know Jesus better, we will become more able to have this attitude of unity.

The Paper Chase   *The correct answer is B.*

DISCUSSION QUESTIONS:
1. How do you handle the "pressure" to complete a project on time? Do you panic? Do you ask your parents for help?
2. Read Isaiah 40:29-31. How does knowing that God will give "strength to the weary" help you?
3. What would you tell a friend who is having difficulty with a big project?

Everyone faces deadlines for projects, book reports, and term papers at school. Sometimes, meeting constant deadlines can feel overwhelming—we get tired, discouraged, and want to quit. But the good news is that God never gets tired. His power and strength never become less. His strength is our source of strength. When you are feeling desperate, remember you can call upon God to renew your strength and lift you above life's difficulties.

Mother's Day   *The best answers are C and D.*

DISCUSSION QUESTIONS:
1. Wouldn't Chuck's mother understand if he didn't have time to go out and buy a gift?
2. What would you do in Chuck's situation?
3. What is the key to resolving Chuck's dilemma?

We all have so many demands upon our time—after-school activities, homework, practicing instruments, sports. At times, it feels as though we can't fit in one more thing. That's when it's important to decide what is the best use of our time and how to use our time wisely. God's Word teaches that a wise person thinks first—and then acts! Waiting until the last minute only serves to expose our foolishness.

Never Too Young   *The correct answer is A.*

DISCUSSION QUESTIONS:
1. At what age can people get involved with missions? Is missions work only for adults who have spent years training for the field?
2. In what ways can you get involved without leaving the country?
3. Why should you participate in missions work?

Adults often overlook young people, assuming that they are too young to get involved in God's work. But the Bible tells of the many times that God used children and young people. Paul's nephew, although only a boy, played an important role in protecting Paul's life. God can use anyone of any age, who is willing to obey him. Are you willing to be used by God? If so, he has a job for you!

Saturday Chores   *The correct answer is A.*

DISCUSSION QUESTIONS:
1. How do you usually respond when your parents ask you to help out with chores?
2. How does a person's attitude affect his or her work? What are some possible consequences of a bad attitude?
3. How can Nate adopt a better attitude?

Doing chores never tops anybody's Top Ten Favorite Things to Do on Saturday—including your parents' list! But that doesn't mean we should stop doing chores. (Imagine if your mom stopped doing the laundry!) Proverbs teaches that we will be recognized for the work we do. A good worker is worth much in the eyes of a king—and Mom and Dad.

Down, but Not Out   *The correct answer is D.*

DISCUSSION QUESTIONS:
1. How would you describe what Caleb is feeling now?
2. When you and your family have faced bad times, how did you feel?
3. How can knowing God help Caleb through this difficult time?

God never promises that his people won't experience bad times or difficulties. But what God does promise is that he will never stop loving them or break his "covenant of blessing." His mercy never fails, and he will see us through the difficult times.

Study Guide   *The correct answer is B.*

DISCUSSION QUESTIONS:
1. Why should Clint listen and take his mom's advice?
2. What are the benefits of studying over the weekend rather than waiting until Monday night?
3. When you have a big test coming up, how do you plan your studying?

Kids may not always want to hear this, but at times, parents, teachers, and coaches have good advice that can help them. You will do well to listen to instruction and advice because, as the proverb says, that is the way to success.

The Last Game   *The correct answer is B.*

DISCUSSION QUESTIONS:
1. What is Skip feeling? Do you think he has a right to be angry? Why or why not?
2. When you are angry, what usually happens? Do you yell at others? Sulk?
3. Read Psalm 37:8-9. What will happen to those who get angry and worry? What will happen to those who don't? What do you think it means to inherit the land?

Anger and worry are two strong and harmful emotions. They show a lack of faith in the truth that God loves us and is in control. When we focus on our problems, we become worried and angry. But when we focus on God, we find peace. On what are you focusing?

The Guilty Goalie   *The correct answer is B.*

DISCUSSION QUESTIONS:
1. Why do you think Shelia should tell the ref what actually happened?
2. When you have been tempted to hide the truth, what did you do?
3. How do you think Shelia would really feel, knowing that her team won unjustly?

There is a right way and a wrong way to do anything, including winning a soccer game. We should strive to be honest in all of our dealings. Passing a test, earning a teacher's praise, or winning a championship unjustly will never bring God's blessing or lasting happiness.

The Camp-Out   *The correct answer is E.*

DISCUSSION QUESTIONS:
1. Why is it important for everyone in a group to pitch in and do their part?
2. What might happen if Brad decides to sneak off and not do his share of the work?
3. How do you feel when someone in a group goofs off and doesn't help out?

You've heard similar warnings: "If you don't study, you'll fail"; "If you don't save now, you won't have money when you need it"; "If you don't pitch in and help prepare the campsite now, you won't eat dinner until late!" As members of a group, we have a responsibility to do our part so the work gets done and *everyone* can enjoy the results.

Sleeping In   *The correct answer is D.*

DISCUSSION QUESTIONS:
1. Why is Minda so angry with her mother? Who is really at fault in this situation?
2. What would you say to Minda if she told you this story at the lunch table?
3. How difficult is it for you to accept instruction from your parents, your teachers, or God? What has happened when you didn't listen?

Sometimes it is not easy to accept instruction from our parents, especially when we don't want to hear about it! When we choose not to listen to instructions, we had better be sure we are willing to pay the price. Proverbs clearly teaches that wisdom comes from listening to advice and accepting instruction.

Future Plans   *The correct answer is C.*

DISCUSSION QUESTIONS:
1. What about *your* future excites you? What discourages you? What do you find confusing?
2. Should Chip be worried about his future? Why or why not?
3. Read Jeremiah 29:11. Why would knowing this verse help Chip, or you, in planning for the future?

God is able to stir us to move ahead. He believes that we can do the task he has given us to perform, and he will be with us all of the way. As long as God, who knows the future, plans our steps and goes with us as we do his will, we can have hope. Trust that God will lead *you* in the right direction.

Turning the Other Cheek   *The correct answer is D.*

DISCUSSION QUESTIONS:
1. What should Tina say to her teammates as they begin the second half?
2. What did you *feel* like doing when you were involved in a game where the other team was playing dirty? What did you *do?*
3. How can believers follow Jesus' instructions in Matthew 5:39?

Resisting the natural reaction to get even requires supernatural power! Only God can give us the power to love as he does. The next time you find yourself wanting to get back at someone, pray that God will enable you to do good instead.

Spin the Bottle   *The correct answer is B.*

DISCUSSION QUESTIONS:
1. Why should Juanita not get involved in playing kissing games?
2. What is the harm in playing a game like Spin the Bottle?
3. How does God wants his people to handle relationships with the opposite sex?

A game like Spin the Bottle may seem harmless, but it can lead to dangerous desires and thoughts. It is better, as Paul says, to "have nothing to do" with anything that will cause us to sin in this way. Make a conscious decision to remove anything that supports or feeds these desires, and rely on the Holy Spirit's power to help you resist temptation.

The Science Project   *The correct answer is E.*

DISCUSSION QUESTIONS:
1. When someone "stole" your idea for a class project, how did you react?
2. When have you been tempted to "borrow" an idea for a class project from a classmate?
3. Why is what Caitlin's friend did a form of stealing? Why was it wrong?

It's a natural response to want to get back at a person who wrongs us. But God says that his people should treat their enemies with kindness and return good for evil. God's Word says that it is God's responsibility, not ours, to repay those who deserve it.

The Accident   *The correct answer is B.*

DISCUSSION QUESTIONS:
1. What might be some reasons that Jessie would be afraid to help in this situation?
2. Why do you think it would be wrong for Jessie to ride away?
3. How would you be likely to respond in a similar situation?

There are many excuses we can give to avoid helping someone in need: We're too busy; we're not qualified to help; we don't know what to do; someone else will do it. But Jesus teaches, through his example, that people's needs are more important than any rules or excuses. When we have the opportunity to help another person in need, God expects us to respond. To refuse to do so is a sin in God's eyes.

The Team Captain   *The best answer is B.*

DISCUSSION QUESTIONS:
1. What would you do in Sally's situation? Who would you choose to be on your team?
2. Why wouldn't C be a good solution?
3. What does it mean to "clothe yourselves with tenderhearted mercy, kindness, humility, gentleness, and patience"?

If winning is most important, then this is a no-win situation. If Sally picks only the strongest players, she will hurt her friend. If she picks the weaker players, her team will most likely lose. But winning softball games is not the most important thing to God. How we live, and how we treat others, is much more important. As his "holy people," we should show tenderhearted mercy and kindness to those around us—no matter how good they are at softball.

Beauty Is in the Eye . . .   *The correct answer is B.*

DISCUSSION QUESTIONS:
1. Why do you think Gail should not even try a little makeup, just to check it out?
2. Read 1 Peter 3:3-4. Why do you think it is important not to be obsessed with clothes or hairstyles?
3. What do think is important to remember about appearance?

While we should not be obsessed with fashion, neither should we neglect personal hygiene, neatness, and grooming. But we need to remember that attitude and inner spirit are most important. True beauty begins inside.

Unconditional Love   *The correct answer is A.*

DISCUSSION QUESTIONS:
1. How did you react when you did something for which you felt God could never forgive you?
2. When you hear about kids in your youth group getting into trouble, how do you feel? Do you have a hard time accepting them?

God is a mighty Savior, always merciful, always loving. God *is* faithful and just and will forgive us and cleanse all who trust in Christ and confess their sins to him. God rejoices in his people and sings over them. Don't let unconfessed sin or guilt over past sins keep you from finding forgiveness and comfort in your loving heavenly Father.

Making the First Move   *The correct answer is A.*

DISCUSSION QUESTIONS:
1. Why should Felicia make the first move when it is apparent (or is it?) that the new girl isn't very friendly?
2. When you notice new students in school or at church, how do you respond?

3. What can you do to make new kids feel welcome in your neighborhood, at school, or in church?

When Saul came to Jerusalem, his reputation—as a persecutor of Christians—preceded him. No one could believe that Saul had actually seen the light (literally) and had become a Christian. But Barnabas took him and introduced him to the other believers. You can be a Barnabas to newcomers by welcoming them, introducing them, and encouraging them in a new situation.

MAY 18

Baseball Burnout   *The correct answer is C.*

DISCUSSION QUESTIONS:
1. When you feel pressured to participate in an activity or a sport, how do you respond?
2. Why would it be important for Art to be truthful with his dad about being burned out?
3. What might happen as a result of Art talking with his dad? What might happen if he doesn't?

Paul was able to persevere when he kept his focus on the prize—knowing Jesus. Like an athlete training for an event, Paul laid aside everything that was distracting him from becoming effective. Likewise, when you are facing burnout and feel as though you can't continue, sit down and reevaluate your goals, and then get rid of everything else that is distracting you!

MAY 19

Trash TV   *The correct answer is C.*

DISCUSSION QUESTIONS:
1. Why shouldn't Guy watch the TV show?
2. How do you feel about your parents supervising your TV viewing?
3. Why do your parents consider certain TV shows as inappropriate for your viewing? Do you agree or disagree with their evaluations?

Those who belong to Christ throw off their old way of doing things. Sometimes that includes books, music, or TV shows. Paul says that believers should adopt new thoughts and attitudes that reflect Jesus' character. A good test for what is appropriate is to imagine, *Would I be watching (reading, listening) this if Jesus were in the room?* Allow your parents and the Holy Spirit to guide you in making wise decisions.

MAY 20

Spreading the News   *The correct answer is A.*

DISCUSSION QUESTIONS:
1. Why do you think it would be wrong for Robyn to explain what is wrong with Holly?
2. What do you think is wrong with answers C and E?
3. When someone told you something confidential, what did you do?

Proverbs 25:19 says that putting confidence in an unreliable person can be painful. It is like "chewing with a toothache or walking with a broken foot." When someone tells you something confidential, remember to keep it that way!

The Prayer Chain   *The correct answer is B.*

DISCUSSION QUESTIONS:
1. When you prayed for something for a long time like Derek did, without getting an answer, how did you feel? What did you do?
2. Is there a right and a wrong way to pray?
3. Why should Derek not give up and stop praying?

Luke 18:1-8 tells about Jesus using a parable to teach his disciples that they should always pray and never give up. We need to keep our requests constantly before God, believing that he will answer. God may delay in answering, but his delays always have a good reason. While we wait in prayer, we grow in character, faith, and hope.

It's in the Stars!   *The correct answer is E.*

DISCUSSION QUESTIONS:
1. What do you say when someone asks if you have read your horoscope?
2. What do you think about astrology? Is it a fad and completely harmless?
3. Read Deuteronomy 4:19. Why do you think God is so determined that his people not follow such practices?

When we start looking to other things for guidance—whether it's the stars, tarot cards, or crystals—we are guilty of worshiping created things, rather than the Creator. Avoid such practices, because they are evil to God. The Bible, God's Word, tells us all we need to know about the future. We don't need to turn to the occult for faulty information.

Looks Aren't Everything   *The correct answer is D.*

DISCUSSION QUESTIONS:
1. How do you feel when someone makes fun of the way you look?
2. What do you think is most important—how a person looks or how he or she acts?
3. Read 1 Samuel 16:7. How does knowing this verse help a person who may not be the best-looking kid in school?

When we judge people by how they look, we many overlook other important qualities. Our appearance doesn't always reveal what we are really like—or our true values. Take heart, because God judges by faith and character, not appearance.

Too Hard to Handle?   *The best answers are C and D.*

DISCUSSION QUESTIONS:
1. Why do you know that God *can* handle Christopher's problem?
2. When you are facing a huge problem, how do you handle it? Do you talk to someone about it? Do you talk to God?
3. Why would answer C also be a good action for Christopher to take?

God created everything, including all people. When facing problems that appear insurmountable, remember that nothing is too hard for God.

The Pizza Party   *The correct answer is B.*

DISCUSSION QUESTIONS:
1. Why should Liza have to ask first if she could have some pizza? After all, she is a member of the choir.
2. When you have doubts about whether a certain action is right or wrong, what is the best course of action to take?
3. When someone asks you for advice on whether an action is right or wrong, what can you tell them?

In many situations the Bible is silent as to what to do. That's when you must allow your conscience to guide you. If a particular course of action will leave you with an uneasy conscience, then you should avoid it. When God shows you that something is wrong, do whatever you can to avoid it.

The Hidden Magazines   *The correct answer is D.*

DISCUSSION QUESTIONS:
1. Why should Earl confront his brother about finding the dirty magazines?
2. When you discover a friend or a sibling with dirty magazines or videos, what can you do?
3. Why is it important for others to see Christians live "clean, innocent lives"?

Anything that causes a person to have an unhealthy desire for the opposite sex is clearly sinful. Christians should do everything they can to avoid those types of sins and help others to do so as well. God wants his people to shine out as bright examples of blameless and pure living in a dark, sinful world. Hold tight to what you know about God's truth for your life and be obedient. Then you can be an effective witness for God.

Choosing Friends   *The best answer is B, although Lori could give answer D a try.*

DISCUSSION QUESTIONS:
1. Are your closest friends Christians or unbelievers?
2. Why do you think our relationships are so important to God?
3. If you were in Lori's situation, would you invite your non-Christian friends to church? Why or why not?

Without a doubt, a person's relationships affect his or her faith. We want to be friends with those who don't know God, but often those friendships can lead to unhealthy practices. We need to be friends with unbelievers, but we must not abandon our faith or adopt their behavior.

Your Witness   *The correct answer is B.*

DISCUSSION QUESTIONS:
1. Do you have a friend like Nicole? What happened when you tried to witness to him or her?
2. What would you say to Brittany to help her in this situation?
3. Read Acts 20:24. How does knowing this verse help you?

We need to remember that the most important task we will ever have is to share our faith with others. When we do, we must trust God to take care of the results.

Justice Is Served?   *The correct answer is D.*

DISCUSSION QUESTIONS:
1. Why do you think Bert should tell the aide that Dominic wasn't responsible for breaking the window?
2. Why do you think it is wrong for the school bully to be punished in this situation? After all, he's probably guilty of doing something bad during recess.

The Bible is clear that if we withhold truthful information about a situation, then we are held responsible. What's important in this situation is not that the school bully gets punished but that the truth is spoken. Don't let your feelings about a particular person sway your responsibility to speak the truth.

A Little Help from My Friends   *The correct answer is A.*

DISCUSSION QUESTIONS:
1. How do you feel when your friends promise to help you with something and then not show up?
2. How will it be possible for Blair to forgive her friends?
3. When a friend asks you to help out on a project or a party, do you follow through on your commitment?

Three times in Matthew 26:31-46, Jesus asked his best friends, his disciples, to stay awake and watch while he prayed in terrible suffering before his betrayal. Three times the disciples failed him. But Jesus still loved them and forgave them. Our friends, sooner or later, will disappoint us. They will fail us. When they do, we need to remember Jesus' example. Through him, and because of him, we will be able to forgive our friends and put the disappointment behind us.

"I Spy"   *The correct answer is A.*

DISCUSSION QUESTIONS:
1. Why should Beau forget about this incident?
2. How do you feel when you have inside information that no one else knows? What is the first thing you want to do with that information?
3. Why is it harmful to pass along gossip or unconfirmed rumors?
4. What might have happened if Beau had spread the story about Owen and it wasn't true? What if it was true—does that make a difference?

Jumping to conclusions is easy—especially when we have not taken the time to check out the facts. The tribes of Israel almost began a war against their brothers because they thought the three tribes had built an altar to worship idols rather than God. And Peter was nearly drummed out of the church because he had eaten dinner with a Gentile! Fortunately, in both instances, when the truth was revealed, war was averted, and the people praised God. Before judging the behavior of others, find the truth first—and then keep it to yourself.

Many Thanks   *The correct answer is A.*

DISCUSSION QUESTIONS:
1. Why do you think C would not be a good solution to Jordan's situation?
2. Why do you think it's important to say thank you?
3. How do you feel when someone thanks you for a job well done?

A simple word of thanks goes a long way! Taking time to tell people you appreciate their hard work is very encouraging to those who have invested time in teaching you—whether at school, church, on the soccer field or basketball court. As Proverbs tells us, kind words are "sweet to the soul and healthy to the body."

Family Feud   *The correct answer is D.*

DISCUSSION QUESTIONS:
1. How fair are your parents in handing out punishment?
2. Why do you think Vic deserves the punishment he received?
3. How do you generally respond when you are punished? Do you sulk, get angry, or accept your punishment?

Nobody enjoys being punished. But good parents discipline their children. Like earthly parents, God disciplines his children for their own good. The Bible says that God's discipline, like the discipline of parents, is a sign of his deep love for his people.

The Younger Sister   *The correct answer is A.*

DISCUSSION QUESTIONS:
1. Why should Donna go to the recital? What does Donna need to change before she goes? (And it's not her clothes!)
2. Read 1 Peter 1:2. What does Peter means by "sincere love"? How can we accomplish that?
3. How do you feel about your younger (or older) brother or sister who gets all the attention in the family? How can you learn to "sincerely" love him or her?

When our eyes are focused on ourselves, there is no way we can sincerely love anyone. "Sincere love" involves selfless giving. Only through God's love and forgiveness can we become free to take our eyes off ourselves and meet others' needs. You can love others by following Jesus' example of sacrificial love.

School's Out—Almost!   *The correct answer is A.*

DISCUSSION QUESTIONS:
1. What's so important about Riley going to school on the last day?
2. What do you think Riley is risking by going to the swimming pool instead of school?
3. What should be the most important factor in Riley's decision?

Kids may not always agree with their parents' rules, but as Proverbs says, the wise son or daughter is the one who is obedient. Those who seek out "worthless companions" and disobey will bring shame to their parents. How does your behavior reflect upon your mom and dad?

JUNE 5

Lazy Days of Summer   *The correct answer is D.*

DISCUSSION QUESTIONS:
1. Why should Tiffany volunteer at the day-care center?
2. What is wrong with Tiffany's plans for the summer?
3. How do you view your summer time off from school—like Tiffany, or as an opportunity to explore new things and serve others?

People's values and priorities are reflected in how they use their resources—money, talents, and time. If someone is only concerned about satisfying himself or herself, then it will be reflected in his or her activities. Put God first, and be willing to do the job he has for you. He will reward you by providing for all your needs.

JUNE 6

Making a Good Impression   *The correct answer is C.*

DISCUSSION QUESTIONS:
1. What might be the consequences if Janie's new friends find out she lied to them about her family?
2. When you are around friends who have more than you, how do you act?
3. How do you think Janie can make the best impression on her new friends?
4. How do you feel toward friends who boast about everything they have or do?

Some kids feel the need to invent a "better" family or "bigger" home to make a good impression on others. But, as Abraham discovered when he lied to the Pharaoh in Egypt, lies lead to further complications and problems. Tell the truth, and don't worry about what others think of you.

JUNE 7

Scared Silly   *The correct answer is D.*

DISCUSSION QUESTIONS:
1. When you are afraid of doing something—whether it's a performance or speaking in front of the class—what do you do?
2. What do you think Alysse can do to help conquer her fears?
3. Read Deuteronomy 31:6. How does knowing this verse help you? How can this help Alysse?

The Bible presents story after story displaying God's great power in delivering his people. The same God who guided Moses and the Israelites through the desert and brought them to the Promised Land will also help you in your present and future needs. Remembering God's help in the past will encourage you to face your own battles today.

JUNE 8

Special Delivery   *The correct answer is A.*

DISCUSSION QUESTIONS:
1. Why is it important for Dean to finish the job?
2. When you are given a task, what do you do? Do you finish it, or quit halfway through?
3. Do you think it matters if you take shortcuts (for example, get someone else to finish the task) to get a job done?

In Ezekiel 45:9-11, God commands the princes and people to be just and right, particularly in their business dealings. God's commands hold true today. If someone has been paid to deliver two hundred phone books, then that person should deliver *all* two hundred books, no matter how hot, tired, and frustrated he or she is. God is completely trustworthy, and his followers should be trustworthy too.

JUNE 9

Birthday Shopping   *The correct answer is B.*

DISCUSSION QUESTIONS:
1. Why should Lily buy her mom the music box as planned?
2. When you are shopping for others and see something you want for yourself, how do you usually plan to buy it?
3. What should be the most important factor in Lily's decision on whether or not she should buy the shirt for herself?

Philippians 2:4 says that Christians should not be concerned only with their own interests but to think about others. Use this as your guiding principle, and you will not be easily swayed by your own desires.

JUNE 10

Member of the Club   *The best answer is E.*

DISCUSSION QUESTIONS:
1. Why do you think answer E is an appropriate response? Why do you think Max should explain why he won't go along with the "initiation rite"?
2. Why shouldn't Max just refuse and walk away?
3. What did you do when friends asked you to perform a "harmless" prank against someone?

If we live for Jesus, then our lives will glow like lights, showing others what Jesus is like. We hide that light, though, when we go along with the crowd, or keep silent when we should speak out or not explain our light to others. When someone asks us to do something that is wrong or inappropriate, we need to expose that deed for what it really is and not go along with the crowd.

JUNE 11

Walking the Rails   *The correct answer is A.*

DISCUSSION QUESTIONS:
1. Why should Jamal stick to the safer, yet longer, route home?
2. When your friends suggest something you have been taught is dangerous—like riding bikes on a busy street—how do you handle it?
3. Read Proverbs 22:17-18. What are some of the ways you can help tell the difference between right and wrong?

Discerning right from wrong sometimes is as clear as black and white. Other times, it can be kind of gray, especially when friends are trying to convince you to do something that you're not sure is right. Take some advice from Proverbs, and when you hear good, sound advice, pay attention to it; apply it by obeying it; and remember it so it will come back to mind when you are in doubt.

Whose Money?   *The correct answer is C.*

DISCUSSION QUESTIONS:
1. How do you decide how much money to give to God's work?
2. When you receive a gift of money, how do you feel about giving a portion of that money to God?
3. Why do you think it's important to tithe? (Look at Nehemiah 10:35-39.)

The Israelites decided to donate a tenth of everything they had because they wanted to obey and they didn't want to "neglect the work of the Lord." The same is true for God's people today. God wants us to be faithful and obedient with everything we have—whether it's our money, time, or talents. How are you doing in that department?

JUNE 13

Storm Clouds   *The correct answer is C.*

DISCUSSION QUESTIONS:
1. When you are scared, what helps you feel better?
2. What do you do to help calm others when they are frightened?
3. How does knowing Joshua 1:9 comfort you?

God gives us many promises throughout the Bible. When afraid or facing a difficult situation, perhaps none is more precious than knowing that God will be with us wherever we go. Take comfort in God's promise to you—and remember to pass it along to others when they are frightened!

JUNE 14

Doggone It!   *The correct answer is B.*

DISCUSSION QUESTIONS:
1. How would you respond to someone telling you, "Go ahead and do it. No one will ever know"?
2. Why wouldn't fixing up the garden before Mrs. Henderson gets back be a good solution?
3. Do you think it would be lying if Don doesn't tell Mrs. Henderson what happened? Why or why not?

There is a saying that you can tell a person's true character by how he or she acts when no one is looking. Don may be tempted to think that no one will ever find out what happened to the garden, but God knows. And the Bible tells us in Proverbs that "a liar will not go unpunished." It might help to remember that the next time you think no one is looking!

JUNE 15

Summertime Blues   *The correct answer is C.*

DISCUSSION QUESTIONS:
1. Is Gary is being treated fairly? Why?
2. When you feel you are being treated unfairly, how do you respond?
3. Why do you think Gary shouldn't quit this job and look for a better-paying one?

In Philippians 4:5, Paul says that believers should be "considerate in all they do." This means that we should not seek revenge against those whom we feel are treating us unfairly. Nor should we be overly vocal about our personal rights.

"Oh, Brother!"   *The correct answer is C.*

DISCUSSION QUESTIONS:

1. Why should Chet listen to his brother?
2. Read 1 Peter 5:5. What does it mean to "serve each other in humility"? Do you think this verse is just talking about Chet's attitude, or about his brother's attitude as well?
3. How do you respond when your older sibling is left in charge? Or how do you act when you are in charge of younger sibs?

Both young and old can benefit from Peter's instructions. Older people (including brothers!) can learn from trying to understand young people, and young people can learn by listening to those who are older. Both, says Peter, need to be humble and serve each other. Every believer needs to be humble enough to admit that he or she can learn from others.

The New Baby   *The correct answer is E.*

DISCUSSION QUESTIONS:

1. When you are struggling with a difficult situation, how do deal with your emotions?
2. What does God want to hear from you when you are feeling low? How about your parents?
3. How does talking through your problems and emotions—either with God or parents—help?

Like the psalm writer, God wants his people to pour out their hearts to him, telling him when they are discouraged and depressed. Put your hope and trust in the Lord to see you through difficult times. Then as you focus on his unfailing love, you, too, will be able to praise him.

The Long, Hot Summer   *The correct answer is B.*

DISCUSSION QUESTIONS:

1. Why shouldn't Rodney go along with his friends' plan?
2. What might happen when the boy discovers their scheme?
3. How would you feel if you knew your "friends" were using you to gain something you had?

It is easy to pretend friendship—particularly when we want something. In David's time, many people wanted to be the "friend" of the king to achieve their own goals. Christians should be straightforward and honest in all their relationships.

The Perfect Example   *The correct answer is A.*

DISCUSSION QUESTIONS:

1. Why wouldn't it be all right for Logan to have another ice cream? After all, the instructions were just for the younger kids.
2. Why is it so important for leaders to set a good example?
3. Does setting a good example apply only to the "big" things and not the "little" things?

Leaders should set good examples so that those who look up to them, and follow them, will see their good deeds and imitate them. If you want someone to act a certain way, be sure to live that way yourself. Then you will earn the right to be heard, and your life will reinforce what you say.

The Sunday School Lesson   *The correct answer is C.*

DISCUSSION QUESTIONS:

1. Why should Dexter begin planning now?
2. What's the problem with waiting until the last minute to do a project or assignment?
3. What have been the consequences when you have not properly prepared for an assignment or lesson?

First Corinthians 14:33 says, "God is not a God of disorder but of peace." When you do something, whether it's for Sunday school or the classroom, God wants you to do it orderly and properly. Waiting until the last minute will only lead to disaster.

Teamwork   *The correct answer is E.*

DISCUSSION QUESTIONS:

1. Why would Jackson be reluctant to take his friend as a partner?
2. What are the advantages of working on a project with someone else?

In Ecclesiastes 4:9-10, Solomon states plainly that "two are better than one." Some people prefer to work alone, thinking they can't trust anyone to help them do the job. But God designed us for community and companionship. We are here to serve others, not ourselves. Don't try to go it alone. Be part of the team!

Rainy Day Blues   *The best answers are A and C.*

DISCUSSION QUESTIONS:

1. What do you usually do when you are bored?
2. How do you think Ted will feel if he chooses B or D? What about if he decides to help his parents or work on his piano?
3. What's wrong with sitting around all afternoon watching TV? Do you think it's the best use of Ted's time?

There are some people who spend their lives trying to avoid hard work. But God says that hard work brings about its own rewards. Consider the satisfaction of finally mastering that difficult passage in a piano piece or helping to plant the family garden (especially when enjoying the "fruits of those labors" later in the summer). "Only fools," says the Lord, "idle away their time."

Real Worries   *The correct answer is C.*

DISCUSSION QUESTIONS:

1. When you read about a flood wiping out a family's home, or about people dying in an airplane crash, how do you feel? How often do you worry that something like that will happen to you or your family?
2. How will worrying change things?
3. How can you handle your worries about the future?

Worrying is a waste of time. It accomplishes nothing, and it only shows that we lack faith in God and have little understanding of who God is. When we begin to worry about tomorrow, we need to remember that the God who created all living things can be trusted with the details of our life.

The Rock Concert   *The correct answer is C.*

DISCUSSION QUESTIONS:
1. To what kind of music do you like to listen?
2. Why should Christians avoid music that is anti-Christian?
3. What do you say to your friends who enjoy rock bands that are anti-Christian, use vulgar language, or promote drugs?

Paul issues a strong warning about people who don't live according to Christian values (see 2 Timothy 3:1-5). Paul's descriptive list of behaviors describes many in society today. Check your life and your values against Paul's list. Don't give in to society's pressures, but live the way God wants you to live.

The Voice of Experience   *The correct answer is A.*

DISCUSSION QUESTIONS:
1. Why do you think Corey should listen to the speaker?
2. When someone older speaks to you about issues like taking drugs, drinking, or smoking, how do you respond?
3. Why do you think it's important to live *now* for Jesus and not wait until later?

Solomon did it all. In his own words, he said that he denied himself nothing; he refused no pleasure; he lived the good life. But what was his conclusion? That it was all meaningless. Nothing matters, he said, except fearing God and obeying his commandments—now!

Hard Times   *The best answer is D, although C also would be acceptable.*

DISCUSSION QUESTIONS:
1. When have you wondered, like Jordan, why God allows awful things to happen to people?
2. Why do you think God allows suffering?
3. How do you handle your doubts about God?
4. How can watching a family going through difficult times yet still praising God strengthen your faith?

It's good to talk with your parents or pastor when you have doubts about God. The best response to accepting bad times, however, is to cling to the fact that God is in control. Reaffirm, as Habakkuk did, that despite the circumstances "I will rejoice in the Lord; I will be happy in the God of my salvation."

Summer Help   *The correct answer is D.*

DISCUSSION QUESTIONS:
1. How do you act when you don't get the good assignments?
2. Why isn't answer B a good solution?

3. Do you think what happened to Hannah in this situation is fair? Do you think it matters if it were fair or not?

It can be discouraging to have certain expectations and then have things turn out differently than planned. Galatians 6:9 teaches that believers should not get tired of "doing good." We may not always be thanked for working behind the scenes or doing a small task well, but Paul says that "at the proper time," we will enjoy the fruits of our labor. But only if we don't give up!

JUNE 28

Going Shopping   *The correct answer is E.*

DISCUSSION QUESTIONS:
1. How did you feel when someone challenged your belief in God?
2. What would be a good way for Harriet to respond to her friends when they ask her to go to the store?
3. How would you respond to someone who tells you, "I don't really need Jesus—there are other ways to heaven"?

Eventually you will encounter people whose beliefs will differ from yours. Sometimes your friends may choose to follow these people, just as Harriet's friends did. But God tells his people to stand firm in his truth and to refuse to follow bad examples. As 3 John 1:11 says, "Follow only what is good."

JUNE 29

The Memory Game   *The correct answer is B.*

DISCUSSION QUESTIONS:
1. What would you tell Casey is the value of memorizing Scripture?
2. When has memorizing Scripture been valuable to you?
3. How would you rate yourself in the Scripture-memory department?
4. What might you do to be more effective in memorizing Scripture?

The writer of this psalm says that the way to please God is to read and obey his Word. The only way to do that is to *know* what God's Word says. Memorizing Scripture not only helps you do that, but it can help keep you from sinning against God. If you have trouble with your temper, for example, memorizing verses dealing with anger can remind you to keep your anger in check.

JUNE 30

The Piano Player   *The correct answer is D.*

DISCUSSION QUESTIONS:
1. Why is it important for Vince to use his talents in this ministry?
2. How are you using your gifts and talents to serve God?
3. In what ways could you be using your gifts?

Every believer has God-given gifts. Thus it is important to identify those gifts and then use them. Christians should use their abilities to serve others. When you use your gifts for God, you bring him praise and honor.

JULY 1

The Graffiti Gang   *The correct answer is B.*

DISCUSSION QUESTIONS:
1. Why shouldn't Colin just ride away? After all, he doesn't have positive proof that the boys are responsible for the graffiti.

2. When you caught a classmate doing something wrong, did you report that student to the teacher or the office? Why, or why not?
3. What would you do if you were in Colin's situation?

It is important that we avoid "worthless deeds," but we must go even further. Paul teaches that we must expose these types of deeds. God says that we must be willing to take a stand for what we know is right.

Split Decision   *The correct answer is B.*

DISCUSSION QUESTIONS:
1. In this situation, what should be the most important factor in deciding what service project to adopt?
2. When your ideas are rejected, how do you feel? How do you react?
3. Why do you think Ozzie should not fight to have the group adopt his idea?

When we quarrel, particularly in Sunday school or youth group, we allow divisions to distract us from the most important thing—doing God's work and advancing his kingdom. Let God's desires, not your own, be your guide.

Playing by the Rules   *The correct answer is C.*

DISCUSSION QUESTIONS:
1. Why should Meredith and her group follow the principal's new rule?
2. How do you relate to people in authority over you, such as your teachers, principals, coaches, etc.?
3. Read Romans 13:1-5. What would be helpful for Meredith to know in making her decision?

Paul says that Christians have the responsibility to obey those in authority. We should do so for two reasons: (1) God put these authorities in place. (2) If we disobey them, we disobey God. By obeying them, we keep a clear conscience before God.

Slumber Party Fiasco   *The correct answer is D.*

DISCUSSION QUESTIONS:
1. What did you do when your friends played a mean-spirited trick on you?
2. How difficult will it be for Tricia to forgive her friends? How hard was it for you to forgive your friends?
3. How can you forgive someone when you feel hurt and angry?

It's difficult to love those with whom we are hurt and angry. But God says that Christians should love one another because God loves them. The Holy Spirit gives us the power to love as he lives in our hearts and enables us to be more like Jesus. God's love always involves a choice and an action. We can choose to be angry with our friends—or we can choose to love them. How well do you reflect God's love in your choices?

Boooring! *The correct answer is D.*

DISCUSSION QUESTIONS:

1. Why do you think it is important for Christians to worship together? Why can't believers just worship at home?
2. What should be your attitude toward worship and going to church? What needs to change about your attitude?
3. What could you say to someone who thinks that church is boring?

Christians come together to learn, worship, and strengthen one another. To give up meeting together would mean passing up encouragement and help from other believers. Worshiping together is one of the privileges of being a Christian.

The Grunge Express *The correct answer is D.*

DISCUSSION QUESTIONS:

1. Why shouldn't Stan pretend to know all about the group?
2. When your friends listen to music groups whose music is less than desirable, how do you handle it?
3. Why wouldn't it be OK for Stan to attend the concert and see what this group is all about?

Paul states clearly in 2 Timothy 2:22 that Christians are to run from anything that will cause them to sin. Instead, Christians, should "follow anything that makes [them] want to do right." Music groups that promote wild parties, drinking, or drugs should not be on your Top Ten list. Look for those things that promote God's values—faith, love, and peace.

The Natural *The correct answer is B.*

DISCUSSION QUESTIONS:

1. Every team or activity has a Judson. How do others react to the Judson on your team or activity? How do you feel toward that person?
2. How can we guard against a prideful spirit like Judson's?
3. What are some of the consequences of a prideful spirit?

Pride causes us to look down on others and prevents us from learning anything from them—and from God. Don't allow pride in your achievements to cut you off from God and others.

Pass It On *The correct answer is C.*

DISCUSSION QUESTIONS:

1. When you are going through a difficult time, how important is it to you to receive encouragement from others?
2. Why is it particularly important for Gloria to comfort and encourage her friend?
3. What can you do today to encourage or comfort a friend?

God comforts us in many different ways—and not always by removing our troubles. Being comforted also can mean receiving strength, encouragement, and hope to deal with our troubles. In the same way we receive comfort from God, we, too, are to help comfort those who suffer in similar ways.

The Wicked Stepmother   *The correct answer is D.*

DISCUSSION QUESTIONS:
1. Why should Angelica go back and feed the dog?
2. What might happen if Angelica continues to obey her stepmother—even when she doesn't feel like it?
3. What steps can you take to get along with the difficult parent, stepparent, teacher, coach, or classmate?

Those who truly belong to Jesus will adopt his values and perspective in every area of life. That means having his attitude of love toward others. As you grow in faith, through prayer and Bible study, you will become more able to maintain this attitude of love toward others throughout the day.

Stranger Danger   *The correct answer is E.*

DISCUSSION QUESTIONS:
1. Why should Cyrus walk away and have an adult call the police?
2. How can Cyrus know for sure that the woman is telling him the truth?
3. When you have doubts about people you don't know, what is the best course of action?

It's hard to ignore the plight of someone in distress. But often it is best to let the police handle the situation. Trust your instincts in situations where things don't feel right. Don't be like Samson and allow yourself to be talked into doing something you know is wrong.

The Ballerina   *The correct answer is D.*

DISCUSSION QUESTIONS:
1. How do you think something as harmless as dancing could become a god?
2. What do you spend most of your time doing? Do you think that activity might be a god in your life?
3. What does it mean to allow other things to become gods in our lives?

Sports, music, video games, and yes, even dancing, can become gods in our lives when we concentrate too much on them rather than on God. We may not set out to worship these activities, but little by little, by the amount of time we devote to them, they can begin to control our thoughts and energy. Making sure that God has the central place in your life will prevent these things from becoming gods.

Thank You!   *The correct answer is E.*

DISCUSSION QUESTIONS:
1. Why should Toby take the time to write the thank-you notes now? It has been two months—certainly his relatives have forgotten all about those gifts!
2. Why is it important to have a thankful attitude in all circumstances—even if Toby didn't like his gifts, for example?
3. How can you adopt a more thankful attitude today?

The Bible teaches that it is God's will that his people always be joyful, always keep praying, and always be thankful. These attitudes often go against a person's natural inclinations, particularly when things aren't going right. As you choose to obey God, though, you will begin to see things in a different perspective. Then you will find it easier to be more thankful and joyful.

JULY 13

Soccer Camp   *The correct answer is B.*

DISCUSSION QUESTIONS:
1. How do you respond when someone asks if you believe in Jesus?
2. What are some reasons you are uncomfortable in sharing your faith?
3. What answer do you have for "the reason for the hope that you have"?

It *is* hard to share our faith. We don't want to be laughed at or called names. But when someone asks a question, usually it means that he or she is curious about our faith. We have a responsibility to Jesus and to our friends to honestly, gently, and respectfully answer their questions about what we believe.

JULY 14

Pushing the Right Buttons   *The correct answer is E.*

DISCUSSION QUESTIONS:
1. How do you provoke your siblings? How do they provoke you?
2. How does this kind of behavior affect the rest of your family, particularly your parents?
3. What might be some consequences if Seth helps his brother build another invention?

One of God's greatest resources is family. Families provide security, encouragement, support, guidance, and love. Do everything you can to promote healing, communication, and acceptance rather than arguments, fights, and spiteful teasing.

JULY 15

The Garage Sale   *The correct answer is C.*

DISCUSSION QUESTIONS:
1. Why should Colton donate the bike to charity? Why shouldn't he try and fix it up himself and then sell it?
2. How do you feel when you buy something that breaks down after a few uses?
3. What's wrong with offering less than perfect stuff at a garage sale? Everyone knows garage sales are for dumping junk.

Whether it's a sidewalk lemonade stand, a garage sale, or a fund-raising event at school, God demands honesty in all of your business dealings. You may feel pressured to be dishonest in order to make money for something you want. But if you want to obey God, there is no middle ground. God is completely trustworthy, and you should be, too, in every endeavor.

Finders Keepers, Part 2 *The correct answer is A.*

DISCUSSION QUESTIONS:
1. When you lost something of value, how did you feel? How about when it was returned to you?
2. How do you handle the temptation to keep something you have found—especially something you've wanted?
3. Why wouldn't leaving the knife on the ground be a good solution?

Television advertisements continue to display tons of the neat stuff to buy. The more we watch, the more we want those advertised products. The temptation to get a lot of stuff is all around us. Jesus warns us not to be greedy for the things we don't have. Our lives will be measured not by what we own, but by who owns us—Jesus.

Just Desserts *The correct answer is B.*

DISCUSSION QUESTIONS:
1. How do you react to someone who is the first to grab food at the table?
2. What do you think that says about a person's character?
3. Why do you think God cares about how much food we eat (or take) at a meal?

Too much of anything—whether it's double-chocolate brownies, watching TV, or sleeping—is not good for a person. God says to use self-control in all areas of life, and to stay away from people who lack self-control. Moderation—taking just one brownie instead of stuffing our mouth—is a good rule of thumb to "keep our hearts on the right course."

Drinking Buddy? *The correct answer is E.*

DISCUSSION QUESTIONS:
1. How do you and your friends typically treat the kids who get into trouble?
2. Why are Chase's youth group friends so quick to make fun of him?
3. How do you suppose Chase is feeling? What might happen if the youth group were to treat Chase like he is a terrible sinner?

Those who quickly pass judgment on others are acting as if they have never sinned. God alone is the judge. Our role is to show forgiveness and compassion. The next time you begin judging another person, remember Jesus' words: "Let those who have never sinned throw the first stones!"

The Great Bargain *The correct answer is C.*

DISCUSSION QUESTIONS:
1. Why do you think it would be a good idea for Melissa to wait?
2. What would you do in Melissa's situation? Would you be tempted to ask your parents to buy the CD player for you?
3. When you were saving to buy a big-ticket item, how did you feel when you finally saved up enough money?

Waiting is difficult. Patience is a tough lesson for just about everybody to learn. Waiting, simply put, isn't fun, particularly when we think we're going to miss out on a great opportunity. But if Jesus lives in us, then we have the power and ability to be patient—that's a fruit of the Holy Spirit.

J U L Y   2 0

The Name above All Names   *The correct answer is C.*

DISCUSSION QUESTIONS:
1. What should Dinah say to Melina? How can she tell Melina about Jesus without sounding like a "Holy Roller"?
2. When your friends use God's name in vain, what do you do?
3. Why is it important to speak up about this?

Sometimes using God's name in vain is such a habit that people don't even realize they are doing it. Introduce your friends to the Jesus of the Bible, who is Lord and Savior over all things. Let them know that we *all* will bow down before him some-day—either as his friend or as his enemy. Those who understand who Jesus really is will want to honor his name "above all other names."

J U L Y   2 1

The Farewell Bash   *The best answer is A, although E would also be acceptable.*

DISCUSSION QUESTIONS:
1. What is preventing Leigh from enjoying the party?
2. Why should she change her plans?
3. What should be Leigh's priority for the party—preparing the food or spending time with her friend? Explain your answer.

If you have a tendency to worry about details, then you can learn from Martha. Luke 10:38-42 tells how Martha and her sister Mary were serving Jesus and his friends. While Mary chose to serve Jesus by attending to his personal comfort, Martha tried to make the perfect evening for Jesus—the best food, the most comfort-able surroundings. Because she was so preoccupied with all the little details, Martha found it hard to relax and enjoy her guest. Jesus gently pointed out to Martha that although her priorities were good, they were not the best. Make sure you keep your priorities straight and give your guests the personal attention they deserve.

J U L Y   2 2

Make Up Your Mind!   *The correct answer is A.*

DISCUSSION QUESTIONS:
1. Why don't you think answer C is a good option for Luis—at least until he feels comfortable in his new school?
2. How do you handle pressure from your friends to do things that you know aren't right?
3. Why do you think it's important for Luis to make up his mind what to do *before* he gets to school?

It's easier to resist temptation and pressure to act like everyone else if we think through where we stand before hitting the temptation. Trouble comes when we haven't decided where to draw the line. Before you walk into a tempting situation, decide what your stand will be. Then when the pressure comes, you will be ready to say no.

Video Role   *The best answer is E.*

DISCUSSION QUESTIONS:

1. Why wouldn't calling her parents to take her home be a good solution for Megan? What could be some of the possible consequences of taking that action?
2. How do you handle situations where friends' standards differ from yours?
3. Why wouldn't telling her friends not to watch "garbage like this" be a good solution? What kind of example would Megan be setting for her friends?

Like Megan, we are accountable to God for our own actions and choices—not for the actions of others. Megan can't change the choice of movies her friends make, but she can choose what she watches. God says to "program" our minds with thoughts that are *true, honorable, right, pure, lovely, admirable, excellent, and worthy of praise.* Which of those categories would describe the TV shows, videos, and movies you watch, and the books you read?

The Loyal Friend   *The correct answer is A.*

DISCUSSION QUESTIONS:

1. Why should Hank go camping with Zeke when Zeke is acting like such a jerk?
2. When your friends are going through a bad time, how can you help them?
3. When someone is difficult to be around because of his or her problems, how do you respond?

When the going gets tough, everyone leaves. Is this true about you and your friendships? Proverbs teaches that you should not abandon your friends when times get tough. Loyalty is the true sign of a genuine friend. You need to be available when your friends are experiencing distress or personal struggles. Then in your time of need, you will be able to call upon a friendship that has already weathered some tough times.

The Good Neighbor   *The correct answer is A.*

DISCUSSION QUESTIONS:

1. Since Sean wasn't the one who caused the accident in the first place, why should he stop?
2. What is your responsibility to your neighbors? Who is your neighbor?
3. When you see someone who needs help, what do you do?

Jesus' teachings in Luke 10:30-37 leave no doubt as to the identity of neighbors and how believers should respond to their needs. A neighbor is anyone of any race, age, or social background who is in need. And the believer's only response is to *act* to help meet that person's need. There is no good excuse for doing anything else.

The Cold War   *The correct answer is E.*

DISCUSSION QUESTIONS:
1. Why should Kay take the first step?
2. When you have a fight with your friends, do you wait until they apologize or do you initiate a truce?
3. Why do you think it is difficult to be the one to take the first step in offering an apology?

Christians are called to love each other. Sometimes that will mean swallowing our pride and our hurt feelings in order to reach out to a friend and apologize. It's not easy, but God promises to give you the ability to do just that.

Promises, Promises   *The correct answer is D.*

DISCUSSION QUESTIONS:
1. When you made promises to God, like Devin, did you take your promises seriously?
2. How do you think God views promises like that? Does he *really* expect Devin to hold up his end of the bargain?

Solomon offers some serious words on making foolish promises or vows. It is foolish to make a vow you cannot keep or to play games with God by only partially fulfilling what you promised to do. It's better not to make a vow to God and then break it. It's even better to make a vow and keep it.

The Long Haul   *The correct answer is A.*

DISCUSSION QUESTIONS:
1. Why should Marilee stick with the program?
2. How did you handle situations where things didn't go as expected?
3. Read Acts 20:22-24. What kept Paul on track, even when facing great hardship?

Paul didn't travel an easy road. What kept him going, however, was his attitude. It's easy to feel as though life is a failure or a program is a failure unless it results in fun, recognition, or success. But Paul looked at things differently. He considered life worth nothing unless he was working for God. What he put into life was far more important than what he got out of it. Which is more important to you—what you put into life or what you get out of it?

Just Cruisin'   *The correct answer is A.*

DISCUSSION QUESTIONS:
1. Why do you think it is hard for Ed to be happy for Nick?
2. Why is it so difficult to share in a friend's good fortune, especially if he or she gets something we want?
3. How can we handle feelings of jealousy or envy?

God tells us to share with each other in all situations—in the bad times and in the good times. We should be happy with our friends when something good happens to them—not be jealous or have a pity party for ourselves. And when our friends are sad, we should offer them our shoulder to cry on.

Fun at the Water Park   *The correct answer is C.*

DISCUSSION QUESTIONS:
1. Why is it important that Dorrie return to the group now—regardless what her friends decide to do?
2. How did you feel when your group had to wait for stragglers?
3. How does one or two people disregarding the rules affect the entire group?

When you're having fun with your friends, it's easy to get caught up in the moment and forget that there are other things to consider—such as your chaperones' rules and the group. Don't follow the crowd in doing wrong. Instead, set a good example for others to follow by doing what is right.

The Eldest Elder   *The correct answer is D.*

DISCUSSION QUESTIONS:
1. Why does God want people to respect and honor their elders?
2. How would you describe your attitude towards older people?
3. What do you think you can learn from someone who is eighty?

It's often easy to dismiss the opinions of the elderly and avoid spending time with them. After all, sometimes they dress and speak funny, and sometimes they don't hear very well. But God commands his people to honor the elderly. Take this responsibility seriously and learn from the voices of experience and wisdom.

Leader of the Pack   *The correct answer is C.*

DISCUSSION QUESTIONS:
1. How would you describe your leadership abilities? In what ways can you be a positive leader? How about a negative one?
2. How would you react to the Sunday school teacher's request?
3. What is important to remember when taking on a leadership role?

Second Chronicles 19:4-7 tells of King Jehoshaphat giving very specific instructions to the judges he appointed to lead the people. The most important thing for any leader to remember is that he or she is to lead in a way that pleases God, not classmates. Whenever you are in a leadership position, your behavior and actions should point toward God, not away from him.

The Chat Room   *The correct answer is D.*

DISCUSSION QUESTIONS:
1. Why should Griffin answer truthfully? No one on the Internet will ever know the difference.
2. Why do you think God's rules apply to today's constantly changing technology?
3. How do you handle conversations on the Internet? Do you think they are different from face-to-face encounters?

The technology may change, but God's Word remains the same. We should approach our conversations and our words the same—whether we are talking over the telephone, over the computer, or in the school lunchroom. If we love God, we will watch our tongues and keep from lying, no matter what the situation.

Admit One   *The correct answer is C.*

DISCUSSION QUESTIONS:
1. What should Tom do if the ticket person does, in fact, charge him for a child's ticket?
2. Why do you think trying to get in to a show with a cheaper ticket is wrong?
3. How do you react when your friends try to do this?

Trying to sneak in to a show or fair with a cheaper ticket may seem like a small thing, but God values honesty! When we start to lie to others, we will begin to lie to ourselves, too. How can we possibly have a relationship with God if we are caught up in lies? Without honesty, a close relationship with God is impossible.

That Wild and Crazy Guy   *The correct answer is E.*

DISCUSSION QUESTIONS:
1. Why do you think the members of the youth group are having such a hard time accepting Martin?
2. What kids could you not possibly imagine coming to church or youth group? Why?
3. How do you think God views Martin?

In the early church, the last people anyone expected to receive the gospel were Gentiles (non-Jews). Nevertheless, God told Peter to share the Good News with a Roman soldier. God made it very clear to Peter that the Gospel is for everyone. Language, culture, education, or reputation should not keep someone from hearing about Jesus.

Cleanup Detail   *The correct answer is D.*

DISCUSSION QUESTIONS:
1. Why do you think Marissa should step forward as one volunteer to clean the latrines?
2. When you are with a group, what happens when the "dirty" jobs nobody wants to do come up?
3. What example should you be setting in these situations?

Jesus provides a new perspective on being a leader. A real leader has a servant's heart and is ready to serve others. As leaders, we need to realize others' worth and that we are not above any job—including cleaning the latrines. If you see something that needs to be done—take the initiative and do it!

Roughing It   *The correct answer is C.*

DISCUSSION QUESTIONS:
1. How do you react when you are out of your comfort zone?
2. How do you think Eileen can, in fact, make the best of a difficult situation?
3. Read Philippians 4:12-13. What do you think is Paul's secret "of being content in any and every situation"?

Paul wrote these verses while in prison, but Paul was content because he could see life from God's point of view. He was focused on what he was supposed to *do*, not on what he felt he should have. Paul had his priorities straight. When you find yourself grumbling about your circumstances, check your priorities and your source of power. Then you will find true contentment.

AUGUST 7

Movie Madness   *The correct answer is B.*

DISCUSSION QUESTIONS:
1. Why do you suppose Mark's family has rules about what movies he can watch? What rules does your family have about movies?
2. What would you do in Mark's situation?
3. Why does God care about what movies we watch?

God cares about what we watch, what we read, and what we listen to. It is wise to set limits in these areas of our lives and to not copy what friends do—especially when our friends' values are not the same as God's values. We must please God, not our friends.

AUGUST 8

Learning to Ride   *The correct answer is D.*

DISCUSSION QUESTIONS:
1. How should Becky react to her brother's first bike-riding efforts?
2. How do you feel when first trying something new? What helps you keep trying?
3. How can you show kindness and compassion to others today?

Learning anything new can be difficult. Add the fear of having people laugh at you, and sometimes it seems easier to just give up. You can help others get over their fears and potential embarrassment by treating them with kindness and compassion.

AUGUST 9

Put on a Happy Face   *The correct answer is B.*

DISCUSSION QUESTIONS:
1. Ever have a day like Stella's? What's your attitude on days when nothing seems to go right?
2. What's it like being around someone like Stella when they are in a bad mood?
3. Who, or what, can make the difference in a person's attitude toward his or her circumstances?

An attitude can color a person's entire personality. No one can choose many of the things that happen—rained-out softball games or bad hair days—but they can choose their attitudes in each situation. The secret to a cheerful heart is thinking about all the good things of life, not the bad. Check your attitude right now. Maybe you need to make some changes.

Worship Time   *The correct answer is E.*

DISCUSSION QUESTIONS:
1. What do you think it means to worship God with "holy fear and awe"? What does that look like?
2. When you sit with your friends in church, how do you and your friends act?
3. If your friends were acting up in church, what would you do?

There is a time and place for goofing around with friends, but in church we should be actively engaged in one thing—worshiping God. We should be focusing on God's goodness, glory, strength, and holiness. When we do that, we give God the respect due him as Lord of all.

It's a Dog's Life   *The correct answer is C.*

DISCUSSION QUESTIONS:
1. Why would it be wrong for Dara to take the dog and care for it herself?
2. Why would it be important for Dara to pray about this situation before acting? (Read Proverbs 3:5-6.)
3. If the dog finally gets the proper care and attention it needs, does it really matter how it was accomplished?

When we have an important decision to make or we face a difficult situation, we often think we can't trust anyone to help us—not even God! But God knows what is best for us. We must learn to trust him completely with our problems and our decisions. We must not be wise in our own eyes but learn to listen to, and be corrected by, God's Word and wise counselors. Then we will know the proper actions to take.

No Big Deal?   *The correct answer is B.*

DISCUSSION QUESTIONS:
1. When a friend asks you to lie for him or her, how do you respond?
2. Do you think there is such a thing as a "little lie"? Explain your answer.
3. How do you think God views our lies—big and small?

Ezra 9:2-7 tells about Ezra mourning for his people's sins. He recognized that sin is serious and that no one sins without affecting others. It often is easy to view sin lightly in a world that doesn't take sin seriously. But we need to remember Ezra's example and take all sin as seriously as he did.

The Ketchup Caper   *The correct answer is E.*

DISCUSSION QUESTIONS:
1. Why do you think Dennis will be lying if he doesn't say anything?
2. How can telling a half-truth be harmful?

We give "false testimony" when we leave something out of a story, tell a half-truth, twist the truth, or withhold the truth. God warns against using such deception.

Cashing In   *The correct answer is A.*

DISCUSSION QUESTIONS:
1. Why wouldn't giving the money to charity be a good solution for Danielle?
2. If the cashier made the mistake, why should Danielle take the money back?
3. Why would it be a form of stealing for Danielle to keep the money?
4. When you benefited from a mistake by a store cashier, what did you do?

Proverbs teaches plainly that God hates all forms of dishonesty. God says that his people should be guided by their honesty in all areas of their lives. Cheating in one small area of life can easily spill over into other areas. Dishonesty can destroy us.

Holding a Grudge   *The correct answer is E.*

DISCUSSION QUESTIONS:
1. Why is it difficult to forgive a person who has offended you?
2. When you tell someone you have forgiven him or her, do you forget about the incident or do you, from time to time, remind the person about it?

Matthew 18:21-22 tells how Jesus says that believers are to forgive each other seventy-seven times! We are not to keep track of how many times we forgive someone, or of the person's offense. If a person is truly sorry for what he or she has done, we need to forgive that person as many times as he or she asks, and then forget it.

Just a Little Sin   *The correct answer is A.*

DISCUSSION QUESTIONS:
1. Why is there no such thing as a "little sin"?
2. Why does it matter to God how his people express themselves—especially when they use language that everyone else seems to use?
3. When you hear friends and classmates swearing, how do you react? Do you say anything or just let it go?

In James 3:7-10, James calls the tongue "a restless evil, full of deadly poison." Tongues are used to praise God, but also to curse others made in God's image. As James says, "Surely, my brothers and sisters, this is not right!" Christians need to "tame" their tongues by controlling what they say. The only way to do this is through the power of the Holy Spirit; he will give the self-control to use only words that please God. The tongue may be a small part of the body, but it can cause major damage.

The Right Choice   *The best answers are B and C.*

DISCUSSION QUESTIONS:
1. Why should Carlie to go to practice and then catch up with her friends?
2. Why do you think asking her friends to consider another movie is reasonable? What should Carlie do if they don't agree to find another movie?
3. When you were in a similar situation, what did you do?

We face difficult choices every day. The most important question to ask in making those decisions is, "What would be pleasing God?" If you use God's Word to help you decide what is right, you will always have a clear conscience before God and everyone else.

AUGUST 18

The Big Celebration   *The correct answer is D.*

DISCUSSION QUESTIONS:
1. Why do you think Dana shouldn't be paid for her work?
2. Do you expect your parents to pay you for every chore you do? Why or why not?
3. Do you consider the chores you do around the house a duty or a job?

In Luke 17:7-10, Jesus is talking about obedience to God. But the same idea applies to obeying our parents. Obedience is not something extra we do; it is our duty. We don't deserve extra credit for doing our duty by obeying our parents and doing our part to help out.

AUGUST 19

The Competition   *The correct answer is C.*

DISCUSSION QUESTIONS:
1. Why do you think Gavin is having a hard time on the soccer field?
2. How do you handle competing against an older brother or sister?
3. If you were Gavin's friend, what advice would you give him? What is the most important thing for Gavin to know?

Everything a Christian does—whether it's playing soccer, studying the Bible, or doing volunteer work at church—should be done in such a way that it brings honor to Jesus. Don't worry about competing with older siblings or your friends. Just do your best for Jesus, bringing honor to him.

AUGUST 20

Family Devotions   *The correct answer is C.*

DISCUSSION QUESTIONS:
1. What is the value of reading and studying Scripture?
2. When has a Scripture verse helped you with a problem?
3. What do you need to do to make God's Word practical in your life?

Reading God's Word, whether during family devotions or on your own, is only part of the equation. It is not enough to simply hear God's Word and then forget about it. The wise person not only hears God's Word, but he or she also puts it into practice. Practicing obedience then becomes the solid foundation for weathering storms. Look for ways you can put God's Word into action today.

AUGUST 21

The Pool Party   *The correct answer is A.*

DISCUSSION QUESTIONS:
1. When you see your friends about to do something wrong, what do you do?
2. Why do you think it is important that as representatives of their youth group, Mason and his friends obey the rules?
3. Should Mason be the one to say something, or should he wait for the group leader to tell the boys what to do?

Wherever they are, Christians represent Jesus. So we need to make sure that Jesus is honored by our behavior. If our friends seem inclined to do something wrong, then it is our responsibility to set the example. Don't wait for someone else higher up to correct the situation when you clearly know what is required.

The Church Choir Clown   *The correct answer is A.*

DISCUSSION QUESTIONS:
1. Why should Chet respect the choir director? After all, he is right, *this* isn't school?
2. How should you act in activities outside of school, like choir or Scouts?
3. When you see a friend acting up, what do you say to him or her?

God's Word says that Christians should pray for all people, particularly those in authority. We need to pray for them so that the business at hand can be conducted in "peace and quietness, godliness and dignity." We have a responsibility to contribute to the peace, not disruption, of the group. So when you see someone ready to act up, you should gently remind that person of this responsibility.

The Bonus Offer   *The correct answer is C.*

DISCUSSION QUESTIONS:
1. To what lengths will you go to get something you just have to buy?
2. Why do you think Sheldon should wait?
3. What is the difference between a "need" and a "want"? How can knowing that help you in managing your money?

Greed—the desire for more things—can lead to all sorts of problems. It can cause people to make wrong choices and to do strange things to get what they want. Don't be a slave to your desires for things you think you need. Choose to be content without having all you want.

Love Your Enemies   *The correct answer is E.*

DISCUSSION QUESTIONS:
1. How do you usually feel like treating someone who cuts you down all the time?
2. Why shouldn't Jenna tell Peggy to forget it? (See answer A.)
3. How is it possible to "do good to those who hate you"?

When Jesus says to "love our enemies," he's not talking about having affection for them. Instead, he is talking about choosing to find ways to help our them. We should pray for our enemies and grant them the same respect and rights as we desire for ourselves.

At Your Service   *The correct answer is B.*

DISCUSSION QUESTIONS:
1. Why do you think Tracy considers it an honor to serve in this ministry? Why is serving others an honor?
2. How do you respond when people ask you to serve in some capacity? Do you look for excuses, or are you eager to serve?
3. In what ways could you serve others—at church, at home, and at school?

Paul tells us that nothing we do for the Lord is useless—every good deed, kind word, or service that we do in the Lord's name counts for God. We might not always see results or feel like we have accomplished anything, but that should not stop us from working. Look for every opportunity to serve and do good, because it's God's work.

Follow the Leader   *The correct answer is C.*

DISCUSSION QUESTIONS:
1. If you are dared to do something, how do you respond?
2. What should be the most important consideration in Trent's decision?
3. Why should Trent refuse to take the dare? Do you think he will lose the respect of his friends for not taking the dare—or taking it?

The more we know about Jesus, the more we are obedient in doing his will, the more we follow the influence of other Christians, the more we will have the desire to obey Jesus. God helps us want to obey him, not others, and he will give us the power to do so as we grow in his Word and in obedience. As we grow in Jesus, we will be able to resist the foolish ideas of others.

His Brother's Keeper   *The correct answer is D.*

DISCUSSION QUESTIONS:
1. How would you describe your relationship with your siblings? What changes do you think you need to make?
2. Why do you think it is important for Duane to not just take his brother with him but to include him?

God delights when Christians live with their brothers and with others in harmony. Do everything possible to promote unity, not discord, in your household between you and your siblings.

Sweet Rewards   *The correct answer is A.*

DISCUSSION QUESTIONS:
1. Why would it be wrong for Vance to cash in on this golden opportunity?
2. Why does it matter if Mrs. Solcumb never finds out who took the candies?
3. How can you always keep a clear conscience?

Every time we deliberately ignore our conscience and do what is wrong, we harden our hearts toward God. As we continue to do this, we will find it more and more difficult to tell right from wrong. To avoid that, be sure to act on those inner tugs that tell you the right thing to do. Then you can keep a clear conscience before God.

The New Kid on the Block   *The correct answer is C.*

DISCUSSION QUESTIONS:
1. When you walk into a new situation where you don't know a lot of people, how do you feel?
2. What is the best way to make friends? What would you advise Cassandra to do?

3. What do you think is wrong with Cassandra's other choices for making new friends?

Paul says that believers should not "live to make a good impression on others." Fancy parties, the latest fashions, or acting cool may turn a few heads, but the real way to win friends is by showing a genuine interest in people and letting them know they are important.

AUGUST 30

Brotherly Love?   *The correct answer is D.*

DISCUSSION QUESTIONS:
1. Why shouldn't Jim try and convince his brother to go along with his choice?
2. How does your family decide what to do when family members disagree?
3. Do you think that flipping a coin would be a fair way to decide what to do? Why, or why not?

It's very difficult to let someone else go first—whether it's having the first choice of an activity, being first in line in a game, or even getting the first piece of cake. God not only wants us to put others before ourselves, but he also helps us *want* to do that as we grow to become more like Jesus.

AUGUST 31

The Competitor   *The correct answer is A.*

DISCUSSION QUESTIONS:
1. What's wrong with Ike wanting to win and be competitive? Is winning, like some people believe, the "only thing" that's important?
2. How would you describe yourself as a competitor? Do you want to win at any cost?
3. What might happen if Ike does lose his temper?
4. What do you think of professional athletes who can't control their emotions during the game?

Success in the classroom or on the volleyball court can be ruined when you lose control of your temper. Count it a great personal victory when you are able to control your anger. Remember, when you feel you're about to explode, losing control may cause you to forfeit what you want the most.

SEPTEMBER 1

A Good Steward   *The correct answer is A.*

DISCUSSION QUESTIONS:
1. Why do you think Ariel should tell her friend what happened—and not just replace the missing CDs?
2. What do you think is the principle Jesus is teaching in Luke 16:11-12?
3. When you borrow something from a friend, how do you take care of it?

God calls us to be honest in all areas of our life, even the small matters. Borrowing from a friend is one of those small areas. If something happens to the borrowed item—we lose it or damage it—we need to be honest about what happened and offer immediately to replace the item. When we take care of these smaller matters, our integrity will not fail us when the bigger issues hit.

The New Job   *The correct answer is C.*

DISCUSSION QUESTIONS:
1. Lana has a real attitude problem. In what ways do you find yourself with a similar attitude at home? Do you expect your parents to do most of the work at home?
2. What might you be able to do to pitch in and help your parents at home?
3. If you were Lana's friend, listening to her complain about her mom, what advice would you give her?

Sometimes, like Lana, we need a nudge in the right direction. We have a responsibility to one another to encourage each other and to find ways that we can help each other through "outbursts of love and good deeds." Grumbling and complaining aren't the answers; having a loving attitude and pitching in are.

Stick of Gum   *The correct answer is C.*

DISCUSSION QUESTIONS:
1. How would you feel if one of your friends, like Andrew, wouldn't share something with you?
2. How would you feel about sharing something with a friend like Andrew, who hordes his possessions?
3. Why wouldn't it be all right for Andrew to promise his friend a piece of gum later when he has more?

God wants us to be generous and cheerful givers. He warns us that if we are so concerned about holding on to the things we have, we may end up with nothing. The person who gives a little will only get a little in return.

The Missing Bike   *The correct answer is E.*

DISCUSSION QUESTIONS:
1. What is the real source of Joel's anger? Who is he most concerned about in this situation?
2. Why is being "quick to listen, slow to speak, and slow to get angry" good advice? In what situation would this have helped you?
3. How can Joel be "slow to get angry" in this situation?

Often anger erupts when a person's ego is hurt or his or her "rights" have been ignored. We *should* become angry when others are being hurt or injustice occurs. But selfish anger never helps anybody. The next time you feel an "anger attack" coming on, make sure you listen first and speak later!

The Friend   *The correct answer is E.*

DISCUSSION QUESTIONS:
1. When have you had a friend like Jason, who wasn't accepted by the popular kids? How did you treat that friend when you both were around other people?
2. Why wouldn't it be all right for Jerome just to remain quiet and hope that someone would change the subject?
3. Why might it be difficult for Jerome to speak up? What would you do in his situation?

God says that the greatest evidence of a genuine friend is loyalty—enduring "through every circumstance"—no matter what the situation. Too often, people are fair-weather friends. They stick around as long as the friendship helps them, and they move on when a better "opportunity" comes along. What kind of friend are you?

SEPTEMBER 6

Forgive and Forget   *The correct answer is E.*

DISCUSSION QUESTIONS:
1. Why should Lydia forgive Carmen?
2. Can you forgive someone who has hurt you deeply?
3. How can knowing that Jesus forgives you help you to forgive others?

The Bible teaches that because God freely forgives all our sins, we should not withhold forgiveness from others. Realizing the completeness of Jesus' forgiveness should produce a free and generous attitude of forgiveness toward others. Those who don't forgive set themselves outside of Jesus' law.

SEPTEMBER 7

The Teacher's Kid   *The correct answer is A.*

DISCUSSION QUESTIONS:
1. Why shouldn't Gus do anything about Mr. Blackwell?
2. What do you do when you have a teacher who enjoys singling you out? What about when that happens to a friend? What advice would you give to your friend?
3. What might happen if Gus continues to work his hardest in Mr. Blackwell's class and not cause any trouble?

Everyone encounters people—whether in the classroom, on the job, or in church—with whom they just don't click. But when someone is giving you a hard time unfairly, don't push back. Instead, continue to do your best, quietly and without boasting. You may find you will win over your opposition without a word!

SEPTEMBER 8

Vote for Me!   *The correct answer is E.*

DISCUSSION QUESTIONS:
1. Why should June tell Cleo the truth about her vote—after all, it is a secret ballot?
2. When you are called upon to choose a classmate for a responsible position, what usually influences your vote?

The truth can hurt sometimes, especially when friends are involved. But it is far better to be honest with friends than to lie to them and have them discover the lies later. Be sure to build your relationships on honesty and understanding—not lies and deceit. As David says in Psalm 51, God desires "honesty from the heart."

SEPTEMBER 9

Braggin' Rights   *The correct answer is B.*

DISCUSSION QUESTIONS:
1. What do you do when your friends start boasting about their accomplishments? Do you try to keep up with them or do you keep quiet?
2. What would you like people to admire the most about you?

3. Why do you think Darnell would be wrong to mention only a few of his accomplishments?

In our society, we tend to value people who have the most power, who are the strongest or best-looking, or who have accomplished the most. But what God values is our relationship with him and how we live. Don't get caught up in "can you top this" with others. That puts the focus on you, rather than on God.

SEPTEMBER 10

Passing Notes   *The correct answer is B.*

DISCUSSION QUESTIONS:
1. When someone else was blamed for something you did, what did you do?
2. Why should Elly come forward and accept the blame?

God makes it clear what he requires of his people: to do what is right and just, and to show mercy to others. Christians need to be fair in all of their dealings and to be humble before others. Then, if someone is falsely accused for a believer's actions, the believer will step forward and accept the consequences.

SEPTEMBER 11

Finding Time for God   *The correct answer is A.*

DISCUSSION QUESTIONS:
1. Nobody can be as busy as Lorraine! Or can they? How does your schedule stack up against hers?
2. How much time do you manage to spend with God each week? Why should a person plan to spend time with God?
3. What do you need to do to make time with God part of your daily activities?

Even though Daniel knew it was against the king's law to pray, he remained committed to praying three times a day. Daniel had a disciplined prayer life that he was not going to abandon—even by the threat of death. Christians' prayer lives these days are interrupted not by threats but by busy schedules. Find time for regular prayer with God because prayer is your lifeline to him.

SEPTEMBER 12

Going the Distance   *The correct answer is A.*

DISCUSSION QUESTIONS:
1. How do you think Simon felt as the last one to finish the race?
2. How did you feel when someone encouraged you when you were struggling?
3. Why do you think it is important to "encourage one another" as Paul says in 1 Thessalonians 5:11?

A word of encouragement offered at the right time can mean the difference between finishing well or collapsing—whether it's in a race, in the classroom, or during a personal struggle. Be sensitive to others' need for encouragement, and offer supportive words or actions.

Four-Eyes! *The correct answer is E.*

DISCUSSION QUESTIONS:

1. What advice would you give to Maggie to help her in this situation?
2. Why is it important not to judge others by their physical appearance?
3. What can you do to feel more confident about your physical appearance?

When we judge others by their physical appearance, we can overlook their other good qualities. Physical appearance doesn't reveal what a person is really like or that person's true worth. Fortunately, God sees every person's inner character and heart. You may not measure up to the world's standards for physical beauty, but you can be beautiful before God.

A Bad Attitude *The correct answer is B.*

DISCUSSION QUESTIONS:

1. When asked to help someone younger, how do you usually respond? Is it a nuisance, or are you eager to help?
2. Why might someone think that he or she is too important to help someone else?

Been there, done that. Boring! Is that an attitude that sounds familiar? Paul says that believers must never think that they are too important to help one another. No one, whether it's the senior pastor or the principal of the school, is too important to help another person. We should all work for the good of everyone.

The New Teacher *The correct answer is E.*

DISCUSSION QUESTIONS:

1. Why wouldn't answer C be an appropriate response? What is wrong with not saying *anything* about Mr. Hamilton?
2. What's wrong with a little exaggeration? How do you feel about someone who seems to exaggerate quite a bit?
3. Why do you think it is so important to commit to telling the truth?

When we exaggerate, pass on rumors or gossip, or say things to build up our own image, we destroy trust. If we are committed to Jesus, we must get rid of all attitudes and types of speech that break down relationships.

The Newspaper Staff *The correct answer is D.*

DISCUSSION QUESTIONS:

1. When you are learning something new, how do you want to be treated?
2. In this situation, do you think it is more important to get the school newspaper out on time or to teach the new staff members the correct procedures?
3. How do you react when you're part of a group where some of the members don't do the assignment correctly?

When you are put in charge of a task—whether it is publishing a school paper or a group assignment at school—make sure you are willing to teach and encourage the members of your team. Paul instructs leaders to "correct, rebuke, and encourage" with great patience and careful instruction. Is that the way you lead?

The Matchmaker   *The correct answer is D.*

DISCUSSION QUESTIONS:
1. Why should Deanna turn down her friend's offer?
2. What would be wrong with Deanna going with the boy just so she can have a date for the dance?
3. What do you think God wants for our relationships?

God desires honesty, kindness, and the type of love that puts others' interests first. To toy with members of the opposite sex, just to say we have a boyfriend or girl-friend, is to ignore God's commands. Do everything with kindness and love as your underlying motives.

The Older Sister   *The correct answer is B.*

DISCUSSION QUESTIONS:
1. How do you feel when you are compared to a brother or sister? Do you find yourself following in his or her footsteps?
2. Why do you think it is important not to make comparisons?
3. How would you respond to someone who begins to compare you to someone else?

Don't fall into the trap of comparing yourself with others—whether it's an older brother or your best friend. When you're tempted to compare, look to Jesus. His example will inspire you to do your very best, and his loving acceptance will comfort you when you fall short.

The Recycling Rap   *The correct answer is A.*

DISCUSSION QUESTIONS:
1. When others respond less than enthusiastically to your ideas, do you want to quit or press on?
2. What would you advise Maggie to do?
3. What are some good steps to follow when you face an overwhelming task? (Hint: Read Nehemiah 4 to find out how Nehemiah handled one!)

Not only did Nehemiah have an overwhelming task to accomplish (rebuilding the city wall around Jerusalem), but he also faced fierce opposition. Probably no one would blame him much if he had given up. But Nehemiah combined constant prayer with preparation and planning to get the job done. Remember this winning combination the next time you face a large project!

Earning Trust   *The correct answer is D.*

DISCUSSION QUESTIONS:
1. Why shouldn't George stop—even for a few minutes?
2. How would you handle this situation?
3. What might be the consequences if George does stop—and his mom finds out?

God expects us to be honest even in the small details—and even if we don't think anyone will ever find out. As Jesus says, if we can't be trusted in small matters, how do we expect to be trusted with bigger matters? If you have integrity in the seemingly insignificant situations, you will have it later, in the important decisions.

Making a Quick Profit   *The correct answer is B.*

DISCUSSION QUESTIONS:
1. Why should Jeremy's friend have nothing to do with his scheme?
2. If Jeremy's friend goes along with the plan, why is he as responsible as Jeremy for ripping off kids?
3. What might be some consequences if the principal does catch wind of the scheme?
4. Do you think the possible consequences are worth the profits Jeremy might make?

Doing what is right is far more valuable than making a profit, but we don't always act that way. The offer to make some easy cash—especially when we don't have much—can be very tempting. But if we know and love God, then having little or no cash is a small price to pay for clean living before him.

The Handicapped Student   *The correct answer is D.*

DISCUSSION QUESTIONS:
1. In what other ways can Monica help her classmates get to know this new girl?
2. When you see someone in your school with physical or mental disabilities, how do you treat him or her?
3. Why do you think people react strangely to people who walk, speak, or think differently than they do?

Throughout Jesus' ministry on earth, he spent time with the unlovely, the crippled, the blind, the lame, and the sick. He had great compassion for people who often were shunned, despised, and neglected by the majority. Christians today can do no less than follow Jesus' example and have compassion for all people, especially those avoided by others.

The Right Friends?   *The correct answer is C.*

DISCUSSION QUESTIONS:
1. Why do you think Bethany should find other friends?
2. Do your friends reflect your values, or do you reflect your friends' values?
3. What is important to you in choosing friends?
4. What do you think you should look for in a good friend?

Our friends can have a big influence on us, often in ways we are not always aware of. If you are friends with kids who mock what God considers important, you might sin by ignoring God. For a quick test, ask yourself this question: Do my friends build up my faith, or do they tear it down? True friends help bring you closer to God.

Class Elections *The correct answer is B.*

DISCUSSION QUESTIONS:
1. How do you think showing favoritism affects others? Where do you see favoritism taking place at your school?
2. Why would some people want to endorse Josh?
3. In what situations do you think you have shown favoritism?

Everyone likes to associate with winners, and sometimes we find ourselves falling into the trap of playing favorites with those who are the most popular, have the most money, or look the best. But James says that this attitude is sinful. God does not play favorites. He views all people as equals, and we should follow his example.

The Litterbugs *The correct answer is E.*

DISCUSSION QUESTIONS:
1. Why should Shane throw away the litter before going home?
2. When you see trash on the ground, what do you do?
3. Why do you think Christians have a special responsibility to take care of the environment?

God created the world and everything in it. God delegated some of his authority to the human race to take responsibility for the environment and the creatures on earth. God was careful how he made this planet. It is our responsibility to take care of it.

The Guilt Trip *The answer is D.*

DISCUSSION QUESTIONS:
1. Why was Catherine wrong to take the towel? After all, no one else had claimed it for several days.
2. The pool season is over. Why should Catherine continue to feel guilty about the towel?
3. When you feel guilty about something, whom do you tell? Your parents? A friend? God?

God is "faithful and just," and he will forgive our sins when we confess them to him. God wants us to confess when we have sinned. Confessing sins to God shows that we agree with him that our sin truly is sin, and that we are willing to turn from it.

Great Performances *The correct answer is C.*

DISCUSSION QUESTIONS:
1. Why should Barbara revise her schedule?
2. What usually happens to you when you don't get enough rest?
3. What do you think is significant about the fact that even God rested from his work?

From the very beginning, God demonstrated that rest is very important. If God himself needed rest from work, then it must be right for us to rest as well. Jesus demonstrated this, too, when he and the disciples left to find rest from the crowds. If you get the proper rest you need, you will find yourself refreshed to tackle the day's activities.

Loyal Friends   *The correct answer is A.*

DISCUSSION QUESTIONS:
1. Why should Lois stick up for Camille?
2. How would you describe yourself as a friend? Are you a loyal friend or a fair-weather friend?
3. When a friend was dropped from the group, how did you react?

The greatest evidence of a true friend is loyalty—being available to help in the tough times and sticking around when everyone else is ganging up on you. Too many people are fair-weather friends, however, who leave at the first sign of trouble or when the friendship no longer serves their purpose. Check your friendship barometer. Are you the kind of true friend the Bible encourages?

The Detour   *The correct answer is C.*

DISCUSSION QUESTIONS:
1. Why should Les continue the course as planned and not take the shortcut?
2. Are there any shortcuts to being a winner? What would be the consequences if Les's shortcut was discovered?
3. What should be your top priority in any endeavor?

The Bible teaches that believers should be very careful to do what is right, not only in God's eyes, but in people's eyes as well. If you do your best in whatever you attempt, and avoid the quick fix to problems, you will accomplish both.

Losing Effort   *The correct answer is B.*

DISCUSSION QUESTIONS:
1. When you perform poorly in school or in athletics, how do you respond to constructive criticism?
2. What do you think is the difference between constructive criticism and a critical spirit?
3. Why do you think someone who listens to constructive criticism will be "at home among the wise"?

After a poor performance, whether on a test or on the playing field, people tend to make excuses. It's difficult to listen to a coach or teacher tell us what we did wrong. But Proverbs says that a wise person will listen carefully to *constructive* criticism and learn from his or her mistakes.

Forbidden Fruit   *The correct answer is A.*

DISCUSSION QUESTIONS:
1. What would you do in Grant's situation?
2. What is wrong with "just looking" at a dirty magazine?
3. How do you handle temptation when no one is looking? Is no one really looking?

The deliberate and repeated filling of the mind with fantasies that could result from looking at dirty magazines is clearly wrong—even if the person never acts upon those fantasies. Sinful desires can be just as damaging. If left unchecked, our sinful desires may lead us to wrong actions and away from God. Clearly, the wise thing to do is avoid those temptations by never looking.

OCTOBER 2

The Editor   *The correct answer is B.*

DISCUSSION QUESTIONS:
1. When a teacher or your parent corrects your work, how do you typically respond?
2. If we are unwilling to listen to others, what might result?
3. Why do you think it is hard to accept correction, especially if you worked hard on something? How do you need to change your attitude in this area?

People who are willing to listen are the ones most likely to learn. It is a sign of strength, not weakness, to pay attention to what others have to say. By listening and accepting correction, we are able to grow and learn more. Listening is a good habit to develop for the rest of your life!

OCTOBER 3

Gang Turf   *The correct answer is D.*

DISCUSSION QUESTIONS:
1. Why shouldn't Sanford cave in to the pressure to join a gang?
2. What would help Sanford withstand this pressure?
3. What can you do to resist temptation?

Sanford's situation is a bleak reality for many students today. He faces a strong temptation to join a gang just to survive going to school! But in 1 Corinthians 10:13, the Bible offers strong words of encouragement about facing temptation. Remember these truths: Temptations happen to everyone, so you should not feel singled out; others have resisted temptations, and so can you; God will help you resist temptations. He will help you recognize those situations and people who give you trouble, help you run from anything that is wrong, and give you friends who help you resist.

OCTOBER 4

The Progress Report   *The correct answer is D.*

DISCUSSION QUESTIONS:
1. What should Torrie do with her progress report?
2. What will be the consequences if Torrie tries to hide her poor grades from her parents?
3. When you do poorly on a test or on your report card, how do you handle it with your parents?

Trying to hide unpleasant news from parents will only lead to further trouble. Eventually, the truth will come out, and you will be trapped by your lies. Avoid such traps by being truthful. As Proverbs says, "The godly escape such trouble."

Blowing Smoke   *The correct answer is C.*

DISCUSSION QUESTIONS:
1. What would you say to your friends if they started smoking around you?
2. What do you think it means to honor God with your body?
3. What do you think it means that our bodies belong to God?

Many people think that they have the right to do whatever they want with their bodies. But the Bible teaches differently. If we are followers of Christ, our bodies are the temples of the Holy Spirit. We no longer "own" our bodies because Christ lives in us. Therefore, we must live up to God's standards for our bodies, not our own.

The Food Drive   *The correct answer is B.*

DISCUSSION QUESTIONS:
1. Why would answer A not be a good response? What are the possible consequences of switching times now?
2. Why do you think Bruce should attend the food drive instead of going to the football game?
3. Why does it matter to the youth director if one person doesn't show up?

God's people should be productive. Paul writes that they should devote themselves to doing good and helping others who have urgent needs. Take advantage of every opportunity God gives you to help someone.

Keeping Secrets   *The correct answer is A.*

DISCUSSION QUESTIONS:
1. Why is important for Bonnie to tell the truth in this situation?
2. When you found yourself in a similar situation to Bonnie, did you hide your plans or tell the truth?
3. What might happen if Bonnie does not tell her friend the truth?

We have a responsibility to one another to tell the truth. Lying creates conflicts and destroys trust. It tears apart relationships, rather than keeping them together. Do your part to guard your friendships by always telling the truth.

High Standards   *The correct answer is C.*

DISCUSSION QUESTIONS:
1. Why do you think Pierce should redo his paper?
2. When you were asked to redo a paper or a project, how did you feel? What did you do?
3. What do you think it means to work as "though for the Lord . . ."?

Paul talks about slaves and masters in Ephesians 6:5-7, but a master can be anyone in authority—whether it's a coach, a boss, or a teacher. Remember that as a Christian, your ultimate boss is Jesus, and you should work enthusiastically as if you were working for him.

The Birthday Sweater   *The correct answer is E.*

DISCUSSION QUESTIONS:
1. When you received a gift you didn't particularly care for, what did you do?
2. Is it necessary to make a big fuss about it or to gently tell the person that this particular gift is not your style?
3. What might you say to the grandmother if you were Lorna?

As it says in John 14:6, Jesus is the truth. Followers of Jesus need to be committed to the truth. That means that both words and actions should reflect Jesus's character. Speaking the truth in love may not be always pleasant or convenient, but it must be done if you are to remain obedient to Jesus.

The Missing Brother   *The answer is E.*

DISCUSSION QUESTIONS:
1. When asked to take on a family responsibility, how do you react?
2. In this situation, why would it be important for Francie to go back and look for her brother?
3. Why are family responsibilities so important?

Family relationships are very important in God's eyes. Paul says that a person who neglects caring for the members of his family has denied his or her faith. Make sure that you are doing your part to help care for your family members' needs.

The Egghead   *The correct answer is E.*

DISCUSSION QUESTIONS:
1. Why should Nora tell the truth about what she got on the test?
2. When you do well on a test that everyone else flunks, why do you try and hide what you did?
3. When you are singled out, for whatever reason, how do you feel? What do you want to do?

When facing opposition from others, whether it is because of getting the only A on a test or because of your ideas, remember who is in control. Words spoken against you can often be the most painful attack you may have to face. But you can trust God to protect you from hurtful words.

The Cookie Caper   *The correct answer is A, although B is probably what will most likely happen. (Ask any dad!)*

DISCUSSION QUESTIONS:
1. Why do you think it's important that Carolyn brings the cookies to the meeting?
2. Do you think it would be OK for Carolyn to go without the cookies but be honest and say she forgot? Why, or why not?
3. When you were in a situation where someone promised to do something and didn't do it, how did that affect the group? How did you feel about it?

Think back on the previous week or even yesterday. How many promises did you make to do something? Every day we make—or break—promises to friends, teachers, parents, brothers, or sisters. No matter how small the promise may be, it is important to God that we keep our word and do what we said we would. God *delights* in people who keep their word.

OCTOBER 13

"I Told You So"   *The correct answer is A.*

DISCUSSION QUESTIONS:
1. Why should Drew resist the urge to say, "I told you so"? After all, he did tell them so!
2. If Drew insists on rubbing it in that he was right, will this make the group more likely or less likely to listen to him next time? Why?
3. When your advice turns out to be right (and the group ignores it!), what do you feel like doing?

Acts 27:10-25 tells about Paul warning the Roman soldiers about sailing. But his advice was ignored. Later, Paul reminded them of his warning, but not as an "I told you so" taunt. Rather, Paul was reminding them that with God's guidance, he had predicted the problem. Afterwards, when Paul had something to say, the crew listened. In the same way, Christians who reflect God's attitude and love towards others, rather than a boastful attitude, will find a more attentive audience the next time around.

OCTOBER 14

The Party Animals   *The correct answer is C.*

DISCUSSION QUESTIONS:
1. Why do you think Winston should stay away from this "wild" party?
2. Why do you think it's difficult to withstand peer pressure to drink and smoke?
3. What would you do with an invitation to a party where you knew drinking and drugs would be the main source of entertainment?

Peter offers a very convincing argument for avoiding places where "evil things" take place, like drinking and wild parties, because the kids there will "be surprised when you don't join in" and "will say evil things about you." Peer pressure can be very difficult to withstand, especially if everybody seems to be doing it. Save yourself the trouble and avoid these situations.

OCTOBER 15

Cinderella, Cinderella!   *The correct answer is C.*

DISCUSSION QUESTIONS:
1. What do you do when handed a long list of chores to do? What happened when you tried to duck out of doing your chores?
2. Why do you think a person's attitude toward doing chores is as important as doing the chores themselves?
3. Why do you think it is important for every family member to share in the workload at home?

Family members have a responsibility to each other. Children are told to obey their parents, and parents should not discourage their children with nagging or insults. Every home needs an atmosphere of mutual respect and love. How is your relationship with your parents? What can you do to honor and obey them?

The Soccer Tournament   *The correct answer is A.*

DISCUSSION QUESTIONS:
1. When your team suffered a disappointing loss, how did you react?
2. How did you feel when another team rubbed a loss in your face?
3. Why do you think God doesn't want his people to gloat over other's misfortunes—even if they seem to deserve it?

To gloat over someone's misfortune or defeat is to make yourself the avenger rather than God. God alone is the judge of the earth. The nation of Edom, in Obadiah 1:12, rejoiced over the defeat of Israel, so God punished them for their terrible attitude. Make sure you are gracious in defeat *and* victory.

The Shopping Spree   *The correct answer is A.*

DISCUSSION QUESTIONS:
1. How do you react to pressure to have the latest fashion in clothes—whether it's jeans or gym shoes?
2. Why should Mimi not cave in to her friend's pressure to buy the jeans?
3. What can you do to prevent yourself from becoming a victim of the "fad police"?

If you keep God and his will always before you, you will become more able to make the right decision and live as God desires. To do that, you need to focus on God's standards and not the world's. Then "you will not be shaken," and you can resist conforming to the world.

Dating Dilemma   *The correct answer is D.*

DISCUSSION QUESTIONS:
1. Why is it better for Heidi to just be friends with this boy?
2. Why do you think going out is not a wise choice?
3. How would you describe *going out* as defined by you and your friends? Does it describe a relationship, or is it more a status symbol—something everyone does?

Paul's advice is to live "not as fools, but as those who are wise." We should not act thoughtlessly, but we should consider what Jesus would have us do. Jesus wants our relationships to be based on honesty, respect, and genuine affection. Does that sound like a relationship based on going out? Be wise, and allow your relationships with the opposite sex to develop slowly.

The Geeky Stepbrother   *The correct answer is C.*

DISCUSSION QUESTIONS:
1. What do you do when you see bigger kids picking on weaker ones?
2. Why should Neal help his stepbrother?
3. In what ways do you think all Christians are responsible for "weaker brothers"?

God reveals his heart toward the needy, the afflicted, and the weak in Psalm 72:12-14. They are precious to him; he hears their cries and will rescue them. If God feels so strongly about these needy ones and loves them so deeply, how can we ignore them? Christians must do everything they can to reach out to the weak and needy with God's love.

The Substitute Horn   *The correct answer is C.*

DISCUSSION QUESTIONS:
1. Why should Hallie stick around and help Mr. Brady?
2. When you have been asked to help out in an emergency, what did you do?
3. In Romans 8:5, what are "things that please the Holy Spirit"?

Once a person has said yes to Jesus, that person will want to continue to follow him and to choose to live according to the Bible's guidelines. Believers will want to do those things that please Jesus because his way leads to life and peace. In every situation, consider what Jesus would want you to do. When you are available to help out, you should do so. Don't let your sinful nature control you. Choose daily to focus on what the Holy Spirit points out, and you will always make the right decisions.

Smoke Signals   *The correct answer is E.*

DISCUSSION QUESTIONS:
1. How could Edy have avoided this entire situation?
2. Why should Edy tell her mother the truth—and risk getting everyone else mad at her?
3. When a friend asks you to cover for him or her when he or she has done something wrong, how do you respond?

Sometimes it can be easy to justify a lie when it is under the guise of helping out a friend. If you want to succeed in God's eyes, however, you will hate lies of any kind, for any reason, and pursue the truth. These qualities will promote success and a good reputation before God, your parents, and your friends.

Be True to Your School   *The correct answer is A.*

DISCUSSION QUESTIONS:
1. How might his rivals react if Woody just smiles and congratulates them?
2. When you (or your school) is the object of taunts, how do you respond? What do you feel like doing?
3. What is the best way to get rid of an enemy? (Hint: Look up Proverbs 25:21-22 and Romans 12:20-1.)

When someone is obnoxious and getting in your face, it's not easy to respond with kindness. But the Bible teaches that Christians should do just that. When they are treated with kindness, enemies become ashamed and turn from their sin. The best way to get rid of enemies is to turn them into friends!

Just Listen!   *The correct answer is D.*

DISCUSSION QUESTIONS:
1. When a friend comes to you with a problem, how do you respond? Do you give solutions or just listen?
2. Why do you think it is important to just listen?

3. Do you think Earl is expecting Larry to solve his problem? Explain your answer.

Sometimes the best—and only—response to a friend's suffering is silence. Often people feel that they need to say something spiritual to a hurting friend. But sometimes what that person needs the most is just our presence, showing that we care.

OCTOBER 24

Fixing the Blame   *The correct answer is A.*

DISCUSSION QUESTIONS:
1. Why do you think Michelle shouldn't tell the homeroom teacher of her suspicions?
2. Does Michelle have a good reason to suspect the boy?
3. Why shouldn't believers judges others based on rumors or reputation?

Be very careful in accusing another person of anything. Before you do, make sure you have *all* the facts. Don't base your judgment on rumors, suspicions, and past history.

OCTOBER 25

Great Job!   *The correct answer is D.*

DISCUSSION QUESTIONS:
1. How did you feel when you lost out to a rival? What did you feel like doing or saying to that person?
2. How can Celina possibly offer Norbert her congratulations after such a bitter disappointment?
3. What can you do to help build others up for their good?

Paul teaches that Christians should do whatever they can to please and help others. This does not mean being "people pleasers" and saying whatever people want to hear. Rather, it means setting aside one's own self-centered desires and actions for the sake of building others up for good. Are the things you say and do helping to build others up, or tear them down?

OCTOBER 26

Losing a Friend   *The correct answer is A.*

DISCUSSION QUESTIONS:
1. How do you react to a friend who is in great distress or grieving?
2. What should Jip to say to his friend?
3. What do you think is the best thing you—or Jip—could do in this situation?

John 11:30-36 shows that God cares. He weeps with his people and has compassion on them in their sorrow. He welcomes them to honestly share their feelings with him. He understands those feelings because he experienced them too. In the same way, believers need to show compassion to grieving friends, allowing them the same freedom to express their true feelings. You don't need to say a word—your presence, like Jesus', will show that you care.

OCTOBER 27

Sloppy Homework   *The correct answer is A.*

DISCUSSION QUESTIONS:
1. Why should Carlin take his time to do his homework right—even if it means he won't get it done?

2. When you are pressed for time to get your homework done, what do you do?
3. What is the importance of doing a job well—to you, to your parents, to your teachers, to God?

In Ecclesiastes 9:10, Solomon offers a very cynical view of working hard—do your best now because this is your only shot at it. Once you die, it's all over. But Paul gives you even more reason to do your best—because you are working to please Jesus. And, Paul promises, you will receive a reward for your work! How do you view the work you are assigned to do? Take Paul's advice and "work hard and cheerfully at whatever you do."

OCTOBER 28

A Hairy Experience!   *The correct answer is C.*

DISCUSSION QUESTIONS:
1. How do you handle pressure from your friends to do something you don't want to do?
2. How would you advise Cassie in this situation?
3. How would knowing Ephesians 6:13-15 help in a situation like this?

Three times in Ephesians 6:13-15, Paul tells believers to stand: stand their ground; stand after they have done everything else; and stand firm. You can stand your ground when you come fully prepared to do "battle" with the belt of truth, the armor of God's righteousness, and fitted with shoes that come from the peace of knowing God's Word. Fully armed and prepared, you can stand against pressure from your friends and the world.

OCTOBER 29

Home Sweet Home?   *The correct answer is D.*

DISCUSSION QUESTIONS:
1. When others have more than you—whether it's a bigger house, a newer car, nicer clothes—how do you feel about their possessions?
2. How can you combat feelings of jealousy and envy?
3. Why shouldn't Brenda worry about what her friends think?

It's easy to get trapped into wrong feelings like jealousy and selfishness by what society tells says we need and by what our friends have. But remember, jealousy and selfishness are inspired by the devil. Seek God's wisdom and he will deliver you from the need to compare yourself with others and to want what they have.

OCTOBER 30

The Presidential Debate   *The correct answer is E.*

DISCUSSION QUESTIONS:
1. Why shouldn't you criticize and ridicule political leaders and others in authority?
2. Why does it really matter—everybody else does it?
3. How else can Kenton get his point across to his friends?

When the conversation turns to politics, it doesn't take long for the critics to emerge and offer their view of the country's leaders. Everybody has an opinion—good or bad—when it comes to political figures. Christians, however, are to follow God's principles regarding social responsibility. The Bible clearly teaches that believers should not "curse" those who rule over them.

The Club Treasurer   *The correct answer is A.*

DISCUSSION QUESTIONS:
1. Why shouldn't Penny use the club money to buy something personal?
2. In what other ways can you misuse the responsibility entrusted to you?
3. What do your money-management practices say about your character?

The way you handle money says a lot about your character. The "wicked person" mentioned in Psalm 37:21 steals under the guise of borrowing, but the godly person mentioned in Psalm 112:5-6 is generous, lends freely, and conducts his or her business fairly. Instead of using your money just for yourself and what you can gain, manage your money to help others.

Center of Attention   *The correct answer is D.*

DISCUSSION QUESTIONS:
1. When you are faced with competition, how do you react?
2. Does tough competition make you want to try harder, or quit?
3. Read Philippians 2:3. In what ways is it difficult to think of others as better than yourself? What can you do to put this verse into practice?

To find the perfect example of how we should regard others, study Jesus' life and how he treated people. He did not demand his rights or consider himself better than others. In the same way, we need to lay aside our selfishness and treat people with respect and common courtesy. When we think of other's interests as more important than our own, we link ourselves to Jesus.

On Top of the World   *The correct answer is B, along with C as a good alternative plan!*

DISCUSSION QUESTIONS:
1. Why should Reed attend the church retreat? Does he really need "church stuff" when things are going so well?
2. When things are going well for you, do you stop to thank God? How about when things aren't going as well?
3. If a friend were to say that he or she doesn't need that "God stuff" now, how could you respond?

When things are going your way, you can easily forget who has showered you with blessings. Don't let your blessings make you feel self-sufficient and forgetful of God. Rather, let the blessings that God has brought into your life make you thankful to God and draw you closer to him.

Piecrust Promises   *The correct answer is C.*

DISCUSSION QUESTIONS:
1. Why should Lamont take his brother to the fun fair?
2. What might result if you make it a habit to make quick promises that you don't intend to keep?
3. What is preventing Lamont from keeping his promise to his brother?

Take a look at John 6:38. Jesus came to earth fully human. He could have ignored his Father's purpose for him and followed his own desires. But Jesus told his disciples that his entire purpose in coming to earth was to do his Father's will. When you follow Jesus, your purpose should be the same—to do God's will. Instead of working to satisfy your own desires, work at reflecting Jesus' love by serving others.

NOVEMBER 4

The Inferiority Complex   *The correct answer is D.*

DISCUSSION QUESTIONS:
1. From where does Wes's true value come? Is it from making the basketball team or passing history?
2. What do you think is important for Wes (and you) to remember to keep from feeling worthless?
3. Read Luke 12:6-7. How would knowing these verses help Wes? How does it help you?

A person's true value is God's estimate of that person's worth, not a peer's, a coach's, or a teacher's. People evaluate on performance, achievements, or appearance. But God cares for his people because he made them in his image and because they belong to him. You are very valuable to God.

NOVEMBER 5

The Basketball Shoes   *The correct answer is A.*

DISCUSSION QUESTIONS:
1. If this guy has so many basketball shoes already and is careless about the ones he owns, why shouldn't Brady help himself?
2. What might be a few alternatives for Brady to earn a pair of shoes for himself?
3. Why does it matter if we "take" something from someone who has a lot?

It's hard to see others who have the latest basketball shoes or the latest fashions when we can't afford the same things. It's our human nature to want what the other person has. But we can get into trouble real fast if we start thinking it's all right to take something from a kid who has a lot because he (or she) can afford to buy another pair. Stealing is stealing in the eyes of the Lord. Don't do it!

NOVEMBER 6

The Problem with Math   *The correct answer is A.*

DISCUSSION QUESTIONS:
1. How do you handle a very difficult class?
2. What attitude should you have in tackling a tough assignment?
3. Why should Martha stick with the class and work with her teacher?

When the first sign of trouble comes along, many people are ready to surrender. In James, the Bible teaches that believers shouldn't turn tail and run; instead, they should welcome trials because trials will help build character. Instead of complaining about your struggles, look at them as opportunities for growth. And remember that God will never leave you alone; he will be with you at all times.

Science Says . . .   *The correct answer is A.*

DISCUSSION QUESTIONS:
1. When classmates and teachers dispute your beliefs as a Christian, how do you respond?
2. Why should Wade speak up?
3. How do you respond when your views on creation are challenged?

The Bible clearly teaches that God is the creator of the heavens, the world, and humankind. Paul warns Christians to beware of false teachings that are based on human ideas and experiences and that credit humanity, not God. Use your mind, keep your eyes on Christ, and always be prepared to give an answer based on the truth that is found in the Bible.

Mad Money   *The correct answer is B.*

DISCUSSION QUESTIONS:
1. Why should have Jocelyn listened to her mom's advice? Why should she admit her mistake now?
2. What are some reasons that prevent you from listening to your parents' advice?
3. What lessons have you had to learn the hard way?

Jocelyn learned the hard way that she should have listened to her mom's advice. It cost her a new crisp fifty-dollar bill, but sometimes the price paid for ignoring parents' instructions can be even more costly. Proverbs teaches that those who listen and learn from their parents will be crowned with grace and clothed with honor.

The Pity Party   *The correct answer is E.*

DISCUSSION QUESTIONS:
1. How do you handle disappointment, especially when you expect to win?
2. Why does thinking about God keep people from feeling sorry for themselves? (Hint: Read 1 Samuel 12:24.)
3. What advice can you give a friend who is having his or her own pity party?

When things don't go your way and you begin to feel sorry for yourself, take time to reflect on God's goodness. It will strengthen your faith and help you move forward with gratitude.

Lazybones   *The correct answer is B.*

DISCUSSION QUESTIONS:
1. What's the difference between laziness and rest? (Consider what God has to say about the two.)
2. What are some of the consequences of laziness? (Look at Caleb's situation and others you may be aware of.)
3. How would you rate yourself on the laziness scale, with one being asleep and ten being supercharged? What changes do you need to make?

God gave his creation a weekly day of rest and restoration. But we should not rest when we should be working—whether in school, or at home, or for someone else.

If laziness prevents us from fulfilling our responsibilities, we may find ourselves barred from the rest or reward we should enjoy. Think of what you might be missing because of laziness.

NOVEMBER 11

The Phone Fib   *The correct answer is C.*

DISCUSSION QUESTIONS:
1. Why is it important that Spencer not lie in this situation?
2. When you have been put in a situation like this, especially by a parent, how did you handle it?
3. Who do you think Spencer should be obeying in this situation—God or his dad?

Tough situations sometimes arise where we cannot obey human beings and God at the same time. We must try and live at peace with everyone—especially our parents!—but ultimately, God says we are to obey him rather than humans. When you are in a situation where you are asked to go against what God has said in the Bible, remember to keep your priorities straight. Obey God and trust his Word.

NOVEMBER 12

Activity Overload   *The correct answer is A.*

DISCUSSION QUESTIONS:
1. Why should Bev tell her youth group leader she can't make it? Why shouldn't she cancel one of her other activities?
2. How does your schedule look compared to Bev's? What changes might you need to make?
3. How can you avoid activity overload?

When David wrote Psalm 69, he was in some pretty hot water. So he responded in the only way he could—praying to God to rescue him. When you feel overwhelmed by a busy schedule or difficult problem, keep praying. Remember, as David did, that God's unfailing love and his plentiful mercy will rescue you and give you peace.

NOVEMBER 13

Best Friends   *The correct answer is E.*

DISCUSSION QUESTIONS:
1. What should be the most important factor in Jay's decision?
2. What might happen if Jay attends the Bible study? What might happen if he doesn't?
3. Do you tend to influence your friends, or do they influence you?

Christians have the responsibility to grow in their faith. Second Peter 1:5-8 lists several of faith's actions: learning to know God better, developing perseverance, doing God's will, loving others. These actions don't come automatically. It takes a lot of hard work to develop them. Don't allow anything, including your friendships, to keep you from growing in your faith.

NOVEMBER 14

Better Business   *The correct answer is C.*

DISCUSSION QUESTIONS:
1. Why would be wrong for Buzz to give the candy bar to his friends?
2. What is the most important thing for Buzz to keep in mind in this

situation? Should he be most concerned about his friends or the school business?

3. Why is should Christians be honest in their business dealings?

We know what is honest and what is dishonest in business—whether we are buying or selling something, or offering a service. While we sometimes may feel pressured to be dishonest, remember that God sets the standard. Obeying God has no middle ground—be honest.

NOVEMBER 15

Just Say No! *The correct answer is D.*

DISCUSSION QUESTIONS:

1. When you are pressured by your friends to do something wild or crazy, how do you "just say no"?
2. Read Isaiah 50:7. How can this verse help you in situations like this?
3. What is the best way to talk a friend out of doing something stupid?

Isaiah offers two thoughts on standing your ground against pressure from others: One, know that God is there to help guard you and keep you from doing wrong; two, knowing this, you can set your face like stone and determine to do God's will. If you do that, God promises you will "not be put to shame."

NOVEMBER 16

Pet Care *The correct answer is B.*

DISCUSSION QUESTIONS:

1. How can Trey show that he will be more responsible in caring for his pet?
2. What responsibilities do you have at home? How well do you take care of what you are given?
3. Does Trey have any real excuse for not taking care of his pet? Do you have any excuses for not taking care of your responsibilities?

In Matthew 25:14-29 Jesus teaches us about using God-given resources. God entrusts his people with time, talent, and money that he wants them to use wisely. Their responsibility is to take care of what they have been given and not abuse it. Christians shouldn't make excuses for not doing what God has called them to do. This may include taking care of a pet, getting homework done on time, or doing chores at home. How well are you taking care of business?

NOVEMBER 17

Lost and Found *The correct answer is C.*

DISCUSSION QUESTIONS:

1. Why should Tyrone take the pen and show it to his friend?
2. What could happen if Tyrone delays in showing his friend the pen?
3. If you were to find a valuable item, what could you do to find the owner?

Delaying to do good is inconsiderate and unfair. If it is in your power to act, whether it's repaying a loan, returning a lost item, or fulfilling a promise, do what you can without delay. Be as eager to do good as you are eager for people to do good to you.

Future Plans   *The correct answer is B.*

DISCUSSION QUESTIONS:
1. Why should Archie trust that God has a plan for him? What is Archie's role in discovering God's plan?
2. When you think of the future, do you look ahead with anxiety or with confidence?
3. What can you do to face the future with confidence?

God *does* have a plan for your future, but first, you must want to be guided by God. Then, you must understand that God's guidance is found in his Word. By spending time studying and learning from God's Word, you will gain the wisdom to perceive God's direction for your life. You may be tempted to demand answers, but, like David, seek God's direction instead.

Something Borrowed, Something New   *The correct answer is B.*

DISCUSSION QUESTIONS:
1. Why do you think Gwen is angry with this girl?
2. How do you feel when your help is not appreciated (according to you)?
3. What do you need to remember when you help others?

In Ruth 2:15-16 Boaz is a model of doing the right thing at the right time. He showed a sensitivity to Ruth's needs by telling his workers to leave more grain behind for her to pick and to not embarrass her. When you are in a position to give to others, be like Boaz, and give with a generous and sensitive heart. In Matthew 25:31-40, Jesus shows the proper motivation for helping others: to serve them as if serving Jesus himself.

Share and Share Alike   *The correct answer is E.*

DISCUSSION QUESTIONS:
1. Why should Sadie let her sister wear the sweater?
2. When friends or siblings want to borrow your things, how do you respond?
3. What should be your attitude toward sharing with others? In what ways do you need to change your attitude about sharing?

Where is your treasure stored—in heaven or in the clothes hanging in your closet, or in the newest Nintendo set in the basement, or in your ever growing CD collection? Luke 12:32-34 teaches that God's love should touch your possessions and your money so that you will give generously, share with others, and serve God. Then you will store lasting treasures in heaven.

Get a Whiff of That   *The correct answer is C.*

DISCUSSION QUESTIONS:
1. Why is it important that Garth not even take a small whiff of the Wite-Out solution?
2. When kids try to entice you into trying drugs or alcohol, how do you respond?
3. How can you stand against these temptations?

Romans 13:11-14 warns about becoming involved in wild parties or getting drunk or high. Instead, Christians are instructed to let Jesus take control of their lives so that they exemplify his qualities—love, humility, truth, and service. Don't give your desires an opportunity to sin. Avoid any situation that will open the door to wrong behaviors.

Keeps on Ticking   *The correct answer is E.*

DISCUSSION QUESTIONS:
1. Why shouldn't Luis hide his broken watch from his parents?
2. Is Luis more concerned about doing the right thing or getting caught with a broken watch?
3. When have you gotten into a situation where you were afraid of getting caught? Did you? What happened?

How you react in certain situations often exposes your hidden agenda. When faced with a moral dilemma, are you more concerned with getting caught (like Jacob or Luis) or in doing what is right? If your concern is about getting caught, you probably are involved in something less than honest. Let your fear of getting caught act as a warning to do what is right!

The Knife Fight   *The correct answer is C.*

DISCUSSION QUESTIONS:
1. Why should Keenan report the incident to the dean of students?
2. What might happen if Keenan does nothing?
3. If you were to receive information that might avert a dangerous situation, what should you do?

In the story in Esther 4:12-14, Queen Esther could have ignored Mordecai's plea to talk to the king about his decree to kill the Jews. She could have saved herself, or she could have waited for God to intervene. Instead, she saw that she had been put in her position as queen to help her people. When it is possible for you to help avert a dangerous situation, don't withdraw, behave selfishly, or get discouraged. Ask God for direction and then act!

A Call for Help   *The correct answer is D.*

DISCUSSION QUESTIONS:
1. Why should Reba take time to talk with Nan?
2. When your plans are unexpectedly interrupted, how do you feel? What do you do?
3. How can you change your schedule so you will have time for your friends or for interruptions?

Sometimes getting a call from a needy friend can throw a huge monkey wrench into our plans. Life becomes so scheduled that often little time is available to sit and chat with a friend. Find time to spend with your friends so you can comfort and encourage them *when* they need it, not when it's convenient for you.

Dirty Politics   *The correct answer is B.*

DISCUSSION QUESTIONS:
1. What's wrong with Leo putting his own "spin" on Nelson's words? Nelson *did* say that girls were stupid, didn't he?
2. What might be the consequences if Leo were to conduct a smear campaign? How would that reflect on Leo?
3. When you hear gossip or half-truths about someone you know, what do you do? What if it's someone you don't like?

Imagine taking an ax and hitting one of your classmates. Or stabbing someone with a knife. These images are shocking, but that's what Proverbs says telling lies about another person is like. Lying is vicious, and its effects can be as permanent as those of a sword or ax. Next time you are tempted to participate in gossip, think about stabbing that victim of your remarks with a sword. The image may shock you into silence.

What's for Lunch?   *The correct answer is B.*

DISCUSSION QUESTIONS:
1. Why is it important to eat the right foods?
2. When given a choice at lunch, what foods do you typically buy?
3. What can you do to stick to a healthy diet?

Daniel and his friends, although tempted with the king's rich food and wine, stuck to their resolve to eat only vegetables and water. The healthy diet paid off when the king's attendant noticed that Daniel and his friends were healthier and better nourished than the others. You can keep a better watch over your diet if you follow Daniel's example. Commit yourself first to a course of action; then when temptation strikes to eat a lunch of brownies, french fries, and soda pop, you will be ready to say no!

Line Up!   *The correct answer is C.*

DISCUSSION QUESTIONS:
1. Simone isn't the choir director or the assistant, so why should she try to get everyone back in line?
2. Read Proverbs 27:18. What does it mean for "workers to protect their employer's interests"? How does that apply here?
3. In what ways can you assist your teachers, parents, and volunteer leaders by looking after their interests?

Undoubtedly you've seen this situation before—as soon as the teacher (choir director, band leader, etc.) leaves the room, the class erupts into chaos. In these instances Christians should "look after the interests" of their "masters" to the best of their ability. That doesn't mean telling on classmates but helping to restore order by quietly promoting the kind of behavior that reflects Jesus' teachings.

The Saturday Couch Potato   *The correct answer is E.*

DISCUSSION QUESTIONS:
1. Why should Addie opt for the bike ride with her family?

2. How do you like to spend your free afternoons? Is spending time with your family high on the list? Why or why not?
3. What can help you decide the best use of your time?

Ephesians 5:15-17 gives guidelines on making the best use of time. Christians need to keep the standards high, act wisely, and make the most of every opportunity for doing good, always keeping in mind what the Lord wants them to do. In Addie's situation, the choices become clearer as she chooses to honor her parents (Ephesians 6:2-3) by considering what will make them happy.

NOVEMBER 29

Practice Time   *The correct answer is A.*

DISCUSSION QUESTIONS:
1. Why should Georgette pick up the horn and practice?
2. How do you respond when you are expected to do something?
3. What might happen if your mom or dad waited until they were told to fix dinner, wash the car, mow the grass, etc.? What can you do to make things run smoother at your house?

Technically, Georgette might have a good case for not practicing. After all, her mom *didn't* tell her to practice like she usually does. But we can get into big-time trouble if we are always looking for loopholes in doing what is right. King Saul lost a kingdom when he selectively obeyed God's commands, even though he *knew* God's heart. Remember, selective obedience is just another form of disobedience.

NOVEMBER 30

All Alone   *The correct answer is D.*

DISCUSSION QUESTIONS:
1. What advice could you give Troy to help him in this situation?
2. When you have been the new kid on the block, how did God answer your prayers for new friends?
3. As an old-timer in your school or church, how can you be sensitive to newcomers and encourage them?

After stealing the birthright from his twin brother, Jacob was forced to leave his home. Even though Jacob was all alone in a strange country, however, God had not forgotten about him. In Jacob's loneliness, God promised that he would never leave him and that he would watch over him. God promises to do the same for you. He knows your needs, and as he promised Jacob thousands of years ago, he will watch over you.

DECEMBER 1

Those Lucky Laces   *The correct answer is D.*

DISCUSSION QUESTIONS:
1. What's wrong with having a pair of lucky shoelaces or a rabbit's foot?
2. What superstitions do you have? (Wear the same pair of socks to soccer games; always sit in the same seat for important tests, etc.)
3. What can Christians do to stop from following, as the writer of Hebrews puts it, "strange, new ideas"?

Don't trust in a practice or object like laces, a rabbit's foot, or a four-leaf clover. Worship the Creator rather than the created things and recognize that God, and God alone, controls everything. Remember that spiritual strength comes from God and not something like a pair of shoelaces.

Gaining an In-Sight   *The correct answer is A.*

DISCUSSION QUESTIONS:
1. Why should Ferguson tell the choral director that he saw the selection?
2. What is the best way for Ferguson to achieve his goals?
3. When you had an "opportunity" to take a look at a test, what did you do?

Maybe Ferguson would make the state choral group if he studied the sight-reading selection ahead of time. Maybe you would get that much needed A in history if you sneaked a peek at the questions on the final exam. But eventually, Proverbs teaches, you would be found out, and the consequences would far outweigh any gains you might make. Take the right path, making sure that whatever you do is accomplished with complete honesty.

The Scary Flick Fest   *The correct answer is E.*

DISCUSSION QUESTIONS:
1. How could Fiona have avoided this entire situation?
2. What types of movies, books, and music are off-limits to you?
3. In what ways do you show good planning and insight? In what ways don't you?

The Bible teaches that in order to be wise a person needs both discernment and sound judgment. Discernment is the ability God gives to people to think and make correct choices. But God only gives sound judgment to those who follow him. Sound judgment includes discernment, but it also includes knowledge that comes from knowing and applying God's Word. Do you have the necessary sound judgment to make good decisions? If not, ask God and he will show you how to get it.

The Christmas Pageant   *The correct answer is C.*

DISCUSSION QUESTIONS:
1. How do you feel when given a big responsibility? Do you run from it or welcome it?
2. What would you say to April to encourage her?
3. What gives you encouragement when a job seems just too big to handle?

Joshua 1:5-9 tells about Joshua being given a huge challenge—leading more than two million people into a strange land and conquering it. What a challenge—even for a Bible hero! But three times God told Joshua to "be strong and courageous," for God would never leave him or forget about him. Although God probably won't ask you to conquer new lands, he promises that whatever he asks and in every situation, he will always be with you.

Come Clean!   *The correct answer is D.*

DISCUSSION QUESTIONS:
1. Why don't you think Albert should report Rusty to the band director? What about asking his father for advice?
2. What did you do when a friend confessed to you something wrong that he or she had done?
3. Why do you think it is important to confess our sins to God?

When you have done something wrong, God doesn't want a superficial "I'm sorry." He is looking at your heart. When you come before him, truly sorry for what you have done, God is gracious and kind. He will forgive you and always love you.

DECEMBER 6

The Naysayer   *The correct answer is D.*

DISCUSSION QUESTIONS:
1. Every group always has a Talbot—the doom-and-gloom guy. How do you handle such people in your group?
2. If you disagree with what the group is doing, what is the best way to express your opinions?
3. If you are always negative and do not offer any constructive solutions, will your opinion carry any weight? Why or why not?

When you are involved in a group decision, make sure you focus on the positives—not the negatives. The naysayers among the Israelites literally condemned the people to another forty years in the desert because of their negative reports of the land God had promised to the people. Don't let fears and problems immobilize you. Instead, focus on God's direction and promise—and then move out in faith.

DECEMBER 7

My Grandmother   *The correct answer is B.*

DISCUSSION QUESTIONS:
1. Why is it all right to tell God you are angry with him?
2. When you are hurt and angry with God, what do you do? Do you avoid God and stop praying, or do you run to him?
3. How can letting God know how you feel help in a situation like Rhoda's?

David was feeling very bad when he wrote Psalm 13. Four times, he pleaded with God "how long?" indicating his deep distress. Yet, in expressing his feelings, David found strength from God. By the end of the prayer, David was able to express trust and hope in God again. Through prayer, you can tell God exactly how you are feeling and talk out your problem. Then God can help you gain the right perspective and give you peace.

DECEMBER 8

The Houseguest   *The correct answer is D.*

DISCUSSION QUESTIONS:
1. Why should Millie make the best of this situation? It certainly seems hopeless.
2. When you find yourself in less than desirable circumstances, what do you do?
3. How can you learn to make the best of your situation?

One way to learn to overcome difficulties is by understanding that God is using these situations to build character. The difficulties you are experiencing now will help you grow in your faith. The Bible teaches that problems help develop endurance. That, in turn, strengthens character, deepens trust in God, and gives greater confidence. As you see God build your character, you truly will be able to rejoice when you run into problems!

A Judgment Call   *The correct answer is E.*

DISCUSSION QUESTIONS:
1. Why should Jonah relate his suspicions to an adult? Is it any of his concern?
2. How would you handle Jonah's situation? What other ways could you help someone like Vera?
3. What are some of the dangers of getting involved in a situation like this? Should that prevent you from helping? Why or why not?

Genesis 14:14-16 tells about Abram learning that his nephew, Lot, had been taken a prisoner. To rescue Lot meant facing a powerful foe and risking the lives of his men. Most likely, it would have been easier and safer not to get involved. But Abram chose to act quickly and decisively. In order to help someone, sometimes you will need to get involved in a messy and painful situation. With God's direction and strength, you should be willing to help immediately.

Math Buddies   *The correct answer is B.*

DISCUSSION QUESTIONS:
1. Ethan's not the teacher, so why should he take the time to teach Lennie the metric system?
2. How do you respond when you have a partner in class who is less capable than you?
3. What happens when you begin to think too highly of yourself and your abilities?

Mark 9:33-35 tells about when Jesus caught the disciples in an argument over who was the greatest. The disciples had pushed aside obedience and service and had allowed pride and insecurity to cause them to place a higher value on their position and prestige. You can avoid that pitfall by making sure that your motives are the same as Jesus'—to serve others and advance God's kingdom, not your own.

Bus Stop   *The correct answer is A.*

DISCUSSION QUESTIONS:
1. When you see kids acting up in class, on the bus, or at a church activity, how do you respond? Do you say something to them to try and get them to stop, or do you join in?
2. Why do you think people, like bus drivers or school cafeteria workers, deserve respect from the students they serve? Are they really in a position of authority?
3. How can you model the principles expressed in 1 Peter 2:17.

Peter doesn't say we should respect just the king, other believers, or God. Rather, we are to respect *everyone*—including our bus drivers, school janitors, cafeteria workers, etc. We show respect when we treat people courteously, behave responsibly, and help others to do the same.

The Tutor   *The correct answer is E.*

DISCUSSION QUESTIONS:
1. How can Newt overcome the distraction of Miss Birdwell's birthmark?
2. When you see someone in school or in public with a deformity of some kind, how do you react?
3. What does God want you to remember about appearances?

In a society that focuses on youth and beauty, it is sometimes hard to get past appearances. But Proverbs teaches that we shouldn't base the worth of people on how they look, because beauty doesn't last forever. Instead, we should look at a person's character and qualities such as hard work, honesty, care for others, encouragement, and fear of God. That's what truly counts.

The Pastor's Daughter   *The correct answer is C.*

DISCUSSION QUESTIONS:
1. How do you respond when other kids make fun of your faith? Do you feel like punching them out or praying for them?
2. Read 1 Peter 3:9. How can you effectively put this into practice?

Hurling insults back at this boy is unacceptable behavior in God's kingdom. Followers of Jesus need to rise above feelings of wanting to get back at people who hurt them. Instead of reacting angrily, pray for these people.

Double Trouble   *The correct answer is D.*

DISCUSSION QUESTIONS:
1. Why should Gretchen clean up the mess?
2. What might result if Gretchen decides to sit back and watch videos with a bowl of ice cream (that she doesn't clean up)? What about if the Thompsons come home to find the house spotless?
3. How do you react when faced with a task that seems too dirty for you to do?

When Ruth was faced with the tough, tiring, menial (and probably degrading) task of gathering the leftover grain, she didn't flinch. Instead, the Bible tells us she worked steadily without complaint. Her life reflected many admirable qualities: She was hardworking, loving, kind, and faithful. These qualities earned her a good reputation because she displayed them consistently. Your reputation is formed by the people who watch you at school, at church, while baby-sitting, and so forth. What do people see *consistently* in your behavior? Consistently do what is right, and you, like Ruth, will earn a good reputation.

The Blizzard   *The correct answer is D.*

DISCUSSION QUESTIONS:
1. Why should Davis finish the job and shovel the walkways?
2. What should be Davis's motivation for finishing the job?
3. How do you feel about doing extra chores for someone else?

Helping others probably won't be at the top of your agenda every day. But what better motivation would you need than knowing that God himself is pleased when you do good and share with others. Even when your good deeds go unnoticed on earth, don't forget that God sees all you do and will reward you.

DECEMBER 16

The New Outfit   *The correct answer is C.*

DISCUSSION QUESTIONS:
1. Since Noelle looks good in the outfit, why shouldn't she just go ahead and get it?
2. How would you respond to this statement: "Clothes make the person."
3. What things are important to you in selecting clothes? Being in style, making a statement, comfort?

The Bible doesn't say it is wrong to dress nicely and look attractive. But the Bible does teach that true beauty begins inside. A gentle, modest, loving character is more important than wearing the latest fashion. Dress in such a way that reflects your character and style—and not the latest fashions. The hippest style will be artificial if it doesn't reflect your inner character.

DECEMBER 17

The Grandparent Dilemma   *The correct answer is D.*

DISCUSSION QUESTIONS:
1. Why should Abe choose to visit his grandparents instead of going to the concert?
2. When you are faced with a decision like Abe's, what factors should you consider?
3. How can you make the most of each day God has given you?

Life is short; play hard, right? That's not exactly what the Bible teaches. But the Bible does teach that life is short. You don't know what is ahead, and you shouldn't be deceived into thinking that you have lots of time to be with loved ones or to do what you know you should do. Life is short—live for God today! Then you can be confident that you won't neglect what is truly important.

DECEMBER 18

Youth Group Rap   *The correct answer is C.*

DISCUSSION QUESTIONS:
1. Why should Faye ignore her friends' rude behavior?
2. What might happen if Faye erupts and starts screaming at her so-called friends?
3. When your friends act rude, how do you react?

When you are insulted or annoyed, it is natural to want to get back at the person, to get even. But Proverbs 12:16 says that a wise person will stay calm when insulted. Reacting in anger doesn't solve anything and most likely will result in more trouble. Instead, react slowly and quietly to insults. Your positive response will achieve positive results.

DECEMBER 19

Trading Cards   *The correct answer is C.*

DISCUSSION QUESTIONS:
1. Bud's new cards are ruined! Why should he accept the cards now?
2. When you have been wronged, what does your human nature want to do in response?

3. What might happen if Bud were to try to get back at his friend for ruining the cards?

Judges 15 tells about the Philistines raiding the villages of Judah because Samson had paid them back for what they had done to him. Revenge can become an ugly, uncontrollable monster. Each act of revenge brings another one. The vicious cycle of revenge can only be broken by forgiveness. The Bible teaches that forgiveness is at the cornerstone of a person's relationship with God. God has forgiven you, so you should forgive those who have wronged you.

DECEMBER 20

Meet My Brother   *The correct answer is B.*

DISCUSSION QUESTIONS:
1. Why should Raquel not be embarrassed by her friends' reaction to her brother?
2. When do you feel embarrassed by your siblings (or parents)—either because of their behavior or appearance? How can you combat those feelings?
3. How does knowing the truth expressed in Psalm 139:13-14 help you know your worth? The worth of others?

God's character is reflected in each and every person. When you are feeling worthless or are tempted to make fun of someone else, remember that God's spirit is ready and willing to work in you and in others. You should have as much respect for yourself and for others as God does. Then you can praise God because his workmanship is truly wonderful!

DECEMBER 21

The Honors Classes   *The correct answer is A.*

DISCUSSION QUESTIONS:
1. Why should Carlton take the honors classes and possibly mess up his good record?
2. When you have a choice between a challenging class and an easy one, which do you choose? Why?
3. What might be the consequences of always taking the easy way out?

The Bible makes it clear that diligence—being willing to work hard and doing the best at any task given you—is a important part of wise living. If you are willing to work hard, you will reap the rewards—whether that means good grades, recognition from your teachers or parents, or admission into a good college. Remember, however, that you should work hard to serve God by doing your very best, not for the other rewards.

DECEMBER 22

The Party Poopers   *The correct answer is B.*

DISCUSSION QUESTIONS:
1. Why should Alvin apologize? Isn't being humiliated in front of his friends enough?
2. Who is really at fault in this situation?
3. When you are in the wrong and are embarrassed, how do you respond?

When God used a donkey to save Balaam's life (an Old Testament character who thought he could obey God *and* make a profit), Balaam looked pretty foolish. So Balaam got angry with the donkey. Sometimes, when people are embarrassed and their pride is hurt, they also lash out and blame those who get in their way.

Becoming angry with others, however, is a sign that something is wrong. Don't allow pride to lead you to hurt someone.

DECEMBER 23

Talk of the School   *The correct answer is C.*

DISCUSSION QUESTIONS:
1. Why should Edwin keep quiet?
2. How do you respond when classmates spread false rumors about you?
3. What can you do to combat the effects of false rumors and gossip?

David found himself surrounded by enemies who were spreading vicious lies about him. Psalm 57:4 describes those enemies as "fierce lions who greedily devour human prey—whose teeth pierce like spears and arrows, and whose tongues cut like swords." David found the solution to his problem in God. Rather than answering with hateful words, David took his hurt and his problems to the Lord. Learn from David. When confronted with verbal attacks, the best defense is to be quiet and praise God, realizing that your confidence rests in his love and faithfulness.

DECEMBER 24

Working behind the Scenery   *The correct answer is B.*

DISCUSSION QUESTIONS:
1. Why shouldn't Rena point out to others the work she did on the scenery?
2. When you have worked hard on a project, how do you respond when no one recognizes your work?
3. In what ways can recognition be dangerous?

When you do something well, there is a great temptation to tell others and then bask in their praise. Recognition can be dangerous, however, when it leads to inflated pride. When you do something well, seek the praise of God instead of people. Then, when you are praised, you can freely give the credit to God.

DECEMBER 25

Roommates   *The correct answer is C.*

DISCUSSION QUESTIONS:
1. Why should Jayna try to resolve her differences with her sister? What might happen if she doesn't try to work out a solution?
2. When you have a disagreement with a sibling or a friend, what do you usually do?
3. What are some things you can do to work out your differences with a friend?

In Matthew 5:25, the Bible talks about working out differences with others before matters get to court. Your disagreements probably won't take you that far, but still you should resolve your differences with others before their anger causes more trouble. Even your small conflicts can mend more easily if you try to make peace right away.

DECEMBER 26

Go Ask Mom   *The correct answer is C.*

DISCUSSION QUESTIONS:
1. Why shouldn't Otis send in his brother to pester his mother?
2. What happened when you used the tag-team approach to get your parents to do something?

3. Why is plotting something almost as bad as doing it?

Plotting to do something wrong is bad because what a person thinks determines what that person will do. Wrong desires often lead to sin if left unchecked. Even if you don't carry through with your scheme, you will have sinned in your bad attitude. When you find yourself planning to do something wrong, stop and confess your sin to God.

DECEMBER 27

The Killer Cat   *The correct answer is E.*

DISCUSSION QUESTIONS:
1. Why should Lina talk with her neighbors about the cat first?
2. When your neighbors do something that annoys you, what do you do?
3. How can you show love to your neighbors—especially when they are annoying?

The Bible teaches that the one debt believers will always have outstanding is to love their neighbors. Christians are permanently in debt because of the love Jesus has lavished upon them. The only way to repay this debt is to love others. This doesn't mean that you must have affection for your neighbors; it doesn't even mean that you have to like your neighbors. But it does mean that you will *act* in your neighbors' best interests and not do them any harm.

DECEMBER 28

Off-Limits!   *The correct answer is B.*

DISCUSSION QUESTIONS:
1. If Jed's mom will never find out, why is it so important that Jed not allow anyone to go into her office?
2. How do you resist pressure from your friends to do something wrong?
3. What would be the easiest thing for Jed to do?

Genesis 3:1-7 tells about Satan tempting Eve and getting her to sin. What can *we* do to resist temptation? First, we should pray for strength to resist temptation; secondly, we should run (sometimes literally!) from temptation; and third, we should say no. God richly rewards those who don't give in when tempted.

DECEMBER 29

It's Just a Joke   *The correct answer is E.*

DISCUSSION QUESTIONS:
1. Why shouldn't Bryce tell his uncle's joke?
2. When you hear a joke about someone of a different race, how do you respond?
3. What's wrong with jokes that make fun of ethnic or racial groups?

Obscene stories, foolish talk, and coarse jokes are so common that we often take them for granted. But such talk should have no place in our conversations. When we tell obscene stories or coarse jokes, we are not reflecting God's presence in us. The Bible teaches that a believer's conversation should be "gracious and effective."

TV Trauma   *The correct answer is D.*

DISCUSSION QUESTIONS:
1. Why shouldn't Arden insist that she watch the TV show while her friend does something else?
2. When your friends aren't permitted to do something you are, how do you react?
3. What should be your attitude toward a friend who doesn't have the same rules as you do?

First Corinthians 10:9 teaches that Christians should always act in others' best interests. While a certain action may be OK for you, it may not be beneficial to your friend—especially if that friend's parents have specific rules about it. You need to be sensitive to your friend's needs and be gracious. Don't insist on your own way but put others first.

Mind Your Own Business   *The correct answer is C.*

DISCUSSION QUESTIONS:
1. How could Manny have avoided this situation?
2. Why should Manny drop the subject now and forget about it?
3. What can you do to avoid saying the wrong things?

If you want to be self-controlled, then you need to learn to control your tongue. Words that slip out of your mouth have the power to cut down a friend or destroy a reputation. Stop and think before you react or speak, and you will be able to control this most powerful member of the body.

INDEX OF VERSES

Psalm 39:4, December 17, "The Grandparent Dilemma"
Psalm 42, June 17, "The New Baby"
Psalm 42:5-6, April 22, "Third Chair"
Psalm 51:3-4, March 22, "Exposed!"
Psalm 51:6, January 6, "Found Treasure"; September 8, "Vote for Me!"
Psalm 57:1-7, December 23, "Talk of the School"
Psalm 62:8, April 20, "The Hospital"
Psalm 64, October 11, "The Egghead"
Psalm 69:13-17, November 12, "Activity Overload"
Psalm 70, January 4, "We're Here to Praise Him!"
Psalm 72:12-14, October 19, "The Geeky Stepbrother"
Psalm 82:4, February, 27, "Making Fun"
Psalm 101:5-6, January 7, "My Hero?"
Psalm 101:7, January 17, "The Final Exam"
Psalm 112:5-6, October 31, "The Club Treasurer"
Psalm 119:9-11, June 29, "The Memory Game"
Psalm 119:65-66, November 2, "On Top of the World"
Psalm 127:2, September 27, "Great Performances"
Psalm 133:1, August 27, "His Brother's Keeper"
Psalm 139:13-14, December 20, "Meet My Brother"

Proverbs

Proverbs 1:8-9, November 8, "Mad Money"
Proverbs 1:10, January 29, "Egg-spectations"
Proverbs 3:3-4, February 18, "The Clique"
Proverbs 3:5-6, August 11, "It's a Dog's Life"
Proverbs 3:21-24, December 3, "The Scary Flick Fest"
Proverbs 3:27-28, November 17, "Lost and Found"
Proverbs 3:30, October 24, "Fixing the Blame"
Proverbs 3:31, February 5, "The Tough Guy"
Proverbs 4:3-4, December 3, "The Scary Flick Fest"
Proverbs 6:6-8, December 21, "The Honors Classes"
Proverbs 6:6-11, November 10, "Lazybones"
Proverbs 8:1-8, April 13, "And the Answer Is . . ."
Proverbs 10:9, December 2, "Gaining an In-Sight"
Proverbs 10:16, February 10, "The Windfall"
Proverbs 11:1, April 1, "Pop Quiz!"
Proverbs 11:2, February 11, "Looking for Answers"
Proverbs 11:3, August 14, "Cashing In"
Proverbs 11:20, April 6, "The Party Invitations"
Proverbs 11:28, August 23, "The Bonus Offer"
Proverbs 11:29, July 14, "Pushing the Right Buttons"
Proverbs 12:10, February 23, "Pet Peeves"
Proverbs 12:11, June 22, "Rainy Day Blues"
Proverbs 12:13, October 4, "The Progress Report"
Proverbs 12:15, February 8, "The Good Old Days"
Proverbs 12:16, December 18, "Youth Group Rap"
Proverbs 12:17, January 9, "Secret Notes"
Proverbs 12:18, March 24, "Reckless Words"
Proverbs 12:19, July 16, "The Woodcutter"
Proverbs 12:22, February 13, "Math Problem"; October 12,
    "The Cookie Caper"
Proverbs 13:2, March 9, "Finders Keepers, Part 2"

Matthew 5:28, October 1, "Forbidden Fruit"
Matthew 5:39, May 10, "Turning the Other Cheek"
Matthew 6:14-15, September 6, "Forgive and Forget"
Matthew 6:34, June 23, "Real Worries"
Matthew 7:12, January 22, "Lights Out!"
Matthew 7:24-27, August 20, "Family Devotions"
Matthew 18:21-22, August 15, "Holding a Grudge"
Matthew 20:26-27, August 5, "Cleanup Detail"
Matthew 20:29-34, September 22, "The Handicapped Student"
Matthew 25:14-29, November 16, "Pet Care"
Matthew 25:31-40, November 19, "Something Borrowed, Something New"
Matthew 26:30-46, May 30, "A Little Help from My Friends"

Mark
Mark 6:30-31, September 27, "Great Performances"
Mark 9:33-35, December 10, "Math Buddies"

Luke
Luke 6:27-36, January 2, "Getting Even"; February 1, "The Terminator"
Luke 6:27, August 24, "Love Your Enemies"
Luke 6:34, January 21, "The Loan"
Luke 6:37-38, March 4, "The Cutting Edge"
Luke 9:26, February 24, "And Today's Topic Is . . ."
Luke 10:30-37, February 26, "The Big Hurt"; July 25, "The Good Neighbor"
Luke 10:38-42, July 21, "The Farewell Bash"
Luke 11:4, December 19, "Trading Cards"
Luke 12:6-7, November 4, "The Inferiority Complex"
Luke 12:15, February 28, "Finders Keepers, Part 1"; April 16, "The Grass Looks Greener"
Luke 12:32-34, November 20, "Share and Share Alike"
Luke 16:10, September 20, "Earning Trust"
Luke 16:11-12, September 1, "A Good Steward"
Luke 17:7-10, August 18, "The Big Celebration"
Luke 18:1-8, May 21, "The Prayer Chain"
Luke 18:9-14, July 7, "The Natural"

John
John 4:4-30, March 30, "The Real Race"
John 6:38, November 3, "Piecrust Promises"
John 8:1-7, July 18, "Drinking Buddy?"
John 11:30-36, October 26, "Losing a Friend"

Acts
Acts 5:29, November 11, "The Phone Fib"
Acts 9:26-28, May 17, "Making the First Move"
Acts 10:34, August 4, "That Wild and Crazy Guy"
Acts 11:1-4, 15-18, May 31, "I Spy"
Acts 16:11-15, 38-40, March 10, "Great Expectations"
Acts 18:24-28, January 23, "All the Right Moves"
Acts 20:22-24, July 28, "The Long Haul"
Acts 20:24, May 28, "Your Witness"
Acts 23:12-22, May 1, "Never Too Young"

Acts 24:16, August 17, "The Right Choice"
Acts 27:10-25, October 13, ""I Told You So""

Romans

Romans 1:16, April 8, "The Bible Study"
Romans 2:5-8, January 10, "A Double Life"
Romans 5:3-5, December 8, "The Houseguest"
Romans 8:5, October 20, "The Substitute Horn"
Romans 8:28, March 31, "Benched!"
Romans 12:2, August 7, "Movie Madness"; October 17,
   "The Shopping Spree"
Romans 12:3, March 17, "The Talent Show"
Romans 12:10, March 27, "Singing the Blues"; September 17,
   "The Matchmaker"
Romans 12:13, April 17, "Sharing"
Romans 12:14, March 21, "Standing Firm"
Romans 12:15, July 29, "Just Cruisin'"
Romans 12:16, January 12, "The "In" Crowd"
Romans 12:19-20, January 11, "The Locker"
Romans 12:20-21, November 26, "Be True to Your School"
Romans 13:1-5, July 3, "Playing by the Rules"
Romans 13:8-10, December 27, "The Killer Cat"
Romans 13:11-14, November 21, "Get a Whiff of That"
Romans 14:23, May 25, "The Pizza Party"
Romans 15:2, October 25, "Great Job!"
Romans 15:5, July 9, "The Wicked Stepmother"
Romans 15:7, April 28, "New and Unusual"

1 Corinthians

1 Corinthians 1:31, September 9, "Braggin' Rights"
1 Corinthians 3:3, July 2, "Split Decision"
1 Corinthians 6:19-20, October 5, "Blowing Smoke"
1 Corinthians 9:22, April 10, "Common Ground"
1 Corinthians 10:13, October 3, "Gang Turf"
1 Corinthians 10:23-24, December 30, "TV Trauma"
1 Corinthians 12:5, April 14, "Behind the Scenes"
1 Corinthians 13:4-5, January 18, "The Substitute"
1 Corinthians 13:4, January 1, "The Ring"
1 Corinthians 13:5, August 30, "Brotherly Love?"
1 Corinthians 13:6-7, February 6, "Don't Believe It"
1 Corinthians 13:7, September 5, "The Friend"
1 Corinthians 14:1, January 14, "The Invitation"
1 Corinthians 14:33, 40, June 20, "The Sunday School Lesson"
1 Corinthians 15:58, August 25, "At Your Service"
1 Corinthians 16:13-14, September 17, "The Matchmaker"

2 Corinthians

2 Corinthians 1:3-7, July 8, "Pass It On"
2 Corinthians 6:4-7, May 27, "Choosing Friends"
2 Corinthians 8:21, September 29, "The Detour"
2 Corinthians 9:6, September 3, "Stick of Gum"
2 Corinthians 10:17-18, December 24, "Working behind
the Scenery"

1 Thessalonians

1 Thessalonians 4:18, November 24, "A Call for Help"
1 Thessalonians 5:11, September 12, "Going the Distance"
1 Thessalonians 5:12-13, March 18, "The New Pastor"
1 Thessalonians 5:14, February 14, "The Group Project"
1 Thessalonians 5:16-18, July 12, "Thank You!"

2 Thessalonians

2 Thessalonians 3:6-7, February 19, "The Stock Boy"

1 Timothy

1 Timothy 1:18-19, August 28, "Sweet Rewards"
1 Timothy 2:1-2, August 22, "The Church Choir Clown"
1 Timothy 2:9-10, December 16, "The New Outfit"
1 Timothy 4:12, February 25, "The Birthday Gift"
1 Timothy 5:8, October 10, "The Missing Brother"
1 Timothy 6:11, March 15, "Surfing the Net"
1 Timothy 6:11-12, January 20, "The Comic Book King"

2 Timothy

2 Timothy 1:8, March 13, "Going to Church"
2 Timothy 2:15, March 14, "The Birthday Present"
2 Timothy 2:22, July 6, "The Grunge Express"
2 Timothy 2:23, April 15, "The Great Debate"
2 Timothy 3:1-5, June 24, "The Rock Concert"
2 Timothy 4:2, September 16, "The Newspaper Staff"

Titus

Titus 2:1, November 27, "Line Up!"
Titus 2:7, June 19, "The Perfect Example"
Titus 3:2, February 17, "The Slumber Party"
Titus 3:8, April 12, "Unlocked Secrets"
Titus 3:14, October 6, "The Food Drive"

Hebrews

Hebrews 4:13, July 23, "Video Role"; November 11, "The Phone Fib"
Hebrews 10:24, September 2, "The New Job"
Hebrews 10:25, July 5, "Boooring!"
Hebrews 12:10-11, June 2, "Family Feud"
Hebrews 12:11, January 16, "The Sunday Matinee"
Hebrews 12:28, August 10, "Worship Time"
Hebrews 13:9, December 1, "Those Lucky Laces"
Hebrews 13:16, June 5, "Lazy Days of Summer"; December 15, "The Blizzard"

James

James 1:2-4, November 6, "The Problem with Math"
James 1:5, March 16, "Decisions, Decisions"
James 1:12, December 28, "Off-Limits!"
James 1:13-16, April 21, "After-School Activity"
James 1:19-20, September 4, "The Missing Bike"
James 1:22-27, January 15, "A Friend in Need"
James 2:1-4, September 24, "Class Elections"
James 3:6, March 24, "Reckless Words"

James 3:7-10, August 16, "Just a Little Sin"
James 3:13-16, October 29, "Home Sweet Home?"
James 3:18, April 23, "In the Middle"
James 4:6, March 20, "We're Number One!"
James 4:13-15, December 17, "The Grandparent Dilemma"
James 4:17, January 24, "The Sick Classmate"; May 13, "The Accident"

1 Peter

1 Peter 1:21-22, June 3, "The Younger Sister"
1 Peter 2:13, January 31, "Show a Little Respect"
1 Peter 2:17, December 11, "Bus Stop"
1 Peter 3:3-4, May 15, "Beauty Is in the Eye . . ."
1 Peter 3:9, December 13, "The Pastor's Daughter"
1 Peter 3:15, February 21, "Spreading the Word"; July 13, "Soccer Camp"; November 7, "Science Says . . ."
1 Peter 3:16, April 11, "The Accused"
1 Peter 4:3-5, October 14, "The Party Animals"
1 Peter 4:8, July 26, "The Cold War"
1 Peter 4:9, January 27, "Guess Who's Coming to Dinner?"
1 Peter 4:10, June 30, "The Piano Player"
1 Peter 5:5, June 16, "Oh, Brother!"
1 Peter 5:7, April 25, "Moving On"

2 Peter

2 Peter 1:5-8, November 13, "Best Friends"

1 John

1 John 1:9, May 16, "Unconditional Love"; September 26, "The Guilt Trip"
1 John 3:18, April 24, "The Sick Mom"
1 John 4:7-11, July 4, "Slumber Party Fiasco"

3 John

3 John 1:11, June 28, "Going Shopping"

Jude

Jude 1:22, January 25, "Doubting Ray"